WELCOME

D0197164

"Maui no ka oi" is what locals say—it's the best, the most, the top of the heap. To those who know Maui well, there are good reasons for the superlatives. The island's miles of perfect beaches, lush green valleys, and volcanic landscapes, as well as its historic villages, top-notch water sports, and stellar restaurants and resorts, have made it an international favorite. Maui is also home to rich culture and stunning ethnic diversity, as reflected in the island's wide range of food and traditional activities.

TOP REASONS TO GO

★ **Beaches:** From black-sand beauties to palm-lined strands, each beach is unique.

★ **Resorts:** Opulent spas, pools, gardens, and golf courses deliver pampering aplenty.

★ **Hawaiian Culture:** From hula to luaus, you can experience Maui's diverse culture.

★ **Road to Hana:** This famed winding road offers stunning views of coast and ocean.

★ **Whale-Watching:** Humpback whales congregate each winter right off Maui's shores.

★ **Water Sports:** Surfing, snorkeling, and sailing are just a few top options.

Fodor's MAUI 2014

Publisher: Amanda D'Acierno, *Senior Vice-President*

Editorial: Arabella Bowen, *Executive Editorial Director*; Linda Cabasin, *Editorial Director*

Design: Fabrizio La Rocca, *Vice-President, Creative Director*; Tina Malaney, *Associate Art Director*; Chie Ushio, *Senior Designer*; Ann McBride, *Production Designer*

Photography: Melanie Marin, *Associate Director of Photography*; Jessica Parkhill and Jennifer Romains, *Researchers*

Maps: Rebecca Baer, *Map Editor*; Mark Stroud, Moon Street Cartography, and David Lindroth, *Cartographers*

Production: Linda Schmidt, *Managing Editor*; Evangelos Vasilakis, *Associate Managing Editor*; Angela L. McLean, *Senior Production Manager*

Sales: Jacqueline Lebow, *Sales Director*

Marketing & Publicity: Heather Dalton, *Marketing Director*; Katherine Fleming, *Senior Publicist*

Business & Operations: Susan Livingston, *Vice-President, Strategic Business Planning*; Sue Daulton, *Vice-President, Operations*

Fodors.com: Megan Bell, *Executive Director, Revenue & Business Development*; Yasmin Marinaro, *Senior Director, Marketing & Partnerships*

Copyright © 2014 by Fodor's Travel, a division of Random House, Inc.

Writers: Eliza Escaño-Vasquez, Bonnie Friedman, Heidi Pool, Joana Varawa

Editors: Luke Epplin, Mark Sullivan, Linda Cabasin

Production Editor: Carrie Parker, *senior production editor*

ISBN 978-0-7704-3213-3

ISSN 1559-0798

SPECIAL SALES

This book is available at special discounts for bulk purchases for sales promotions or premiums. For more information, e-mail specialmarkets@randomhouse.com

PRINTED IN CHINA

10 9 8 7 6 5 4 3 2 1

CONTENTS

ABOUT
THIS GUIDE

Fodor's Recommendations

Everything in this guide is worth doing—we don't cover what isn't—but exceptional sights, hotels, and restaurants are recognized with additional accolades. Fodor's Choice★ indicates our top recommendations; and **Best Bets** call attention to notable hotels and restaurants in various categories. Care to nominate a new place? Visit Fodors.com/contact-us.

Trip Costs

We list prices wherever possible to help you budget well. Hotel and restaurant price categories from **$** to **$$$$** are noted alongside each recommendation. For hotels, we include the lowest cost of a standard double room in high season. For restaurants, we cite the average price of a main course at dinner or, if dinner isn't served, at lunch. For attractions, we always list adult admission fees; discounts are usually available for children, students, and senior citizens.

Hotels

Our local writers vet every hotel to recommend the best overnights in each price category, from budget to expensive. Unless otherwise specified, you can expect private bath, phone, and TV in your room. For expanded hotel reviews, facilities, and deals visit Fodors.com.

Restaurants

Unless we state otherwise, restaurants are open for lunch and dinner daily. We mention dress code only when there's a specific requirement and reservations only when they're essential or not accepted. To make restaurant reservations, visit Fodors.com.

Credit Cards

The hotels and restaurants in this guide typically accept credit cards. If not, we'll say so.

Top Picks
★ Fodor's Choice

Listings
- ⊠ Address
- ⊠ Branch address
- ☎ Telephone
- 🖷 Fax
- ⊕ Website
- ✉ E-mail
- 🎫 Admission fee
- ☉ Open/closed times
- Ⓜ Subway
- ✛ Directions or Map coordinates

Hotels & Restaurants
- 🏨 Hotel
- ⤶ Number of rooms
- ⅋◯⅋ Meal plans
- ✕ Restaurant
- ⚲ Reservations
- 🏛 Dress code
- ▭ No credit cards
- Ⓢ Price

Other
- ⇨ See also
- ☞ Take note
- 🏌 Golf facilities

Experience Maui

1

WHAT'S WHERE

1 West Maui. This leeward, sunny area with excellent beaches is ringed by upscale resorts and condominiums in areas such as Kaanapali and, farther north, Kapalua. Also on the coast is the busy, tourist-oriented town of Lahaina, a former whaling center with plenty of shops and good restaurants that's a base for snorkel and other tours.

2 South Shore. The leeward side of Maui's eastern half is what most people mean when they say South Shore. This popular area is sunny and warm year-round; Kihei, a fast-growing town, and Wailea, a luxurious resort area with some outstanding hotels, are here. Notable beaches include Makena, mostly undeveloped and spectacular, and Wailea, fronting the resorts.

3 Central Maui. Between Maui's two mountain areas is Central Maui, home to the county seat of Wailuku and the commercial center of Kahului. Kahului Airport, Maui's main terminal, is here, along with convenient shopping malls and a good selection of reasonably priced restaurants. In addition, local museums such as the Bailey House provide good background on Maui's history.

4 Upcountry. Island residents have a name they use affectionately to describe the regions climbing up the slope of Haleakala Crater: Upcountry. A visit to Haleakala National Park to see the volcanic crater is a must-do. The town of Makawao retains its country charm but also has interesting shopping. Upcountry is a great place for agricultural tours, too—you can visit a lavender farm or an organic farm, for example.

5 North Shore. The North Shore has no large resorts, just plenty of picturesque, laid-back small towns like Paia and Haiku—and great windsurfing action at Hookipa Beach. Baldwin Beach is a local favorite just off the highway. The towns are good spots for a break if you're heading out along the Road to Hana. Inland, this part of Maui is lush and wild.

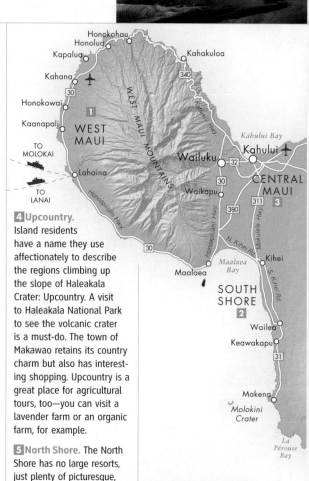

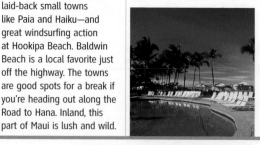

6 Road to Hana. The island's northeastern, windward side is largely one great rain forest, traversed by the stunning road to Hana. Exploring this iconic, winding road with its dramatic coastal views can be the highlight of a trip. The tiny town of Hana preserves the slow pace of the past; if you want to escape from it all, consider an overnight stay here.

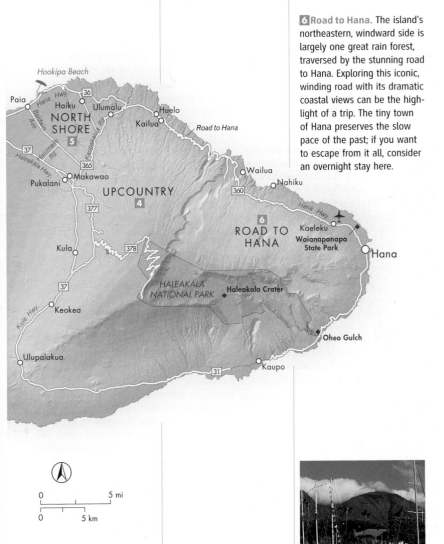

Hookipa Beach

Paia

Haiku
Ulumalu
Huelo
Kailua

Road to Hana

NORTH SHORE 5

37

365

Makawao

Pukalani

Wailua

Nahiku

UPCOUNTRY 4

360

Hana Hwy.

377

6
ROAD TO HANA

Kaeleku

Kula

378

Waianapanapa State Park

Hana

37

HALEAKALA NATIONAL PARK

Haleakala Crater

Keokea

Oheo Gulch

Ulupalakua

31

Kaupo

0 ____ 5 mi
0 ____ 5 km

MAUI AND HAWAII TODAY

When you experience Maui firsthand, it's hard not to gush about the long, perfect beaches, dramatic cliffs, greener-than-green rain forests, and the fragrance of plumeria that hangs over it all. Add to that the amazing marine life and the culture and history of the Hawaiian people, and it's easy to see why Maui is so popular.

The island consists of two distinct circular landmasses: the western area includes the rain-chiseled West Maui Mountains, and the larger eastern landmass includes Haleakala, with its cloud-wreathed volcanic peak. Maui has very different areas, from the resorts of sunny West Maui and the South Shore to the funky small towns of the North Shore, the ranches and farms of Upcountry, and the remote village of Hana in unspoiled East Maui.

Hawaiian culture and tradition here have experienced a renaissance over the last few decades. There's a real effort to revive traditions and to respect history as the Islands go through major changes. New developments often have a Hawaiian cultural expert on staff to ensure cultural sensitivity and to educate newcomers.

Nonetheless, development remains a huge issue for all islanders—land prices are skyrocketing, putting many areas out of reach for the native population. Traffic is becoming a problem on roads that were not designed to accommodate all the new drivers, and the Islands' limited natural resources are being seriously tapped. The government, though sluggish to respond at first, is trying to make development in Hawaii as sustainable as possible.

Sustainability

Although sustainability is an effective buzzword and authentic direction for the Islands' dining establishments, 90% of Hawaii's food and energy is imported.

Most of the land was used for monocropping of pineapple or sugarcane, both of which have all but vanished. Sugarcane is now produced in only two plants on Kauai and Maui, while pineapple production has dropped precipitously. Dole, once the largest pineapple company in Hawaii, closed its plants in 1991, and after 90 years Del Monte stopped pineapple production in 2008. The next year, Maui Land and Pineapple Company also ceased its Maui Gold pineapple operation, although in early 2010 a group of executives took over one third of the land and created a new company. Low cost of labor and transportation from Latin American and Southeast Asian pineapple producers are factors contributing to the industry's demise in Hawaii. Although this proves daunting, it also sets the stage for great agricultural change to be explored.

Back-to-Basics Agriculture

Emulating how the Hawaiian ancestors lived and returning to their simple ways of growing and sharing a variety of foods has become a statewide initiative. Hawaii has the natural conditions and talent to produce far more diversity in agriculture than it currently does.

The seed of this movement thrives through various farmers' markets and partnerships between restaurants and local farmers. Localized efforts such as the Hawaii Farm Bureau Federation are collectively leading the organic and sustainable agricultural renaissance. From home-cooked meals to casual plate lunches to fine-dining cuisine, these sustainable trailblazers enrich

the culinary tapestry of Hawaii and uplift the Islands' overall quality of life.

Tourism and the Economy

The $10+ billion tourism industry represents a third of Hawaii's state income. Naturally, this dependency causes economic hardship as the financial meltdown of recent years affects tourists' ability to visit and spend.

One way the industry has changed has been to adopt more eco-conscious practices, as many Hawaiians feel that development shouldn't happen without regard for impact to local communities and their natural environment.

Belief that an industry based on the Hawaiians' *aloha* should protect, promote, and empower local culture and provide more entrepreneurial opportunities for local people has become more important to tourism businesses. More companies are incorporating authentic Hawaiiana in their programs with the aim of not only providing a commercially viable tour but also ensuring that the visitor leaves feeling connected to his or her host.

The concept of *kuleana*, a word for both privilege and responsibility, is upheld. Having the privilege to live in such a sublime place comes with the responsibility to protect it.

Sovereignty

Political issues of sovereignty continue to divide Native Hawaiians, who have formed myriad organizations, each operating with a separate agenda and lacking one collectively defined goal. Ranging from achieving complete independence to solidifying a nation within a nation, existing sovereignty models remain fractured and their future unresolved.

The introduction of the Native Hawaiian Government Reorganization Act of 2009 attempts to set up a legal framework in which Native Hawaiians can attain federal recognition and coexist as a self-governed entity. Also known as the Akaka Bill after Senator Daniel Akaka of Hawaii, this pending bill has been presented before Congress and is still awaiting a vote at the time of this writing.

Rise of Hawaiian Pride

After the overthrow of the monarchy in 1893, a process of Americanization began. Traditions were duly silenced in the name of citizenship. Teaching Hawaiian language was banned from schools and children were distanced from their local customs.

But Hawaiians are resilient people, and with the rise of the civil rights movement they began to reflect on their own national identity, bringing an astonishing renaissance of the Hawaiian culture to fruition.

The people rediscovered language, hula, chanting, and even the traditional Polynesian arts of canoe building and wayfinding (navigation by the stars without use of instruments). This cultural resurrection is now firmly established in Hawaiian life, with a palpable pride that exudes from Hawaiians young and old.

The election of President Barack Obama definitely increased Hawaiian pride and inspired a ubiquitous hope for a better future. The president's strong connection and commitment to Hawaiian values of diversity, spirituality, family, and conservation have restored confidence that Hawaii can inspire a more peaceful, tolerant, and environmentally conscious world.

MAUI PLANNER

When You Arrive

Most visitors arrive at Kahului Airport in Central Maui. A rental car is the best way to get from the airport to your destination. The major car-rental companies have desks at the airport and can provide a map and directions to your hotel. ■ TIP→ Flights to Maui tend to land around the same time, leading to long lines at car-rental windows. If possible, send one person to pick up the car while the others wait for the baggage.

Visitor Information

The Hawaii Visitors & Convention Bureau (HVCB) has plenty of general and vacation-planning information for Maui and all the Islands, and offers a free official vacation planner. The Maui Visitors and Convention Bureau website includes information on accommodations, sights, events, and suggested itineraries.

Hawaii Visitors & Convention Bureau ✉ *2270 Kalakaua Ave., Suite 801, Honolulu* ☎ *808/923–1811, 800/464–2924 to order free visitor guide* ⊕ *www.gohawaii.com.*

Maui Visitors and Convention Bureau ⊕ *www.gohawaii.com/maui.*

Getting Here and Around

If you want to travel around on your own schedule, a rental car is a must on Maui. It's also one of your biggest trip expenses, especially given the price of gasoline—higher on Maui than on Oahu or the mainland. *See Travel Smart for details of renting a car and driving.* If you need to ask for directions, try your best to pronounce the multivowel road names. Locals don't use (or know) highway route numbers and will respond with looks as blank as yours. Also, they will give you directions by the time it takes to get somewhere rather than by the mileage.

Island Driving Times

Driving from one point on Maui to another can take longer than the mileage indicates. It's 52 miles from Kahului Airport to Hana, but the drive will take you about three hours if you stop to smell the flowers, which you certainly should do. As for driving to Haleakala, the 38-mile drive from sea level to the summit will take about two hours. The roads are narrow and winding; you must travel slowly. Kahului is the transportation hub—the main airport and largest harbor are here. Traffic on Maui's roads can be heavy, especially during the rush hours of 6 am to 8:30 am and 3:30 pm to 6:30 pm. Here are average driving times.

Kahului to Wailea	17 miles/30 mins
Kahului to Kaanapali	25 miles/45 mins
Kahului to Kapalua	36 miles/1 hr, 15 mins
Kahului to Makawao	13 miles/25 mins
Kapalua to Haleakala	73 miles/3 hrs
Kaanapali to Haleakala	62 miles/2 hrs, 30 mins
Wailea to Haleakala	54 miles/2 hrs, 30 mins
Kapalua to Hana	88 miles/5 hrs
Kaanapali to Hana	77 miles/5 hrs
Wailea to Hana	69 miles/4 hrs, 30 mins
Wailea to Lahaina	20 miles/45 mins
Kapalua to Lahaina	12 miles/25 mins

Island Hopping

If you have a week or more on Maui, you may want to set aside a day or two for a trip to Molokai or Lanai. Tour operators such as Trilogy offer day-trip packages to Lanai, which include snorkeling and a van tour of the island. Ferries are available to both islands and have room for your golf clubs and mountain bike. (The Molokai channel can be rough, so avoid ferry travel on a blustery day.)

If you prefer to travel to Molokai or Lanai by air, and you're not averse to flying on 4- to 12-seaters, your best bet is a small air taxi. Book with Pacific Wings *(see Air Travel in Getting Here and Around in Travel Smart)* for flights to Hana, Maui, or Kalaupapa and Molokai, as well as the main airports.

Dining and Lodging on Maui

Hawaii is a melting pot of cultures, and nowhere is this more apparent than in its cuisines. From luau and "plate lunches" to sushi and teriyaki steak, there's no shortage of interesting flavors and presentations. Restaurant atmosphere varies, too, from casual local spots to elegantly decorated resort restaurants.

Whether you're looking for a quick snack or a multicourse meal, we can help you find the best eating experiences the island has to offer. Jump in and enjoy!

Choosing lodging is a tough decision, but fret not—our expert writers and editors have done most of the legwork.

To help narrow your choices, consider what type of property you'd like to stay at (big resort, quiet bed-and-breakfast, or condo rental) and what type of island climate you're looking for (beachfront strand or remote rain forest). We give you all the details you need to book a place that suits your style.

■ TIP→ **Reserve your room well in advance, and ask about discounts and packages. Hotel websites often have Internet-only deals.**

Money Savers

There are ways to travel to paradise even on a budget.

Accommodations: No matter what the season, ask about deals—a free night after three or four or five paid nights, kids stay free, meal credits. Condos are less expensive and bigger than hotel rooms and are perfect for families or groups of friends. If you pass up the ocean view, you'll save money on your hotel or condo. September, October, and May are off-peak months with many hotels offering reduced rates.

Food: Eat a big breakfast and skip lunch. You'll probably be sightseeing or at the beach anyway. It's easy to get by with a smoothie or fruit and yogurt. If you eat lunch out, go to that high-end restaurant. Lunch will be less expensive. If you're staying in a condo, eat in or pack a picnic as often as you can.

Activities: Pick up free publications at the airport and at racks all over the island; many of them are filled with money-saving coupons; also check newspapers. Activity desks—there are dozens around Kaanapali and Wailea as well as in Lahaina and Kihei—are good places to check on deals and discounts if you're not booking in advance. However, advance booking will ensure you get the activity you want; sometimes you can save 10% or more if you book on outfitters' websites.

MAUI
TOP ATTRACTIONS

Hike Haleakala

(A) Take time to trek down one of the trails into Haleakala National Park's massive bowl and see proof, at this dormant volcano, of how powerful the earth's exhalations can be. The cinder cones have beautiful swirls of subtle colors that can sparkle in the sunlight. You won't see a landscape like this anywhere, outside of visiting the moon. The barren terrain is deceptive, however—many of the world's rarest plants, birds, and insects live here.

Take the Road to Hana

(B) Spectacular views of waterfalls, lush forests, and the sparkling ocean are part of the pleasure of the twisting drive along the North Shore to tiny, timeless Hana in East Maui. The journey is the destination, but once you arrive, kick back and enjoy. Wave to pedestrians, "talk story" with locals in line at the Hasegawa store, and explore the multicolor beaches. An overnight stay here allows for the most

relaxed experience, though; a day trip is a big push. You may decide to drive just part of the way as an alternative.

Discover the Joy of Snorkeling

(C) Snorkeling is a must, either on your own with a buddy or on a snorkel cruise. Maui has snorkel boats of all sizes to take you to spots such as the Molokini Crater. Wherever you duck under, you'll be inducted into a mesmerizing world underwater. Slow down and keep your eyes open; even fish dressed in camouflage can be spotted when they snatch at food passing by. Some great spots to try right near the shore are Honolua Bay and Kekaa (known as Black Rock, it's in front of the Sheraton Maui) in West Maui; there are also good spots on the rocky fringes of Wailea's beaches on the South Shore.

Stretch Out on Makena

(D) This South Shore beauty is the sand dreams are made of: deep, golden, and pillowy. Don't be discouraged by the

crammed parking lots; there's more than enough room. Makena (Oneloa in Hawaiian) is still relatively wild. There are no hotels, minimarts, or public restrooms nearby—instead there's crystal-clear water, the occasional pod of dolphins, and drop-dead-gorgeous scenery (including the sunbathers). You can grab a fish taco and a drink at a nearby truck for a tasty lunch.

Buy Tropical Fruit at a Roadside Stand
(E) Your first taste of ripe guava or mango is something to remember. Delicious lychee, mangoes, star fruit, bananas, passion fruit, pineapple, and papaya can be bought on the side of the road with the change in your pocket. Go on, let the juice run down your chin. Farmers' markets are another place to seek out taste treats—just be sure to ask if what you crave is, indeed, local.

Try the Resorts and Spas
(F) Indulge your inner rock star at the posh, pampering resorts and spas around the island. Sip a "Tommy Girl" in the hot tub at the Four Seasons or get massaged poolside at the Grand Wailea. Even if you don't stay the night, you can enjoy the opulent gardens, restaurants, art collections, and perfectly cordial staff. For pure relaxation, book a spa treatment from the extensive menus.

Escape to a Bed-and-Breakfast
(G) Being a shut-in isn't so bad at a secluded B&B. It's a sure way to get a taste of what it's like to live in paradise: trees hanging with ripe fruit outside your door, late-night tropical rainstorms, a wild chicken or two. Rather than blasting the air-conditioning in a hotel room, relax with the windows open in a plantation house designed to capture sea breezes.

Whale-Watch

(H) Maui is the cradle for hundreds of humpback whales that return every year from late December through April to frolic in the warm waters and give birth. Watch a mama whale teach her one-ton calf how to tail-wave. You can eavesdrop on them, too: book a tour boat with a hydrophone or just plunk your head underwater to hear the strange squeaks, groans, and chortles of the cetaceans. Tours are good, but you can also easily watch whales from the beach.

Listen to Hawaiian Music

(I) Before his untimely death in 1997, Israel Kamakawiwoole, or "IZ," woke the world to the sound of modern Hawaiian music. Don't leave without hearing it live. The Maui Arts & Cultural Center in Kahului has top Hawaiian entertainers regularly, and so do many island bars and restaurants. The Wednesday-night George Kahumoku Jr.'s Slack Key Show: Masters of Hawaiian Music concert series at the Napili Kai Beach Resort in West Maui is excellent. The Hawaiian Slack Key Guitar Festival (check ⊕ *www.slackkeyfestival. com*) features guest performers who play Hawaii's signature style.

Go Surfing on West Maui

(J) Feel the thrill of a wave rushing beneath your feet at any one of the beginner's breaks along Honoapiilani Highway. Ask local surf schools about the best locations for beginners and consider taking a lesson or two. You can bring surf wax home as a souvenir. Stand-up paddle surfing is popular now, too.

Attend the Old Lahaina Luau

(K) The Old Lahaina Luau has a warm heart—and seriously good *poke* (diced raw tuna tossed with herbs and other seasonings). Tuck a flower behind your ear, mix a dab of *poi* (taro-root paste) with your *lomilomi* salmon (rubbed with onions and herbs), and you'll be living like

a local. Different styles of hula are part of the performance; the fire dancers are not traditional, but they are fun. Reserve well in advance.

Tee Off in Paradise

(L) Spectacular views, great weather year-round, and challenging courses created by the game's top designers make Maui an inspiring place to play golf. The Kapulua Resort on West Maui and the Wailea and Makena resort courses on the South Shore offer memorable rounds. Check about twilight fees to save some money.

Tour Upcountry

(M) Beach lovers might need some arm-twisting to head up the mountain for a day, but the views and the fresh-smelling countryside are ample reward. On the roads winding through ranchlands, crisp, high-altitude air is scented with eucalyptus and the fragrances of the forest. Stop for an agricultural tour and learn about

where the island's bounty comes from; you can sample it, too.

Dig into Ono Kine Grinds

(N) *"Ono kine grinds"* is local slang for delicious food you'll find at dozens of restaurants island-wide. Maui chefs take their work seriously, and they have good material to start with: sun-ripened produce and seafood caught the very same morning. Try a plate lunch, that reminder of the state's cultural mix, at a casual spot. Sample as many types of fish as you can and don't be shy: try it raw. And try shave ice flavored with tropical fruit syrups.

Windsurf at Kanaha or Hookipa

(O) You might not be a water-sports legend, but that doesn't mean you can't give it a try. In the early morning some of windsurfing's big-wave spots are safe for beginners. Don't settle for the pond in front of your hotel—book a lesson on the North Shore and impress yourself by hanging tough where the action is.

WHEN TO GO

Long days of sunshine and fairly mild year-round temperatures make Hawaii, including Maui, an all-season destination. Most resort areas are at sea level, with average afternoon temperatures of 75°F to 80°F during the coldest months of December and January; during the hottest months of August and September the temperature often reaches 90°F. Higher Upcountry elevations have cooler and often misty conditions. Only at mountain summits does it reach freezing.

Typically the weather on Maui is drier in summer (more guaranteed beach days) and rainier in winter (greener foliage, better waterfalls). Throughout the year, West Maui and the South Shore (the leeward areas) are the driest, sunniest areas on the island—that's why the resorts are there. The North Shore and East Maui and Hana (the windward areas) get the most rain, are densely forested, and abound with waterfalls and rainbows.

Many travelers head to the Islands in winter, especially during Christmas and spring break; room rates average 10% to 15% higher during these times than the rest of the year. The best months for bargains are May, September, and October.

Seasonal Specialties

In winter Maui is *the* spot for whale-watching. The humpback whales start arriving in December, are in full force by February, and are gone by early May. The biggest North Shore waves show up in winter: kiteboarders and windsurfers get their thrills in the windy, late summer months.

Only-in-Hawaii Holidays

Hawaiians appreciate any occasion to celebrate; not only are indigenous Hawaiian holidays honored, so are those of the state's early immigrant cultures. If you happen to be in the Islands on March 26 or June 11, you'll notice light traffic and busy beaches—these are state holidays. March 26 recognizes the birthday of Prince Jonah Kuhio Kalanianaole, a member of the royal line who spearheaded the effort to set aside homelands for Hawaiian people. June 11 honors the first island-wide monarch, Kamehameha the Great; locals drape his statues with lei and stage elaborate parades. May 1 isn't an official holiday, but it's Lei Day in Hawaii, when schools and civic groups celebrate the flower lei with lei-making contests and pageants. Statehood Day is celebrated on the third Friday in August (Admission Day was August 21, 1959). Most Japanese and Chinese holidays are widely observed. On Chinese New Year, in winter, homes and businesses sprout red good-luck mottoes and everybody eats *gau* (steamed pudding) and *jai* (vegetarian stew). Good Friday is a state holiday in spring, a favorite for picnics. Summertime is for Obon festivals and the July 4 Rodeo; the Maui County Fair and Aloha Festivals are in fall.

Climate

The following are average maximum and minimum temperatures for Lahaina in West Maui; the temperatures throughout the Hawaiian Islands are similar.

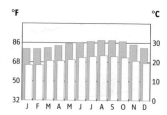

GREAT ITINERARIES

Maui's landscape is incredibly diverse, offering everything from underwater encounters with eagle rays to treks across moonlike terrain. Although daydreaming at the pool or on the beach may fulfill your initial island fantasy, Maui has much more to offer. The following one-day itineraries will take you to our favorite spots on the island.

Beach Day in West Maui

West Maui has some of the island's most beautiful beaches, though many of them are hidden by megaresorts. If you get an early start, you can begin your day snorkeling at Slaughterhouse Beach (in winter, D.T. Fleming Beach is a better option as it's less rough). Then spend the day beach hopping through Kapalua, Napili, and Kaanapali as you make your way south. You'll want to get to Lahaina before dark so you can spend some time exploring the historic whaling town before choosing a restaurant for a sunset dinner.

Focus on Marine Life on the South Shore

Start your South Shore trip early in the morning, and head out past Makena into the rough lava fields of rugged La Pérouse Bay. At the road's end there are areas of the Ahihi-Kinau Marine Preserve open to the public (others are closed indefinitely) that offer good snorkeling. If that's a bit too far afield for you, there's excellent snorkeling at Polo Beach. Head to the right (your right while facing the ocean) for plenty of fish and beautiful coral. Head back north to Kihei for lunch, and then enjoy the afternoon learning more about Maui's marine life at the outstanding Maui Ocean Center at Maalaea.

Haleakala National Park, Upcountry, and the North Shore

If you don't plan to spend an entire day hiking in the crater at Haleakala National Park, this itinerary will at least allow you to take a peek at it. Get up early and head straight for the summit of Haleakala (if you're jet-lagged and waking up in the middle of the night, you may want to get there in time for sunrise). Bring water, sunscreen, and warm clothing; it's freezing at sunrise. Plan to spend a couple of hours exploring the various lookout points in the park. On your way down the mountain, turn right on Makawao Avenue and head into the little town of Makawao. You can have lunch here, or make a left on Baldwin Avenue and head downhill to the North Shore town of Paia, which has a number of great lunch spots and shops to explore. Spend the rest of your afternoon at Paia's main strip of sand, Hookipa Beach.

The Road to Hana

This cliff-side driving tour through rainforest canopy reveals Maui's lushest and most tropical terrain. It will take a full day to explore this part of the North Shore and East Maui, especially if you plan to make it all the way to Oheo Gulch. You'll pass through communities where Old Hawaii still thrives, and where the forest runs unchecked from the sea to the summit. You'll want to make frequent exploratory stops. To really soak in the magic of this place, consider staying overnight in Hana town. That way you can spend a full day winding toward Hana, hiking and exploring along the way, and the next day traveling leisurely back to civilization.

MAUI'S TOP BEACHES

Ah, Maui's beaches: it's hard to single out just a few because the island's strands are so varied. The leeward shores of West and South Maui have calm beaches and some great snorkeling, but experienced surfers and windsurfers gravitate to the windward (North Shore and East Maui) beaches that face the open ocean. Here are some favorites for different interests from around the island.

Best for Families

Baldwin Beach, the North Shore. The long, shallow, calm end closest to Kahului is safe even for toddlers—with adult supervision, of course.

Kamaole III, the South Shore. Sand, gentle surf, a playground, volleyball net, and barbecues all add up to great family fun.

Napili Beach, West Maui. Kids will love the turtles that snack on the *limu* (seaweed) growing on the lava rocks. This intimate crescent-shape beach offers sunbathing, snorkeling, swimming, bodysurfing, and startling sunsets.

Best Offshore Snorkeling

Olowalu, West Maui. The water remains shallow far offshore, and there's plenty to see.

Ulua, the South Shore. It's beautiful and the kids can enjoy the tide pools while the adults experience the excellent snorkeling.

Best Surfing

Hookipa, the North Shore. This is the place to see great surfers and windsurfers: it's not for beginners or for swimmers, but Hookipa is great for experienced wave riders and also for anyone who wants to take in the North Shore scene.

Honolua Bay, West Maui. One bay over from Slaughterhouse (Mokuleia) Beach north of Kapalua you can find one of the best surf breaks in Hawaii.

Best Sunsets

Kapalua Bay, West Maui. The ambience here is as stunning as the sunset.

Keawakapu, the South Shore. Most active beachgoers enjoy this gorgeous spot before midafternoon, when the wind picks up, so it's never crowded at sunset.

Best for Seeing and Being Seen

Kaanapali Beach, West Maui. Backed by resorts, condos, and restaurants, this is not the beach for solitude. But the sand is soft, the waters are gentle, and the action varies from good snorkeling at Black Rock (Kekaa) to people-watching in front of Whalers Village—not for nothing is this section called "Dig Me Beach."

Wailea Beach, the South Shore. At this beach fronting the ultraluxurious Four Seasons and Grand Wailea resorts, you never know who might be "hiding" in that private cabana.

Best Setting

Makena (Oneloa), South Shore. Don't forget the camera for this beauty, a state park away from the Wailea resort area. Finding it is worth the effort—a long, wide stretch of golden sand and translucent offshore water. The icing on the cake is that this long beach is never crowded. Use caution for swimming, because the steep, onshore break can get big.

Waianapanapa State Park, East Maui. This rustic black-sand beach will capture your heart—it's framed by lava cliffs and backed by bright green beach *naupaka* bushes. Ocean currents can be strong, so enjoy the views and cool off in one of two freshwater pools. Get an early start, because your day's destination is just shy of Hana.

HAWAIIAN HISTORY

Hawaiian history is long and complex; a brief survey can put into context the ongoing renaissance of native arts and culture.

The Polynesians

Long before both Christopher Columbus and the Vikings, Polynesian seafarers set out to explore the vast stretches of the open ocean in double-hulled canoes. From western Polynesia they traveled back and forth between Samoa, Fiji, Tahiti, the Marquesas, and the Society Isles, settling on the outer reaches of the Pacific, Hawaii, and Easter Island, as early as AD 300. The golden era of Polynesian voyaging peaked around AD 1200, after which the distant Hawaiian Islands were left to develop their own unique cultural practices and subsistence in relative isolation.

The island's symbiotic society was deeply intertwined with religion, mythology, science, and artistry. Ruled by an *alii*, or chief, each settlement was nestled in an *ahupuaa*, a pie-shaped land division from the uplands where the alii lived, through the valleys and down to the shores where the commoners resided. Everyone contributed, whether it was by building canoes, catching fish, making tools, or farming land.

A United Kingdom

When the British explorer Captain James Cook arrived in 1778, he was revered as a god upon his arrival. With guns and ammunition purchased from Cook, the Big Island chief, Kamehameha the Great, gained a significant advantage over the other alii. He united Hawaii into one kingdom in 1810, bringing an end to the frequent interisland battles that dominated Hawaiian life.

Tragically, the new kingdom was beset with troubles. Native religion was abandoned, and *kapu* (laws and regulations) were eventually abolished. The European explorers brought foreign diseases with them, and within a few short decades the Native Hawaiian population was decimated.

New laws regarding land ownership and religious practices eroded the underpinnings of pre-contact Hawaii. Each successor to the Hawaiian throne sacrificed more control over the island kingdom. As Westerners permeated Hawaiian culture, Hawaii became more riddled with layers of racial issues, injustice, and social unrest.

Modern Hawaii

In 1893 the last Hawaiian monarch, Queen Liliuokalani, was overthrown by a group of Americans and European businessmen and government officials, aided by an armed militia. This led to the creation of the Republic of Hawaii, and it became a U.S. territory for the next 60 years. The loss of Hawaiian sovereignty and the conditions of annexation have haunted the Hawaiian people since the monarchy was deposed.

Pearl Harbor was attacked in 1941, which engaged the United States immediately into World War II. Tourism, from its beginnings in the early 1900s, flourished after the war and naturally inspired rapid real-estate development in Waikiki. In 1959 Hawaii officially became the 50th state. Statehood paved the way for Hawaiians to participate in the American democratic process. With the rise of the civil rights movement in the 1960s, Hawaiians began to reclaim their own identity, from language to hula.

THE HAWAIIAN ISLANDS

Oahu. The state's capital, Honolulu, is on Oahu; this is the center of Hawaii's economy and by far the most populated island in the chain—953,000 residents add up to 71% of the state's population. At 597 square miles Oahu is the third largest island in the chain; the majority of residents live in or around Honolulu, so the rest of the island still fits neatly into the tropical, untouched vision of Hawaii. Situated southeast of Kauai and northwest of Maui, Oahu is a central location for island hopping. Pearl Harbor, iconic Waikiki Beach, and surfing contests on the legendary North Shore are all here.

Maui. The second largest island in the chain, Maui is northwest of the Big Island and close enough to be visible from its beaches on a clear day. The island's 729 square miles are home to only 155,000 people but host more than 2 million tourists every year. With its restaurants and lively nightlife, Maui is the only island that competes with Oahu in terms of entertainment; its charm lies in the fact that although entertainment is available, Maui's towns still feel like island villages compared to the heaving modern city of Honolulu.

Hawaii (The Big Island). The Big Island has the second largest population of the Islands (almost 190,000) but feels sparsely settled due to its size. It's 4,038 square miles and growing—all the other Islands could fit onto the Big Island and there would still be room left over. The southernmost island in the chain (slightly southeast of Maui), the Big Island is home to Kilauea, the most active volcano on the planet. It percolates within Volcanoes National Park, which draws nearly 3 million visitors every year.

Kauai. The northernmost island in the chain (northwest of Oahu), Kauai is, at approximately 622 square miles, the fourth largest of all the Islands and the least populated of the larger Islands, with 67,000 residents. Known as the Garden Isle, this island is home to lush botanical gardens as well as the stunning Napali Coast and Waimea Canyon. The island is a favorite with honeymooners and others wanting to get away from it all—lush and peaceful, it's the perfect escape from the modern world.

Molokai. North of Lanai and Maui, and east of Oahu, Molokai is Hawaii's fifth-largest island, encompassing 260 square miles. On a clear night, the lights of Honolulu are visible from Molokai's western shore. Molokai is sparsely populated, with about 7,300 residents, the majority of whom are Native Hawaiians. Most of the island's 79,000 annual visitors travel from Maui or Oahu to spend the day exploring its beaches, cliffs, and former leper colony on Kalaupapa Peninsula.

Lanai. Lying just off Maui's western coast, Lanai looks nothing like its sister Islands, with pine trees and deserts in place of palm trees and beaches. Still, the tiny 140-square-mile island is home to about 3,200 residents and draws an average of 75,000 visitors each year to two resorts (one in the mountains and one at the shore), both operated by Four Seasons, and the small, 11-room Hotel Lanai.

Hawaii's Geology

The Hawaiian Islands comprise more than just the islands inhabited and visited by humans. A total of 19 islands and atolls constitute the State of Hawaii, with a total landmass of 6,423.4 square miles.

The Islands are actually exposed peaks of a submersed mountain range called

the Hawaiian Ridge-Emperor Seamounts chain. The range was formed as the Pacific plate moves very slowly (around 32 miles every million years—or about as much as your fingernails grow in one year) over a hot spot in the Earth's mantle. Because the plate moves northwestwardly, the Islands in the northwest portion of the archipelago (chain) are older, which is also why they're smaller—they have been eroding longer and have actually sunk back into the sea floor.

The Big Island is the youngest, and thus the largest, island in the chain. It is built from five different volcanoes, including Mauna Loa, which is the largest mountain on the planet (when measured from the bottom of the sea floor). Mauna Loa and Kilauea are the only Hawaiian volcanoes still erupting with any sort of frequency. Mauna Loa last erupted in 1984. Kilauea has been continuously erupting since 1983.

Mauna Kea (Big Island), Hualalai (Big Island), and Haleakala (Maui) are all in what's called the post-shield-building stage of volcanic development—eruptions decrease steadily for up to a million years before ceasing entirely. Kohala (Big Island), Lanai (Lanai), and Waianae (Oahu) are considered extinct volcanoes, in the erosional stage of development; Koolau (Oahu) and West Maui (Maui) volcanoes are extinct volcanoes in the rejuvenation stage—after lying dormant for hundreds of thousands of years, they began erupting again, but only once every several thousand years.

There is currently an active undersea volcano to the south and east of the Big Island called Kamaehu that has been erupting regularly. If it continues its current pattern, it should breach the ocean's surface in tens of thousands of years.

Hawaii's Flora and Fauna

More than 90% of native Hawaiian flora and fauna are endemic (they evolved into unique species here), like the koa tree and the yellow hibiscus. Long-dormant volcanic craters are perfect hiding places for rare native plants. The silversword, a rare cousin of the sunflower, grows on Hawaii's three tallest peaks: Haleakala, Mauna Kea, and Mauna Loa, and nowhere else on Earth. Ohia trees—thought to be the favorite of Pele, the volcano goddess—bury their roots in fields of once-molten lava, and one variety sprouts ruby pom-pom–like lehua blossoms. The deep yellow petals of ilima (once reserved for royalty) are tiny discs, which make the most elegant lei.

But most of the plants you see while walking around aren't Hawaiian at all and came from Tahitian, Samoan, or European visitors. Plumeria is ubiquitous; alien orchids run rampant on the Big Island; bright orange relatives of the ilima light up the mountains of Oahu. Though these flowers are not native, they give the Hawaiian lei their color and fragrance.

Hawaii's state bird, the nene goose, is making a comeback from its former endangered status. It roams freely in parts of Maui, Kauai, and the Big Island. Rare Hawaiian monk seals breed in the northwestern Islands. With only 1,500 left in the wild, you probably won't catch many lounging on the beaches, though they have been spotted on the shores of Kauai in recent years. Spinner dolphins and sea turtles can be found off the coast of all the Islands; and every year from November to April, the humpback whales migrate past Hawaii in droves.

HAWAIIAN PEOPLE AND THEIR CULTURE

By October 2012, Hawaii's population was more than 1.3 million with the majority of residents living on Oahu. Ten percent are Hawaiian or other Pacific Islander, almost 40% are Asian American, 9% are Latino, and about 26% Caucasian. Nearly a fifth of the population list two or more races, making Hawaii the most diverse state in the United States.

Among individuals 18 and older, about 89% finished high school, half attained some college, and 29% completed a bachelor's degree or higher.

The Role of Tradition

The kingdom of Hawaii was ruled by a spiritual class system. Although the *alii,* or chief, was believed to be the direct descendent of a deity or god, high priests, known as *kahuna,* presided over every imaginable aspect of life and *kapu* (taboos) that strictly governed the commoners.

Each part of nature and ritual was connected to a deity—Kane was the highest of all deities, symbolizing sunlight and creation; Ku was the god of war; Lono represented fertility, rainfall, music, and peace; Kanaloa was the god of the underworld or darker spirits. Probably the most well known by outsiders is Pele, the goddess of fire.

The kapu not only provided social order, they also swayed the people to act with reverence for the environment. Any abuse was met with extreme punishment, often death, as it put the land and people's *mana,* or spiritual power, in peril.

Ancient deities play a huge role in Hawaiian life today—not just in daily rituals, but in the Hawaiians' reverence for their land. Gods and goddesses tend to be associated with particular parts of the land, and most of them are connected with

many places, thanks to the body of stories built up around each.

One of the most important ways the ancient Hawaiians showed respect for their gods and goddesses was through the hula. Various forms of the hula were performed as prayers to the gods and as praise to the chiefs. Performances were taken very seriously, as a mistake was thought to invalidate the prayer, or even to offend the god or chief in question. Hula is still performed both as entertainment and as prayer; it is not uncommon for a hula performance to be included in an official government ceremony.

Who Are the Hawaiians Today?

To define the Hawaiians in a page, let alone a paragraph, is nearly impossible. Those considered to be indigenous Hawaiians are descendants of the ancient Polynesians who crossed the vast ocean and settled Hawaii. According to the government, there are Native Hawaiians or native Hawaiians (note the change in capitalization), depending on a person's background.

Federal and state agencies apply different methods to determine Hawaiian lineage, from measuring blood percentage to mapping genealogy. This has caused turmoil within the community because it excludes many who claim Hawaiian heritage. It almost guarantees that, as races intermingle, even those considered Native Hawaiian now will eventually disappear on paper, displacing generations to come.

Modern Hawaiian Culture

Perfect weather aside, Hawaii might be the warmest place anyone can visit. The Hawaii experience begins and ends with *aloha,* a word that envelops love, affection, and mercy, and has become a salutation for hello and good-bye. Broken

down, *alo* means "presence" and *ha* means "breath"—the presence of breath. It's to live with love and respect for self and others with every breath. Past the manicured resorts and tour buses, aloha is a moral compass that binds all of Hawaii's people.

Hawaii is blessed with some of the most unspoiled natural wonders, and aloha extends to the land, or *aina*. Hawaiians are raised outdoors and have strong ties to nature. They realize as children that the ocean and land are the delicate sources of all life. Even ancient gods were embodied by nature, and this reverence has been passed down to present generations who believe in *kuleana*, their privilege and responsibility.

Hawaii's diverse cultures unfold in a beautiful montage of customs and arts—from music, to dance, to food. Musical genres range from slack key to *Jawaiian* (Hawaiian reggae) to *hapa-haole* (Hawaiian music with English words). From George Kahumoku's Grammy-worthy laid-back strumming to the late Iz Kamakawiwoole's "Somewhere over the Rainbow" to Jack Johnson's more mainstream tunes, contemporary Hawaiian music has definitely carved its ever-evolving niche.

The Merrie Monarch Festival is celebrating almost 50 years of worldwide hula competition and education. The fine-dining culinary scene, especially in Honolulu, has a rich tapestry of ethnic influences and talent. But the real gems are the humble hole-in-the-wall eateries that serve authentic cuisines of many ethnic origins in one plate, a deliciously mixed plate indeed.

And perhaps, the most striking quality in today's Hawaiian culture is the sense of family, or *ohana*. Sooner or later, almost everyone you meet becomes an uncle or auntie, and it is not uncommon for near strangers to be welcomed into a home as a member of the family.

Until the last century, the practice of *hanai*, in which a family essentially adopts a child, usually a grandchild, without formalities, was still prevalent. While still practiced to a somewhat lesser degree, the *hanai*, which means to feed or nourish, still resonates within most families and communities.

How to Act Like a Local

Adopting local customs is a firsthand introduction to the Islands' unique culture. So live in T-shirts and shorts. Wear cheap rubber flip-flops, but call them slippers. Wave people into your lane on the highway, and, when someone lets you in, give them a wave of thanks in return. Never, ever blow your horn, even when the pickup truck in front of you is stopped for a long session of "talk story" right in the middle of the road.

Holoholo means to go out for the fun of it—an aimless stroll, ride, or drive. "Wheah you goin', braddah?" "Oh, holoholo." It's local speak for Sunday drive, no plan, it's not the destination but the journey. Try setting out without an itinerary. Learn to *shaka*: pinky and thumb extended, middle fingers curled in, waggle sideways. Eat white rice with everything. When someone says, "Aloha!" answer, "Aloha no!" ("And a real big aloha back to you"). And, as the locals say, "No make big body" ("Try not to act like you own the place").

TOP 10 HAWAIIAN FOODS TO TRY

Food in Hawaii is a reflection of the state's diverse cultural makeup and tropical location. Fresh seafood, organic fruits and vegetables, free-range beef, and locally grown products are the hallmarks of Hawaii regional cuisine. Its preparations are drawn from across the Pacific Rim, including Japan, the Philippines, Korea, and Thailand—and "local food" is a cuisine in its own right. Don't miss Hawaiian-grown coffee, either, whether it's smooth Kona from the Big Island or coffee grown on other islands.

Saimin

The ultimate hangover cure and the perfect comfort food during Hawaii's mild winters, *saimin* ranks at the top of the list of local favorites. In fact, it's one of the few dishes deemed truly local, having been highlighted in cookbooks since the 1930s. Saimin is an Asian-style noodle soup so ubiquitous, it's even on McDonald's menus statewide. In mom-and-pop shops, a large melamine bowl is filled with homemade *dashi*, or broth, and wheat-flour noodles and then topped off with strips of omelet, green onions, bright pink fish cake and *char siu* (Chinese roast pork) or canned luncheon meat, such as SPAM. Add shoyu (the "local" name for soy sauce) and chili pepper water, lift your chopsticks, and slurp away.

SPAM

Speaking of SPAM, Hawaii's most prevalent grab-and-go snack is SPAM *musubi*. Often displayed next to cash registers at groceries and convenience stores, the glorified rice ball is rectangular, topped with a slice of fried SPAM and wrapped in *nori* (seaweed). Musubi is a bite-sized meal in itself. But just like sushi, the rice part hardens when refrigerated. So it's best to gobble it up right after purchase.

Hormel Company's SPAM actually deserves its own recognition—way beyond as a mere musubi topping. About 5 million cans are sold per year in Hawaii, and the Aloha State even hosts a festival in its honor. It's inexpensive protein and goes a long way when mixed with rice, scrambled eggs, noodles or, well, anything. The spiced luncheon meat gained popularity in World War II days, when fish was rationed. Gourmets and those with aversions to salt, high cholesterol, or high blood pressure may cringe at the thought of eating it, but SPAM in Hawaii is here to stay.

Manapua

Another savory snack is *manapua*, fist-sized dough balls fashioned after Chinese *bao* (a traditional Chinese bun) and stuffed with fillings such as *char siu* (Chinese roast pork) and then steamed. Many mom-and-pop stores sell them in commercial steamer display cases along with pork hash and other dim sum. Modern-day fillings include curry chicken.

Fresh Ahi or Tako Poke

There's nothing like fresh ahi or *tako* (octopus) *poke* to break the ice at a backyard party, except, of course, the cold beer handed to you from the cooler. The perfect pupu, poke (pronounced poh-kay) is basically raw seafood cut into bite-sized chunks and mixed with everything from green onions to roasted and ground kukui nuts. Other variations include mixing the fish with chopped round onion, sesame oil, seaweed, and chili pepper water. Shoyu is the constant. These days, grocery stores sell a rainbow of varieties such as kimchi crab and anything goes, from adding mayonnaise to tobiko caviar. Fish lovers who want to take it to the next level order sashimi, the best cuts of ahi

sliced and dipped in a mixture of shoyu and wasabi.

Tropical Fruits

Tropical fruits such as apple banana and strawberry papaya are plucked from trees in Island neighborhoods and eaten for breakfast—plain or with a squeeze of fresh lime. Give them a try; the banana tastes like an apple and the papaya's rosy flesh explains its name. Locals also love to add their own creative touches to exotic fruits. Green mangoes are pickled with Chinese five-spice, and Maui Gold pineapples are topped with li hing mui powder (heck, even margarita glasses are rimmed with it). Green papaya is tossed in a Vietnamese salad with fish paste and fresh prawns.

Plate Lunch

It would be remiss not to mention the plate lunch as one of the most beloved dishes in Hawaii. It generally includes two scoops of sticky white rice, a scoop of macaroni or macaroni-potato salad, heavy on the mayo, and perhaps kimchi or *koko* (salted cabbage). There are countless choices of main protein such as chicken *katsu* (fried cutlet), fried mahimahi and beef tomato. The king of all plate lunches is the Hawaiian plate. The main item is laulau or kalua pig and cabbage along with poi, *lomilomi* salmon, chicken long rice, and sticky white rice.

Bento Box

The bento box gained popularity back in the plantation days, when workers toiled in the sugarcane fields. No one brought sandwiches to work then. Instead it was a lunch box with the ever-present steamed white rice, pickled *ume* (plum) to preserve the rice, and main meats such as fried chicken or fish. Today, many stores sell prepackaged bentos or you may go to an

okazuya (Japanese deli) with a hot buffet counter and create your own.

Malasadas

The Portuguese have contributed much to Hawaii cuisine in the form of sausage, soup, and sweetbread. But their most revered food is *malasadas*, hot, deep-fried doughnuts rolled in sugar. Malasadas are crowd-pleasers. Buy them by the dozen, hot from the fryer, placed in brown paper bags to absorb the grease. Or bite into gourmet malasadas at restaurants, filled with vanilla or chocolate cream.

Shave Ice

Much more than just a snow cone, shave ice is what locals crave after a blazing day at the beach or a hot-as-Hades game of soccer. If you're lucky, you'll find a neighborhood store that hand-shaves the ice, but it's rare. Either way, the counter person will ask you first if you'd like ice cream and/or adzuki beans scooped into the bottom of the cone or cup. Then they shape the ice to a giant mound and add colorful fruit syrups. First-timers should order the Rainbow, of course.

Crack Seed

There are dozens of varieties of crack seed in dwindling specialty shops and at the drugstores. Chinese call the preserved fruits and nuts *see mui* but somehow the Pidgin English version is what Hawaiians prefer. Those who like hard candy and salty foods will love li hing mangoes and rock salt plums, and those with an itchy throat will feel relief from the lemon strips. Peruse large glass jars of crack seed sold in bulk or smaller hanging bags—the latter make good gifts to give to friends back home.

ONLY IN HAWAII

Traveling to Hawaii is as close as an American can get to visiting another country while staying within the United States. There's much to learn and understand about the state's indigenous culture, the hundred years of immigration that resulted in today's blended society, and the tradition of aloha that has welcomed millions of visitors over the years.

Aloha Shirt

To go to Hawaii without taking an aloha shirt home is almost sacrilege. The first aloha shirts from the 1920s and 1930s—called "silkies"—were classic canvases of art and tailored for the tourists. Popular culture caught on in the 1950s, and they became a fashion craze. With the 1960s' more subdued designs, Aloha Friday was born, and the shirt became appropriate clothing for work, play, and formal occasions. Because of its soaring popularity, cheaper and mass-produced versions became available.

Hawaiian Quilt

Although ancient Hawaiians were already known to produce fine *kapa* (bark) cloth, the actual art of quilting originated from the missionaries. Hawaiians have created designs to reflect their own aesthetic, and bold patterns evolved over time. They can be pricey because the quilts are intricately made by hand and can take years to finish. These masterpieces are considered precious heirlooms that reflect the history and beauty of Hawaii.

Popular Souvenirs

Souvenir shopping can be intimidating. There's a sea of Islands-inspired and often kitschy merchandise, so we'd like to give you a breakdown of popular and fun gifts that you might encounter and consider bringing home. If authenticity is important to you, be sure to check labels and ask shopkeepers. Museum shops are good places for authentic, Hawaiian-made souvenirs.

Fabrics. Purchased by the yard or already made into everything from napkins to bedspreads, modern Hawaiian fabrics make wonderful keepsakes.

Home accessories. Deck out your kitchen or dining room in festive luau style with bottle openers, pineapple mugs, tiki glasses, shot glasses, slipper and surfboard magnets, and salt-and-pepper shakers.

Lei and shell necklaces. From silk or polyester flower lei to kukui or puka shell necklaces, lei have been traditionally used as a welcome offering to guests (although the artificial ones are more for fun, as real flowers are always preferable).

Lauhala products. *Lauhala* weaving is a traditional Hawaiian art. The leaves come from the hala, or pandanus, tree and are hand-woven to create lovely gift boxes, baskets, bags, and picture frames.

Spa products. Relive your spa treatment at home with Hawaiian bath and body products, many of them manufactured with ingredients found only on the Islands.

Vintage Hawaii. You can find vintage photos, reproductions of vintage postcards or paintings, heirloom jewelry, and vintage aloha wear in many specialty stores.

Luau

The luau's origin, which was a celebratory feast, can be traced back to the earliest Hawaiian civilizations. In the traditional luau, the taboo or *kapu* laws were very strict, requiring men and women to eat separately. However, in 1819 King Kamehameha II broke the great taboo and shared a feast with women and commoners, ushering in the modern-era luau. Today, traditional luau usually commemorate a child's

first birthday, graduation, wedding, or other family occasion. They also are a Hawaiian experience that most visitors enjoy, and resorts and other companies have incorporated the fire-knife dance and other Polynesian dances into their elaborate presentations.

Nose flutes

The nose flute is an instrument used in ancient times to serenade a lover. For the Hawaiians, the nose is romantic, sacred, and pure. The Hawaiian word for kiss is *honi*. Similar to an Eskimo's kiss, the noses touch on each side sharing one's spiritual energy or breath. The Hawaiian term, *ohe hano ihu*, simply translated to "bamboo," with which the instrument is made; "breathe," because one has to gently breathe through it to make soothing music; and "nose," as it is made for the nose and not the mouth.

Slack-Key Guitar and the Paniolo

Kihoalu, or slack-key music, evolved in the early 1800s when King Kamehameha III brought in Mexican and Spanish vaqueros to manage the overpopulated cattle that had run wild on the Islands. The vaqueros brought their guitars and would play music around the campfire after work. When they left, supposedly leaving their guitars to their new friends, the Hawaiian *paniolo,* or cowboys, began to infuse what they learned from the vaqueros with their native music and chants, and so the art of slack-key music was born.

Today, the paniolo culture thrives where ranchers have settled.

Ukulele

The word *ukulele* literally translates to the "the jumping flea" and came to Hawaii in the 1880s by way of the Portuguese and Spanish. Once a fading art form, today it brings international kudos as a solo instrument, thanks to tireless musicians and teachers who have worked hard to keep it by our fingertips.

One such teacher is Roy Sakuma. Founder of four ukulele schools and a legend in his own right, Sakuma and his wife Kathy produced Oahu's first Ukulele Festival in 1971. Since then, they've brought the tradition to the Big Island, Kauai, and Maui. The free event annually draws thousands of artists and fans from all over the globe.

Hula

"Hula is the language of the heart, therefore the heartbeat of the Hawaiian people." —Kalakaua, the Merrie Monarch.

Thousands—from tots to seniors—devote hours each week to hula classes. All these dancers need some place to show off their stuff. The result is a network of hula competitions (generally free or very inexpensive) and free performances in malls and other public spaces. Many resorts offer hula instruction.

HAWAII AND THE ENVIRONMENT

Sustainability—it's a word rolling off everyone's tongues these days. In a place known as the most remote island chain in the world (check your globe), Hawaii relies heavily on the outside world for food and material goods—estimates put the percentage of food arriving on container ships as high as 90. Like many places, though, efforts are afoot to change that. And you can help.

Shop Local Farms and Markets

From Kauai to the Big Island, farmers' markets are cropping up, providing a place for growers to sell fresh fruits and vegetables. There is no reason to buy imported mangoes, papayas, avocadoes, and bananas at grocery stores, when the ones you'll find at farmers' markets are not only fresher but tastier, too. Some markets allow the sale of fresh-packaged foods—salsa, say, or smoothies—and the on-site preparation of food—like pork *laulau* (pork, beef and fish or chicken with taro, or luau, leaves wrapped and steamed in *ti* leaves) or roasted corn on the cob—so you can make your run to the market a dining experience.

Not only is the locavore movement vibrantly alive at farmers' markets, but Hawaii's top chefs are sourcing more of their produce—and fish, beef, chicken, and cheese—from local providers as well. You'll notice this movement on restaurant menus, featuring Kilauea greens or Hamakua tomatoes or locally caught mahimahi.

And while most people are familiar with Kona coffee farm tours on Big Island, if you're interested in the growing slow-food movement in Hawaii, you'll be heartened to know many farmers are opening up their operations for tours—as well as sumptuous meals.

Support Hawaii's Merchants

Food isn't the only sustainable effort in Hawaii. Buying local goods like art and jewelry, Hawaiian heritage products, crafts, music, and apparel is another way to "green up" the local economy. The County of Kauai helps make it easy with a program called **Kauai Made** (⊕ *www. kauaimade.net*), which showcases products made on Kauai, by Kauai people, using Kauai materials. The Maui Chamber of Commerce does something similar with **Made in Maui** (⊕ *www.madeinmaui. com*). Think of both as the Good Housekeeping Seal of Approval for locally made goods.

Then there are the crafty entrepreneurs who are diverting items from the trash heap by repurposing garbage. Take Oahu's **Muumuu Heaven** (⊕ *www.muumuuheaven. com*). They got their start by reincarnating vintage aloha apparel into hip new fashions.

Choose Green Tour Operators

Conscious decisions when it comes to Island activities go a long way to protecting Hawaii's natural world. The **Hawaii Ecotourism Association** (⊕ *www.hawaiiecotourism. org*) recognizes tour operators for, among other things, their environmental stewardship. The **Hawaii Tourism Authority** (⊕ *www. hawaiitourismauthority.org*) recognizes outfitters for their cultural sensitivity. Winners of these awards are good choices when it comes to guided tours and activities.

FOR KIDS AND FAMILIES

With dozens of adventures to take, discoveries to make, and loads of kid-friendly beaches, Maui is a blast for families with children. The entire family, parents included, will enjoy surfing, discovering a waterfall in the rain forest, and snorkeling with sea turtles. And there are organized activities for kids that will free parents' time for a few romantic beach strolls.

Choosing a Place to Stay

Resorts. All the big resorts make kids' programs a priority. When booking your room, ask about "kids eat free" deals and the number of kids' pools at the resort. Also check out the ages and sizes of groups in the children's programs and find out whether the cost of the programs includes lunch, equipment, and activities.

On the South Shore, the best bet for families is the Fairmont Kea Lani Maui, where the accommodations are spacious suites. Kids will love the beach right in front of the Mana Kai Maui on the island's south side. The Westin Maui Resort & Spa, with its long list of activity programs for kids and adults, is a good choice in the Kaanapali Resort. Also in West Maui, Napili Kai Beach Resort sits on a protected crescent of white-sand beach that is perfect for body boarding, playing in the water, and sunbathing.

Condos. Condo and vacation rentals are a fantastic value for families vacationing in Hawaii. You can cook your own food, which is much less expensive than eating out, and often easier, and you'll get twice the space of a hotel room for about a quarter of the price.

If you decide to go the condo route, be sure to ask about the size of the complex's pool (some try to pawn off a tiny soaking tub as a pool) and whether barbecues are available. One of the best parts of staying in your own place is having a sunset family barbecue by the pool or overlooking the ocean.

On West Maui all the Aston Hotels & Resorts properties, like Papakea Resort, offer children's packages such as "Kids Stay, Play and Eat Free," and have a *keiki* (child) activity program that ranges from sandcastle building to sightseeing excursions.

On the South Shore Kamaole Sands is a family favorite, with an excellent location right across from three beach parks that are good for swimming and have grassy fields good for games and picnics.

Ocean Activities

Hawaii is all about getting your kids outside—away from video games. And who could resist the turquoise water, the promise of spotting dolphins or whales, and the fun of body boarding or surfing?

On the Beach. Most people like being in the water, but toddlers and school-age kids are often completely captivated. The swimming pool at your condo or hotel is always an option, but don't be afraid to hit the beach with a little one in tow. Several beaches in Hawaii are nearly as safe as a pool—completely protected bays with pleasant white-sand beaches. As always, use your judgment, and heed all posted signs and lifeguard warnings.

The leeward side of Maui has many calm beaches to try. Good ones include Wailea Beach in front of the Grand Wailea and Four Seasons resorts and Kamaole beach parks on the South Shore. Napili Bay in West Maui is great for kids and also for body boarding. On the North Shore, at the Kahului end of Baldwin Beach Park, check out the shallow pool known as Baby Beach.

On the Waves. Surf lessons are a great idea for older kids, especially if Mom and Dad want a little quiet time. Beginner lessons are always on safe and easy waves and last anywhere from two to four hours.

The world-class waves of Maui's North Shore are best left to the pros. The gentle swells off West Maui are where the Nancy Emerson School of Surfing provides lessons designed for beginners. Big Kahuna Adventures will also show you how to ride the waves in the calm mornings off Kalama Beach Park in Kihei on the South Shore.

The Underwater World. If your kids are ready to try snorkeling, Hawaii is a great place to introduce them to the underwater world. Even without the mask and snorkel, they'll be able to see colorful fish, and they may also spot turtles and dolphins at many of the island's beaches.

It's easy (and inexpensive) to learn the basics and see amazing underwater life immediately at Kaanapali Beach in front of the Sheraton Maui on the island's west side. For guided snorkel tours that offer beginner instruction, try Trilogy Excursions, a family-oriented day trip from Lahaina to Lanai, or Maui Classic Charters out of Maalaea Harbor.

Land Activities

In addition to beach experiences, Hawaii has rain forests, botanical gardens (the Big Island and Maui have the best), numerous aquariums (Oahu's and Maui's take the cake), and even petting zoos and hands-on children's museums that will keep your kids entertained and out of the sun for a day. Older kids (over 10) may be interested in a zipline adventure.

Central Maui abounds with activities for children, including the Alexander & Baldwin Sugar Museum with its interactive displays and the hands-on Hawaii Nature Center next to Heritage Gardens Kepaniwai Park at the entrance to Iao Valley.

If the weather's not great for seeing marine life in the ocean, see it at the excellent Maui Ocean Center in Maalaea on the South Shore, where all manner of live marine creatures including reef fish, sea turtles, manta rays, and sharks swim behind glass. It's expensive, but kids (and adults) can learn a lot from the displays.

To discover all there is to know about Maui's biggest annual visitor, the humpback whale, children will enjoy the Hawaiian Islands Humpback Whale National Marine Sanctuary on the South Shore and the worthwhile free museum at Whalers Village shopping center in Kaanapali on West Maui.

For a moving experience, hop aboard the Sugar Cane Train that chugs between Lahaina and Kaanapali and features a singing conductor. Yup, it's corny, but the train is a favorite with kids of all ages.

After Dark

At nighttime, younger kids get a kick out of luau, and many of the shows incorporate young audience members, adding to the fun. Older kids might find it all a bit lame, but there are a handful of new shows in the Islands that are more modern, incorporating acrobatics and lively music.

We think the best luau is the Old Lahaina Luau, which takes place nightly on the oceanfront at the north end of Lahaina. The show is traditional, lively, and colorful; it will keep the whole family entertained. Book in advance to avoid disappointment; this is extremely popular.

WEDDINGS AND HONEYMOONS

There's no question that Hawaii is one of the country's foremost honeymoon destinations. Romance is in the air here, and the white, sandy beaches, turquoise water, swaying palm trees, balmy tropical breezes, and perpetual sunshine put people in the mood for love. It's easy to understand why Hawaii is fast becoming a popular wedding destination as well, especially as the cost of airfare is often discounted, new resorts and hotels entice visitors, and as of January 2012 the state now recognizes and grants civil unions. A destination wedding is no longer exclusive to celebrities and the superrich. You can plan a traditional ceremony in a place of worship followed by a reception at an elegant resort, or you can go barefoot on the beach and celebrate at a luau. There are almost as many wedding planners in the Islands as real estate agents, which makes it oh-so-easy to wed in paradise, and then, once the knot is tied, stay and honeymoon as well.

The Big Day

Choosing the Perfect Place. When choosing a location, remember that you really have two choices to make: the ceremony location and where to have the reception, if you're having one. For the former, there are beaches, bluffs overlooking beaches, gardens, private residences, resort lawns, and, of course, places of worship. As for the reception, there are these same choices, as well as restaurants and even luau. If you decide to go outdoors, remember the seasons—yes, Hawaii has seasons. If you're planning a winter wedding outdoors, be sure you have a backup plan (such as a tent), in case it rains. Also, if you're planning an outdoor wedding at sunset—which is very popular—be sure you match the time of your ceremony to the time the sun sets at that time of year. If

you choose an indoor spot, be sure to ask for pictures of the location when you're planning. You don't want to plan a pink wedding, say, and wind up in a room that's predominantly red. Or maybe you do. The point is, it should be your choice.

Finding a Wedding Planner. If you're planning to invite more than a minister and your loved one to your wedding ceremony, seriously consider an on-island wedding planner who can help select a location, help design the floral scheme and recommend a florist as well as a photographer, help plan the menu and choose a restaurant, caterer, or resort, and suggest any Hawaiian traditions to incorporate into your ceremony. And more: Will you need tents, a cake, music? Maybe transportation and lodging? Many planners have relationships with vendors, providing packages—which mean savings.

If you're planning a resort wedding, most have on-site wedding coordinators; however, there are many independents around the Islands and even those who specialize in certain types of ceremonies—by locale, size, religious affiliation, and so on. A simple "Hawaii weddings" Google search will reveal dozens. What's important is that you feel comfortable with your coordinator. Ask for references—and call them. Share your budget. Get a proposal—in writing. Ask how long they've been in business, how much they charge, how often you'll meet with them, and how they select vendors. Request a detailed list of the exact services they'll provide. If your idea of your wedding doesn't match their services, try someone else. If you can afford it, you might want to meet the planner in person.

Getting Your License. The good news about marrying in Hawaii is that no

waiting period, no residency or citizenship requirements, and no blood tests or shots are required. You can apply and pay the fee online; however, both the bride and groom must appear together in person before a marriage-license agent to receive the marriage license (the permit to get married). You'll need proof of age—the legal age to marry is 18. (If you're 19 or older, a valid driver's license will suffice; if you're 18, a certified birth certificate is required.) Upon approval, a marriage license is immediately issued and costs $60 (credit cards accepted online and in-person; cash accepted in-person only). After the ceremony, your officiant will mail the marriage certificate (proof of marriage) to the state. Approximately four months later, you will receive a copy in the mail. (For $10 extra, you can expedite this process. Ask your marriage-license agent when you apply.) For more detailed information, visit ⊕ *https:// marriage.ehawaii.gov.*

Also—this is important—the person performing your wedding must be licensed by the Hawaii Department of Health, even if he or she is a licensed minister. Be sure to ask.

Wedding Attire. In Hawaii, basically anything goes, from long, formal dresses with trains to white bikinis. Floral sundresses are fine, too. For the men, tuxedos are not the norm; a pair of solid-colored slacks with a nice aloha shirt is. In fact, tradition in Hawaii for the groom is a plain white aloha shirt (they do exist) with slacks or long shorts and a colored sash around the waist. If you're planning a wedding on the beach, barefoot is the way to go.

If you decide to marry in a formal dress and tuxedo, you're better off making your selections on the mainland and

hand-carrying them aboard the plane. Yes, it can be a pain, but ask your wedding-gown retailer to provide a special carrying bag. After all, you don't want to chance losing your wedding dress in a wayward piece of luggage.

Local customs. The most obvious traditional Hawaiian wedding custom is the lei exchange in which the bride and groom take turns placing a lei around the neck of the other—with a kiss. Bridal lei are usually floral, whereas the groom's is typically made of *maile*, a green leafy garland that drapes around the neck and is open at the ends. Brides often also wear a *lei poo*—a circular floral headpiece. Other Hawaiian customs include the blowing of the conch shell, hula, chanting, and Hawaiian music.

The Honeymoon

Do you want champagne and strawberries delivered to your room each morning? A breathtaking swimming pool in which to float? A five-star restaurant in which to dine? Then a resort is the way to go. If, however, you prefer the comforts of a home, try a bed-and-breakfast. A small inn is also good if you're on a tight budget or don't plan to spend much time in your room. On the other hand, maybe you want your own private home in which to romp naked—or just laze around recovering from the wedding planning. Maybe you want your own kitchen so you can whip up a gourmet meal for your loved one. In that case, a private vacation-rental home is the answer. Or maybe a condominium resort. That's another beautiful thing about Hawaii: the lodging accommodations are almost as plentiful as the beaches, and there's one that will perfectly match your tastes and your budget.

CRUISING THE HAWAIIAN ISLANDS

Cruising has become popular in Hawaii. Cruises are a comparatively inexpensive way to see all of Hawaii, and you'll save travel time by not having to check-in at hotels and airports on each island. The limited amount of time in each port can be an argument against cruising, but you can make reservations for tours, activities, rental cars, and more aboard the cruise ship. This will also give you more time for sightseeing and shopping at ports.

The larger cruise lines such as Carnival, Princess, and Holland America offer itineraries of 10–16 days departing from the West Coast of the United States, most with stops at all the major Hawaiian Islands. Some cruise lines, such as Crystal, Cunard, and Disney, include ports in Hawaii on around-the-world cruises. All have plenty on board to keep you busy during the 4–5 days that you are at sea between the U.S. mainland and Hawaii.

Cruise ships plying the Pacific from the continental United States to Hawaii are floating resorts complete with pools, spas, rock-climbing walls, restaurants, nightclubs, shops, casinos, children's programs, and much more. Most hold thousands of passengers with an average staff-to-passenger ratio of three to one.

Prices for cruises are based on accommodation type: interior (no window, in an inside corridor); outside (includes a window or porthole); balcony (allows you to go outside without using a public deck); and suite (larger cabin, more amenities and perks). Passages start at about $1,000 per person for the lowest class accommodation (interior) and include room, on-board entertainment, and food. Ocean-view, balcony, and suite accommodations can run up to $6,500 and beyond per person.

Cruising to Hawaii

Carnival Cruises is great for families, with plenty of kid-friendly activities. Departing from Los Angeles or Vancouver, Carnival's "fun ships" show your family a good time, both on board and on shore (☎ 888/227–6482 ⊕ www.carnival.com). The grand dame of cruise lines, Holland America has a reputation for service and elegance. Their 14-day Hawaii cruises leave from and return to San Diego, with a brief stop at Ensenada (☎ 877/932–4259 ⊕ www.hollandamerica.com). More affordable luxury is what Princess Cruises offers. While their prices seem a little higher, you get more bells and whistles on your trip (more affordable balcony rooms, more restaurants to chose from, personalized service) (☎ 800/774–6237 ⊕ www.princess.com).

Cruising within Hawaii

Norwegian Cruise Lines is the only major operator to begin and end cruises in Hawaii. Pride of Hawaii (vintage America theme, family focus with lots of connecting staterooms and suites) offers a seven-day itinerary that includes stops on Maui, Oahu, the Big Island, and Kauai. This is the only ship to cruise Hawaii that does not spend days at sea visiting a foreign port, allowing you more time to explore destinations (☎ 800/327–7030 ⊕ www2.ncl.com). Ocean conditions in the channels between islands can be a consideration when booking an interisland cruise on a smaller vessel such as American Safari Cruises—a stately yacht accommodating only 36 passengers. This yacht's small size allows it to dock at less frequented islands such as Molokai and Lanai. The cruise is billed as "all inclusive"—your passage includes shore excursions, water activities, and a massage (☎ 888/862–8881 ⊕ www.innerseadiscoveries.com).

EXPLORING MAUI

Updated by Bonnie Friedman

To those who know Maui well, there are good reasons for all the superlatives it's earned. The island's miles of perfect beaches, lush green valleys, historic villages, top-notch windsurfing and diving, stellar restaurants and resorts, and variety of cultural activities have made it an international favorite.

Maui is more than sandy beaches and palm trees: The natural bounty of this place is impressive. Puu Kukui, the 5,788-foot interior of the West Maui Mountains, also known as Mauna Kahalawai, is one of Earth's wettest spots—annual rainfall of 400 inches has sculpted the land into impassable gorges and razor-sharp ridges. On the opposite side of the island, the blistering lava fields at Ahihi-Kinau receive scant rain. Just above this desertlike landscape, *paniolo* (Hawaiian cowboys) herd cattle on rolling, fertile ranchlands. On the island's rugged east side is the lush, tropical Hawaii of travel posters.

Nature isn't all Maui has to offer: it's also home to a rich culture and stunning ethnic diversity. In small towns like Paia and Hana you can see remnants of the past mingling with modern-day life. Ancient *heiau* (stone platforms once used as places of worship) line busy roadways. Old coral and brick missionary homes now house broadcasting networks. The antique smokestacks of sugar mills tower above communities where the children blend English, Hawaiian, Japanese, Chinese, Portuguese, Filipino, and more into one colorful language. Hawaii is a melting pot like no other. Visiting an eclectic mom-and-pop shop—such as Upcountry Makawao's Komoda Store & Bakery—can feel like stepping into another country, or back in time. The more you look here, the more you find.

At 729 square miles, Maui is the second-largest Hawaiian Island, but offers more miles of swimmable beaches than any of its neighbors. Despite rapid growth over the past few decades, the local population still totals only 155,000.

GEOLOGY

Maui is made up of two volcanoes, one now extinct and the other dormant but which erupted long ago, joined into one island. The resulting depression between the two is what gives the island its nickname, the Valley Isle. West Maui's 5,788-foot Puu Kukui was the first volcano to form, a distinction that gives that area's mountainous topography a more weathered look. Rainbows seem to grow wild over this terrain as gentle mists fill the deeply eroded canyons. The Valley Isle's second volcano is the 10,023-foot Haleakala, where desertlike terrain butts up against tropical forests.

HISTORY

Maui's history is full of firsts—Lahaina was the first capital of Hawaii and the first destination of the whaling industry (early 1800s), which explains why the town still has that seafaring vibe. Lahaina was also the first stop for missionaries on Maui (1823). Although they suppressed aspects of Hawaiian culture, the missionaries did help invent the Hawaiian alphabet and built a printing press—the first west of the Rockies— that rolled out the news in Hawaiian, as well as, not surprisingly, Hawaii's first Bibles. Maui also boasts the first sugar plantation in Hawaii (1849) and the first Hawaiian luxury resort (1946), now called the Travaasa Hana.

ON MAUI TODAY

In the mid-1970s savvy marketers saw a way to improve Maui's economy by promoting the Valley Isle to golfers and luxury travelers. The ploy worked well; Maui's visitor count is about 2.5 million annually. Impatient traffic now threatens to overtake the ubiquitous aloha spirit, development encroaches on agricultural lands, and county planners struggle to meet the needs of a burgeoning population. But Maui is still carpeted with an eyeful of green, and for every tailgater there's a local on "Maui time" who stops for each pedestrian and sunset.

WEST MAUI

Separated from the remainder of the island by steep *pali* (cliffs), West Maui has a reputation for attitude and action. Once upon a time this was the haunt of whalers, missionaries, and the kings and queens of Hawaii. Today the main drag, Front Street, is crowded with T-shirt and trinket shops, art galleries, and restaurants. Farther north is Kaanapali, Maui's first planned resort area. Its first hotel, the Sheraton, opened in 1963. Since then, massive resorts, luxury condos, and a shopping center have sprung up along the white-sand beaches, with championship golf courses across the road. A few miles farther up the coast is the ultimate in West Maui luxury, the resort area of Kapalua. In between, dozens of strip malls line both the *makai* (toward the sea) and *mauka* (toward the mountains) sides of the highway. There are gems here, too, like Napili Bay and its crescent of sand.

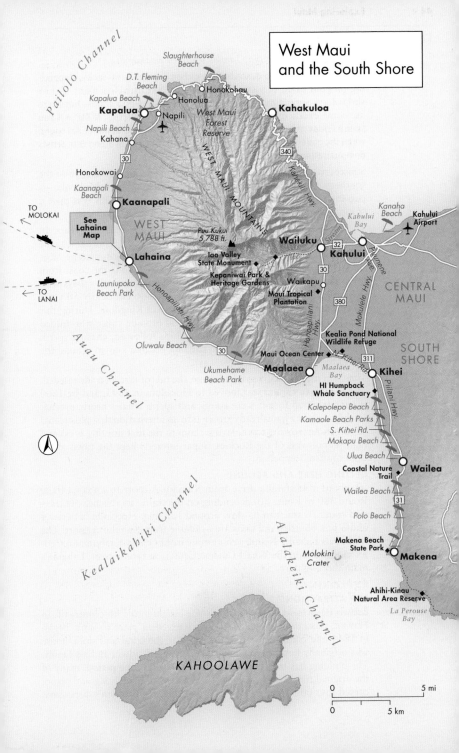

LAHAINA

27 miles west of Kahului; 4 miles south of Kaanapali.

Lahaina may best be described as either charming or tacky, depending on your point of view—and opinions do differ. Too many T-shirt shops have supplanted the traditional mom-and-pop shops, but there are some excellent restaurants and interesting galleries. ■ TIP➜ **If you spend Friday afternoon exploring Front Street, hang around for Art Night, when the galleries stay open late and offer entertainment along with artists demonstrating their work.**

Sunset cruises and other excursions depart from Lahaina Harbor. At the southern end of town an important archaeological site—Mokuula—is currently being researched, excavated, and restored. This was once a spiritual and political center, as well as home to Maui's chiefs.

The town has been welcoming visitors for more than 200 years. In 1798, after waging war to unite the Hawaiian Islands, Kamehameha the Great chose Lahaina, then called Lele, as the seat of his monarchy. Warriors from Kamehameha's 800 canoes, stretched along the coast from Olowalu to Honokowai, turned inland and filled the lush valleys with networks of stream-fed *loi kalo,* or taro patches. For nearly 50 years Lahaina remained the capital of the Hawaiian Kingdom. During this period, the scent of Hawaiian sandalwood brought those who traded with China to these waters. Whaling ships followed, chasing sperm whales from Japan to the Arctic. Lahaina became known around the world for its rough-and-tumble ways.

Then, almost as quickly as it had come, the tide of foreign trade receded. The Hawaiian capital was moved to Honolulu in 1845, and by 1860 the sandalwood forests were empty and sperm whales nearly extinct. Luckily, Lahaina had already grown into an international, sophisticated (if sometimes rowdy) town, laying claim to the first printing press and high school west of the Rockies. Sugar interests kept the town afloat until tourism stepped in.

GETTING HERE AND AROUND

It's about a 45-minute drive from Kahului Airport to Lahaina (take Route 380 to Route 30) depending on the traffic on this heavily traveled route. Traffic can be slow around Lahaina, especially between 4 and 6 pm. Shuttles and taxis are available from Kahului Airport. The Maui Bus Lahaina Islander route runs from Queen Kaahumanu Center in Kahului to the Wharf Cinema Center on Front Street, Lahaina's main thoroughfare.

EXPLORING

TOP ATTRACTIONS

Fodor's Choice ★   **Baldwin Home Museum.** If you want some insight into 19th-century life in Hawaii, this informative museum is an excellent place to start. Begun in 1834 and completed the following year, the coral and stone house was originally home to missionary Dr. Dwight Baldwin and his family. The building has been carefully restored to reflect the period; many of the original furnishings remain. You can view the family's grand piano, carved four-poster bed, and most interesting, Dr. Baldwin's dispensary.

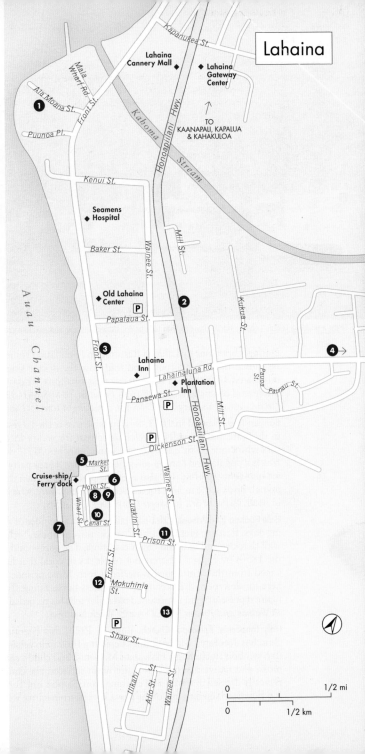

Lahaina

Once a whaling center, Lahaina Harbor bustles with tour boats, fishing vessels, and pleasure craft.

During a brief tour by Lahaina Restoration Foundation volunteers, you'll be shown the "thunderpot" and told how the doctor single-handedly inoculated 10,000 Maui residents against smallpox. Friday at 6:30 pm are special candlelight tours. ⊠ *696 Front St.* ☎ *808/661–3262* ⊕ *www. lahainarestoration.org* ⧐ *$7, $8 for candlelight tour* ⊙ *Daily 10–4.*

Banyan Tree. Planted in 1873, this massive tree is the largest of its kind in the state and provides a welcome retreat for weary locals and visitors who come to sit under its awesome branches. ■ **TIP→ The Banyan Tree is a popular and hard-to-miss meeting place if your party splits up for independent exploring.** It's also a terrific place to be when the sun sets— mynah birds settle in here for a screeching symphony, which is an event in itself. ⊠ *Front St., between Hotel and Canal Sts.*

Hale Paahao (Old Prison). Lahaina's jailhouse is a reminder of rowdy whaling days. Its name literally means "stuck-in-irons house," referring to the wall shackles and ball-and-chain restraints. The compound was built in the 1850s by convict laborers out of blocks of coral that had been salvaged from the demolished waterfront fort. Most prisoners were sent here for desertion, drunkenness, or reckless horse riding. Today, a wax figure representing an imprisoned old sailor tells his recorded tale of woe. ⊠ *Wainee and Prison Sts.* ⧐ *Free* ⊙ *Weekdays 8–3.*

Holy Innocents' Episcopal Church. Built in 1927, this beautiful open-air church is decorated with paintings depicting Hawaiian versions of Christian symbols (including a Hawaiian Madonna and child), rare or extinct birds, and native plants. At the afternoon services, the congregation is typically dressed in traditional clothing from Samoa and Tonga. Anyone is welcome to slip into one of the pews, carved from native woods. Queen

Liliuokalani, Hawaii's last reigning monarch, lived in a large grass house on this site as a child. ✉ *561 Front St., near Mokuhina St.* ☎ *808/661–4202* ⊕ *www.holyimaui.org* ☜ *Free* ⊙ *Daily 8–5.*

Lahaina Court House. The Lahaina Arts Society and the Lahaina Heritage Museum occupy this charming old government building in the center of town. Wander among the terrific displays, pump the knowledgeable museum staff for interesting trivia, and ask for the walking-tour brochure covering historic Lahaina sites. The nonprofit Lahaina Town Action Committee, which oversees Lahaina's

attractions, can also be found here. Erected in 1859 and restored in 1999, the building has served as a customs and court house, governor's office, post office, vault and collector's office, and police court. On August 12, 1898, its postmaster witnessed the lowering of the Hawaiian flag when Hawaii became a U.S. territory. The flag now hangs above the stairway. ■ TIP➔ There's a public restroom in the building. ✉ *648 Wharf St.* ☎ *808/661–0111 Lahaina Arts Society, 808/667–9175 Lahaina Town Action Committee* ⊕ *www.lahaina-arts.com* ☜ *Free* ⊙ *Daily 9–5.*

Fodor'sChoice
★ **Waiola Church and Wainee Cemetery.** Immortalized in James Michener's *Hawaii*, the original building from the early 1800s was destroyed once by fire and twice by fierce windstorms. Repositioned and rebuilt in 1954, the church was renamed Waiola ("water of life") and has been standing proudly ever since. The adjacent cemetery was the region's first Christian cemetery and is the final resting place of many of Hawaii's most important monarchs, including Kamehameha the Great's wife, Queen Keopuolani, who was baptized during her final illness. ✉ *535 Wainee St.* ☎ *808/661–4349* ⊕ *www.waiolachurch.org.* ☜ *Free* ⊙ *Daily 9–4.*

Fodor'sChoice
★ **Wo Hing Museum.** Smack-dab in the center of Front Street, this eye-catching Chinese temple reflects the importance of early Chinese immigrants to Lahaina. Built by the Wo Hing Society in 1912, the museum contains beautiful artifacts, historic photos of old Lahaina, and a Taoist altar. Don't miss the films playing in the rustic theater next door—some of Thomas Edison's first films, shot in Hawaii circa 1898, show Hawaiian wranglers herding steer onto ships. Ask the docent for some star fruit from the tree outside, for the altar or for yourself. ✉ *858 Front St.* ☎ *808/661–5553* ☜ *$7* ⊙ *Sat.–Thurs. 10–4, Fri. 1–8 pm.*

WORTH NOTING

Fort. Stone ruins are all that remain at the site that served mostly as a prison. It was built from 1831 to 1832 after sailors, angered by a law forbidding local women from swimming out to ships, lobbed cannonballs into town the previous year. The fort was finally torn down in the 1850s and the stones used to construct the new prison. Cannons raised from the wreck of a warship in Honolulu Harbor were brought to Lahaina and placed in front of the fort, where they still sit today. ⊠ *Canal and Wharf Sts.*

Hale Pai. Protestant missionaries established Lahainaluna Seminary as a center of learning and enlightenment in 1831. Six years later, they built this printing shop, where they and their young Hawaiian scholars created a written Hawaiian language and used it to produce a Bible, history texts, and a newspaper. An exhibit displays a replica of the original Rampage press and facsimiles of early printing. The oldest U.S. educational institution west of the Rockies, the seminary now serves as Lahaina's public high school. ⊠ *980 Lahainaluna Rd.* ☎ *808/661–3262* 🖃 *Donations accepted* ۞ *Mon.–Wed. 10–4; Thurs. and Fri. by appointment.*

Hauola Stone. Just visible above the tide is a gigantic stone, perfectly molded into the shape of a low-backed chair and believed by Hawaiians to hold healing powers. It sits in the harbor where the sea and the underground freshwater meet. ⊠ *Front St., behind public library* 🖃 *Free.*

Jodo Mission. Established at the turn of the 20th century by Japanese contract workers, this Buddhist mission is one of Lahaina's most popular sites, thanks to its idyllic setting and spectacular views across the channel. Although the buildings are not open to the public, you can stroll the grounds and enjoy glimpses of the 90-foot-high pagoda, as well as a great 3.5-ton copper and bronze statue of the Amida Buddha (erected in 1968). If you're nearby at 8 any evening, listen for the temple bell to toll 11 times; each peal has a specific significance. ⊠ *12 Ala Moana St., near Lahaina Cannery Mall* ☎ *808/661–4304* 🖃 *Free.*

Lahaina Harbor. For centuries, Lahaina has drawn ships of all sizes to its calm harbor: King Kamehameha's conquering fleet of 800 carved *koa* canoes gave way to Chinese trading ships, Boston whalers, United States Navy frigates, and, finally, a slew of pleasure craft. The picturesque harbor is the departure point for ferries headed to nearby islands, sailing charters, deep-sea fishing trips, and snorkeling excursions. ⊠ *Wharf St.* 🖃 *Free.*

FAMILY **Lahaina–Kaanapali and Pacific Railroad.** Affectionately called the Sugar Cane Train, Maui's only passenger train is an 1890s-vintage railway that once shuttled crops but now moves sightseers between Kaanapali and Lahaina. This quaint little attraction with its singing conductor is a big deal for Hawaii but probably not much of a thrill for those more accustomed to trains (though kids like it no matter where they grew up).

✉ *Honoapiilani Hwy. at Hinau St., 1½ blocks north of Lahainaluna Rd. stoplight* ☎ *808/661–0080* ⊕ *www.sugarcanetrain.com* 🎫 *$22.95* 🕐 *Weekdays 10:15–4.*

KAANAPALI AND VICINITY

Kaanapali is 4 miles north of Lahaina.

As you drive north from Lahaina, the first resort community you reach is Kaanapali, a cluster of high-rise hotels framing a beautiful white-sand beach. This is part of West Maui's famous resort strip. A little farther up the road lie the condo-filled beach towns of Honokowai, Kahana, and Napili, followed by Kapalua.

GETTING HERE AND AROUND

Shuttles and taxis are available from Kahului and West Maui airports. Resorts offer free shuttles between properties, and some hotels also provide free shuttles into Lahaina. In the Maui Bus system the Napili Islander begins and ends at Whalers Village in Kaanapali and stops at most condos along the coastal road as far north as Napili Bay.

EXPLORING

Farmers' Market of Maui–Honokowai. From pineapples to corn, the produce at this West Maui open-air market is local and flavorful. Prices are good, too. Colorful tropical flowers and handcrafted items are also available. ✉ *Honoapiilani Hwy., across from Honokowai Park, Honokowai* ☎ *808/669–7004* 🕐 *Mon., Wed., and Fri. 7 am–11 am.*

Kaanapali. The theatrical look of Hawaii tourism—planned resort communities where luxury homes mix with high-rise hotels, fantasy swimming pools, and a theme-park landscape—all began right here in the 1960s, when clever marketers built this sunny shoreline into a playground for the world's vacationers. Three miles of uninterrupted white-sand beach and placid water form the front yard for this artificial utopia, with its 40 tennis courts and two championship golf courses.

In ancient times, this area was known for its bountiful fishing (especially lobster) and its seaside cliffs. Puu Kekaa, today incorrectly referred to as "Black Rock," was a *lele*, a place in ancient Hawaii from which souls leaped into the afterlife. (Today this site is near the Sheraton Maui.) But times changed and the sleepy fishing village was washed away by the wave of Hawaii's new economy: tourism. ✉ *Kaanapali.*

Whalers Village. While the kids hit Honolua Surf Company, their parents can peruse such shops as Louis Vuitton, Sephora, and Coach, as well as interesting art galleries and several fine jewelry stores, at this casual, classy mall fronting Kaanapali Beach. Pizza and Häagen-Dazs ice cream are available in the center courtyard. At the beach entrance is a wonderful restaurant, Hula Grill. ✉ *2435 Kaanapali Pkwy., Kaanapali* ☎ *808/661–4567* ⊕ *www.whalersvillage.com.*

FAMILY **Whalers Village Museum.** The skeleton of a massive whale leads the way to the Whale Center of the Pacific on the second floor of Whalers Village. Here you can learn about the hard life of whalers during the 19th-century Moby-Dick era. A replica of their living quarters, their

On the north end of West Maui, remote Kahakuloa is a reminder of Old Hawaii.

tools and equipment, their letters and business papers, and other artifacts are on display. Many historical photos illustrate how the whalers chased and captured these giants of the deep and how they processed their catch while out at sea. Several short films run continuously, including one about Hawaiian turtles and the folklore surrounding them. ⊠ *2435 Kaanapali Pkwy., Suite H16, Kaanapali* ☎ *808/661–5992* ⊕ *www.whalersvillage.com/museum.htm* ☎ *$3* ⊗ *Daily 10–6.*

KAPALUA AND VICINITY

Kapalua is 10 miles north of Kaanapali and 36 miles west of Kahului.

Upscale Kapalua is north of the Kaanapali resorts, past Napili. Farther along the Honoapiilani Highway you'll find the remote village of Kahakuloa, a reminder of Old Hawaii.

GETTING HERE AND AROUND

Shuttles and taxis are available from Kahului and West Maui airports. The Ritz-Carlton, Kapalua has a resort shuttle within the Kapalua Resort.

EXPLORING

Kahakuloa. The wild side of West Maui and untouched by progress, this tiny village at the north end of Honoapiilani Highway is a relic of pre-jet-travel Maui. Remote villages similar to Kahakuloa were once tucked away in several valleys in this area. Many residents still grow taro and live in the old Hawaiian way. Driving this route is not for the faint of heart: the unimproved road weaves along coastal cliffs, and there are lots of blind curves; it's not wide enough for two cars to pass in places.

Watch out for stray cattle, roosters, and falling rocks. True adventurers will find terrific snorkeling and swimming along this drive, as well as some good hiking trails. ⊠ *Kahakuloa.*

QUICK
BITES

Julia's Best Banana Bread. Follow the signs in Kahakuloa village to this bright green roadside stand, which offers really delicious banana bread, coconut candy, passion fruit butter, taro chips, and other treats. The stand is open daily from 9 to 5:30 or until the goodies are sold out. ⊠ *7465 Kahekili Hwy., Kahakuloa* ⊕ *www.juliasbananabread.com.*

Kapalua. Beautiful and secluded, Kapalua is West Maui's northernmost, most exclusive resort community. First developed in the late 1970s, the resort now includes the Ritz-Carlton, posh residential complexes, two golf courses, and the surrounding pineapple fields. The area's distinctive shops and restaurants cater to dedicated golfers, celebrities who want to be left alone, and some of the world's richest folks. In addition to golf, recreational activities include hiking and snorkeling. Mists regularly envelop the landscape of tall Cook pines and rolling fairways in Kapalua, which is cooler and quieter than its southern neighbors. The beaches here, including Kapalua and D.T. Fleming, are among Maui's finest.

QUICK
BITES

Honolua Store. In contrast to Kapalua's many high-end retailers, the old Honolua Store still plies the groceries, household goods, and fishing nets it did in plantation times. Hefty plates of *ono* (delicious) local foods are served at the deli until 3 pm. The plate lunches are the quintessential local meal and very popular. ⊠ *502 Office Rd., Kapalua* ☏ *808/665–9105.*

SOUTH SHORE

Blessed by more than its fair share of sun, the southern shore of Haleakala was an undeveloped wilderness until the 1970s. Then the sun worshippers found it; now restaurants, condos, and luxury resorts line the coast from the world-class aquarium at Maalaea Harbor, through working-class Kihei, to lovely Wailea, a resort community rivaling its counterpart, Kaanapali, on West Maui. Farther south, the road disappears and unspoiled wilderness still has its way.

Because the South Shore includes so many fine beach choices, a trip here (if you're staying elsewhere on the island) is an all-day excursion—especially if you include a visit to the aquarium. Get active in the morning with exploring and snorkeling, then shower in a beach park, dress up a little, and enjoy the cool luxury of the Wailea resorts. At sunset, settle in for dinner at one of the area's many fine restaurants.

MAALAEA

13 miles south of Kahului; 6 miles west of Kihei; 14 miles southeast of Lahaina.

Pronounced Mah-*ah*-lye-*ah,* this spot is not much more than a few condos, an aquarium, and a wind-blasted harbor—but that's more than enough for some visitors. Humpback whales seem to think Maalaea is tops for meeting mates, and green sea turtles treat it like their own personal spa, regularly seeking appointments with cleaner wrasses in the harbor. Surfers revere this spot for "freight train," reportedly the world's fastest wave.

A small Shinto shrine stands at the shore here, dedicated to the fishing god Ebisu Sama. Across the street, a giant hook often swings heavy with the sea's bounty, proving the worth of the shrine. At the end of Hauoli Street (the town's single road), a small community garden is sometimes privy to traditional Hawaiian ceremonies. That's all; there's not much else. But the few residents here like it that way.

GETTING HERE AND AROUND

To reach Maalaea from Kahului Airport, take Route 380 to Route 30. The town is also a transfer point for many Maui Bus routes.

EXPLORING

Maalaea Small Boat Harbor. With so many good reasons to head out onto the water, this active little harbor is quite busy. Many snorkeling and whale-watching excursions depart from here. There was a plan to expand the facility, but surfers argued that would have destroyed their surf breaks. In fact, the surf here is world-renowned. The elusive spot to the left of the harbor, called "freight train," rarely breaks, but when it does, it's said to be the fastest anywhere. Shops, restaurants, and a museum front the harbor. ⊠ *101 Maalaea Boat Harbor Rd., off Honoapiilani Hwy., Maalaea.*

FAMILY
Fodor's Choice
★

Maui Ocean Center. You'll feel as though you're walking from the seashore down to the bottom of the reef at this aquarium, which focuses on creatures of the Pacific. Vibrant exhibits let you get close to turtles, rays, sharks, and the unusual creatures of the tide pools; allow two hours or so to explore it all. It's not an enormous facility, but it does provide an excellent (though pricey) introduction to the sea life that makes Hawaii special. The center is part of a complex of retail shops and restaurants overlooking the harbor. Enter from Honoapiilani Highway as it curves past Maalaea Harbor. ⊠ *192 Maalaea Rd., off Honoapiilani Hwy., Maalaea* ☎ *808/270–7000* ⊕ *www. mauioceancenter.com* ✉ *$25.50* ☉ *Sept.–June, daily 9–5; July and Aug., daily 9–6.*

Ono Organic Farms Farmers' Market. The family-owned Ono Farms offers certified organic produce at this roadside market at an old gas station. You may find such unusual delicacies as *rambutan* (resembling grapes), jackfruit (taste like bananas), and *lilikoi* (passion fruit). ⊠ *Hana Hwy., near Hasegawa General Store, Hana* ☎ *808/248–7779* ⊕ *www. onofarms.com* ☉ *Daily 10–6.*

KIHEI

9 miles south of Kahului; 20 miles east of Lahaina.

Traffic lights and shopping malls may not fit your notion of paradise, but Kihei offers dependably warm sun, excellent beaches, and a front-row seat to marine life of all sorts. Besides all the sun and sand, the town's relatively inexpensive condos and excellent restaurants make this a home base for many Maui visitors.

The county beach parks such as Kamaole I, II, and III have lawns, showers, and picnic tables. ■TIP→ Remember: Beach park or no beach park, the public has a right to the entire coastal strand but not to cross private property to get to it.

GETTING HERE AND AROUND
Kihei is a 20-minute ride south of Kahului once you're past the heavy traffic on Dairy Road and get on the four-lane Mokulele Highway (Route 311).

EXPLORING

> ### FUN THINGS TO DO ON THE SOUTH SHORE
>
> ■ Observe the green sea turtles while snorkeling at Ulua beach.
>
> ■ Spike a volleyball at Kalama Park.
>
> ■ Witness the hammerheads feeding at the excellent Maui Ocean Center.
>
> ■ Follow the Hoapili Trail through an ancient Hawaiian village.
>
> ■ Sink into Makena's soft sand.
>
> ■ Decipher whale song at the Hawaiian Islands Humpback Whale Sanctuary.

Farmers' Market of Maui–Kihei. Tropical flowers, tempting produce, and locally made preserves, baked goods, and crafts are among the bargains at this South Shore market. It's in the west end of Kihei, next to the ABC Store. ⊠ *61 S. Kihei Rd., Kihei* ☎ *808/875–0949* ☺ *Weekdays 8 am–4 pm.*

FAMILY
Fodor's Choice
★

Hawaiian Islands Humpback Whale National Marine Sanctuary. This nature center sits in prime humpback-viewing territory beside a restored ancient Hawaiian fishpond. Whether the whales are here or not, the education center is a great stop for youngsters curious to know more about underwater life. Interactive displays and informative naturalists will explain it all. Throughout the year, the center hosts intriguing activities including "Forty-Five-Ton Talks." The sanctuary itself includes virtually all the waters surrounding the archipelago. ⊠ *726 S. Kihei Rd., Kihei* ☎ *808/879–2818, 800/831–4888* ⊕ *www.hawaiihumpbackwhale.noaa. gov* ⊠ *Free* ☺ *Weekdays 10–3.*

FAMILY

Kealia Pond National Wildlife Refuge. Natural wetlands have become rare in the Islands, and the 700 acres of this reserve attract migratory birds and other wildlife. Long-legged stilts casually dip their beaks into the shallow waters as traffic shuttles by. Sharp-eyed birders may catch sight of migratory visitors such as osprey. Interpretive signs on the boardwalk explain how the endangered hawksbill turtles return to the sandy dunes year after year. The boardwalk stretches along the coast by North Kihei Road; the main entrance to the reserve is on Mokulele Highway. A new visitor center with the reserve headquarters and exhibits provides a good introduction. ⊠ *Mokulele Hwy., mile marker 6, Kihei* ☎ *808/875–1582* ⊕ *www.fws.gov/kealiapond* ⊠ *Free* ☺ *Weekdays 7:30–4.*

WAILEA AND FARTHER SOUTH

15 miles south of Kahului, at the southern border of Kihei.

The South Shore's resort community, Wailea is slightly quieter and drier than its West Maui sister, Kaanapali. Many visitors cannot pick a favorite, so they stay at both. The luxury of the resorts (edging on the excessive) and the simple grandeur of the coastal views make the otherwise stark landscape an outstanding destination; take time to stroll the coastal beach path. A handful of perfect little beaches, all with public access, front the resorts.

The first two resorts were built here in the late 1970s. Soon a cluster of upscale properties sprang up, including the Four Seasons and the Fairmont Kea Lani. Check out the Grand Wailea Resort's chapel, which tells a Hawaiian love story in stained glass.

GETTING HERE AND AROUND

From Kahului Airport, take Route 311 (Mokulele Highway) to Route 31 (Piilani Highway) until it ends in Wailea. Shuttles and taxis are available at the airport. If you're traveling by Maui Bus, the Kihei Islander route runs between the Shops at Wailea and Kaahumanu Center in Kahului. There's a resort shuttle, and a paved shore path goes between the hotels.

EXPLORING

Ahihi-Kinau Natural Area Reserve. South of Makena Beach, the road fades away into a vast territory of black-lava flows, the result of Haleakala's last eruption and now a place for exploration on land and below the water. Before it ends, the road passes through the Ahihi-Kinau Natural Area Reserve, an excellent place for morning snorkel adventures *(see Chapter 4, Water Sports and Tours)*. The area was so popular that it had to be temporarily closed in 2008. At this writing it was scheduled to reopen in July 2014. Parts that remain open include the coastal area along Ahihi Bay, including the "Dumps" surf break. This area is the start of the Hoapili Trail, where you can hike through the remains of one of Maui's ancient villages. ■TIP➔ Bring water and a hat, as there are no public facilities and little shade, and tread carefully over this culturally important landscape. ⊠ *Just before end of Makena Alanui Rd.* ⊕ *hawaii.gov/dlnr.*

Coastal Nature Trail. A 1.5-mile-long paved beach walk allows you to stroll among Wailea's prettiest properties, restaurants, and rocky coves. The trail teems with joggers in the morning hours. The *makai*, or ocean side, is landscaped with exceptionally rare native plants. Look for the silvery *hinahina*, named after the Hawaiian moon goddess because of its color. In winter this is a great place to watch whales. The trail is also accessible from Polo Beach. ⊠ *Wailea Beach, Wailea Alanui Dr., south of Grand Wailea Resort.*

Fodor's Choice ★ Makena Beach State Park. Although it's commonly known as Big Beach, this part of the shoreline is correctly called Oneloa, meaning "long sand." That's exactly what it is—a huge stretch of heavenly golden powder without a house or hotel in sight. More than a decade ago, Maui citizens campaigned successfully to preserve this beloved beach

DID YOU KNOW?

Snorkel cruises are popular on Maui, but you can also find great snorkeling on your own. Try the rocky borders of beaches on the South Shore in places such as Kihei (shown here) or Wailea.

from development. It's still wild, lacking in modern amenities (such as plumbing) but frequented by dolphins and turtles; sunsets are glorious. At the end of the beach farthest from Wailea, skim boarders catch air. On the opposite end rises the beautiful hill called Puu Olai, a perfect cinder cone. A climb over the steep rocks at this end leads to Little Beach, which, although technically illegal, is clothing-optional. On Sunday, it's a mecca for drummers and island gypsies. On any day of the week watch out for the mean shore break—those crisp, aquamarine waves are responsible for more than one broken arm. ⊠ *End of Wailea Alanui Dr.* ⊕ *www.hawaiistateparks.org* 🖃 *Free* ☉ *Weekdays 6–6.*

The Shops at Wailea. Louis Vuitton, Tiffany & Co., and the sumptuous Cos Bar lure shoppers to this elegant mall with more than 65 shops. Honolulu Coffee brews perfect shots of espresso to fuel those "shop-'til-you-drop" types. The kids can buy island-themed T-shirts while their parents ponder vacation ownership upstairs. Tommy Bahama's, Ruth's Chris, and Longhi's are all good dining options. ⊠ *3750 Wailea Alanui Dr.* ☎ *808/891–6770* ⊕ *www.shopsatwailea.com.*

CENTRAL MAUI

Kahului, where you most likely landed when you arrived on Maui, is the industrial and commercial center of the island. West of Kahului is Wailuku, the county seat since 1950 and the most charming town in Central Maui, with some good, inexpensive restaurants. Outside these towns are attractions from museums and historic sites to gardens.

You can combine sightseeing in Central Maui with some shopping at the Queen Kaahumanu Center, Maui Mall, and Maui Marketplace *(see Chapter 6, Shops and Spas).* This is one of the best areas on the island to stock up on groceries and supplies, thanks to major retailers including Walmart, Kmart, and Costco. Note that grocery prices are much higher than on the mainland.

KAHULUI

3 miles west of Kahului Airport; 9 miles north of Kihei; 31 miles east of Kaanapali; 51 miles west of Hana.

With the island's largest airport and commercial harbor, Kahului is Maui's commercial hub. But it also offers plenty of natural and cultural attractions. The town was developed in the early 1950s to meet the housing needs of the large sugarcane interests here, specifically those of Alexander & Baldwin. The company was tired of playing landlord to its many plantation workers and sold land to a developer who promised to create affordable housing. The scheme worked and "Dream City," the first planned city in Hawaii, was born.

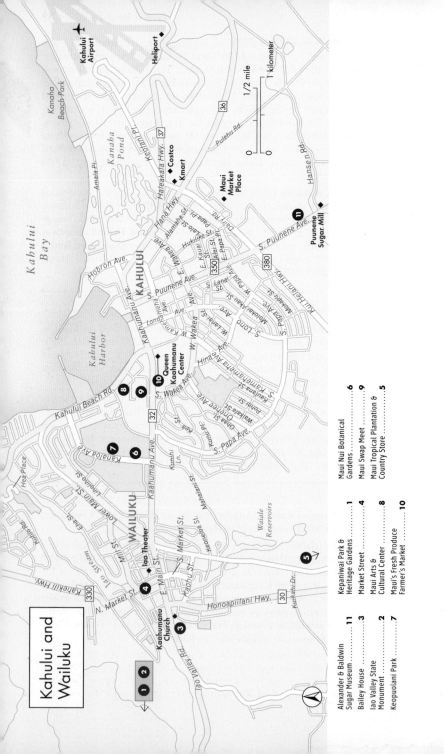

Kahului and Wailuku

Kahului Airport

Heliport

Kanaha Beach Park

Kanaha Pond

Costco
Kmart

Maui Market Place

Puunene Sugar Mill **11**

Kahului Bay

Kahului Harbor

KAHULUI

Queen Kaahumanu Center **10**

8
9

Hobron Ave.
Kaahumanu Ave.
S. Puunene Ave.
Lonomena Ave.
Kamehameha Ave.
S. Wakea Ave.
W. Wakea
W. Lanai St.
Kahului Beach Rd.
32

Hana Hwy.
Alamaha St.
Lalo Pl.
Papa Pl.
Dairy Rd.
E. Kauai St.
Hukilike St.
Aiki St.
E. Papa Av.
E. Lanai St.
S. Lono Ave.
Mokauea St.
S. Papa Ave.
Mehani St.
Kahului
350
380

Kaahumanu Ave.
Kanaloa Ave. **7** **6**

W. Kaahumanu Ave.
Hina Ave.
S. Kamehameha Ave.
Onehee Ave.
Wahani St.
Papili St.
Kaulana St.
S. Papa Ave.

WAILUKU
Iao Theater
S. Market St.
Mill St.
Lower Main St.
Lunalilo St.
Eha St.
Keoneloa St.
Mahalani St.
Kuikahi Dr.
Kunihi Ln.
Kunihi
Kenoi St.

Hea Place

Iao Stream
N. Market St.
Kahekili Hwy. **330**
Iao Valley Rd.
E. Main St.
Kaohu St.
Kaahumanu Church
3
4

Honoapiilani Hwy. **30**

Waiale Reservoirs

5

Maui's Fresh Produce Farmer's Market **10**

Keoiani Pl.
37
36
Pulehu Rd.
Hansen Rd.
Kuihelani Hwy.

0   1/2 mile
0   1 kilometer

1 **2**

Alexander & Baldwin
Sugar Museum **11**
Bailey House **3**
Iao Valley State
Monument **2**
Keopuolani Park **7**

Kepaniwai Park &
Heritage Gardens **1**
Market Street **4**
Maui Arts &
Cultural Center **8**
Maui's Fresh Produce
Farmer's Market **10**

Maui Nui Botanical
Gardens **6**
Maui Swap Meet **9**
Maui Tropical Plantation &
Country Store **5**

GETTING HERE AND AROUND

From the airport, take Keolani Place to Route 36 (Hana Highway), which becomes Kaahumanu Avenue, Kahului's main drag. Run by Maui Bus, the Kahului Loop route traverses all of the town's major shopping centers. The fare is $2.

EXPLORING

TOP ATTRACTIONS

Fodor'sChoice **Alexander & Baldwin Sugar Museum.**
★ Maui's largest landowner, A&B was one of the "Big Five" companies that spearheaded the planting, harvesting, and processing of sugarcane. At this museum, historic photos, artifacts, and documents explain the introduction of sugarcane to Hawaii. Exhibits reveal how plantations brought in laborers from other countries, forever changing the Islands' ethnic mix. Although Hawaiian cane sugar is now being supplanted by cheaper foreign versions—as well as by sugar derived from inexpensive sugar beets—the crop was for many years the mainstay of the local economy. You can find the museum in a small, restored plantation manager's house across the street from the post office and the still-operating sugar refinery, where smoke billows up when cane is being processed. ⊠ 3957 Hansen Rd., Puunene ☎ 808/871–8058 ⊕ www.sugarmuseum.com ☎ $7 ⊗ Daily 9:30–4:30; last admission at 4.

Maui Arts & Cultural Center. At the MACC (as it's called) you can enjoy a concert under the glass-capped Yokouchi Pavilion, rock music at the A&B Amphitheater, or theatrical and dance performances in the multitiered, 1,200-seat Castle Theater. A major draw is the free Schaeffer International Gallery, which houses superb rotating art exhibits. The complex, surrounded by a lava-rock wall, incorporates works by Maui artists. ⊠ 1 Cameron Way, off Kahului Beach Rd., Kahului ☎ 808/242–7469 box office ⊕ www.mauiarts.org ⊗ Weekdays 9–5.

WORTH NOTING

Maui's Fresh Produce Farmers' Market. Local purveyors showcase their fruits, vegetables, orchids, and crafts in the central courtyard at the Queen Kaahumanu Shopping Center. If "strictly local" is critical to you, it's a good idea to ask about the particular produce/flowers/items you want to purchase. ⊠ Queen Kaahumanu Shopping Center, 275 W. Kaahumanu Ave., Kahului ☎ 808/877–4325 ⊗ Tues., Wed., and Fri. 8–4.

FAMILY **Maui Nui Botanical Gardens.** Hawaiian and Polynesian species are cultivated at this fascinating 7-acre garden, including Hawaiian bananas, local varieties of sweet potatoes and sugarcane, native poppies, hibiscus, and *anapanapa*, a plant that makes a natural shampoo when rubbed

---

FUN THINGS TO DO IN CENTRAL MAUI

■ Unwind to slack-key guitar at a Maui Arts & Cultural Center concert.

■ Marvel at the indigenous plant life at Maui Nui Botanical Gardens.

■ Pick your way through Iao Valley's guava and ginger forest.

■ Imagine mastering the ancient weapons at the Bailey House.

■ Boost your fortune with a pair of foo dogs purchased on Market Street.

between your hands. Reserve ahead for the ethnobotany tours that are offered four times a week. Self-guided tour booklets cost $4. ✉ *150 Kanaloa Ave., Kahului* ☎ *808/249–2798* ⊕ *www.mnbg.org* 🏷 *Free* ⏱ *Mon.–Sat. 8–4.*

Maui Swap Meet. Even locals get up early to go to the Maui Swap Meet for fresh produce and floral bouquets. Hundreds of stalls sell everything from quilts to didgeridoos. Enter the parking lot from the traffic light at Kahului Beach Road. ✉ *University of Hawaii Maui, 310 Kaahumanu Ave., Kahului* ☎ *808/244–3100* ⊕ *www.mauiexposition. com* ⏱ *Sat. 7–1.*

WAILUKU

4 miles west of Kahului; 12 miles north of Kihei; 21 miles east of Lahaina.

Wailuku is peaceful now—though it wasn't always so. Its name means "Water of Destruction," after the fateful battle in Iao Valley that pitted King Kamehameha the Great against Maui warriors. Wailuku was a politically important town until the sugar industry began to decline in the 1960s and tourism took hold. Businesses left the cradle of the West Maui Mountains and followed the new market (and tourists) to the shores. Wailuku houses the county government but has the feel of a town that's been asleep for several decades.

The shops and offices now inhabiting Market Street's plantation-style buildings serve as reminders of a bygone era, and continued attempts at "gentrification," at the very least, open the way for unique eateries, shops, and galleries. Drop by on the first Friday of the month for First Friday, when Market Street is closed to traffic and turns into a festival with live music, performances, food, and more.

GETTING HERE AND AROUND

Heading to Wailuku from the airport, Hana Highway turns into Kaahumanu Avenue, the main thoroughfare between Kahului and Wailuku. Maui Bus system's Wailuku Loop stops at shopping centers, medical facilities, and government buildings. The fare is $2.

EXPLORING

Fodor'sChoice ★ **Bailey House.** This repository of the largest and best collection of Hawaiian artifacts on Maui includes objects from the sacred island of Kahoolawe. Built in 1833 on the site of the compound of Kahekili (the last ruling chief of Maui), it was occupied by the family of missionary teachers Edward and Caroline Bailey until 1888. Edward Bailey was something of a Renaissance man: beyond being a missionary, he was also a surveyor, a naturalist, and an excellent artist. The museum displays a number of Bailey's landscape paintings, which provide a snapshot of the island during his time. There is missionary-period furniture, and the grounds include gardens with native Hawaiian plants and a fine example of a traditional canoe. ▇TIP➔ **The gift shop is one of the best sources on Maui for items that are actually made in Hawaii.** ✉ *2375A Main St.* ☎ *808/244–3326* ⊕ *www.mauimuseum.org* 🏷 *$7* ⏱ *Mon.–Sat. 10–4.*

2

Fodor's Choice **Iao Valley State Monument.** When Mark Twain saw this park, he dubbed
★ it the Yosemite of the Pacific. Yosemite it's not, but it is a lovely deep
valley with the curious "**Iao Needle**," a spire that rises more than 2,000
feet from the valley floor. You can walk from the parking lot across
Iao Stream and explore the thick, junglelike topography. This park
has some lovely short strolls on paved paths, where you can stop and
meditate by the edge of a stream or marvel at the native plants. Locals
come to jump from the rocks or bridge into the stream—this isn't
recommended. Mist often rises if there has been a rain, which makes
being here even more magical. Parking is $5. ⊠ *Western end of Rte. 32*
⊕ *www.hawaiistateparks.org* ⊠ *Free* ☉ *Daily 7–7.*

FAMILY **Kepaniwai Park & Heritage Gardens.** Picnic facilities dot the landscape
of this county park, a memorial to Maui's cultural roots. Among the
interesting displays are an early-Hawaiian *hale* (house), a New England–style saltbox, a Portuguese-style villa with gardens, and dwellings
from such other cultures as China and the Philippines. Next door, the
Hawaii Nature Center has excellent interactive exhibits and hikes easy
enough for children.

The peacefulness here belies the history of the area. In 1790, King
Kamehameha the Great from the Island of Hawaii waged a successful and bloody battle against Kahekili, the son of Maui's chief. An
earlier battle at the site had pitted Kahekili himself against an older
Hawaii Island chief, Kalaniopuu. Kahekili prevailed, but the carnage
was so great that the nearby stream became known as *Wailuku* (water
of destruction), and the place where fallen warriors choked the stream's
flow was called *Kepaniwai* (damming of the waters). ⊠ *870 Iao Valley
Rd.* ⊠ *Free* ☉ *Daily 7–7.*

Market Street. An idiosyncratic assortment of shops makes Wailuku's
Market Street a delightful place for a stroll. Brown-Kobayashi and the
Bird of Paradise Unique Antiques are the best shops for interesting collectibles and furnishings. Wailuku Coffee Company houses works by
local artists and occasionally offers live entertainment in the evening.
On the first Friday of every month Market Street closes to traffic from
5:30 to 9 for Wailuku's First Friday celebration. The fun includes street
vendors, live entertainment, and food.

WORTH NOTING

FAMILY **Keopuolani Park.** Originally named Maui Central Park, Keopuolani Park
got its name after schoolchildren argued before the county council that
it be named for Hawaii's most revered queen, who was born near here
and was forced to flee across the mountains before the arrival of Kamehameha the Great's army. This 101-acre park includes seven playing
fields and a running path, gym, pool, skate park, and grass amphitheater. ⊠ *Kanaloa Ave.* ☉ *Daily 7–7.*

FAMILY **Maui Tropical Plantation & Country Store.** When Maui's cash crop declined
in importance, a group of visionaries opened an agricultural theme park
on the site of this former sugarcane field. The 60-acre preserve offers a
30-minute tram ride with an informative narration covering the growing process and plant types. Children will enjoy such hands-on activities
as coconut husking. Also here are an art gallery, a restaurant, and a

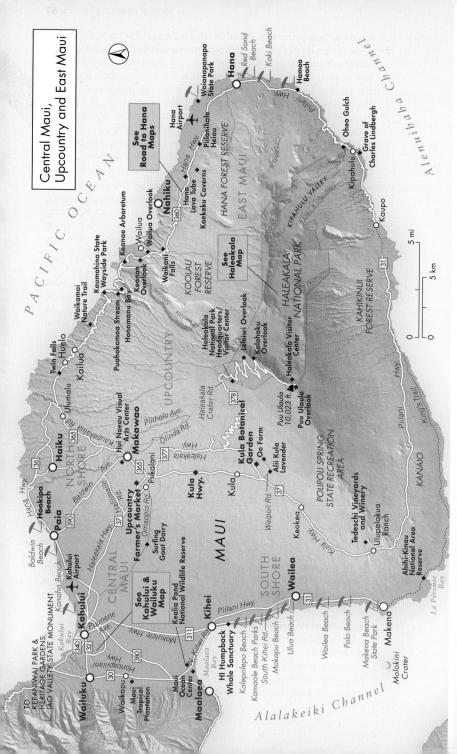

store specializing in "Made in Maui" products. ⊠ *1670 Honoapiilani Hwy., Waikapu* ☎ *808/244–7643* ⊕ *www.mauitropicalplantation.com* ⊠ *Free; $15 for tram ride* ⊙ *Daily 9–5.*

UPCOUNTRY

2

The west-facing upper slopes of Haleakala are locally called "Upcountry." This region is responsible for much of Maui's produce—lettuce, tomatoes, strawberries, sweet Maui onions, and much, much more. You'll notice cactus thickets mingled with purple jacaranda, wild hibiscus, and towering eucalyptus trees. Keep an eye out for *pueo*, Hawaii's native owl, which hunts these fields during daylight hours.

Upcountry is also fertile ranch land; cowboys still work the fields of the historic 20,000-acre Ulupalakua Ranch and the 32,000-acre Haleakala Ranch. ■ TIP➔ **Take an agricultural tour and learn more about the island's bounty. Lavender and wine are among the offerings.**

A drive to Upcountry Maui from Wailea (South Shore) or Kaanapali (West Maui) can be an all-day outing if you take the time to visit Tedeschi Vineyards and the tiny but entertaining town of Makawao. You may want to cut these side trips short and combine your Upcountry tour with a visit to Haleakala National Park *(see Haleakala National Park feature)*. It's a Maui must-see. If you leave early enough to catch the sunrise from the summit of Haleakala, you'll have plenty of time to explore the mountain, have lunch in Kula or at Ulupalakua Ranch, and end your day with dinner in Makawao.

THE KULA HIGHWAY

15 miles east of Kahului; 44 miles east of Kaanapali; 28 miles east of Wailea.

Kula: Most Mauians say it with a hint of a sigh. Why? It's just that much closer to heaven. Explore it for yourself on some of the area's agricultural tours.

On the broad shoulder of Haleakala, this is blessed country. From the Kula Highway most of Central Maui is visible—from the lava-scarred plains of Kenaio to the cruise-ship-lighted waters of Kahului Harbor. Beyond the central valley's sugarcane fields, the plunging profile of the West Maui Mountains can be seen in its entirety, wreathed in ethereal mist. If this sounds too dramatic a description, you haven't been here yet. These views, coveted by many, continue to drive real-estate prices further skyward. Luckily, you can still have them for free—just pull over on the roadside and drink them in.

GETTING HERE AND AROUND

From Kahului, take Route 37 (Haleakala Highway), which runs into Route 377 (Kula Highway). Upper and Lower Kula highways are both numbered 377, but join each other at two points.

MAUI SIGHTSEEING TOURS

Maui is really too big to see all in one day, so tour companies offer specialized tours, visiting either Haleakala or Hana and its environs. A tour of Haleakala and Upcountry is usually a half-day excursion and is offered in several versions by different companies for $75 and up. The trip often includes stops at Tedeschi Vineyards, Maui's only winery.

A Haleakala sunrise tour starts before dawn so that you can get to the top of the dormant volcano before the sun peeks over the horizon. Because trips offer hotel pickup around the island, many sunrise trips leave around 2:30 am.

A tour of Hana is almost always done in a van, since the winding Road to Hana just isn't built for bigger buses. Guides decide where you stop for photos. Tours run from $100 to $140.

The key is to ask how many stops you get and how many other passengers will be on board—otherwise you could end up on a packed bus, sightseeing through a window.

Most of the tour guides have been in the business for years, and some have taken classes to learn more about the culture and lore. They expect a tip ($1 per person at least), but they're just as cordial without one.

Maui Pineapple Tours. This tour gives you a first-hand look at the cultivation and shipping of pineapples. You'll start by heading into the fields to sample fresh fruit, and at the end you'll get a free pineapple to take home. Tours depart weekday mornings from Haliimaile Plantation at 9:30 and 11:45 and cost $68. For an extra $15, you can enjoy lunch at the Haliimaile General Store next door. ⊠ *875 Haliimaile Rd., Haliimaile* ☎ *808/665–5491* ⊕ *www.mauipineappletour.com.*

Polynesian Adventure Tours. This company uses large buses with floor-to-ceiling windows. The drivers are fun and, because they have extensive training, really know the island. Some Haleakala tours also include visits to Iao Valley and Lahaina. ☎ *808/877–4242, 800/622–3011* ⊕ *www.polyad.com.*

Roberts Hawaii Tours. This is one of the state's largest tour companies and offers numerous experiences. Its staff can arrange tours with bilingual guides if requested ahead of time. Eleven-hour trips venture out to Kaupo, the wild area past Hana. ☎ *808/871–6226, 866/898–2519* ⊕ *www.robertshawaii.com.*

Temptation Tours. An affluent older crowd is the market for this company. Tours in plush eight-passenger limo-vans explore Haleakala and Hana, and range from $210 to $360 per person. The "Hana Sky-Trek" includes a return trip via helicopter. ☎ *808/877–8888, 800/817–1234* ⊕ *www.temptationtours.com.*

Tour da Food Maui. Maui resident Bonnie Friedman (a Fodor's contributor) guides small, customized ethnic food tours through Wailuku and Upcountry that include a couple of holes-in-the-wall some locals don't even know about. Newest is her GAS-tronomy tour—yes, good eats at island gas stations. Tours leave Tuesday, Wednesday, and Thursday mornings; all-inclusive prices start at $120 per person. ☎ *808/242–8383* ⊕ *www.tourdafoodmaui.com.*

EXPLORING
TOP ATTRACTIONS

Alii Kula Lavender. Reserve a spot for tea or lunch at this lavender farm with a falcon's view: It's *the* relaxing remedy for those suffering from too much sun, shopping, or golf. Knowledgeable guides lead tours through winding paths of therapeutic lavender varieties, protea, succulents, and rare Maui wormwood. The gift shop abounds with many locally made lavender products such as brownies, moisturizing lotions, and fragrant sachets. ⊠ *1100 Waipoli Rd.* ☎ *808/878–3004* ⊕ *www.aklmaui. com* ⊠ *$3; $12 for walking tours* ☉ *Daily 9–4.*

FUN THINGS TO DO UPCOUNTRY

■ Nibble lavender scones with a view of the Valley Isle at Alii Kula Lavender Farm.

■ Open the car windows wide and breathe in the fresh, cool country air.

■ Taste pineapple wine at Tedeschi Vineyards and Winery.

■ Watch a plein-air painter work on the grounds at the Hui Noeau Visual Arts Center in Makawao.

Oo Farm. About a mile from Alii Kula Lavender are 8 acres of salad greens, herbs, vegetables, fruits, and berries—all of it headed directly to restaurants in Lahaina. Owned and operated by the restaurateurs, more than 300 pounds of fresh Oo Farm produce ends up on diners' plates every week. Tours include an informational walk around the gorgeous grounds and a pick-your-own lunch, supervised by a chef. Reservations are necessary. ⊠ *651 Waipoli Rd.* ☎ *808/667–4341* ⊕ *www.oofarm.com* ⊠ *$50* ☉ *Mon.–Thurs. 10:30–2.*

Fodor's Choice ★ **Tedeschi Vineyards and Winery.** You can tour Maui's only winery and its historic grounds, the former Rose Ranch, and sample such wines as Ulupalakua Red and Upcountry Gold. The top seller, naturally, is the pineapple wine, Maui Blanc. The tasting room is a cottage built in the late 1800s for the frequent visits of King Kalakaua. The cottage also contains the **Ulupalakua Ranch History Room,** which tells colorful stories of the ranch's owners, the *paniolo* (Hawaiian cowboy) tradition that developed here, and Maui's polo teams. The old Ranch Store across the road may look like a museum, but in fact it's an excellent pit stop. ▉TIP➔ The elk burgers are fantastic. ⊠ *Kula Hwy.* ☎ *808/878–6058* ⊕ *www.mauiwine.com* ⊠ *Free* ☉ *Daily 10–5; tours at 10:30 and 1:30.*

WORTH NOTING

Keokea. More of a friendly gesture than a town, this tiny outpost is the last bit of civilization before Kula Highway becomes a winding back road. A coffee tree pushes through the sunny deck at Grandma's Maui Coffee, the morning watering hole for Maui's cowboys who work at Ulupalakua or Kaupo Ranch. Keokea Gallery next door sells cool, quirky artwork. And two tiny stores—Fong's and Ching's—are testament to the Chinese immigrants who settled the area in the late 19th Century. ▉TIP➔ The only restroom for miles is in the public park, and the view makes stretching your legs worth it.

Kula Botanical Gardens. This well-kept garden has assimilated itself naturally into its craggy 8-acre habitat. There are 2,500 species of plants and trees here including native koa (prized by woodworkers) and *kukui* (the state tree, a symbol of enlightenment). There is also a good selection of proteas, the flowering shrubs that have become a signature flower crop of Upcountry Maui. A flowing stream feeds into a koi pond; nene and ducks roam; and a paved pathway dotted with benches meanders throughout the grounds. ✉ *638 Kekaulike Hwy.* ☎ *808/878–1715* ⊕ *www.kulabotanicalgarden.com* ⛬ *$10* ⊙ *Daily 9–4.*

FAMILY **Surfing Goat Dairy.** It takes goats to make goat cheese, and they've got plenty of both at this 42-acre farm. Tours range from "casual" to "grand," and any of them delight kids as well as adults. If you have the time, the "Evening Chores and Milking Tour" is educational and fun. The owners make more than two-dozen kinds of goat cheese, from the plain, creamy "Udderly Delicious" to more exotic varieties that include tropical ingredients. All are available in the dairy store, along with gift baskets and even goat-milk soaps. ✉ *3651 Omaopio Rd.* ☎ *808/878–2870* ⊕ *www.surfinggoatdairy.com* ⛬ *Free; tours $10–$25* ⊙ *Mon.–Sat. 9–5, Sun. 9–2.*

Upcountry Farmers' Market. Most of Maui's produce is grown Upcountry, which is why everything is fresh at this outdoor market at the football field parking lot in Kulamalu Town Center. Farmers offer fruits, vegetables, and flowers, as well as jellies and breads. Go early, as nearly everything sells out. ✉ *Rte. 37, near Longs Drugs* ⊕ *ww.upcountryfamersmarket.com* ⊙ *Sat. 7 am–10:30 am.*

MAKAWAO

10 miles east of Kahului; 10 miles southeast of Paia.

At the intersection of Baldwin and Makawao avenues, this once-tiny town has managed to hang on to its country charm (and eccentricity) as it has grown in popularity. Its good selection of specialized shops makes Makawao a fun place to spend some time.

The district was originally settled by Portuguese and Japanese immigrants who came to Maui to work the sugar plantations and then moved Upcountry to establish small farms, ranches, and stores. Descendants now work the neighboring Haleakala and Ulupalakua ranches. Every July 4 weekend the *paniolo* set comes out in force for the Makawao Rodeo.

The crossroads of town—lined with shops and down-home eateries—reflects a growing population of people who came here just because they liked it. For those seeking greenery rather than beachside accommodations, there are secluded B&Bs around the town.

GETTING HERE AND AROUND

To get to Makawao by car, take Route 37 (Haleakala Highway) to Pukalanai, then turn left on Makawao Avenue. You can also take Route 36 (Hana Highway) to Paia and make a right onto Baldwin Avenue. Either way, you'll arrive in the heart of Makawao.

Continued on page 73

HALEAKALA NATIONAL PARK

HALEAKALA CRATER

From the Tropics to the Moon! Two hours, 38 miles, 10,023 feet—those are the unlikely numbers involved in reaching Maui's highest point, the summit of the volcano Haleakala. Nowhere else on earth can you drive from sea level (Kahului) to 10,023 feet (the summit) in only 38 miles. And what's more shocking—in that short vertical ascent, you'll journey from lush, tropical-island landscape to the stark, moonlike basin of the volcano's enormous, otherworldly crater.

Established in 1916, Haleakala National Park covers an astonishing 27,284 acres. Haleakala "Crater" is the centerpiece of the park though it's not actually a crater. Technically, it's an erosional valley, flushed out by water pouring from the summit through two enormous gaps. The mountain has terrific camping and hiking, including a trail that loops through the crater, but the chance to witness this unearthly landscape is reason enough for a visit.

THE CLIMB TO THE SUMMIT

To reach Haleakala National Park and the mountain's breathtaking summit, take Route 36 east of Kahului to the Haleakala Highway (Route 37). Head east, up the mountain to the unlikely intersection of Haleakala Highway and Haleakala Highway. If you continue straight the road's name changes to Kula Highway (still Route 37). Instead, turn left onto Haleakala Highway—this is now Route 377. After about 6 miles, make a left onto

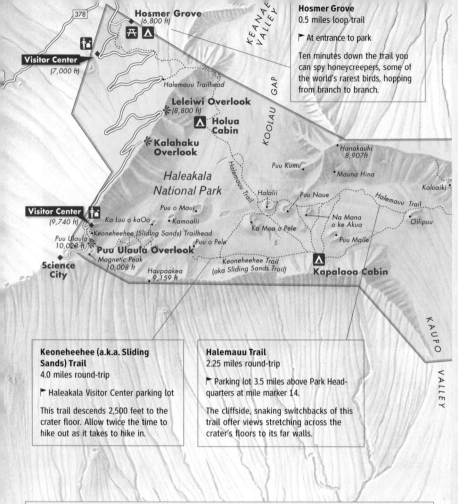

Hosmer Grove

0.5 miles loop trail

▶ At entrance to park

Ten minutes down the trail you can spy honeycreepers, some of the world's rarest birds, hopping from branch to branch.

378
Hosmer Grove
(6,800 ft)
Visitor Center
(7,000 ft)

KEANAE VALLEY

Halemauu Trailhead

Leleiwi Overlook
(8,800 ft)
Holua Cabin

KOOLAU GAP

Kalahaku Overlook

Haleakala National Park

Hanakauhi
8,907 ft

Puu Kumu

Mauna Hina

Halemauu Trail

Halalii

Puu Naue

Puu o Maui
Ka Luu o kaOo
Kamoalii

Kaluaiki

Halemauu Trail

Oilipuu

Na Mana o ke Akua

Visitor Center
(9,740 ft)
Puu Ulaula
10,023 ft

Ka Moa o Pele

Puu Maile

Keoneheehee (Sliding Sands) Trailhead

Puu o Pele

Puu Ulaula Overlook

Science City

Magnetic Peak
10,008 ft

Haupaakea
9,159 ft

Keoneheehee Trail
(aka Sliding Sands Trail)

Kapalaoa Cabin

KAUPO VALLEY

Keoneheehee (a.k.a. Sliding Sands) Trail

4.0 miles round-trip

▶ Haleakala Visitor Center parking lot

This trail descends 2,500 feet to the crater floor. Allow twice the time to hike out as it takes to hike in.

Halemauu Trail

2.25 miles round-trip

▶ Parking lot 3.5 miles above Park Head-quarters at mile marker 14.

The cliffside, snaking switchbacks of this trail offer views stretching across the crater's floors to its far walls.

Crater Road (Route 378). After several long switchbacks (look out for downhill bikers!) you'll come to the park entrance.

■TIP→ Before you head up Haleakala, call for the latest park weather conditions (☎ 866/944–5025). Extreme gusty winds, heavy rain, and even snow in winter are not uncommon. Because of the high altitude, the mountaintop temperature is often as much as 30 degrees cooler than that at sea level. Be sure to bring a jacket. Also make sure you have a full tank of gas. No service stations exist beyond Kula.

There's a $10 per car fee to enter the park; but it's good for three days and

can be used at Oheo Gulch (Kipahulu), so save your receipt.

6,800 feet, Hosmer Grove. Just as you enter the park, Hosmer Grove has campsites and interpretive trails (*see* Hiking & Camping *on the following pages*). Park rangers maintain a changing schedule of talks and hikes both here and at the top of the mountain. Call the park for current schedules.

7,000 feet, Park Headquarters/Visitor Center. Not far from Hosmer Grove, the Park Headquarters/Visitor Center (open daily from 6:30 am to 3:45) has trail maps and displays about the vol-

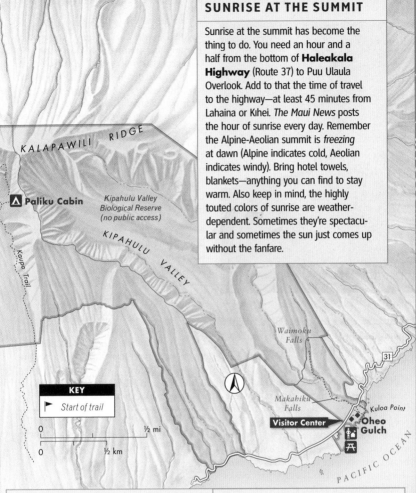

SUNRISE AT THE SUMMIT

Sunrise at the summit has become the thing to do. You need an hour and a half from the bottom of **Haleakala Highway** (Route 37) to Puu Ulaula Overlook. Add to that the time of travel to the highway—at least 45 minutes from Lahaina or Kihei. *The Maui News* posts the hour of sunrise every day. Remember the Alpine-Aeolian summit is *freezing* at dawn (Alpine indicates cold, Aeolian indicates windy). Bring hotel towels, blankets—anything you can find to stay warm. Also keep in mind, the highly touted colors of sunrise are weather-dependent. Sometimes they're spectacular and sometimes the sun just comes up without the fanfare.

KALAPAWILI RIDGE

▲ Paliku Cabin

Kipahulu Valley Biological Reserve (no public access)

KIPAHULU VALLEY

Kaupo Trail

Waimoku Falls

31

Makahiku Falls

Kuloa Point

Visitor Center

◆ Oheo Gulch

PACIFIC OCEAN

KEY

▶ *Start of trail*

0   ½ mi

0   ½ km

cano's origins and eruption history. Hikers and campers should check-in here before heading up the mountain. Maps, posters, and other memorabilia are available at the gift shop.

8,800 feet, Leleiwi Overlook. Continuing up the mountain, you come to Leleiwi Overlook. A short walk to the end of the parking lot reveals your first awe-inspiring view of the crater. The small hills in the basin are volcanic cinder cones (called *puu* in Hawaiian), each with a small crater at its top, and each the site of a former eruption.

WHERE TO EAT

KULA LODGE (✉ Haleakala Hwy., Kula ☎ 808/878–2517) serves hearty breakfasts from 7 to 11 am, a favorite with hikers coming down from a sunrise visit to Haleakala's summit, as well as those on their way up for a late-morning tramp in the crater. Spectacular ocean views fill the windows of this mountainside lodge.

If you're here in the late afternoon, it's possible you'll experience a phenomenon called the Brocken Specter. Named after a similar occurrence in East Germany's Harz Mountains, the "specter"

allows you to see yourself reflected on the clouds and encircled by a rainbow. Don't wait all day for this because it's not a daily occurrence.

9,000 feet, Kalahaku Overlook. The next stopping point is Kalahaku Overlook. The view here offers a different perspective of the crater, and at this elevation the famous silversword plant grows amid the cinders. This odd, endangered beauty grows only here and at the same elevation on the Big Island's two peaks. It begins life as a silver, spiny-leaf rosette and is the sole home of a variety of native insects (it's the only shelter around). The silversword reaches maturity between 7 and 17 years, when it sends forth a 3- to 8-foot-tall stalk with several hundred tiny sunflowers. It blooms once, then dies.

9,740 feet, Haleakala Visitor Center. Another mile up is the Haleakala Visitor Center, open daily from sunrise to 3 pm except Christmas and New Year's. There are exhibits inside, and a trail from here leads to White Hill—a short easy walk that will give you an even better view of the valley.

10,023 feet, Puu Ulaula Overlook. The highest point on Maui is the Puu Ulaula Overlook, at the 10,023-foot summit. Here you find a glass-enclosed lookout with a 360-degree view. The building is open 24 hours a day, and this is where visitors gather for the best sunrise view. Dawn begins between 5:45 and 7, depending on the time of year. On a clear day you can see the islands of Molokai, Lanai, Kahoolawe, and Hawaii (the Big Island). On a *really* clear day you can even spot Oahu glimmering in the distance.

■TIP→ The air is very thin at 10,000 feet. Don't be surprised if you feel a little breathless while walking around the summit. Take it easy and drink lots of water. Anyone who has been scuba diving within the last 24 hours should not make the trip up Haleakala.

On a small hill nearby, you can see **Science City,** an off-limits research and communications center straight out of an espionage thriller. The University of Hawaii maintains an observatory here, and the Department of Defense tracks satellites.

For more information about Haleakala National Park, contact the **National Park Service** (☎ 808/572–4400 ⊕ www.nps.gov/hale).

HIKING AND CAMPING

Exploring Haleakala Crater is one of the best hiking experiences on Maui. The volcanic terrain offers an impressive diversity of colors, textures, and shapes—almost as if the lava has been artfully sculpted. The barren landscape is home to many plants, insects, and birds that exist nowhere else on earth and have developed intriguing survival mechanisms, such as the sun-reflecting, hairy leaves of the silversword, which allow it to survive the intense climate.

Stop at park headquarters to register and pick up trail maps on your way into the park.

1-Hour Hike. Just as you enter Haleakala National Park, **Hosmer Grove** offers a short 10-minute hike and an hour-long, $1/2$-mile loop trail that will give you insight into Hawaii's fragile ecology. Anyone can go on these hikes, whereas a longer trail through the Waikamoi Cloud Forest is accessible only with park ranger–guided hikes. Call park headquarters for the schedule. Facilities here include six campsites (no permit needed, available on a first-come, first-served basis), pit toilets, drinking water, and cooking shelters.

4-Hour Hikes. Two half-day hikes involve descending into the crater and returning the way you came. The first, **Halemauu Trail** (trailhead is between mile markers 14 and 15), is 2.25 miles round-trip. The cliffside, snaking switchbacks of this trail offer views stretching across the crater's puu-speckled floor to its far walls. On clear days you can peer through the Koolau Gap to Hana. Native flowers and shrubs grow along the trail, which is typically misty and cool (though still exposed to the sun). When you reach the gate at the bottom, head back up.

The other hike, which is 5 miles round-trip, descends down **Keoneheehee (a.k.a. Sliding Sands) Trail** (trailhead is at the Haleakala Visitor Center) into an alien landscape of reddish black cinders, lava bombs, and silverswords. It's easy to imagine life before humans in the solitude and silence of this place. Turn back when you hit the crater floor.

■ TIP→ Bring water, sunscreen, and a reliable jacket. These are demanding hikes. Take it slowly to acclimate, and allow additional time for the uphill return trip.

8-Hour Hike. The recommended way to explore the crater in a single, but full day is to go in two cars and ferry yourselves back and forth between the head of **Halemauu Trail** and the summit. This way, you can hike from the summit down **Keoneheehee Trail**, cross the crater's floor, investigate the **Bottomless Pit** and **Pele's Paint Pot**, then climb out on the **switchback trail (Halemauu)**. When you emerge, the shelter of your waiting car will be very welcome (this is an 11.2-mile hike). If you don't have two cars, hitching a ride from Halemauu back to the summit should be relatively safe and easy.

■ TIP→ Take a backpack with lunch, water, sunscreen, and a reliable jacket for the beginning and end of the 8-hour hike. This is a demanding trip, but you will never regret or forget it.

Overnight Hike. Staying overnight in one of Haleakala's three cabins or two wilderness campgrounds is an experience like no other. You'll feel like the only person on earth when you wake up inside this enchanted, strange landscape. The cabins, each tucked in a different corner of the crater's floor, are equipped with 12 bunk beds, wood-burning stoves, fake logs, and kitchen gear.

Holua cabin is the shortest hike, less than 4 hours (3.7 miles) from Halemauu Trail. **Kapalaoa** is about 5 hours (5.5 miles) down Keoneheehee Trail. The most cherished cabin is **Paliku**, an eight-hour (9.3-miles) hike starting from either trail. It's nestled against the cliffs above Kaupo Gap. Cabin reservations can be made up to 90 days in advance through the Friends of Haleakala National Park's Web site (⊕ *fhnp. org/wcr*) or by calling the National Park Service (☎ *808/572–4400*) between 1 and 3 pm HST. Tent campsites at Holua and Paliku are free and easy to reserve on a first-come, first-served basis.

■ TIP→ Toilets and nonpotable water are available—bring iodine tablets to purify the water. Open fires are not allowed and packing out your trash is mandatory.

For more information on hiking or camping, contact the National Park Service (✉ Box 369, Makawao 96768 ☎ 808/572-4459 ⊕ www.nps.gov/hale).

OPTIONS FOR EXPLORING

If you're short on time you can drive to the summit, take a peek inside, and drive back down. But the "House of the Sun" is really worth a day, whether you explore by foot, horseback, or helicopter.

BIKING

At this writing, all guided bike tours inside park boundaries were suspended indefinitely. However, the tours continue but now start outside the boundary of the park. These can provide a speedy, satisfying downhill trip. The park is still open to individual bikes for a $5 fee. There are no bike paths, however—just the same road that is used by vehicular traffic. Whether you're on your own or with a tour, be careful!

HELICOPTER TOURS

Viewing Haleakala from above can be a mind-altering experience, if you don't mind dropping $225+ per person for a few blissful moments above the crater. Most tours buzz Haleakala, where airspace is regulated, then head over to Hana in search of waterfalls.

HORSEBACK RIDING

Several companies offer half-day, full-day, and even overnight rides into the crater. On one half-day ride you descend into the crater on Keoneheehee Trail and have lunch before you head back.

For complete information on any of these activities, ⇨ see Golf, Hiking and Outdoor Activities.

2

EXPLORING

Fodor's Choice **Hui Noeau Visual Arts Center.** The grande dame of Maui's visual arts
★ scene, "The Hui" hosts exhibits that are always satisfying. Located
just outside Makawao, the center's main building is an elegant two-
story Mediterranean-style villa designed in 1917 by the defining Hawaii
architect of the era, C.W. Dickey. You can arrange a $12 tour of the
lovely grounds—which feature many dozens of species of plants and
trees—with at least 24 hours notice. A self-guided tour booklet is available for $6. ⊠ *2841 Baldwin Ave.* ☎ *808/572–6560* ⊕ *www.huinoeau.
com* ✆ *Free* ⊗ *Mon.–Sat. 10–4.*

QUICK
BITES
Komoda Store and Bakery. One of Makawao's landmarks is Komoda Store
and Bakery, a classic mom-and-pop shop that has changed little in three-
quarters of a century. You can get an incredible "stick" donut or delicious
cream puff if you arrive early enough. They make hundreds, but sell out
everyday. ⊠ *3674 Baldwin Ave.* ☎ *808/572–7261.*

THE NORTH SHORE

Blasted by winter swells and wind, Maui's North Shore draws water-
sports thrill seekers from around the world. But there's much more to
this area of Maui than coastline. Inland, a lush, waterfall-fed Garden
of Eden beckons. In forested pockets, wealthy hermits have carved out
a little piece of paradise for themselves.

North Shore action centers around the colorful town of Paia and the
windsurfing mecca of Hookipa Beach. It's a far cry from the more
developed resort areas of West Maui and the South Shore. Paia is also
a starting point for one of the most popular excursions in Maui, the
Road to Hana *(see Road to Hana feature in this chapter).* Waterfalls,
phenomenal views of the coast and ocean, and lush rain forest are all
part of the spectacular 55-mile drive into East Maui.

PAIA

9 miles east of Kahului; 4 miles west of Haiku.

Fodor's Choice At the intersection of Hana Highway and Baldwin Avenue, Paia has
★ eclectic boutiques that supply everything from high fashion to hemp-oil
candles. Some of Maui's best shops for surf trunks, Brazilian bikinis,
and other beachwear are here. Restaurants provide excellent people-
watching and an array of dining and takeout options from flatbread
to fresh fish. The abundance is helpful because Paia is the last place to
snack before the pilgrimage to Hana and the first stop for the famished
on the return trip.

This little town on Maui's North Shore was once a sugarcane enclave,
with a mill, plantation camps, and shops. The old sugar mill finally
closed, but the town continues to thrive. In the 1970s Paia became a hip-
pie town, as dropouts headed for Maui to open boutiques, galleries, and
unusual eateries. In the 1980s windsurfers—many of them European—
discovered nearby Hookipa Beach and brought an international flavor

to Paia. Today this historic town is hip and happening.

GETTING HERE AND AROUND

Route 36 (Hana Highway) runs directly though Paia; 4 miles east of town, follow the sign to Haiku, a short detour off the highway. You can take the Maui Bus from the airport and Queen Kaahumanu Shopping Center in Kahului to Paia and on to Haiku.

EXPLORING

Fodor's Choice ★ **Hookipa Beach.** There's no better place on this or any other island to watch the world's finest windsurfers and kiteboarders in action. They know the five different surf breaks here by name. Unless it's a rare day

without wind or waves, you're sure to get a show. ■TIP→ It's not safe to park on the shoulder. Use the ample parking lot at the county park entrance. ⊠ *Rte. 36, Paia.*

QUICK BITES

Anthony's Coffee. This place roasts its own beans, sells Maui's Rose-lani ice cream and picnic lunches, and is a great place to eavesdrop on the windsurfing crowd. ⊠ *90 Hana Hwy., Paia* ☎ *808/579–8340* ⊕ *www.anthonyscoffee.com.*

Charley's Restaurant. Charley's Restaurant is an easygoing saloon-type hangout where locals gather in the bar to watch football games on big-screen TVs. Breakfasts are big and delicious. ⊠ *142 Hana Hwy., Paia* ☎ *808/579–9453* ⊕ *www.charleysmaui.com.*

Mana Foods. The North Shore's natural-foods store, Mana Foods has an inspired deli with hot and cold items. ⊠ *49 Baldwin Ave., Paia* ☎ *808/579–8078* ⊕ *www.manafoodsmaui.com.*

Paia Fishmarket Restaurant. The long line at Paia Fishmarket Restaurant attests to the popularity of the tasty fresh-fish sandwiches, plates, and tacos. ⊠ *2A Baldwin Ave., Paia* ☎ *808/579–8030* ⊕ *www.paiafishmarket.com.*

HAIKU

13 miles east of Kahului; 4 miles east of Paia.

At one time this area vibrated around a couple of enormous pineapple canneries. Both have been transformed into rustic warehouse malls. Because of the post office next door, Old Haiku Cannery earned the title of town center. Here you can try eateries offering everything from plate lunches to vegetarian dishes to juicy burgers and fantastic sushi. Follow windy Haiku Road to Pauwela Cannery, the other

Continued on page 84

ROAD TO HANA

As you round the impossibly tight turn, a one-lane bridge comes into view. Beneath its worn surface, a lush forested gulch plummets toward the coast. The sound of rushing water fills the air, compelling you to search the over-grown hillside for waterfalls. This is the Road to Hana, a 55-mile journey into the unspoiled heart of Maui. Tracing a centuries-old path, the road begins as a well-paved highway in Kahului and ends in the tiny town of Hana on the island's rain-gouged windward side.

Fodor's Choice Despite the twists and turns, the road to Hana is not as frightening as it may sound. You're bound to be a little nervous approaching it the first time; but afterwards you'll wonder if somebody out there is making it sound tough just to keep out the hordes. The challenging part of the road takes only an hour and a half, but you'll want to stop often and let the driver enjoy the view, too. Don't expect a booming city when you get to Hana. Its lure is its quiet timelessness. As the adage says, the journey *is* the destination.

During high season, the road to Hana tends to clog—well, not clog exactly, but develop little choo-choo trains of cars, with everyone in a line of six or a dozen driving as slowly as the first car. The solution: leave early (dawn) and return late (dusk). And if you find yourself playing the role of locomotive, pull over and let the other drivers pass. You can also let someone else take the turns for you—several companies offer van tours, which make stops all along the way (*see Maui Sightseeing Tours box in this chapter*).

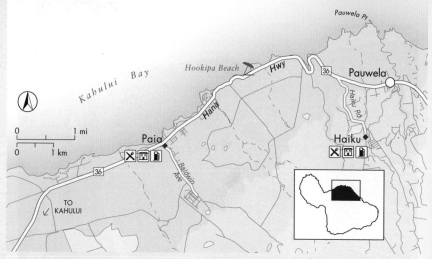

DRIVING THE ROAD TO HANA

Begin your journey in Paia, the little town on Maui's North Shore. Be sure to fill up your gas tank here. There are no gas stations along Hana Highway, and the station in Hana closes by 6 pm. You should also pick up a picnic lunch. Lunch and snack choices along the way are limited to rustic fruit stands.

About 10 miles past Paia, at the bottom of Kaupakalua Road, the roadside mileposts begin measuring the 36 miles to Hana town. The road's trademark noodling starts about 3 miles after that. Once the road gets twisty, remember that many residents make this trip frequently. You'll recognize them because they're the ones zipping around every curve. They've seen this so many times before they don't care to linger. Pull over to let them pass.

All along this stretch of road, waterfalls are abundant. Roll down your windows. Breathe in the scent of guava and ginger. You can almost hear the bamboo growing. There are plenty of places to pull completely off the road and park safely. Do this often, since the road's curves make driving without a break difficult. ■ TIP→ If you're prone to carsickness, be sure to take medication before you start this drive. You may also want to stop periodicially.

❶ **Twin Falls.** Keep an eye out for the fruit stand just after mile marker 2. Stop here and treat yourself to some fresh sugarcane juice. If you're feeling adventurous, follow the path beyond the stand to the paradisiacal waterfalls known as Twin Falls. Once a rough trail plastered with "no trespassing" signs, this treasured spot is now easily accessible. In fact, there's usually a mass of cars surrounding the fruit stand at the trail head. Several deep, emerald pools sparkle beneath waterfalls and offer excellent swimming and photo opportunities.

While this is still private property, the "no trespassing" signs have been replaced by colorfully painted arrows pointing away from residences and toward the falls. ■ TIP→ Bring water shoes for crossing streams along the way. Swim at your own risk and beware: flash floods here and in all East Maui stream areas can be sudden and deadly. Check the weather before you go.

❷ **Huelo and Kailua.** Dry off and drive on past the sleepy country villages of Huelo (near mile marker 5) and Kailua (near mile marker 6). The little farm town of Huelo has two quaint churches. If you linger awhile, you could meet local residents and learn about a rural lifestyle you might not expect to find on the Islands.

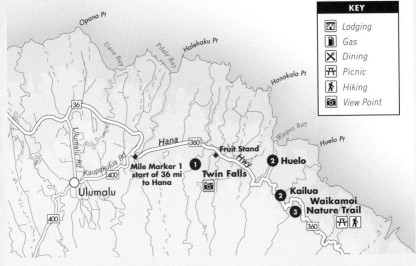

KEY

🏨	Lodging
⛽	Gas
✕	Dining
⛑	Picnic
🚶	Hiking
📷	View Point

The same can be said for nearby Kailua, home to Alexander & Baldwin's irrigation employees.

❸ Waikamoi Nature Trail. Between mile markers 9 and 10, the Waikamoi Nature Trail sign beckons you to stretch your car-weary limbs. A short (if muddy) trail leads through tall eucalyptus trees to a coastal vantage point with a picnic table. Signage reminds visitors QUIET, TREES AT WORK and BAMBOO PICKING PERMIT REQUIRED. *Awapuhi*, or Hawaiian shampoo ginger, sends up fragrant shoots along the trail.

❹ Puohokamoa Stream. About a mile farther, near mile marker 11, you can stop at the bridge over Puohokamoa Stream. This is one of many bridges you cross en route from Paia to Hana. It spans pools and waterfalls. Picnic tables are available, but there are no restrooms.

❺ Kaumahina State Wayside Park. If you'd rather stretch your legs and use a flush toilet, continue another mile to Kaumahina State Wayside Park (at mile marker 12). The park has a picnic area, restrooms, and a lovely overlook to the Keanae Peninsula. The park is open from 6 am to 6 pm and admission is free. ☎ *808/984–8109.*

🕐 **TIMING TIPS**

With short stops, the drive from Paia to Hana should take you between two and three hours one-way. Lunching in Hana, hiking, and swimming can easily turn the round-trip into a full-day outing, especially if you continue past Hana to Oheo Gulch and Kipahulu. If you go that far, you might consider continuing around the "back side" for the return trip. The scenery is completely different and you'll end up in beautiful Upcountry Maui. Since there's so much scenery to take in, we recommend staying overnight in Hana. It's worth taking time to enjoy the waterfalls and beaches without being in a hurry. Try to plan your trip for a day that promises fair, sunny weather—though the drive can be even more beautiful when it's raining.

Keanae Peninsula

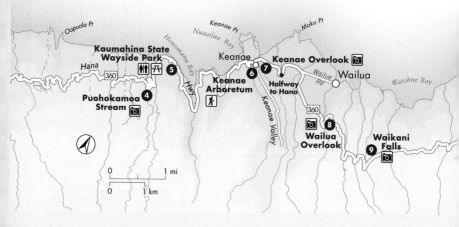

Near mile marker 14, before Keanae, you find yourself driving along a cliff side down into deep, lush Honomanu Bay, an enormous valley, with a rocky black-sand beach.

The Honomanu Valley was carved by erosion during Haleakala's first dormant period. At the canyon's head there are 3,000-foot cliffs and a 1,000-foot waterfall, but don't try to reach them. There's not much of a trail, and what does exist is practically impassable.

6 Keanae Arboretum. Another 4 miles brings you to mile marker 17 and the Keanae Arboretum where you can add to your botanical education or enjoy a challenging hike into a forest. Signs help you learn the names of the many plants and trees now considered native to Hawaii. The meandering Piinaau Stream adds a graceful touch to the arboretum and provides a swimming pond.

You can take a fairly rigorous hike from the arboretum if you can find the trail at one side of the large taro patch. Be careful not to lose the trail once you're on it. A lovely forest waits at the end of the 25-minute hike. Access to the arboretum is free.

You can explore the lovely Keanae Peninsula by driving on the unmarked road shortly past the arboretum. It will take you to a small settlement that is a piece of traditional

Hawaii, and beyond that to a beach park with crashing surf.

7 Keanae Overlook. A half mile farther down Hana Highway you can stop at the Keanae Overlook. From this observation point, you can take in the quilt-like effect the taro patches create below. The people of Keanae are working hard to revive this Hawaiian agricultural art and the traditional cultural values that the crop represents. The ocean provides a dramatic backdrop for the patches. In the other direction there are awesome views of Haleakala through the foliage.

■ TIP→ Coming up is the halfway mark to Hana. If you've had enough scenery, this is as good a time as any to turn around and head back to civilization.

Taro patch viewed from Hana Highway

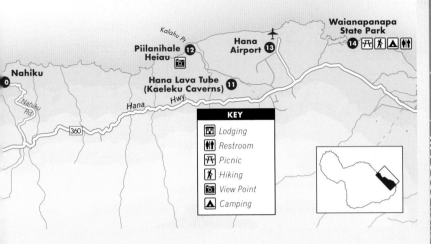

8 Wailua Overlook. Shortly before mile marker 19, on the mountain side, you find Wailua Overlook. From the parking lot you can see Wailua Canyon, but you have to walk up steps to get a view of Wailua Village. The landmark in Wailua Village is a church made of coral, built in 1860. Once called St. Gabriel's Catholic Church, the current Our Lady of Fatima Shrine has an interesting legend surrounding it. As the story goes, a storm washed enough coral up onto shore to build the church and then took any extra coral back to sea.

Just after mile marker 19, there is another overlook on the ocean side.

9 Waikani Falls. Past mile marker 21, you hit the best falls on the entire drive to Hana, Waikani Falls. Though not necessarily bigger or taller than the other falls, these are the most dramatic falls you'll find in East Maui. That's partly because the water is not diverted for sugar irrigation; the taro farmers in Wailua need all the runoff. This is a particularly good spot for photos.

10 Nahiku. At about mile marker 25 you see a road that heads down toward the ocean and the village of Nahiku. In ancient times this was a busy settlement with hundreds of residents. Now only about 80 people live in Nahiku, mostly native Hawaiians

and some back-to-the-land types. A rubber grower planted trees here in the early 1900s, but the experiment didn't work out, and Nahiku was essentially abandoned. The road ends at the sea in a pretty landing. This is the rainiest, densest part of the East Maui rain forest.

Coffee Break. Back on the Hana Highway, about 10 minutes before Hana town, you can stop for—of all things—espresso. The tiny, colorful **Nahiku Ti Gallery and Coffee Shop** (between mile markers 28 and 29) sells local coffee, dried fruits and candies, and delicious (if pricey) banana bread. Sometimes the barbecue is fired up and you can try baked breadfruit (an island favorite nearly impossible to find elsewhere). The Ti Gallery sells Hawaiian crafts.

11 Hana Lava Tube (Kaeleku Caverns). If you're interested in exploring underground, turn left onto Ulaino Road, just after mile marker 31, and follow the signs to the Hana Lava Tube. The site is a mile down Ulaino Rd. Visitors get a brief orientation before heading into Maui's largest lava tube, which is accentuated with colorful underworld formations.

You can take a self-guided, 30- to 40-minute tour daily, from 10:30 to 4 pm, for $12.50 per person. LED flashlights are provided. ☎ 808/248–7308 ⊕ www.mauicave.com

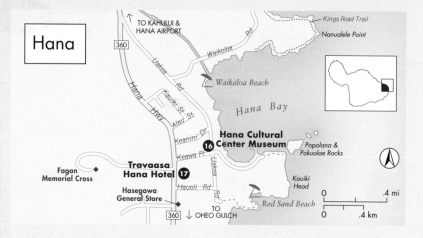

Hana

TO KAHULUI &
HANA AIRPORT

Kings Road Trail

Nanualele Point

Waikaloa Beach

Hana Bay

**Hana Cultural
Center Museum** ⑯

*Popolana &
Pokuolae Rocks*

**Travaasa
Hana Hotel** ⑰

Fagan
Memorial Cross

Hasegawa
General Store

*Kauiki
Head*

Red Sand Beach

TO
OHEO GULCH

0   .4 mi

0   .4 km

★ ⑫ **Piilanihale Heiau.** Continue on Ulaino Road, which doubles back for a mile, loses its pavement, and even crosses a stream before reaching Kahanu Garden and Piilanihale Heiau, the largest pre-contact monument in Hawaii. This temple platform was built for a great 16th-century Maui king named Piilani and his heirs. This king also supervised the construction of a 10-foot-wide road that completely encircled the island. (That's why his name is part of most of Maui's highway titles.)

Hawaiian families continue to maintain and protect this sacred site as they have for centuries, and they have not been eager to turn it into a tourist attraction. However, they now offer a brochure so you can tour the property yourself for $10 per person. Tours include the 122-acre **Kahanu Garden,** a federally funded research center focusing on the ethno-botany of the Pacific (best for those seriously interested in plants). The heiau and garden are open weekdays from 9 am to 2 pm. For a guided tour on Saturday at 10, reserve through www.ntbg. org. ☎ *808/248–8912*

⑬ **Hana Airport.** Back on the Hana Highway, and less than ½ miles farther, is the turnoff for the Hana Airport. Think of Amelia Earhart. Think of Waldo Pepper.

If these picket-fence runways don't turn your thoughts to the derring-do of barnstorming pilots, you haven't seen enough old movies. Only the smallest planes can land and depart here, and when none of them happens to be around, the lonely wind sock is the only evidence that this is a working airfield. ☎ *808/248–8471*

★ ⑭ **Waianapanapa State Park.** Just beyond mile marker 32 you reach Waianapanapa State Park, home to one of Maui's only black-sand beaches and some freshwater caves for adventurous swimmers to explore. The park is right on the ocean, and it's a lovely spot in which to picnic, camp, hike, or swim. To the left you'll find the black-sand beach, picnic tables, and cave pools. To the right you'll find cabins and an ancient trail which snakes along the ocean past blowholes, sea arches, and archaeological sites.

The tide pools here turn red several times a year. Scientists say it's explained by the arrival of small shrimp, but legend claims the color represents the blood of Popoalaea, a princess said to have been murdered in one of the caves by her husband, Chief Kaakea. Whichever you choose to believe, the drama of the landscape itself—black sand, green beach vines, azure water—is bound to leave a lasting impression.

With a permit you can stay in state-run cabins here for less than $99 a night—the price varies depending on the number of people—but reserve early online. They often book up a year in advance. ☎ *808/984–8109* ⊕ *www.hawaiistateparks.org*

🔟 **Hana.** By now the relaxed pace of life that Hana residents enjoy should have you in its grasp, so you won't be discouraged to learn that "town" is little more than a gas station, a post office, a grocery, and the Hasegawa General Store (stuffed with all kinds of oddities and practical items).

Hana, in many ways, is the heart of Maui. It's one of the few places where the slow pulse of island life is still strong. The town centers on its lovely circular bay, dominated on the right-hand shore by a puu called Kauiki. A short trail here leads to a cave, the birthplace of Queen Kaahumanu. This area is rich in Hawaiian history and legend. Two miles beyond town another puu presides over a loop road that passes two of Hana's best beaches—Koki and Hamoa. The hill is called Ka Iwi O Pele (Pele's Bone). Offshore here, at tiny Alau Island, the demigod Maui supposedly fished up the Hawaiian islands.

Sugar was once the mainstay of Hana's economy; the last plantation shut down in

the '40s. In 1946 rancher Paul Fagan built the **Hotel Hana-Maui** (now Travaasa Hana) and stocked the surrounding pastureland with cattle. The cross you see on the hill above the hotel was put there in memory of Fagan. Now it's the ranch and hotel that put food on most tables, though many families still farm, fish, and hunt as in the old days. Houses around town are decorated with glass balls and nets, which indicate a fisherman's lodging.

🔟 **Hana Cultural Center Museum.** If you're determined to spend some time and money in Hana after the long drive, a single turn off the highway onto Uakea Street, in the center of town, will take you to the Hana Cultural Center Museum. Besides operating a well-stocked gift shop, it displays artifacts, quilts, a replica of an authentic *kauhale* (an ancient Hawaiian living complex, with thatch huts and food gardens), and other Hawaiiana. The knowledgeable staff can explain it all to you. The center is open Mon.–Thurs. 10 am to 4 pm. ⊠ *4974 Uakea Rd.* ☎ *808/248–8622* ⛱ *$3* ⊕ *www. hanaculturalcenter.org*

🔟 **Travaasa Hana Hotel.** With its surrounding ranch, the upscale hotel is the mainstay around this beautifully rustic property. The library houses interesting, authentic local Hawaiian artifacts. In the evening, while local musicians play in the lobby bar their

Hala Trees, Waianapanapa State Park

Hāna

friends jump up to dance hula. The Sea Ranch cottages across the road, built to look like authentic plantation housing from the outside, are also part of the hotel. *See Where to Stay for more information.*

Don't be suprised if the mile markers suddenly start descending as you head past Hana. Technically, Hana Highway (Route 360) ends at the Hana Bay. The road that continues south is Piilani Highway (Route 31)—though everyone still refers to it as the Hana Highway.

18 Hamoa Beach. Just outside Hana, take a left on Haneoo Loop to explore lovely Hamoa. Indulge in swimming or body-surfing at this beautiful salt-and-pepper beach. Picnic tables, restrooms, and showers beneath the idyllic shade of coconut trees offer a more than comfortable rest stop.

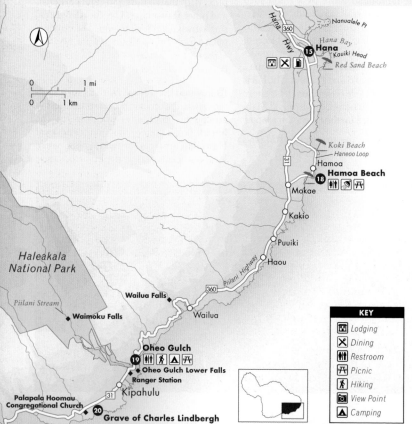

KEY
🏨 Lodging
✕ Dining
🚻 Restroom
⛱ Picnic
🥾 Hiking
📷 View Point
⛺ Camping

The road leading to Hamoa also takes you to **Koki Beach,** where you can watch the Hana surfers mastering the swells and strong currents, and the seabirds darting over **Alau,** the palm-fringed islet off the coast. The swimming is safer at Hamoa.

★ ⑲ **Oheo Gulch.** Ten miles past town, at mile marker 42, you'll find the pools at Oheo Gulch. One branch of Haleakala National Park runs down the mountain from the crater and reaches the sea here, where a basalt-lined stream cascades from one pool to the next. Some tour guides still call this area Seven Sacred Pools, but in truth there are more than seven, and they've never been considered sacred. You can park here—for a $10 fee—and walk to the lowest pools for a cool swim. The place gets crowded, since most people who drive the Hana Highway make this their last stop.

If you enjoy hiking, go up the stream on the 2-mile hike to **Waimoku Falls.** The trail crosses a spectacular gorge, then turns into a boardwalk that takes you through an amazing bamboo forest. You can pitch a tent in the grassy campground down by the sea. *See Hiking in Golf, Hiking, and Outdoor Activities.*

⑳ **Grave of Charles Lindbergh.** Many people travel the mile past Oheo Gulch to see the Grave of Charles Lindbergh. You see a ruined sugar mill with a big chimney on the right side of the road and then, on the left, a rutted track leading to Palapala Hoomau Congregational Church. The simple one-room church sits on a bluff over the sea, with the small graveyard on the ocean side. The world-renowned aviator chose to be buried here because he and his wife, writer Anne Morrow Lindbergh, spent a lot of time living in the area. He was buried here in 1974. Since this is a churchyard, be considerate and leave everything exactly as you found it. Next to the churchyard on the ocean side is a small county park, good for a picnic.

Kaupo Road. The road to Hana continues all the way around Haleakala's "back side" through Ulupalakua Ranch and into

TROPICAL DELIGHTS

The drive to Hana wouldn't be as enchanting without a stop or two at one of the countless fruit (and banana bread) and flower stands by the highway. Every 1/2 mile or so a thatched hut tempts passersby with apple bananas (a smaller firmer variety), lilikoi (passion fruit), avocados, or starfruit just plucked from the tree. Leave a few dollars in the can for the folks who live off the land. Huge bouquets of tropical flowers are available for a handful of change, and some farms will ship.

Kula. The desert-like topography, with its grand vistas, is unlike anything else on the island, but some of the road is in bad shape, sometimes impassable in winter, and parts of it are unpaved. Car-rental agencies call it off-limits to their passenger cars and there is no emergency assistance available. The danger and dust from increasing numbers of speeding jeep drivers are making life tough for the residents, especially in Kaupo, with its 4 miles of unpaved road. The small communities around East Maui cling tenuously to the old ways. Please keep that in mind if you do pass this way. If you can't resist the adventure, try to make the drive just before sunset. The light slanting across the mountain is incredible. At night, giant potholes, owls, and loose cattle can make for some difficult driving.

In the past few years bridges and parts of the road have been upgraded. Please note, however, that the road remains rough.

defunct factory-turned-hangout. Don't fret if you get lost. This jungle hillside is a maze of flower-decked roads that seem to double back upon themselves.

GETTING HERE AND AROUND

Haiku is a short detour off Hana Highway (Route 36) just past Hookipa Beach Park on the way to Hana. Haiku Road turns into Kokomo Road at the post office.

EXPLORING

4th Marine Division Memorial Park. Up Kokomo Road you'll find a large *puu* (volcanic cinder cone) capped with a grove of columnar pines and the 4th Marine Division Memorial Park. During World War II, American GIs trained here for battles on Iwo Jima and Saipan. Locals nicknamed the cinder cone "Giggle Hill" because it was a popular hangout for Maui women and their favorite servicemen. ⊠ *Kokomo Rd., Haiku* ⊕ *www.co.maui.hi.us.*

BEACHES

Updated by
Heidi Pool

Of all the beaches on the Hawaiian Islands, Maui's are some of the most diverse. You can find the pristine, palm-lined shores you dreamed of with clear and inviting waters the color of green sea glass, and you can also discover rich red- and black-sand beaches, craggy cliffs with surging whitecaps, and year-round sunsets that quiet the soul.

As on the other islands, all Maui's beaches are public—but that doesn't mean it's not possible to find a secluded cove where you can truly get away from the world.

The island's leeward shores (West Maui and the South Shore) have the calmest, sunniest beaches. Hit the beach early, when the aquamarine waters are calm as bathwater. In summer, afternoon winds can be a sandblasting force and can chase even the most dedicated sun worshippers away. From November through May these beaches are also great spots to watch the humpback whales that spend winter and early spring in Maui's waters.

Windward shores (the North Shore and East Maui) are for the more adventurous. Beaches face the open ocean rather than other islands and tend to be rockier and more prone to powerful swells. This is particularly true in winter, when the North Shore becomes a playground for big-wave riders and windsurfers. Don't let this keep you away, however; some of the island's best beaches are those slivers of volcanic sand found on the windward shore. *For recommendations of top beaches, see Chapter 1.*

In terms of beach gear, Maui is the land of plenty when it comes to stores stocked full of body boards and beach mats. Look for Longs Drugs (in Kihei, Kahului, Lahaina, and Pukalani) or the ABC Stores (in Kaanapali, Lahaina, Kihei, and more) for sunscreen, shades, towels, and umbrellas. If you want better deals and don't mind the drive into town, look for Kmart or Wal-Mart in Kahului. For more extensive gear, check out Sports Authority in Kahului. Equipment rentals are available at shops and resorts, too.

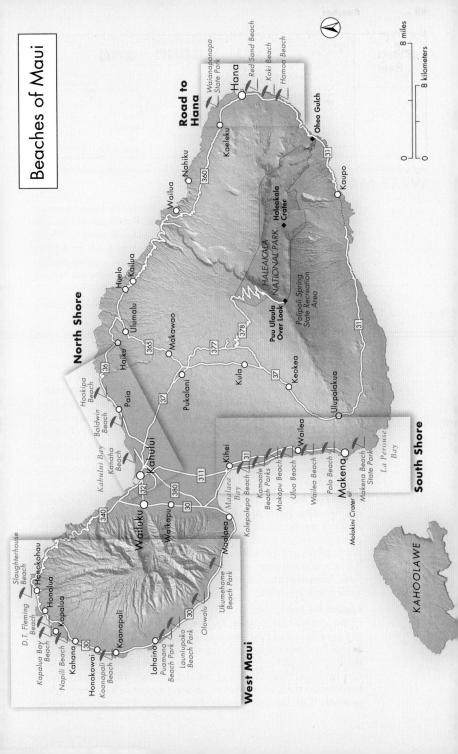

Beaches of Maui

Road to Hana

North Shore

West Maui

South Shore

KAHOOLAWE

Red Sand Beach
Koki Beach
Hamoa Beach
Waianapanapa State Park
Hana
Oheo Gulch
Kaupo
31
Kaeleku
Nahiku
360
Wailua
31
HALEAKALA NATIONAL PARK
Haleakala Crater
Polipoli Spring State Recreation Area
Puu Ulaula Over Look
Huelo
Kailua
Ulumalu
Makawao
365
Haiku
36
378
37
Kula
37
Keokea
Ulupalakua
Hookipa Beach
Paia
Baldwin Beach
Kanaha Beach
Kahului Bay
Kahului
Pukalani
311
La Perouse Bay
Wailea
Makena Beach State Park
Makena
Molokini Crater
Polo Beach
Wailea Beach
Ulua Beach
Mokapu Beach
Kamaole Beach Parks
Kalepolepo Beach
31
Kihei
Maalaea Bay
Maalaea
32
340
Wailuku
Waikapu
380
30
Olowalu
Ukumehame Beach Park
Launiupoko Beach Park
Puamana Beach Park
30
Lahaina
Kaanapali
Kaanapali Beach
Honokowai
Kahana
Napili Beach
30
Kapalua
Kapalua Bay Beach
Honolua
Honokohau
D. T. Fleming Beach
Slaughterhouse Beach

8 miles
8 kilometers

WEST MAUI

The beaches in West Maui are legendary for their glittering aquamarine waters banked by long stretches of golden sand. Reef fronts much of the western shore, making the underwater panorama something to behold. A few tips: parking can be challenging in resort areas. Look for the blue "Shoreline Access" signs to find limited parking and a public path to the beach. Watch out for *kiawe* thorns when you park off-road, because they can puncture tires—and feet.

There are a dozen roadside beaches to choose from on Route 30; these are the ones we like best.

The beaches listed here start in the north at Kapalua and head south past Kaanapali and Lahaina.

"Slaughterhouse" (Mokuleia) Beach. The island's northernmost beach is part of the Honolua-Mokuleia Marine Life Conservation District. "Slaughterhouse" is the surfers' nickname for what is officially Mokuleia. Weather permitting, this is a great place for body surfing and sunbathing. Concrete steps and a green railing help you get down the cliff to the sand. The next bay over, Honolua, has no beach but offers one of the best surf breaks in Hawaii. Competitions are often held there; telltale signs are cars pulled off the road and parked in the pineapple field. **Amenities:** none. **Best for:** sunset; surfing. ⊠ *Rte. 30, mile marker 32, Kapalua.*

D.T. Fleming Beach. Because the current can be quite strong, this charming, mile-long sandy cove is better for sunbathing than for swimming or water sports. Still, it's one of the island's most popular beaches. It's a perfect spot to watch the spectacular Maui sunsets, and there are picnic tables and grills. Part of the beach runs along the front of the Ritz-Carlton Kapalua—a good place to grab a cocktail and enjoy the view. **Amenities:** lifeguards; parking (no fee); showers; toilets. **Best for:** sunset; walking. ⊠ *Rte. 30, 1 mile north of Kapalua, Kapalua.*

Kapalua Bay Beach. Over the years Kapalua has been recognized as one of the world's best beaches, and for good reason: it fronts a pristine bay good for snorkeling, swimming, and general lazing. Just north of Napili Bay, this lovely, sheltered shore often remains calm late into the afternoon, although currents may be strong offshore. Snorkeling is easy here, and there are lots of colorful reef fish. This popular area is bordered by the Kapalua Resort, so don't expect to have the beach to yourself. Walk through the tunnel from the parking lot at the end of

The sandy crescent of Napili Beach on West Maui is a lovely place to wait for sunset.

Kapalua Place to get here. **Amenities:** parking (no fee); showers; toilets. **Best for:** snorkeling; sunset; swimming. ⊠ *Rte. 30, turn onto Kapalua Pl., Kapalua.*

FAMILY
Fodor'sChoice
★

Napili Beach. Surrounded by sleepy condos, this round bay is a turtle-filled pool lined with a sparkling white crescent of sand. Sunbathers love this beach, which is also a terrific sunset spot. The shore break is steep but gentle, so it's great for body boarding and body surfing. It's easy to keep an eye on kids here, as the entire bay is visible from everywhere. The beach is right outside the Napili Kai Beach Club, a popular little resort for honeymooners, only a few miles south of Kapalua. **Amenities:** showers; toilets. **Best for:** sunset; surfing; swimming. ⊠ *5900 Lower Honoapiilani Hwy., look for Napili Pl. or Hui Dr., Napili.*

FAMILY

Kaanapali Beach. Stretching from the northernmost end of the Sheraton Maui to the Hyatt Regency Maui at its southern tip, Kaanapali Beach is lined with resorts, condominiums, restaurants, and shops. If you're looking for quiet and seclusion, this is not the beach for you. But if you want lots of action, spread out your towel here. The center section in front of Whalers Village, also called "Dig Me Beach," is one of Maui's best people-watching spots: folks in catamarans, windsurfers, and stand-up paddleboarders head out from here while the beautiful people take in the scenery. A cement pathway weaves along the length of this 3-mile-long beach, leading from one astounding resort to the next.

The drop-off from Kaanapali's soft, sugary sand is steep, but waves hit the shore with barely a rippling slap. The northern section, known as Kekaa, was, in ancient Hawaii, a *lele,* or jumping-off place for spirits. It's easy to get into the water from the beach to enjoy the prime snorkeling among the lava rock outcroppings.

Throughout the resort, blue "Shoreline Access" signs point the way to a few free-parking stalls and public rights-of-way to the beach. Kaanapali Resort public beach parking can be found between the Hyatt and the Marriott, between the Marriott and the Kaanapali Alii, next to Whalers Village, and at the Sheraton. You can park for a fee at most of the large hotels and at Whalers Village. The merchants in the shopping village will validate your parking ticket if you make a purchase. **Amenities:** parking (no fee); showers; toilets. **Best for:** snorkeling; sunset; swimming; walking. ⊠ *Honoapiilani Hwy., follow any of 3 Kaanapali exits, Kaanapali.*

> ## FREE BEACH ACCESS
>
> All of the island's beaches are free and open to the public—even those that grace the front yards of fancy hotels. Some of the prettiest beaches are often hidden by buildings; look for the blue "Shoreline Access" signs that indicate public rights-of-way through condominiums, resorts, and other private properties.

Puamana Beach Park. This is both a friendly beach park and a surf spot for mellow, longboard rides. With a narrow, sandy beach and a grassy area with plenty of shade, it offers mostly calm swimming conditions and a good view of neighboring Lanai. Smaller than Launiupoko, this beach park tends to attract locals looking to surf and barbecue; it has picnic tables and grills. **Amenities:** parking (no fee); showers; toilets. **Best for:** sunset; surfing; swimming. ⊠ *Rte. 30, ¼ mile south of Lahaina, Lahaina.*

Launiupoko Beach Park. This is the beach park of all beach parks: both a surf break and a beach, it offers a little something for everyone with its inviting stretch of lawn, soft white sand, and gentle waves. The shoreline reef creates a protected wading pool, perfect for small children. Outside the reef, beginner surfers will find good longboard rides. From the long sliver of beach (good for walking), you can enjoy superb views of Neighbor Islands, and, landside, of deep valleys cutting through the West Maui Mountains. Because of its endless sunshine and serenity—not to mention such amenities as picnic tables and grills—Launiupoko draws a crowd on the weekends, but there's space for everyone (and overflow parking across the street). **Amenities:** parking (no fee); showers; toilets. **Best for:** sunset; surfing; swimming; walking. ⊠ *Rte. 30, mile marker 18, Lahaina.*

Olowalu. More an offshore snorkel spot than a beach, Olowalu is also a great place to watch for turtles and whales in season. The beach is literally a pullover from the road, which can make for some unwelcome noise if you're looking for quiet. The entrance can be rocky (reef shoes help), but if you've got your snorkel gear it's a 200-yard swim to an extensive and diverse reef. Shoreline visibility can vary depending on the swell and time of day; late morning is best. Except for during a south swell, the waters are usually calm. A half mile north of mile marker 14 you can find the rocky surf break, also called Olowalu. Snorkeling here is along pathways that wind among coral heads. Note: This is a

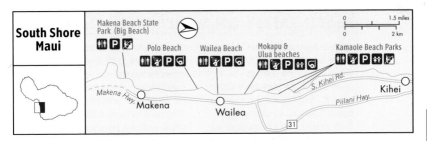

local hangout and can be unfriendly at times. **Amenities:** None. **Best for:** snorkeling. ⊠ *Rte. 30, mile marker 14, south of Olowalu General Store, Olowalu.*

Ukumehame Beach Park. This popular park is also known as Thousand Peaks, because there's barely a break between each wave. Beginning to intermediate surfers say it's a good spot to longboard or body board. It's easy entry into the water, and you don't have to paddle out far. The beach itself leaves something to be desired, because it's more dead grass than sand, but there is some shade, mostly from thorny kiawe trees; footwear is a good idea. Portable toilets are available, along with picnic tables and grills. **Amenities:** parking (no fee); showers; toilets. **Best for:** surfing. ⊠ *Rte. 30, near mile marker 12, Olowalu.*

SOUTH SHORE

Sandy beach fronts nearly the entire southern coastline of Maui. The farther south, the better the beaches get. Kihei has excellent beach parks in town, with white sand, plenty of amenities, and paved parking lots. Good snorkeling can be found along the beaches' rocky borders. As good as Kihei is, Wailea is better. The beaches are cleaner, and the views more impressive. You can take a mile-long walk on a shore path from Ulua to near Polo Beach. Look for blue "Public Shoreline Access" signs for parking along the main thoroughfare, Wailea Alanui. ⚠ **Break-ins have been reported at many parking lots, so don't leave valuables in the car.** As you head to Makena, the terrain gets wilder; bring lunch, water, and sunscreen.

The following South Shore beaches are listed from North Kihei southeast to Makena.

Kalepolepo Beach Park. This tiny beach is the site of the ancient Kalepolepo Village, the prized property of King Kamehameha III in the 1850s. Here the *makaainana* (commoners) farmed, fished, and raised taro. Today, community stewards work to restore the ancient pond. The park has lots of shady trees and stays pretty quiet. However, the beach is only a sprinkling of sand and swimming in the often-murky waters isn't recommended. Kaleopolepo is just south of Hawaiian Islands Humpback Whale National Marine Sanctuary. A portable toilet is available, and there are picnic tables and grills. **Amenities:** parking (free); showers; toilets. **Best for:** solitude. ⊠ *726 S. Kihei Rd., Kihei.*

BEACH SAFETY ON MAUI

Hawaii's beautiful beaches can be dangerous at times due to large waves and strong currents—so much so that the state rates wave hazards using three signs: a yellow square (caution), a red stop sign (high hazard), and a black diamond (extreme hazard). Signs are posted and updated three times daily or as conditions change.

Generally, North Shore beaches (including Slaughterhouse and D.T. Fleming on the west side of the island) can be rough in the winter and not good for swimming or beginner-level water sports. On the south side, Kona storms can cause strong rip currents and powerful shore breaks.

Swim only when there's a normal caution rating, never swim alone, and don't dive into unknown water or shallow breaking waves. If you're unable to swim out of a rip current, tread water and wave your arms in the air to signal for help.

Even in calm conditions, there are other dangerous things in the water to be aware of, including razor-sharp coral, jellyfish, eels, and the occasional shark. Jellyfish cause the most ocean injuries, and signs are posted along beaches when they're present.

Box jellyfish swarm to Hawaii's leeward shores 9 to 10 days after a full moon. Portuguese man-of-wars are usually found when winds blow from the ocean onto land. Reactions to a sting are usually mild (burning sensation, redness); however, in some cases they can be severe (breathing difficulties). If you are stung, pick off the tentacles, rinse the affected area with water, and apply ice. Seek first aid from a lifeguard if you experience severe reactions.

According to state sources, the chances of getting bitten by a shark in Hawaiian waters are low. To reduce your shark-attack risk:

■ Swim, surf, or dive with others at beaches patrolled by lifeguards.

■ Avoid swimming at dawn, dusk, and night.

■ Don't enter the water if you have open wounds or are bleeding.

■ Avoid murky waters, harbor entrances, areas near stream mouths, channels, or steep drop-offs.

■ Don't wear high-contrast swimwear or shiny jewelry.

■ If you spot a shark, leave the water quickly and calmly.

Waipuilani Park. Fronting the Maui Sunset Resort, Waipuilani Park is a spectacular place to sunbathe, relax, or picnic on golf-course-quality grass. A small beach hides behind the dunes, although it's usually speckled with seaweed and shells. This park often hosts local activities, such as volleyball and croquet, and it attracts many dog lovers. There are tennis courts, too. Although the park can be crowded, it's still a perfect place to watch the sunset. From South Kihei Road, turn onto West Waipuilani Road, near the Maui Sunset Resort. **Amenities:** parking (no fee); toilets. **Best for:** partiers; sunset. ⊠ *W. Waipuilani Rd., Kihei.*

Kalama Park. This 36-acre beach park with plenty of shade is great for families and sports lovers. With its extensive lawns and sports fields, the park welcomes volleyball, baseball, and tennis players, and even has a

Catching a wave close to shore can give you an exciting ride.

playground, skateboard park, and a roller hockey rink. Stocked with grills and picnic pavilions, it's a recreational mecca. The beach itself is all but nonexistent, but swimming is fair—though you must brave the rocky steps down to the water. If you aren't completely comfortable with this entrance, stick to the burgers and bocce ball. **Amenities:** parking (no fee); showers; toilets. **Best for:** partiers. ⊠ *S. Kihei Rd., across from Kihei Kalama Village, Kihei.*

Cove Beach Park. Go to the Cove if you want to learn to surf or stand-up paddle. All the surf schools are here in the morning, pushing longboard beginners onto the bunny-slope waves. For spectators there's a grassy area with some shade—and a tiny blink of a beach. If you aren't here to learn to surf, don't bother. The water is sketchy at best and plenty of other beaches are better. **Amenities:** parking (no fee); showers; toilets. **Best for:** surfing. ⊠ *S. Kihei Rd., turn onto Ili Ili Rd., Kihei.*

Charley Young Beach. This secluded 3-acre park sits off the main drag in a residential area. The sand is soft and smooth, with a gentle slope into the ocean. A cloister of lava rocks shelters the beach from heavy after-noon winds, creating a mellow spot to laze around. The usually gentle waves make for good swimming and you can find interesting snorkeling along the rocks on the north end. From South Kihei Road, turn onto Kaiau Street, just north of Kamaole I. **Amenities:** parking (no fee); showers; toilets. **Best for:** snorkeling; swimming. ⊠ *Kaiau St., Kihei.*

FAMILY **Kamaole I, II, and III.** Three steps from South Kihei Road are three golden stretches of sand separated by outcroppings of dark, jagged lava rocks. You can walk the length of all three beaches if you're willing to get your feet wet. The northernmost of the trio, Kamaole I (across from the

ABC Store, in case you forget your sunscreen), offers perfect swimming and an active volleyball court. There's also a great lawn where you can spread out at the south end of the beach. Kamaole II is nearly identical except for the lawn, but there is no parking lot. The last beach, the one with all the people on it, is Kamaole III, perfect for throwing a disk or throwing down a blanket. This is a great family beach, complete with a playground, barbecue grills, kite flying, and, frequently, rented inflatable castles—a must at birthday parties for cool kids.

Locally—and quite disrespectfully, according to native Hawaiians—known as "Kam" I, II, and III, all three beaches have great swimming and lifeguards. In the morning the water can be as still as a lap pool. Kamaole III offers terrific breaks for beginning body surfers. **Amenities:** lifeguards; parking (no fee); showers; toilets. **Best for:** surfing; swimming; walking. ⊠ *S. Kihei Rd., between Alii Ke Alanui and the Hale Kamaole Condominums, Kihei.*

Keawakapu Beach. Everyone loves Keawakapu, with its long stretch of golden sand, near-perfect swimming, and views of Puu Olai cinder cone. It's great fun to walk or jog this beach south into Wailea, as it's lined with over-the-top residences. It's best here in the morning—the winds pick up in the afternoon (beware of sandstorms). Keawakapu has three entrances: one is at the Mana Kai Maui resort (look for the blue "Shoreline Access" sign); the second is directly across from the parking lot on Kilohana Street (the entrance is unmarked); and the third is at the dead end of Kihei Road. Toilets are portable. **Amenities:** parking (no fee); showers; toilets. **Best for:** sunset; swimming; walking. ⊠ *S. Kihei Rd., near Kilohana St., Kihei.*

FAMILY **Mokapu and Ulua.** Look for a little road and public parking lot near the Wailea Marriott if you are heading to Mokapu and Ulua beaches. Though there are no lifeguards, families love this place. Reef formations create tons of tide pools for kids to explore, and the beaches are protected from major swells. Snorkeling is excellent at Ulua, the beach to the left of the entrance. Mokapu, to the right, tends to be less crowded. **Amenities:** parking (free); showers; toilets. **Best for:** snorkeling; swimming. ⊠ *Wailea Alanui Dr., north of the Wailea Marriott, Wailea.*

Wailea Beach. A road near the Grand Wailea Resort takes you to Wailea Beach, a wide, sandy stretch with snorkeling and swimming. If you're not a guest at the Grand Wailea or Four Seasons, the cluster of private umbrellas and chaise lounges can be a little annoying, but any complaint is more than made up for by the calm, unclouded waters and soft, white sand. From the parking lot, walk to the right to get to the main beach; to the left is another, smaller section that fronts the Four Seasons. There are picnic tables and grills away from the beach. **Amenities:** parking (no fee); showers; toilets. **Best for:** snorkeling; swimming. ⊠ *Wailea Alanui Dr., south of Grand Wailea Resort entrance, Wailea.*

Polo Beach. Small and secluded, this crescent fronts the Fairmont Kea Lani. Swimming and snorkeling are great here, and it's a good place to whale-watch. As at Wailea Beach, private umbrellas and chaise lounges occupy the choicest real estate, but there's plenty of room for you and your towel. There's a nice grass picnic area, although it's a considerable

distance from the beach. The pathway connecting the two beaches is a great spot to jog or to take in awesome views of nearby Molokini and Kahoolawe. Rare native plants grow along the ocean, or *makai*, side of the path; the honey-sweet-smelling one is *naio*, or false sandalwood. **Amenities:** parking (no fee); showers; toilets. **Best for:** snorkeling; swimming. ⊠ *Kaukahi St., south of Fairmont Kea Lani entrance, Wailea.*

Fodor's Choice ★   **Makena Beach State Park (Big Beach).** Locals successfully fought to turn Makena—one of Hawaii's most breathtaking beaches—into a state park. This stretch of deep golden sand abutting sparkling aquamarine water is 3,000 feet long and 100 feet wide. It's often mistakenly referred to as "Big Beach," but natives prefer its Hawaiian name, Oneloa. Makena is never crowded, no matter how many cars cram into the lots. The water is fine for swimming, but use caution. ■ TIP→ **The shore drop-off is steep, and swells can get deceptively big.** Despite the infamous "Makena cloud," a blanket that rolls in during the early afternoon and obscures the sun, it rarely rains here. For a dramatic view of the beach, climb Puu Olai, the steep cinder cone near the first entrance you pass if you're driving south. Continue over the cinder cone's side to discover "Little Beach"—clothing optional by popular practice, although this is technically illegal. On Sunday, free spirits of all kinds crowd Little Beach's tiny shoreline for a drumming circle and bonfire. Little Beach has the island's best body surfing (no pun intended). Skim boarders catch air at Makena's third entrance, which is a little tricky to find (it's just a dirt path with street parking). **Amenities:** lifeguards; parking (no fee); toilets. **Best for:** surfing; swimming; walking. ⊠ *Off Wailea Alanui Dr., Makena.*

NORTH SHORE

Many of the people you see jaywalking in Paia sold everything they owned to come to Maui and live a beach bum's life. Beach culture abounds on the North Shore. But these folks aren't sunbathers; they're big-wave riders, windsurfers, or kiteboarders, and the North Shore is their challenging sports arena. Beaches here face the open ocean and tend to be rougher and windier than beaches elsewhere on Maui—but don't let that scare you off. On calm days the reef-speckled waters are truly beautiful and offer a quieter and less commercial beach-going experience than the leeward shore. Be sure to leave your car in a paved parking area so that it doesn't get stuck in soft sand.

Beaches below are listed from Kahului (near the airport) eastward to Hookipa.

Kanaha Beach. Windsurfers, kiteboarders, joggers, and picnicking families like this long, golden strip of sand bordered by a wide grassy area with lots of shade. The winds pick up in the early afternoon, making for the best kiteboarding and windsurfing conditions—if you know what you're doing, that is. The best spot for watching kiteboarders is at the far left end of the beach. From Kaahumanu Avenue, turn *makai* (towards the ocean) onto Hobron Street, then right onto Amala Place. Drive just over a mile through an industrial area and take any of the three entrances into Kanaha. **Amenities:** lifeguard; parking (free); showers; toilets. **Best for:** walking; windsurfing. ⊠ *Amala Pl., Kahului.*

FAMILY **Baldwin Beach.** A local favorite, Baldwin Beach is a big stretch of comfortable golden sand. It's a good place to stretch out, jog, or swim, though the waves can sometimes be choppy and the undertow strong. Don't be afraid of those big brown blobs floating beneath the surface; they're just pieces of seaweed awash in the surf. You can find shade along the beach beneath the ironwood trees, or in the large pavilion, regularly used for local parties and community events. There are picnic tables and grills as well.

The long, shallow pool at the Kahului end of the beach is known as "Baby Beach." Separated from the surf by a flat reef wall, this is where ocean-loving families bring their kids (and sometimes puppies) to practice a few laps. Take a relaxing stroll along the water's edge from one end of Baldwin Beach to Baby Beach and enjoy the scenery. The view of the West Maui Mountains is hauntingly beautiful. **Amenities:** lifeguard; parking (free); showers; toilets. **Best for:** swimming; walking. ⊠ *Hana Hwy., 1 mile west of Baldwin Ave., Paia.*

Fodor's Choice **Hookipa Beach.** To see some of the world's finest windsurfers, hit this ★ beach along the Hana Highway. This beach is also one of Maui's hottest surfing spots, with waves that can be as high as 20 feet. Hookipa is not a good swimming beach, nor the place to learn windsurfing, but it's great for hanging out and watching the pros. There are picnic tables and grills. Bust out your telephoto lens at the cliff-side lookout to capture the aerial acrobatics of board sailors and kiteboarders. **Amenities:** lifeguard; showers; toilets; parking (free). **Best for:** surfing; windsurfing. ⊠ *Rte. 36, 2 miles east of Paia.*

The black sand of small
Waianapanapa State Park on
the Road to Hana is made up
of volcanic pebbles. You can
swim here or hike a memo-
rable coastal path past sea
arches and blowholes.

SUN SAFETY ON MAUI

Hawaii's weather—seemingly never-ending warm, sunny days with gentle trade winds—can be enjoyed year-round with good sun sense. Because of Hawaii's subtropical location, the length of daylight here changes little throughout the year. The sun is particularly strong, with a daily UV average of 14.

The Hawaii Dermatological Society recommends these sun safety tips:

■ Plan your beach, golf, hiking, and other outdoor activities for the early morning or late afternoon, avoiding the sun between 10 am and 4 pm.

■ Apply a broad-spectrum sunscreen with a sun protection factor (SPF) of at least 15. Hawaii lifeguards use sunscreens with an SPF of 30. Cover areas that are most prone to burning

like your nose, shoulders, tops of feet, and ears. And don't forget your lips.

■ Apply sunscreen at least 30 minutes before you plan to be outdoors, and reapply every two hours, even on cloudy days.

■ Wear light, protective clothing, such as a long-sleeve shirt and pants, broad-brimmed hat, and sunglasses.

■ Stay in the shade whenever possible—especially on the beach—by using an umbrella.

■ Children need extra protection from the sun. Apply sunscreen frequently and liberally on children and minimize their time in the sun. Sunscreen is not recommended for children under the age of six months.

ROAD TO HANA

East Maui's and Hana's beaches will literally stop you in your tracks—they're that beautiful. Black and red sands stand out against pewter skies and lush tropical foliage creating picture-perfect scenes, which seem too breathtaking to be real. Rough conditions often preclude swimming, but that doesn't mean you can't explore the shoreline.

Beaches below are listed in order from the west end of Hana town eastward.

Fodor's Choice ★ **Waianapanapa State Park.** Small but rarely crowded, this beach will remain in your memory long after your visit. Fingers of white foam rush onto a black volcanic-pebble beach fringed with green beach vines and palms. Swimming here is both relaxing and invigorating: Strong currents bump smooth stones up against your ankles while seabirds flit above a black, jagged sea arch. There are picnic tables and grills. At the edge of the parking lot a sign tells you the sad story of a doomed Hawaiian princess. Stairs lead through a tunnel of interlocking Polynesian *hau* (a native tree) branches to an icy cave pool—the secret hiding place of the ancient princess. ■ TIP→ You can swim in this pool, but beware of mosquitoes. In the other direction a dramatic 3-mile coastal path continues past sea arches, blowholes, and cultural sites all the way to Hana town. **Amenities:** parking (free); showers; toilets. **Best for:** walking. ⊠ *Hana Hwy., near mile marker 32, Hana* ☎ *808/984–8109.*

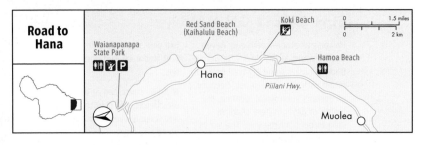

Red Sand Beach (Kaihalulu Beach). Kaihalulu Beach, better known as Red Sand Beach, is unmatched in its raw and remote beauty. It's not simple to find, but when you round the last corner of the trail and are confronted with the sight of it, your jaw is bound to drop. Earthy red cliffs tower above the deep maroon beach, and swimmers bob about in a turquoise lagoon formed by volcanic boulders. The experience is like floating in a giant natural bathtub. It's worth spending a night in Hana so you can get here early to enjoy it before anyone else shows up.

To get here you have to pass through private property—do so at your own risk. The cliff-side cinder path is slippery and constantly eroding. Hiking is not recommended in shoes without traction, or in bad weather. By popular practice, clothing on the beach is optional. The beach is at the end of Uakea Road past the baseball field. Park near the community center and walk through the grass lot to the trail below the cemetery. **Amenities:** None. **Best for:** swimming. ⊠ *Uakea Rd., Hana.*

Koki Beach. You can tell from the trucks parked alongside the road that this is a favorite local surf spot. ■ TIP→ Watch conditions before swimming or body surfing, as riptides can be mean. Look for awesome views of the rugged coastline and a sea arch on the left end. *Iwa,* or white-throated frigate birds, dart like pterodactyls over the offshore Alau Islet. **Amenities:** None. **Best for:** surfing. ⊠ *Haneoo Loop Rd., 2 miles south of Hana town, Hana.*

Hamoa Beach. Why did James Michener describe this stretch of salt-and-pepper sand as the most "South Pacific" beach he'd come across, even though it's in the North Pacific? Maybe it was the perfect half-moon shape, speckled with the shade of palm trees. Perhaps he was intrigued by the jutting black coastline, often outlined by rain showers out at sea, or the pervasive lack of hurry he felt here. Whatever it was, many still feel the lure. The beach can be crowded, but is still relaxing. Early mornings and late afternoons are best for swimming. At times the churning surf might intimidate swimmers, but the body surfing can be great. Hamoa is half a mile past Koki Beach on Haneoo Loop Road, 2 miles south of Hana town. **Amenities:** toilets. **Best for:** surfing; swimming. ⊠ *Haneoo Loop Rd., Hana.*

WATER SPORTS AND TOURS

Updated by Eliza Escaño-Vasquez

Getting into (or onto) the water may well be the highlight of your Maui trip. On the Valley Isle, you can learn to surf, snorkel, or scuba dive, or board a boat for deep-sea fishing, parasailing, and sunset cocktail cruises. From December into May, whale-watching adventures become a top attraction as humpbacks escaping Alaska's frigid winter arrive in Maui's warm waters to frolic, mate, and birth.

Along Maui's leeward coastline, from Kaanapali on the West Shore all the way down to Waiala Cove on the South Shore, you can discover great spots for snorkeling and swimming, some more crowded than others. Thrill seekers can head out to the North Shore and Hookipa, where surfers, kiteboarders, and windsurfers catch big waves and big air.

When your preferred sport calls for flat glassy waters, it is best to start early; the trade winds begin to roll through the valleys in the late morning and pick up speed in the afternoon. You don't want to start kayaking around Olowalu and end up in Tahiti. Visibility when snorkeling is also best early in the morning, although there are times, especially in summer, when it's perfect all day long.

Treat the ocean with respect and know its power. For your safety, choose activities that suit your skill level and health condition. If in doubt, skip the rental and pay for a lesson so you can have proper instructions in navigating through swells and wind, and someone with you in case you get in trouble. The ocean might be beautiful but it can be unpredictable.

Surf can be enjoyed all year, and avid surfers live for the winter swells when the north and west coasts get really "lit up." Whale season on Maui is nothing short of majestic at its peak, around late January to mid-March. You can spot them from the shore, or get up close from a motorized raft or catamaran.

For easy reference, activities are listed in alphabetical order.

BODY BOARDING AND BODYSURFING

Bodysurfing and "sponging" (as body boarding is called by the regulars; boogie boarding is another variation) are great ways to catch some waves without having to master surfing—and there's no balance or coordination required. A body board (or "sponge") is softer than a hard, fiberglass surfboard, which means you can ride safely in the rough-and-tumble surf zone. If you get tossed around (which is half the fun), you don't have a heavy surfboard nearby to bang your head on, but you do have something to hang onto. Serious spongers invest in a single short-clipped fin to help propel them into the wave.

CANOE RACES

Polynesians first traveled to Hawaii by outrigger canoe, and racing the traditional craft is a favorite pastime on the Islands. Canoes were revered in old Hawaii, and no voyage began without a blessing, ceremonial chanting, and a hula performance to ensure a safe journey.

BEST SPOTS

D.T. Fleming Beach. In West Maui, D.T. Fleming Beach offers great surf almost daily along with some nice amenities: ample parking, restrooms, a shower, grills, picnic tables, and a daily lifeguard. Caution is advised, especially during winter months when the current and undertow can get rough. ⊠ *Honoapiilani Hwy., below the Ritz-Carlton, Kapalua.*

Kamaole III. Between Kihei and Wailea on the South Shore, Kamaole III is a good spot for bodysurfing and body boarding. It has a sandy floor, with 1- to 3-foot waves breaking not too far out. It's often crowded late in the day, especially on weekends when local kids are out of school. Don't let that chase you away; the waves are wide enough for everyone. ⊠ *S. Kihei Rd., south of Keonaekai Rd., Kihei.*

Little Beach. If you don't mind public nudity (officially illegal but practiced nonetheless), Little Beach on the South Shore is the best break on the island for body boarding and bodysurfing. The shape of the sandy shoreline creates waves that break a long way out and tumble into shore. Because it's sandy, you only risk stubbing a toe on the few submerged rocks. Don't try body boarding at neighboring Big Beach— waves will slap you onto the steep shore. To get to Little Beach, take the first entrance to Makena State Beach Park; climb the rock wall at the north end of the beach. ⊠ *Makena Rd., Wailea.*

Paia Bay. On the North Shore, Paia Bay has waves suitable for spongers and body surfers. The beach is just before Paia town, beyond the large community building and grass field. ■ TIP→ **Park in the public lot across the street and leave your valuables at home, as this beach is known for break-ins.** ⊠ *Off Rte. 36, Paia.*

EQUIPMENT

Most condos and hotels have body boards available to guests—some in better condition than others (beat-up boards work just as well for beginners). You can also pick up a body board from any discount shop, such as Kmart or Longs Drugs, for upward of $30.

HOW TO CATCH A WAVE

The technique for catching waves is the same with or without a board. Swim out to where the swell is just beginning to break, and position yourself toward shore. When the next wave comes, lie on your body board (if you have one), kick like crazy, and catch it. You'll feel the push of the wave as you glide in front of the gurgling, foamy surf. When bodysurfing, put your arms over your head, bring your index fingers together (so you look like the letter "A"), and stiffen your body like a board to achieve the same effect.

If you don't like to swim too far out, stick with body boarding and body-surfing close to shore. Shore break (if it isn't too steep) can be exhilarating to ride. You'll know it's too steep if you hear the sound of slapping when the waves hit the sand. You're looking for waves that curl over and break farther out, then roll, not slap onto the sand. Always watch first to make sure the conditions aren't too strong.

4

Auntie Snorkel. You can rent decent body boards here for $6 a day or $18 a week. ⊠ *2439 S. Kihei Rd., Kihei* ☎ *808/879–6263* ⊕ *www. auntiesnorkel.com.*

West Maui Sports and Fishing Supply. This old country store has been around since 1987 and has some of the best prices on the west side. Body boards go for $2.50 a day or $15 a week. ⊠ *843 Wainee St., Lahaina* ☎ *808/661–6252* ⊕ *www.westmauisports.com.*

DEEP-SEA FISHING

If fishing is your sport, Maui is your island. In these waters you'll find ahi, *aku* (skipjack tuna), barracuda, bonefish, *kawakawa* (bonito), mahimahi, Pacific blue marlin, ono, and *ulua* (jack crevalle). You can fish year-round and you don't need a license. ■ TIP➔ **Because boats fill up fast during busy seasons, make reservations before coming to Maui.**

Plenty of fishing boats run out of Lahaina and Maalaea harbors. If you charter a private boat, expect to spend in the neighborhood of $700 to $1,000 for a thrilling half day in the swivel seat. You can share a boat for much less if you don't mind close quarters with a stranger who may get seasick, drunk, or worse—lucky! Before you sign up, you should know that some boats keep the catch. Most will, however, fillet a nice piece for you to take home. And if you catch a real beauty, you might even be able to have it professionally mounted.

You're expected to bring your own lunch and beverages in unbreakable containers. (Shop the night before; it's hard to find snacks at 6 am.) Boats supply coolers, ice, and bait. A 7% tax is added to the cost of a trip, and a 10% to 20% tip for the crew is suggested.

BOATS AND CHARTERS

Fodor's Choice ★ **Finest Kind Sportfishing.** A 1,118-pound blue marlin was reeled in by the crew aboard *Finest Kind,* a lovely 37-foot Merritt kept so clean you'd never guess the action it's seen. Captain Dave has been around these waters for about 40 years, long enough to befriend other expert fishers. This family-run company operates four boats and specializes in live bait. Shared charters start at $150 for four hours and go up to $195 for a full day. Private trips go from $800 to $1,100. No bananas on board, please; the captain thinks they're bad luck for fishing. ⊠ *Lahaina Harbor, Slip 7, Lahaina* ☎ *808/661–0338* ⊕ *www. finestkindsportfishing.com.*

Hinatea Sportfishing. This company is well established and has an excellent reputation. The active crew aboard the 41-foot *Hatteras* has one motto: "No boat rides here—we go to catch fish!" Charters go from $150 to $210 for a shared boat and from $800 to $1,100 for a private boat. ⊠ *Lahaina Harbor, Slip 27, Lahaina* ☎ *808/667–7548* ⊕ *www. mauisportfishingcharters.com.*

Jayhawk Charters. This ultraluxe, 48-foot Cabo is available for private charters and takes a maximum of six passengers. It's equipped with air-conditioning, two bathrooms, a salon, and three comfy staterooms with the latest music, video, and satellite TV channels. For serious anglers, the boat also has Shimano rods and reels, a black-box sonar, and the latest in fish finders, GPS, and chart plotters. Rates are $700 an hour, and a full day runs up to $4,800. ⊠ *Lahaina Harbor, Slip 63, Lahaina* ☎ *877/661–0338* ⊕ *www.mauisportfishingcharters.com.*

Kai Palena Sportfishing. Captain Fuzzy Alboro runs a highly recommended operation on the 33-foot *Die Hard*. Check-in is at 1:45 am. He takes a minimum of four and maximum of six people. The cost is from $150 for a shared boat to $1,175 for a private charter. ⊠ *Lahaina Harbor, Slip 10, Lahaina* ☎ *808/878–2362* ⊕ *www. diehardsportfishing.com.*

Start Me Up Sportfishing. With more than 20 years in business, Start Me Up has a fleet of seven boats, all impeccably maintained. These 42-foot Bertram Sportfishers offer some of the most comfortable fishing trips around. The company provides an ice chest, tackle, and equipment. A two-hour shared boat is $99 per person, while a private charter runs from $299 for two hours to $999 for eight hours. There's a six-person maximum. ⊠ *Lahaina Harbor, Slip 12, Lahaina* ☎ *808/667–2774* ⊕ *www.sportfishingmaui.com.*

Strike Zone. This is one of the few charter companies to offer both morning bottom-fishing trips (for smaller fish such as snapper) and deep-sea trips (for the big ones—ono, ahi, mahimahi, and marlin). *Strike Zone* is a 43-foot Delta that offers plenty of room for up to 16 people. Lunch and soft drinks are included. The catch is shared with the entire boat. The cost is $168 per person for a pole; spectators can ride for $78. All trips leave at 6:30 am. ⊠ *Maalaea Harbor, Slip 64, Maalaea* ☎ *808/879–4485* ⊕ *www.strikezonemaui.com.*

KAYAKING

Kayaking is a fantastic and eco-friendly way to experience Maui's coast up close. Floating aboard a "plastic popsicle stick" is easier than you might think, and allows you to cruise out to vibrant, living coral reefs and waters where dolphins and even whales roam. Kayaking can be a leisurely paddle or a challenge of heroic proportions, depending on your ability, the location, and the weather. ■TIP→ **Although you can rent kayaks independently, we recommend hiring a guide.** An apparently calm surface can hide extremely strong ocean currents. Most guides are naturalists who will steer you away from surging surf, lead you to pristine reefs, and point out camouflaged fish, like the stalking hawkfish. Not having to schlep your gear on top of your rental car is a bonus. A half-day tour runs around $75.

If you decide to strike out on your own, tour companies will rent kayaks for the day with paddles, life vests, and roof racks, and many will meet you near your chosen location. Ask for a map of good entries and plan to avoid paddling back to shore against the wind (schedule extra time for the return trip regardless). Read weather conditions, bring binoculars, and take a careful look from the bay before heading in. For beginners, get there early in the day before the trade wind kicks in, and try sticking close to the shore. When you're ready to snorkel, secure your belongings in a dry pack on board and drag your kayak by its bowline behind you. (This isn't as hard as it sounds.)

BEST SPOTS

Makena Landing. This is an excellent starting point for a South Shore adventure. Enter from the paved parking lot or the small sandy beach a little south. The shoreline is lined with million-dollar mansions. The bay itself is virtually empty, but the right edge is flanked with brilliant coral heads and juvenile turtles. If you round the point on the right, you come across Five Caves, a system of enticing underwater arches. In the morning you may see dolphins, and the arches are havens for lobsters, eels, and spectacularly hued butterfly fish. ⊠ *Off Makena Rd., Wailea.*

Ukumehame Beach. In West Maui, past the steep cliffs on the Honoapiilani Highway, there's a long stretch of inviting coastline that includes Ukumehame Beach. This is a good spot for beginners; entry is easy and there's much to see in every direction. Pay attention if trade winds pick up from the late morning onwards; paddling against them can be challenging. If you want to snorkel, the best visibility is farther out at Olowalu Beach. ■TIP→ **Watch for sharp kiawe thorns buried in the sand on the way into the water. Water shoes are recommended.** ⊠ *Rte. 30, near mile marker 12, Lahaina.*

EQUIPMENT, LESSONS, AND TOURS

Kelii's Kayak Tours. One of the highest-rated kayak outfitters on the island, Kelii's offers kayaking trips and combo adventures where you can also surf, snorkel, or hike to a waterfall. Leading groups of up to eight people, the guides show what makes each reef unique. Trips are available on the island's north, south, and west shores, and range from $64 to $160. ⊠ *1993 S. Kihei Rd., Ste. 12, Kihei* ☎ *888/874–7652, 808/874–7652* ⊕ *www.keliiskayak.com.*

Fodor's Choice ★ **South Pacific Kayaks.** These guys pioneered recreational kayaking on Maui, so they know their stuff. Guides are friendly, informative, and eager to help you get the most out of your experience; we're talking true, fun-loving, kayak geeks who will maneuver away from crowds when exploring prime snorkel spots. South Pacific stands out as adventurous *and* environmentally responsible, plus their gear and equipment are well maintained. They offer a variety of trips leaving from both West Maui and South Shore locations. Trips range from $65 to $99. ✉ *95 Halekuai St., Kihei* ☎ *800/776–2326, 808/875–4848* ⊕ *www.southpacifickayaks.com.*

KITEBOARDING

Catapulting up to 40 feet in the air above the breaking surf, kiteboarders hardly seem of this world. Silken kites hold the athletes aloft for precious seconds—long enough for the execution of mind-boggling tricks—then deposit them back in the sea. This new sport is not for the weak-kneed. No matter what people might tell you, it's harder to learn than windsurfing. The unskilled (or unlucky) can be caught in an upwind and carried far out in the ocean, or worse—dropped smack on the shore. Because of insurance (or the lack thereof), companies are not allowed to rent equipment. Beginners must take lessons, and then purchase their own gear. Devotees swear that after your first few lessons, committing to buying your kite is easy.

BEST SPOTS

Kanaha Beach. The steady tracks on Kanaha Beach make this North Shore spot primo for learning. Specific areas are set aside for different water activities, so launch and land only in kiteboarding zones, and kindly give way to swimmers, divers, anglers, and paddlers. ✉ *Amala Pl., Kahului.*

LESSONS

Aqua Sports Maui. A local favorite of kiteboarding schools, Aqua Sports is conveniently located near Kite Beach, at the west end of Kanaha Beach, and offers basic to advanced kiteboarding lessons. Rates start at $240 for a three-hour basics course taught by certified instructors. ✉ *Amala Pl., near Kite Beach, Kahului* ☎ *808/242–8015* ⊕ *www.mauikiteboardinglessons.com.*

Fodor's Choice **Hawaiian Sailboarding Techniques.** Pro kiteboarder and legendary wind-
★ surfer Alan Cadiz will have you safely ripping in no time at lower Kanaha Beach Park. A "Learn to Kitesurf" package starts at $225 for a three-hour private lesson, equipment included. Instead of observing from the shore, instructors paddle after students on a chaseboard to give immediate feedback. The company is part of Hi-Tech Surf Sports, in the Triangle Square shopping center. ✉ *Triangle Square, 425 Koloa St., Kahului* ☎ *808/871–5423, 800/968–5423* ⊕ *www.hstwindsurfing.com.*

Kiteboarding School of Maui. One of the first kiteboarding schools in the United States, KSM offers one-on-one "flight lessons." Pro kiteboarders will induct you at Kite Beach, at the west end of Kanaha Beach, providing instruction, equipment, snacks, and FAA guidelines. (Seriously, there are rules about avoiding airplanes at nearby Kahului Airport.) Rates start at $270 for three hours. KSM is the only school that offers retail gear as well as instruction. They offer a 15 to 25% discount on gear, depending on how many lessons are purchased. ✉ *400 Hana Hwy., Kahului* ☎ *808/873–0015* ⊕ *www.ksmaui.com.*

PARASAILING

Parasailing is an easy, exhilarating way to earn your wings: just strap on a harness attached to a parachute, and a powerboat pulls you up and over the ocean from a launching dock or a boat's platform. ■ TIP➔ **Parasailing is limited to West Maui, and "thrill craft"—including parasails—are prohibited in Maui waters during humpback whale–calving season, December 15 to May 15.**

LESSONS AND TOURS

UFO Parasail. This cheekily named company offers single, tandem, and triple rides at 600 feet ($70), 800 feet ($80), or 1,200 feet ($85). Rides last from 7 to 14 minutes, depending on headcount. It's more fun to take the "dip" (when the boat slows down to let the parachute descend slowly in the water). You'll get a little wet, though you'll probably catch more water while on the boat watching the others take flight. Observers are welcome aboard for $35. ✉ *12 Ulupono St., Lahaina* ☎ *808/661–7836* ⊕ *www.ufoparasail.net.*

West Maui Parasail. Soar at 800 feet above the ocean for a bird's-eye view of Lahaina, or be daring at 1,200 feet for smoother rides and even better views. The captain will be glad to let you experience a "toe dip" or "freefall" if you request it. Hour-long trips departing from Lahaina Harbor and Kaanapali Beach include 8- to 10-minute flights and run from $70 for the 800-foot ride to $80 for the 1,200-foot ride. Observers pay $35 each. ✉ *15 Lahaina Hbr., Lahaina* ☎ *808/661–4060* ⊕ *www.westmauiparasail.com.*

RAFTING

The high-speed, inflatable rafts you find on Maui are nothing like the raft that Huck Finn used to drift down the Mississippi. While passengers grip straps, these rafts fly, skimming and bouncing across the sea. Because they're so maneuverable, they go where the big boats can't—secret coves, sea caves, and remote beaches. Two-hour trips run around $50, half-day trips upward of $100. ■ TIP➔ **Although safe, these trips are not for the faint of heart. If you have back or neck problems or are pregnant, you should reconsider this activity.**

TOURS

Blue Water Rafting. One of the few ways to get to the stunning Kanaio Coast (the roadless southern coastline beyond Ahihi-Kinau), this rafting tour begins trips conveniently at the Kihei boat ramp on the South Shore. Dolphins, turtles, and other marine life are the highlight of this adventure, along with majestic sea caves, lava arches, and views of Haleakala. The Molokini stop is usually timed between the bigger catamarans, so you can enjoy the crater without the usual massive crowd. If conditions permit, you'll be able to snorkel the back wall, which has much more marine life than the inside. Two-hour trips to

MAUI'S TOP 4 WATER ACTIVITIES

Tour Company/ Outfitter	Length	am/ pm	Departure Point	Adult/Kid Price	Kids' Ages	Snack vs. Meal	Alcoholic Beverages Included	Boat Type	Capacity	Worth Noting
KAYAKING										
Keli'i's Kayak Tours	2.5–4.5 hours	am	Makena Landing, Olowalu, D.T. Fleming Beach	$64–$160	minimum age 5 (no kids' prices)	snack/ meal	no	kayak	8–10	Combo trips include snorkeling, hiking, or surfing.
South Pacific Kayaks	2.5–5 hours	am	Various locations	$54–$99/ $41–$75	5–11	snack/ meal	no	kayak	16	Maximum of 8–10 people per guide.
RAFTING										
Blue Water Rafting	2–5.5 hours	am	Kihei Boat Ramp	$190–$125/ $79–$100	4–12	snack/ meal	no	30-foot rigid-hull inflatable	24	Will also do seasonal whale-watch for 1.5 hours.
Ocean Riders	8 hours	am	Mala Wharf	$139/$119	5–12	snack/ meal	no	30' rigid-hull inflatable	18	The only rafting company that circles Lanai.
SCUBA										
Ed Robinson's Diving Adventure	4.5–6.5 hours	am/ pm	Kihei Boat Ramp	$130–$169	minimum age 10	snack/ meal	no	32-foot aluminum dive boat	10–12	10% discount if you book at least 3 charters, 15% for 5.
Lahaina Divers	3.5–10 hours	am/ pm	Lahaina Harbor	$109–$279	minimum age 10	snack	no	46-foot Newton dive boat	30	Nondiving passengers or snorkelers might accompany a certified diver for $69.
Maui Dive Shop	2–8 hours	am/ pm	Maalaea Harbor, West and South shore dives	$93–$170	minimum age 12	snack/ meal	no	48' pro dive boat	24	More suitable for experienced divers.

	Duration	Time	Location	Price	Minimum Age	Snack/Meal	Alcohol	Boat	Passengers	Notes
Mike Severns Diving	5.5–6.5 hours	am	Kihei Boat Ramp	from $145	minimum age 12	snack/meal	no	38-foot aluminum dive boat	12	Dive sites depend on weather and water conditions.
Shaka Divers	2–4 hours	am/pm	Call for exact location.	$69–$99	minimum age 10	snack	no	n/a	8	Offers torpedo-scooter dives and twilight dives.
Tiny Bubbles Scuba	2–2.5 hours	am/pm	West Shore dives	$89–$119	minimum age 10	n/a (water)	no	n/a	4–6 depending on experience	Great for first-time divers. Offers shuttle service.
SNORKELING										
Alii Nui Maui	5 hours	am	Maalaea Harbor	$165–$125	3–12	snack/meal	yes	65-foot power/sail catamaran	49	Kids under 4 are free. Maximum of 60 passengers.
Gemini Sailing Charters	4–4.5 hours	am	Kaanapali Beach	$115	2–12	snack/meal	yes	64-foot power/sail catamaran	49	Videography is available.
Maui Classic Charters	4–5 hours	am/pm	Maalaea Harbor	$42–$112/ $30–$92	3–12	meal	yes	54-foot and 55-foot power catamaran	45 to 120	Four Winds offers snuba and waterslide, ideal for kids.
Teralani Sailing Charters	4–5 hours	am/pm	Whaler's Village	$100–$125/$63–$73	3–12	meal	Yes	65' power sail/catamaran	49	Kids 6 years old and under are free per paying adult.
Trilogy Excursions	3–8 hours	am	Lahaina and Maalaea Harbor	$119–$200/$60–$95	3–15	meal	yes	50–64-foot power/sail catamaran	40–54 on regular snorkel. Up to 100 on the Lanai trip.	Kids ages 3–12 are half-price. Offers an all-day Lanai trip.

Molokini start at $50; longer trips cost $100 to $125 and include a deli lunch. ⊠ *Kihei Boat Ramp, S. Kihei Rd., Kihei* ☎ *808/879–7238* ⊕ *www.bluewaterrafting.com.*

Ocean Riders. Start the day with a spectacular view of the sun rising above the West Maui Mountains, then cross the Au Au Channel to Lanai's Shipwreck Beach. After a short swim at a secluded beach, this tour circles Lanai, allowing you to view the island's 70 miles of remote coast. The "back side" of Lanai is one of Hawaii's unsung marvels, and you can expect to stop at three protected coves for snorkeling. You might chance upon sea turtles, monk seals, and a friendly reef shark, as well as rare varieties of angelfish and butterflyfish. Guides are knowledgeable and slow down long enough for you to marvel at sacred burial caves and interesting rock formations. Sit toward the back bench if you are sensitive to motion sickness. Tours cost $139 per person and include snorkel gear, a fruit breakfast, and a great deli lunch. ⊠ *Mala Wharf, Front St., Lahaina* ☎ *808/661–3586* ⊕ *www.mauioceanriders.com.*

SAILING

With the islands of Molokai, Lanai, Kahoolawe, and Molokini a stone's throw away, Maui waters offer visually arresting backdrops for sailing adventures. Sailing conditions can be fickle, so some operations throw in snorkeling or whale-watching, and others offer sunset cruises. *(For more sunset cruises, see Chapter 7, Entertainment and Nightlife.)* Winds are consistent in summer but variable in winter, and afternoons are generally windier throughout the year. Prices range from around $40 for two-hour trips to $80 for half-day excursions. ■ TIP➜ You won't be sheltered from the elements on the trim racing boats, so be sure to bring a hat that won't blow away, a light jacket, sunglasses, and sunscreen.

BOATS AND CHARTERS

America II. This onetime America's Cup contender offers an exciting, intimate alternative to crowded catamarans. For fast action, try a morning trade-wind sail. All sails are two hours and cost $44.95. Plan to bring a change of clothes, because you will get wet. Snacks and beverages are provided. Not recommended for children under five years old. ⊠ *Lahaina Harbor, Slip 6, Lahaina* ☎ *808/667–2195* ⊕ *www.sailingonmaui.com.*

Paragon. If you want to snorkel and sail, this is your boat. Many snorkel cruises claim to sail but actually motor most of the way; Paragon is an exception. Both Paragon vessels (one catamaran in Lahaina, the other in Maalaea) are ship-shape, and crews are accommodating and friendly. Its mooring in Molokini Crater is particularly good, and tours will often stay after the masses have left. The Lanai trip includes a picnic lunch on Manele Bay, snorkeling, and a quick afternoon blue-water swim. Extras on the trips to Lanai include mai tais, sodas, dessert, and champagne. Hot and cold appetizers come with the sunset sail, which departs from Lahaina Harbor every Monday, Wednesday, and Friday. ⊠ *Maalaea Harbor, Maalaea* ☎ *808/244–2087, 800/441–2087* ⊕ *www.sailmaui.com.*

Scotch Mist Charters. Follow the wind aboard this 50-foot Santa Cruz sailing yacht. The sunset sail, four-hour snorkeling excursion, and two-hour whale-watching trips usually carry fewer than 18 passengers. Two-hour sunset sails start at $59.95 and include soft drinks, wine, beer, champagne, and chocolate-covered macadamia nuts. ⌧ *Lahaina Harbor, Slip 2, Lahaina* ☎ 808/661–0386 ⊕ *www.scotchmistsailingcharters.com.*

Fodor'sChoice ★ **Trilogy Excursions.** With more than 40 years of experience and some good karma from their monthly reef-cleaning campaigns, Trilogy has a great reputation in the community. It's one of only two companies that sail, rather than motor, to Molokini Crater. A two-hour sail starts at $69. The sunset trip includes appetizers, beer, wine, champagne, margaritas, and mai tais. Boarding the catamaran from shore can be tricky—timing is everything and getting wet is inevitable, but after that it's smooth sailing. Tours depart from Lahaina Harbor; Maalaea Harbor; and, in West Maui, in front of the Kaanapali Beach Hotel. ⌧ *180 Lahainaluna Rd., Lahaina* ☎ 808/874–5649, 888/225–6284 ⊕ *www.sailtrilogy.com.*

PRIVATE CHARTERS

Hiring a private charter for a sail will cost you more, but it's one way to avoid crowds. Although almost all sailing vessels offer private charters, a few cater to them specifically.

Cinderella. *Cinderella* is a swift and elegant 50-foot Columbia. ☎ 808/244–0009 ⊕ *www.cinderellasailing.com.*

Island Star. *Island Star* is a 57-foot Columbia offering customized trips out of Maalaea. ⌧ *Maalaea Harbor, Slip 42, Lahaina* ☎ 888/677–7238 ⊕ *www.islandstarexcursions.com.*

Shangri-La. A 65-foot catamaran, *Shangri-La* is the largest and most luxurious boat catering to private charters. ⌧ *Lahaina* ☎ 888/855–9977 ⊕ *www.sailingmaui.com.*

SCUBA DIVING

Maui, just as scenic underwater as it is on dry land, has been rated one of the top 10 dive spots in the United States. It's common on any dive to see huge sea turtles, eagle rays, and small reef sharks, not to mention many varieties of angelfish, parrot fish, eels, and octopuses. Most of the species are unique to this area, making it unlike other popular dive destinations. In addition, the terrain itself is different from other dive spots. Here you can find ancient and intricate lava flows full of nooks where marine life hide and breed. Although the water tends to be a bit rougher—not to mention colder—divers are given a great thrill during humpback-whale season, when you can actually hear whales singing underwater.

Some of the finest diving spots in all of Hawaii lie along the Valley Isle's western and southwestern shores. Dives are best in the morning, when visibility can hold a steady 100 feet. If you're a certified diver, you can rent gear at any Maui dive shop simply by showing your PADI or NAUI card. Unless you're familiar with the area, however, it's probably best to hook up with a dive shop for an underwater tour. Tours include tanks and weights and start around $130. Wet suits and buoyancy

Snorkelers can see adorable green sea turtles around Maui.

compensators are rented separately, for an additional $15 to $30. Shops also offer introductory dives ($100 to $160) for those who aren't certified. ■TIP→ **Before signing on with any outfitter, it's a good idea to ask a few pointed questions about your guide's experience, the weather outlook, and the condition of the equipment.**

Before you head out on your dive, be sure to check conditions. Check the Glenn James weather site, ⊕ *www.hawaiiweathertoday.com,* for a breakdown of the weather, wind, and visibility conditions.

BEST SPOTS

Honolua Bay. This marine preserve in West Maui is alive with many varieties of coral and tame tropical fish, including large *ulua* (jack crevalle), *kahala,* barracuda, and manta rays. With depths of 20 to 50 feet, this is a popular summer dive spot, good for all levels. ■TIP→ **High surf often prohibits winter dives.** ⊠ *Rte. 30, between mile markers 32 and 33, Kapalua.*

Makena Landing. On the South Shore, one of the most popular dive spots is Makena Landing (also called Nahuna Point, Five Graves, or Five Caves). You can revel in underwater delights—caves, ledges, coral heads, and an outer reef home to a large green-sea-turtle colony called Turtle Town. ■TIP→ **Entry is rocky lava, so be careful where you step.** This area is for more experienced divers. ⊠ *Makena Rd., Wailea-Makena.*

Molokini Crater. Three miles offshore from Wailea on the South Shore, Molokini Crater is world renowned for its deep, crystal clear, fish-filled waters. A crescent-shape islet formed by the eroding top of a volcano, the crater is a marine preserve ranging from 10 to 80 feet deep. The numerous tame fish and brilliant coral within the crater make it a

DIVING 101

If you've always wanted gills, Hawaii is a good place to get them. Although the bulky, heavy equipment seems freakish on shore, underwater it allows you to move about freely, almost weightlessly. As you descend into another world, you slowly grow used to the sound of your own breathing and the strangeness of being able to do so 30-plus feet down.

Most resorts offer introductory dive lessons in their pools, which allow you to acclimate to the awkward breathing apparatus before venturing out into the great blue. If you aren't starting from a resort pool, no worries. Most intro dives take off from calm, sandy beaches, such as Ulua or Kaanapali. If you're bitten by the deep-sea bug and want to continue diving, you should get certified. Only certified divers can rent equipment or go on more adventurous dives, such as night dives, open-ocean dives, and cave dives.

There are several certification companies, including PADI, NAUI, and SSI. PADI, the largest, is the most comprehensive. A child must be at least 10 to be certified. Once you begin your certification process, stick with the same company. The dives you log will not apply to another company's certification. (Dives with a PADI instructor, for instance, will not count toward SSI certification.) Remember that you will not be able to fly or go to the airy summit of Haleakala within 24 hours of diving. Open-water certification will take three to four days and cost around $350. From that point on, the sky—or rather, the sea—is the limit!

popular introductory dive site. On calm days, the back side of Molokini Crater (called Back Wall) can be a dramatic sight for advanced divers, with visibility of up to 150 feet. The enormous drop-off into the Alalakeiki Channel offers awesome seascapes, black coral, and chance sightings of larger fish and sharks.

Ahihi Bay. Some of the southern coast's best diving is at Ahihi Bay, part of the Ahihi-Kinau Natural Area Reserve. The area was closed for several years to allow the coral to recover from overuse. At the time of this writing, the closure has been extended through July 2014. The reserve is best known for its "Fishbowl," a small cove right beside the road, next to a hexagonal house. Here you can find excellent underwater scenery, with many types of fish and coral. ■TIP→ Be careful of the rocky-bottom entry (wear reef shoes if you have them). The Fishbowl can get crowded, especially in high season. If you want to steer clear of the crowds, look for a second entry ½ mile farther down the road—a gravel parking lot at the surf spot called Dumps. Entry into the bay here is trickier, as the coastline is all lava. ⊠ *Makena Rd., south of Makena State Park, Wailea-Makena.*

La Pérouse Bay. Formed from the last lava flow two centuries ago, La Pérouse Bay brings you the best variety of fish—more than any other site. The lava rock provides a protective habitat, and all four types of Hawaii's angelfish can be found here. To dive the spot called Pinnacles, enter anywhere along the shore, just past the private entrance to the beach. Wear your reef shoes, as entry is sharp. To the right, you'll be in the Ahihi-Kinau Natural Area Reserve; to the left, you're outside. Look for the white, sandy bottom with massive coral heads. Pinnacles is for experienced divers only. ⊠ *Makena Rd., south of Makena State Park, Wailea.*

EQUIPMENT, LESSONS, AND TOURS

Fodor's Choice ★ **Ed Robinson's Diving Adventures.** Ed Robinson wrote the book, literally, on Molokini. Because he knows so much, he includes a "Biology 101" talk with every dive. An expert marine photographer, he offers diving instruction and boat charters to South Maui and the back side of Molokini Crater. Night dives are available, and there's a discount if you book multiple dives. Prices start at $129.95, plus $20 for the gear. ⊠ *1819 S. Kihei Rd., Kihei* ☎ 808/879–3584, 800/635–1273 ⊕ *www.mauiscuba.com.*

Lahaina Divers. With more than 25 years of diving experience, this West Maui shop offers tours of Maui, Molokini, Molokai, and Lanai. Big charter boats (which can be crowded, with up to 24 divers per boat) leave daily for Molokini Crater, Back Wall, Lanai, Turtle Reef, and other destinations. A Continental breakfast and deli lunch are included. Rates range from $109 to $289. For less experienced divers, there's a daily "Discover Scuba" lesson off the Mala ramp wreckage or one of the Turtle Reef sites, depending on conditions. ⊠ *143 Dickenson St., Lahaina* ☎ 808/667–7496, 800/998–3483 ⊕ *www.lahainadivers.com.*

Maui Dive Shop. With seven locations island-wide, Maui Dive Shop offers scuba charters, diving instruction, and equipment rental. Excursions go to Coral Gardens, Shipwreck Beach, and Cathedrals on Lanai. The manta ray dives off Molokini Crater have a 70% success rate. Night dives and customized trips are available, as are full SSI and PADI certificate programs. ⊠ *1455 S. Kihei Rd., Kihei* ☎ 808/879–3388, 800/542–3483 ⊕ *www.mauidiveshop.com.*

Mike Severns Diving. This company takes groups of up to 12 certified divers with two dive masters to both popular and off-the-beaten-path dive sites. Boat trips leave from Kihei Boat Ramp, and go wherever conditions are best: the Molokini Marine Life Conservation District, Molokini Crater's Back Wall, Makena, La Pérouse Bay, or the Kanaio Coast. Rates start at $145 for a two-tank dive. A private charter costs $1,560. ⊠ *Kihei Boat Ramp, S. Kihei Rd., Kihei* ☎ 808/879–6596 ⊕ *www.mikeseversdiving.com.*

Tiny Bubbles Scuba. Owner and dive master Tim Rollo has led customized, private shore dives along West Maui for 15 years. He'll take only 4 to 6 divers at a time, and can cater to the most novice diver. Intro dives cost $109 and include gear, air, plus shuttle service. Night dives, scooter dives, and scuba certifications are also offered. ⊠ *3350 Lower Honoapiilani Rd., Lahaina* ☎ 808/870-0878 ⊕ *www.tinybubblesscuba.com.*

SNORKELING

No one should leave Maui without ducking underwater to meet a sea turtle, moray eel, or the tongue-twisting humuhumunukunukuapuaa—the state fish. ■TIP→ **Visibility is best in the morning, before the trade winds pick up.**

There are two ways to approach snorkeling—by land or by sea. Daily around 7 am, a parade of boats heads out to Lanai or to Molokini Crater, that ancient cone of volcanic cinder off the coast of Wailea. Boat trips offer some advantages—deeper water, seasonal whale-watching, crew assistance, lunch, and gear. But much of Maui's best snorkeling is found just steps from the road. Nearly the entire leeward coastline from Kapalua south to Ahihi-Kinau offers opportunities to ogle fish and turtles. If you're patient and sharp-eyed, you may glimpse eels, octopuses, lobsters, eagle rays, and even a rare shark or monk seal.

BEST SPOTS

Snorkel sites here are listed from north to south, starting at the north-west corner of the island.

Fodor'sChoice **Honolua Bay.** Just north of Kapalua, the Honolua Bay Marine Life Con-
★ servation District has a superb reef for snorkeling. ■TIP→ **Bring a fish key with you, as you're sure to see many species of triggerfish, filefish, and wrasses.** The coral formations on the right side of the bay are particularly dramatic, with pink, aqua, and orange varieties. On a lucky day, you might even be snorkeling with a pod of dolphins nearby. Take care entering the water; there's no beach and the rocks and concrete ramp can be slippery.

The northeast corner of this windward-facing bay periodically gets hammered by big waves in winter. Avoid the bay then, as well as after heavy rains. ⊠ *Rte. 30, between mile markers 32 and 33, Kapalua.*

Kapalua Bay. Minutes south of Honolua Bay, dependable Kapalua Bay beckons. As beautiful above the water as it is below, Kapalua is exceptionally calm, even when other spots get testy. Needle and butterfly fish dart just past the sandy beach, which is why it's sometimes crowded. ■TIP→ **The sand can be particularly hot here; watch your toes!** ⊠ *Kapalua Pl., Kapalua.*

Fodor'sChoice **Black Rock.** We think Black Rock, in front of the Sheraton Maui Resort
★ & Spa at the northernmost tip of Kaanapali Beach, is great for snorkelers of any skill level. The entry couldn't be easier—dump your towel on the sand and in you go. Beginners can stick close to shore and still see lots of action. Advanced snorkelers can swim to the tip of Black Rock to see larger fish and eagle rays. One of the underwater residents here is a turtle whose hefty size earned him the name Volkswagen. He sits very still, so you have to look closely. Equipment can be rented on-site. Parking, in a small lot adjoining the hotel, is the only hassle. ⊠ *Sheraton Maui Resort & Spa, 2605 Kaanapali Pkwy., Lahaina.*

Hanakaoo Beach Park. Along Honoapiilani Highway there are several favorite snorkel sites, including the area just out from the cemetery at Hanakaoo Beach Park. At depths of 5 and 10 feet, you can see a variety of corals, especially as you head south toward Wahikuli Wayside Park. ⊠ *Rte. 30, near mile marker 23.*

Olowalu. South of Olowalu General Store, the shallow coral reef at Olowalu is good for a quick underwater tour, but if you're willing to venture out about 50 yards, you'll have easy access to an expansive coral reef with abundant turtles and fish—no boat required. Swim offshore toward the pole sticking out of the reef. Except for during a south swell, this area is calm and good for families with small children. Boats sometimes stop here (they refer to this site as "Coral Gardens") when conditions in Honolua Bay are not ideal. During low tide, be extra cautious when hovering above the razor-sharp coral. ⊠ *Rte. 30, at mile marker 14, Lahaina.*

Wailea. Excellent snorkeling is found down the coastline between Kihei and Makena on the South Shore. ■TIP➡ **The best spots are along the rocky fringes of Wailea's beaches—Mokapu, Ulua, Wailea, and Polo—off Wailea Alanui Drive.** Find one of the public parking lots sandwiched between Wailea's luxury resorts (look for a blue sign that says "Shoreline Access" with an arrow pointing to the lot), and enjoy the sandy entries, calm waters with relatively good visibility, and variety of fish. Of the four beaches, Ulua has the best reef. You may listen to snapping shrimp and parrot fish nibbling on coral. ⊠ *Wailea Alanui Dr., Wailea-Makena.*

Molokini Crater. Between Maui and neighboring Kahoolawe you'll find the world-famous Molokini Crater. Its crescent-shape rim acts as a protective cove from the wind and provides a sanctuary for birds and colorful marine life. Most snorkeling tour operators offer a Molokini trip, and it's not unusual for your charter to share this dormant volcano with five or six other boats. The journey to this sunken crater takes more than 90 minutes from Lahaina, an hour from Maalaea, and less than half an hour from the South Shore.

EQUIPMENT

Most hotels and vacation rentals offer free use of snorkel gear. Beachside stands fronting the major resort areas rent equipment by the hour or day. ■TIP➡ **Don't shy away from asking for instructions; a snug fit makes all the difference in the world. A mask fits if it sticks to your face when you inhale deeply through your nose. Fins should cover your entire foot (unlike diving fins, which strap around your heel).** If you're squeamish about using someone else's gear (or need a prescription lens), pick up your own at any discount shop. Costco and Longs Drugs have better prices than ABC stores; dive shops have superior equipment.

Maui Dive Shop. You can rent pro gear (including optical masks, body boards, and wet suits) from seven locations island-wide. Pump these guys for weather info before heading out—they'll know better than last night's news forecaster, and they'll give you the real deal on conditions. ⊠ *1455 S. Kihei Rd., Kihei* ☎ *808/873–3388* ⊕ *www.mauidiveshop.com.*

Snorkel Bob's. Here you can rent fins, masks, and snorkels, and Snorkel Bob's will throw in a carrying bag, map, and snorkel tips for as little as $9 per week. Avoid the circle masks and go for the split-level ($26 per week); it's worth the extra. ⊠ *Napili Village Hotel,*

Continued on page 124

SNORKELING IN HAWAII

The waters surrounding the Hawaiian Islands are filled with life—from giant manta rays cruising off the Big Island's Kona Coast to humpback whales giving birth in Maui's Maalaea Bay. Dip your head beneath the surface to experience a spectacularly colorful world: pairs of milletseed butterflyfish dart back and forth, redlipped parrotfish snack on coral algae, and spotted eagle rays flap past like silent spaceships. Sea turtles bask at the surface while tiny wrasses give them the equivalent of a shave and a haircut. The water quality is typically outstanding; many sites afford 60-foot-plus visibility. On snorkel cruises, you can often stare from the boat rail right down to the bottom.

Certainly few destinations are as accommodating to every level of snorkeler as Hawaii. Beginners can tromp in from sandy beaches while more advanced divers descend to shipwrecks, reefs, craters, and sea arches just offshore. Because of Hawaii's extreme isolation, the island chain has fewer fish species than Fiji or the Caribbean—but many of the fish that live here exist nowhere else. The Hawaiian waters are home to the highest percentage of endemic fish in the world.

The key to enjoying the underwater world is slowing down. Look carefully. Listen. You might hear the strange crackling sound of shrimp tunneling through coral, or you may hear whales singing to one another during winter. A shy octopus may drift along the ocean's floor beneath you. If you're hooked, pick up a waterproof fishkey from Long's Drugs. You can brag later that you've looked the Hawaiian turkeyfish in the eye.

Picasso Triggerfish	Milletseed Butterflyfish*	Yellow Tang
Moorish Idol	Hawaiian Whitespotted Toby*	Saddleback Wrasse*
Redlip Parrotfish	Hawaiian Turkeyfish*	Zebra Moray Eel
Stocky Hawkfish	Green Sea Turtle (Honu)	Spotted Eagle Ray

*endemic to Hawaii

POLYNESIA'S FIRST CELESTIAL NAVIGATORS: HONU

Honu is the Hawaiian name for two native sea turtles, the hawksbill and the green sea turtle. Little is known about these dinosaur-age marine reptiles, though snorkelers regularly see them foraging for *limu* (seaweed) and the occasional jellyfish in Hawaiian waters. Most female honu nest in the uninhabited Northwestern Hawaiian Islands, but a few sociable ladies nest on Maui and Big Island beaches. Scientists suspect that they navigate the seas via magnetism—sensing the earth's poles. Amazingly, they will journey up to 800 miles to nest—it's believed that they return to their own birth sites. After about 60 days of incubation, nestlings emerge from the sand at night and find their way back to the sea by the light of the stars.

SNORKELING

Many of Hawaii's reefs are accessible from shore.

The basics: Sure, you can take a deep breath, hold your nose, squint your eyes, and stick your face in the water in an attempt to view submerged habitats . . . but why not protect your eyes, retain your ability to breathe, and keep your hands free to paddle about when exploring underwater? That's what snorkeling is all about.

Equipment needed: A mask, snorkel (the tube attached to the mask), and fins. In deeper waters (any depth over your head), life jackets are advised.

Steps to success: If you've never snorkeled before, it's natural to feel a bit awkward at first, so don't sweat it. Breathing through a mask and tube, and wearing a pair of fins take getting used to. Like any activity, you build confidence and comfort through practice.

If you're new to snorkeling, begin by submerging your face in shallow water or a swimming pool and breathing calmly through the snorkel while gazing through the mask.

Next you need to learn how to clear water out of your mask and snorkel, an essential skill since splashes can send water into tube openings and masks can leak. Some snorkels have built-in drainage valves, but if a tube clogs, you can force water up and out by exhaling through your mouth. Clearing a mask is similar: lift your head from water while pulling forward on mask to drain. Some masks have built-in purge valves, but those without can be cleared underwater by pressing the top to the forehead and blowing out your nose (charming, isn't it?), allowing air to bubble into the mask, pushing water out the bottom. If it sounds hard, it really isn't. Just try it a few times and you'll soon feel like a pro.

Now your goal is to get friendly with fins—you want them to be snug but not too tight—and learn how to propel yourself with them. Fins won't help you float, but they will give you a leg up, so to speak, on smoothly moving through the water or treading water (even when upright) with less effort.

Flutter stroking is the most efficient underwater kick, and the farther your foot bends forward the more leg power you'll be able to transfer to the water and the farther you'll travel with each stroke. Flutter kicking movements involve alternately separating the legs and then drawing them back together. When your legs separate, the leg surface encounters drag from the water, slowing you down. When your legs are drawn back together, they produce a force pushing you forward. If your kick creates more forward force than it causes drag, you'll move ahead.

Submerge your fins to avoid fatigue rather than having them flailing above the water when you kick, and keep your arms at your side to reduce drag. You are in the water—stretched out, face down, and snorkeling happily away—but that doesn't mean you can't hold your breath and go deeper in the water for a closer look at some fish or whatever catches your attention. Just remember that when you do this, your snorkel will be submerged, too, so you won't be breathing (you'll be holding your breath). You can dive head-first, but going feet-first is easier and less scary for most folks, taking less momentum. Before full immersion, take several long, deep breaths to clear carbon dioxide from your lungs.

If your legs tire, flip onto your back and tread water with inverted fin motions while resting. If your mask fogs, wash condensation from lens and clear water from mask.

TIPS FOR SAFE SNORKELING

- Snorkel with a buddy and stay together.
- Plan your entry and exit points prior to getting in the water.
- Swim into the current on entering and then ride the current back to your exit point.
- Carry your flippers into the water and then put them on, as it's difficult to walk in them, and rocks may be slippery.
- Make sure your mask fits properly and is not too loose.
- Pop your head above the water periodically to ensure you aren't drifting too far out, or too close to rocks.
- Think of the water as someone else's home—don't feed fish, take anything that doesn't belong to you, or leave any trash behind.
- Don't touch any sea creatures; they may sting.
- Wear a rash guard over your swimsuit to help protect you from being fried by the sun.
- When in doubt, don't go without a snorkeling professional; try a guided tour.
- Don't go in if the ocean seems rough.

Green sea turtle (Honu)

5425 Lower Honoapiilani Hwy.,
Napili ☎ *808/669–9603* ⊕ *www.*
snorkelbob.com.

TOURS

The same boats that offer whale-watching, sailing, and diving also offer snorkeling excursions. Trips usually include visits to two locales, lunch, gear, instruction, and possible whale or dolphin sightings. Some captains troll for fish along the way.

Molokini Crater, a crescent about 3 miles offshore from Wailea, is the most popular snorkel cruise destination. You can spend half a day floating above the fish-filled crater for about $80. Some say it's not as good as it's made out to be, and that it's too crowded, but others consider it to be one of the best spots in Hawaii. Visibility is generally outstanding and fish are incredibly tame. Your second stop will be somewhere along the leeward coast, either Turtle Town near Makena or Coral Gardens toward Lahaina. ■TIP→ On blustery mornings there's a good chance the waters will be too rough to moor in Molokini Crater and you'll end up snorkeling some place off the shore, which you could have driven to for free.

If you've tried snorkeling and are tentatively thinking about scuba, you may want to try snuba, a cross between the two. With snuba, you dive down 20 feet below the surface, only you're attached to an air hose from the boat. Many boats now offer snuba (for an extra fee of $45 to $65) as well as snorkeling.

Snorkel cruises vary—some serve mai tais and steaks whereas others offer beer and cold cuts. You might prefer a large ferryboat to a smaller sailboat, or vice versa. Be sure you know where to go to board your vessel; getting lost in the harbor at 6 am is a lousy start. ■TIP→ Bring sunscreen, an underwater camera (they're double the price onboard), a towel, and a cover-up for the windy return trip. Even tropical waters get chilly after hours of swimming, so consider wearing a rash guard. Wet suits can usually be rented for a fee. Hats without straps will blow away, and valuables should be left at home.

Alii Nui Maui. Come as you are (with a bathing suit, of course); towels, sunblock, and all your gear are provided on this 65-foot luxury catamaran. Since the owners also operate Maui Dive Shop, snorkel and dive equipment are top of the line. Wet-suit tops are available to use for sun protection or to keep extra warm in the water. The boat, which holds a maximum of 60 people, is nicely appointed and is often recommended by the island's upscale resorts. A morning snorkel sail (there's a diving option, too) heads to Turtle Town or Molokini Crater and includes a Continental breakfast, lunch, and post-snorkel alcoholic drinks. The trip is $165 per person and includes transportation from your hotel. Videography is available for a fee. ⊠ *Maalaea Harbor, Slip 56, Maalaea* ☎ *800/542–3483, 808/875–0333* ⊕ *www.aliinuimaui.com.*

FAMILY **Gemini Sailing Charters.** One of the main draws of this snorkel excursion is its affordable rate, just $110 per person. The vacation-friendly check-in time of 10:30 am is another plus. Honolua Bay is the primary destination, but Lanai and Olowalu are possible options in case of choppy waters. The hot buffet lunch of lemony ono and tender chicken teriyaki is catered by the Westin Maui Resort & Spa. A videographer is available. You can find the company on Kaanapali Beach near the Westin's activity desk. ✉ *Westin Maui Resort & Spa, 2365 Kaanapali Pkwy.* ☎ *800/820–7245, 808/669–0508* ⊕ *www.geminicharters.com.*

FAMILY **Hawaiian Sailing Canoe Adventure.** Few things could qualify as a more authentic Hawaiian experience than paddling in a sail canoe with this family-run outfit. Get a deep sense of history and mythology as you listen to your guide pray, chant, and bestow a wealth of knowledge about ancient Hawaii during this intimate excursion. The canoe makes a snorkel stop at a nearby reef. The cost is $89 per person, with a maximum of six passengers. Refreshments and equipment are included. You meet at Polo Beach in front of the Fairmont Kea Lani. ✉ *Fairmont Kea Lani, 4100 Wailea Alanui Dr., Wailea* ☎ *808/281–9301* ⊕ *www. mauisailingcanoe.com.*

FAMILY **Maui Classic Charters.** Hop aboard the *Four Winds II,* a 55-foot, glass-bottom catamaran (great fun for kids), for one of the most dependable snorkel trips around. You'll spend more time than the other charter boats do at Molokini Crater and enjoy turtle-watching on the way home. The trip includes optional snuba ($49 extra), Continental breakfast, barbecue lunch, beer, wine, and soda. At a price of $89 per person, it can be popular and crowded. Or try the *Maui Magic,* Maalaea's fastest power cat. This boat holds fewer people than some of the larger vessels, and trips start at $112. ✉ *Maalaea Harbor, Slips 55 and 80, Maalaea* ☎ *808/879–8188, 800/736–5740* ⊕ *www.mauicharters.com.*

Teralani Sailing Charters. Choose between a regular snorkeling trip with a deli lunch or a top-of-the-line excursion that's an hour longer and includes two snorkel sites and a barbecue-style lunch catered by Cilantro Mexican Grill, a popular local restaurant. The company's cats could hold well over 100 people, but 49 is the maximum per trip. The boats are kept in pristine condition. Freshwater showers are available, and so is an open bar after the second snorkel stop. A friendly crew provides all your gear, a flotation device, and a crash course in snorkeling. Boarding is right off Dig Me Beach at Whalers Village in West Maui.

✉ *Whalers Village, 2435 Kaanapali Pkwy., Kaanapali* ☎ *808/661–1230* ⊕ *www.teralani.net.*

Trilogy Excursions. Many people consider a trip with Trilogy Excursions to be a highlight of their vacation. Maui's longest-running operation has comprehensive offerings, with seven beautiful multihull 50- to 64-foot sailing vessels at three departure sites. All excursions are staffed by energetic crews who will keep you well fed and entertained with local stories and corny jokes. A full-day catamaran cruise to Lanai includes a Continental breakfast and barbecue lunch, a guided tour of the island, a "Snorkeling 101" class, and time to snorkel in the waters of Lanai's Hulopoe Marine Preserve (Trilogy Excursions has exclusive commercial access). The company also offers a Molokini Crater and Honolua Bay snorkel cruise that is top-notch. Tours depart from Lahaina Harbor; Maalaea Harbor; and, in West Maui, in front of the Kaanapali Beach Hotel. ✉ *180 Lahainaluna Rd., Lahaina* ☎ *808/874–5649, 888/225–6284* ⊕ *www.sailtrilogy.com.*

STAND-UP PADDLING

Also called stand-up paddle surfing or paddleboarding, stand-up paddling is the "comeback kid" of surf sports; you stand on a longboard and paddle out with a canoe oar. While paddleboarding requires even more balance and coordination than regular surfing, it is still accessible to just about every skill level. Most surf schools now offer stand-up paddle lessons.

The fun thing about stand-up paddling is that you can enjoy it whether the surf is good or the water is flat. However, as with all water sports, it's important to read the environment and be attentive. Look at the sky and assess the wind by how fast the clouds are moving. Take note of where the whitecaps are going. Always point the nose of your board perpendicular to the wave. ■TIP→ Because of the size and speed of a longboard, stand-up paddling can be dangerous to you and those around you, so lessons are highly recommended.

LESSONS

Maui Surfer Girls. Owner and bonafide waterwoman Dustin Tester is known as Mama D to the girls she mentors. While the company started with surf camps, it also offers co-ed stand-up paddle lessons. Locations vary on wind conditions but are usually at beginner-friendly Ukumehame Beach or Thousand Peaks. The lesson includes some history of the ancient sport, gear, and refreshments after the paddle. Lessons begin at $100, with an extra $20 charge for instruction by Dustin, who is accompanied by her dog, Luna. ✉ *Puunene* ☎ *808/214–0606* ⊕ *www.mauisurfergirls.com.*

Stand-Up Paddle Surf School. Maui's first school devoted solely to stand-up paddleboarding was founded by the legendary Maria Souza, the first woman to surf the treacherous waves of "Jaws" on Maui's North Shore. While most surf schools offer stand-up paddling, Maria's classes are in a league of their own. They include a proper warm-up with a hula-hoop and balance ball and a cool-down with some yoga. The cost is $159 for a private session. Locations vary depending on conditions. ⊠ *Lahaina* ☎ *808/579–9231* ⊕ *www.standuppaddlesurfschool.com.*

SURFING

Maui's coastline has surf for every level of waterman or -woman. Waves on leeward-facing shores (West and South Maui) tend to break in gentle sets all summer long. Surf instructors in Kihei and Lahaina can rent you boards, give you onshore instruction, and then lead you out through the channel, where it's safe to enter the surf. They'll shout encouragement while you paddle like mad for the thrill of standing on water—most will give you a helpful shove. These areas are great for beginners; the only danger is whacking a stranger with your board or stubbing your toe against the reef.

The North Shore is another story. Winter waves pound the windward coast, attracting water champions from every corner of the world. Adrenaline addicts are towed in by Jet Ski to a legendary, deep-sea break called "Jaws." Waves here periodically tower upward of 40 feet. The only spot for viewing this phenomenon (which happens just a few times a year) is on private property. So, if you hear the surfers next to you crowing about Jaws "going off," cozy up and get them to take you with them.

> ### SURF REPORT
>
> Before heading out for any water activity, be sure to get a weather and wave report, and make sure the surf report you get is the *full face value* of the wave. "Hawaiian-style" cuts the wave size in half. For instance, a Hawaiian might say a wave is 5 feet high, which means 10 feet if you're from New Jersey or Florida. For years, scientists and surfers were using different measurements, as Hawaii locals measured waves from median sea level to the crest. These days, most surf reports are careful to distinguish between the two.

Whatever your skill, there's a board, a break, and even a surf guru to accommodate you. A two-hour lesson is a good intro to surf culture.

You can get the wave report each day by checking page 2 of the *Maui News*, logging onto the Glenn James weather site at ⊕ *www.hawaiiweathertoday.com*, or calling ☎ *808/871–5054* (for the weather forecast) or ☎ *808/877–3611* (for the surf report).

BEST SPOTS

Cove Park. On the South Shore, beginners can hang 10 at Kihei's Cove Park, a sometimes crowded but reliable 1- to 2-foot break. Boards can easily be rented across the street, or in neighboring Kalama Park parking lot. The only bummer is having to balance the 9-plus-foot board on your head while crossing busy South Kihei Road. ⊠ *S. Kihei Rd., Kihei.*

Hookipa Beach Park. For advanced wave riders, Hookipa Beach Park on the North Shore boasts several well-loved breaks, including "Pavilions," "Lanes," "the Point," and "Middles." Surfers have priority until 11 am, when windsurfers move in on the action. ■TIP→ Competition is stiff here. If you don't know what you're doing, consider watching. ✉ *Hana Hwy., 2 miles past Paia.*

Launiupoko State Wayside. Long- or shortboarders in West Maui can paddle out at Launiupoko State Wayside. The east end of the park has an easy break, good for beginners. ✉ *Honoapiilani Hwy., near mile marker 18, Wailuku.*

Ukumehame. Also called "Thousand Peaks," Ukumehame is one of the better beginner spots in West Maui. You'll soon see how the spot got its name—the waves here break again and again in wide and consistent rows, giving lots of room for beginning and intermediate surfers. ✉ *Honoapiilani Hwy., near mile marker 12, Lahaina.*

WATCHING SURFERS

Even if you aren't a surfer, watching is just as fun (well, almost).

Honolua Bay. Near-perfect waves can be seen at Honolua Bay, on the northern tip of West Maui. To get here, continue 2 miles north of D.T. Fleming Park on Highway 30 and take a left onto the dirt road next to a pineapple field; a path leads down the cliff to the beach. ✉ *Hwy. 30, Kapalua.*

Hookipa Beach Park. Hookipa Beach Park gives you the perfect overlook to see pro surfers, windsurfers, and kiters. ✉ *Hana Hwy., 2 miles past Paia.*

West Maui. Good surf spots in West Maui include "Grandma's" at **Papalaua Park,** just after the *pali* (cliff)—where waves are so easy a grandma could ride 'em; **Puamana Beach Park** for a mellow longboard day; and **Lahaina Harbor,** which offers an excellent inside wave for beginners (called "Breakwall"), as well as the more advanced outside (a great lift if there's a big south swell).

EQUIPMENT AND LESSONS

Surf camps are becoming increasingly popular, especially with women. One- or two-week camps offer a terrific way to build muscle and self-esteem simultaneously.

Big Kahuna Adventures. Rent soft-top longboards here for $20 for two hours, or $30 for the day. The shop also offers surf lessons and rents kayaks and snorkel gear. Across from Cove Park, the company has been around for years. ✉ *1913-C S. Kihei Rd., Kihei* ☎ *808/875–6395* ⊕ *www.bigkahunaadventures.com.*

Goofy Foot. Surfing "goofy foot" means putting your right foot forward. They might be goofy, but we like the right-footed gurus here. This shop is just plain cool and only steps away from "Breakwall," a great beginner's spot in Lahaina. A two-hour class with five or fewer students is $65, and you're guaranteed to be standing by the end or it's free. Owner and "stoke broker" Tim Sherer offers private lessons for $250 and will sometimes ride alongside to record video clips and give more thorough feedback. A private two-hour lesson with another instructor is $150. ✉ *505 Front St., Suite 123, Lahaina* ☎ *808/244–9283* ⊕ *www.goofyfootsurfschool.com.*

Hi-Tech Surf Sports. Locals hold Hi-Tech in the highest regard. It has some of the best boards, advice, and attitude around. It rents even its best surfboards—choose from longboards, shortboards, and hybrids—starting at $25 per day. All rentals come with board bags, roof racks, and wax. ⊠ *425 Koloa St., Kahului* ☎ *808/877–2111* ⊕ *www.htmaui.com.*

Maui Surfer Girls. This highly reputable company immerses adventurous young women in wave-riding wisdom during overnight one- and two-week camps. They also offer daily surf lessons that take place away from the big crowds of Lahaina or Kihei. ⊕ *www.mauisurfergirls.com.*

Nancy Emerson School of Surfing. Instructors here will get even the shakiest novice riding with the school's "Learn to Surf in One Lesson" program. A two-hour group lesson (up to five students) is $78. Private lessons with the patient and meticulous instructors are $165 for two hours. The company provides boards, rash guards, and water shoes, all in impeccable condition—and it's tops in the customer-service department. ⊠ *505 Front St., Suite 201, Lahaina* ☎ *808/244–7873* ⊕ *www.mauisurfclinics.com.*

Outrageous Surf School. If you're not too keen on shore lessons (which usually have you spend 30 minutes simulating surfing instead of doing the real thing), Outrageous might be your best bet. A short instructional video is followed by a quick demo, and down to the Breakwall you go. Lessons start at $60 for a group, $85 for semiprivate, and $120 for a private lesson. Repeat classes are $40. ⊠ *640 Front St., Lahaina* ☎ *808/669–1400* ⊕ *www.youcansurf.com.*

Royal Hawaiian Surf Academy. Owner Kimo Kinimaka grew up rippin' it with his uncle, legendary surfer Titus Kinimaka, so it's no wonder his passion translates to a fun, memorable time at the novice-friendly Lahaina Breakwall. Private lessons are $130, and group lessons cost $65 per person. Rash guards and shoes are provided. ⊠ *117 Prison St., Lahaina* ☎ *808/276–7873* ⊕ *www.royalhawaiiansurfacademy.com.*

Second Wind. Surfboard rentals at this centrally located shop are a deal— good boards go for $22 per day or $120 per week. The shop also rents and sells its own Elua Makani boards (which means "second wind" in Hawaiian). Although the staff doesn't offer lessons, they will book you with the best surfing, windsurfing, and kiteboarding lessons on the island. ⊠ *111 Hana Hwy., Kahului* ☎ *808/877–7467, 800/936–7787* ⊕ *www.secondwindmaui.com.*

WHALE-WATCHING

From December into May whale-watching becomes one of the most popular activities on Maui. During the season *all* outfitters offer whale-watching in addition to their regular activities, and most do an excellent job. Boats leave the wharves at Lahaina and Maalaea in search of humpbacks, allowing you to enjoy the awe-inspiring size of these creatures in closer proximity. From November through May, the Pacific Whale Foundation sponsors the Maui Whale Festival, a variety of whale-related events for locals and visitors; check the calendar at ⊕ *www.mauiwhalefestival.org.*

As it's almost impossible *not* to see whales in winter on Maui, you'll want to prioritize: is adventure or comfort your aim? If close encounters with the giants of the deep are your desire, pick a smaller boat that

The Humpback's Winter Home

The humpback whales' attraction to Maui is legendary, and seeing them between December and May is a highlight for many visitors. More than half the Pacific's humpback population winters in Hawaii, especially in the waters around the Valley Isle, where mothers can be seen just a few hundred feet offshore training their young calves in the fine points of whale etiquette. Watching from shore it's easy to catch sight of whales spouting, or even breaching—when they leap almost entirely out of the sea, slapping back onto the water with a huge splash.

At one time there were thousands of the huge mammals, but a history of overhunting and marine pollution dwindled the world population to about 1,500. In 1966 humpbacks were put on the endangered-species list. Hunting or harassing whales is illegal in the waters of most nations, and in the United States boats and airplanes are restricted from getting too close. The word is still out, however, on the effects military sonar testing has on the marine mammals.

Marine biologists believe the humpbacks (much like the humans) keep returning to Hawaii because of its warmth. Having fattened themselves in subarctic waters all summer, the whales migrate south in the winter to breed, and a rebounding population of thousands cruise Maui waters. Winter is calving time, and the young whales probably couldn't survive in the frigid Alaskan waters. No one has ever seen a whale give birth here, but experts know that calving is their main winter activity, since the 1- and 2-ton youngsters suddenly appear while the whales are in residence.

The first sighting of a humpback whale spout each season is exciting for locals on Maui. A collective sigh of relief can be heard, "Ah, they've returned." In the not-so-far distance, flukes and flippers can be seen rising above the ocean's surface. It's hard not to anthropomorphize the tail waving; it looks like such an amiable gesture. Each fluke is uniquely patterned, like a human's fingerprint, and is used to identify the giants as they travel halfway around the globe and back.

promises sightings. Those who think "green" usually prefer the smaller, quieter vessels that produce the least amount of negative impact to the whales' natural environment. For those wanting to sip mai tais as whales cruise calmly by, stick with a sunset cruise ($40 and up) on a boat with an open bar and *pupu* (Hawaiian tapas). ■TIP→ **Afternoon trips are generally rougher because the wind picks up, but some say this is when the most surface action occurs.**

Every captain aims to please during whale season, getting as close as legally possible (100 yards). Crew members know when a whale is about to dive (after several waves of its heart-shape tail) but rarely can predict breaches (when the whale hurls itself up and almost entirely out of the water). Prime viewing space (on the upper and lower decks, around the railings) is limited, so boats can feel crowded even when half full. If you don't want to squeeze in beside strangers, opt for a smaller boat with fewer bookings. Don't forget to bring sunscreen, sunglasses, a light long-sleeve cover-up, and a hat you can secure. Winter weather

Humpback whale calves are plentiful in winter; this one is breaching off West Maui.

is less predictable and at times can be extreme, especially as the wind picks up. Arrive early to find parking.

BEST SPOTS

Keawakapu Beach. The northern end of Keawakapu Beach on the South Shore seems to be a whale magnet. Situate yourself on the sand or at the nearby restaurant and watch mamas and calves. ⊠ *S. Kihei Rd., near Kilohana Dr., Kihei.*

Papawai Point Lookout. From December 15 to May 1, the Pacific Whale Foundation has naturalists in two places—on the rooftop of its headquarters and at the scenic viewpoint at Papawai Point Lookout. Like the commuting traffic, whales cruise along the *pali,* or cliff side, of West Maui's Honoapiilani Highway all day long. ⚠ **Make sure to park safely before craning your neck out to see them.** ⊠ *Rte. 30, 3 miles west of Maalaea Harbor, Maalaea.*

BOATS AND CHARTERS

Gemini Sailing Charters. Morning and afternoon whale-watching trips off the Kaanapali coast are available on this well-maintained catamaran staffed by an experienced and fun crew. The cost is $60 per person for the morning trip and $70 for the afternoon trip. You can find Gemini on Kaanapali Beach near the Westin Maui Resort's activity desk. ⊠ *Westin Maui Resort & Spa, 2365 Kaanapali Pkwy., Lahaina* ☎ *800/820–7245, 808/669–0508* ⊕ *www.geminicharters.com.*

Maui Adventure Cruises. Whale-watching from this company's raft puts you right above the water surface and on the same level as the whales. You'll forego the cocktail in your hand but you won't have to deal with crowds, even if the vessel is at max with 36 people. The whales can get

up close if they like, and when they do it's absolutely spectacular. These rafts can move with greater speed than a catamaran, so you don't spend much time motoring between whales or pods. Refreshments are included. Prices are $34 for adults and $28 for kids 5–12 years old; children under 4 years old are not admitted. ✉ *Lahaina Harbor, Slip 11, Lahaina* ☎ *808/661–5550* ⊕ *www.mauiadventurecruises.com.*

FAMILY **Pacific Whale Foundation.** With a fleet of nine boats, this nonprofit organization pioneered whale-watching back in 1979. The crew (including a certified marine biologist) offers insights into whale behavior and suggests ways for you to help save marine life worldwide. One of the best things about these trips is the underwater hydrophone that allows you to listen to the whales sing. Trips meet at the organization's store, which sells whale paraphernalia. You'll be sharing the boat with about 100 people in stadium-style seating, but once you catch sight of the wildlife up close, you can't help but be thrilled. ✉ *612 Front St., Lahaina* ☎ *808/249–8811* ⊕ *www.pacificwhale.org.*

Trilogy Excursions. Whale-watching trips with Trilogy Excursions consist of smaller groups of about 20 to 36 passengers and include beverages and snacks, an onboard marine naturalist, and hydrophones that detect underwater sound waves. Trips are $39, and you load at West Maui's Kaanapali Beach Hotel. ✉ *Kaanapali Beach Hotel, 2525 Kaanapali Pkwy., Lahaina* ☎ *808/874–5649, 888/225–6284* ⊕ *www.sailtrilogy.com.*

WINDSURFING TOURNAMENTS

Few places lay claim to as many windsurfing tournaments as Maui. In March the **PWA Hawaiian Pro-Am Windsurfing** competition gets underway at Hookipa Beach. In June the **Da Kine Windsurfing Classic** lures top windsurfers to Kanaha Beach, and in November the **Aloha Classic World Wave Sailing Championships** takes place at Hookipa.

Maui Race Series. For competitions featuring amateurs as well as professionals, check out the Maui Race Series, six events held at Kanaha Beach in Kahului in summer. ☎ *808/877–2111* ⊕ *www.mauiraceseries.com.*

WINDSURFING

Windsurfing, invented in the 1950s, found its true home at Hookipa on Maui's North Shore in 1980. Seemingly overnight, windsurfing pros from around the world flooded the area. Equipment evolved, amazing film footage was captured, and a new sport was born.

If you're new to the action, you can get lessons from the experts islandwide. For a beginner, the best thing about windsurfing is (unlike surfing) you don't have to paddle. Instead, you have to hold on like heck to a flapping sail, as it whisks you into the wind. Needless to say, you're going to need a little coordination and balance to pull this off. Instructors start you out on a beach at Kanaha, where the big boys go. Lessons range from two-hour introductory classes to five-day advanced "flight school."

BEST SPOTS

Hookipa Bay. After Hookipa Bay was discovered by windsurfers three decades ago, this windy North Shore beach 10 miles east of Kahului gained an international reputation. The spot is blessed with optimal wave-sailing wind and sea conditions, and offers the ultimate aerial experience. ✉ *Hana Hwy., 2 miles past Paia.*

Kalepolepo Beach. In summer the windsurfing crowd heads to Kalepolepo Beach on the South Shore. Trade winds build in strength, and by afternoon a swarm of dragonfly-sails can be seen skimming the whitecaps, with the West Maui Mountains as a backdrop. ✉ *S. Kihei Rd., near Ohukai St., Kihei.*

Kanaha Beach Park. A great site for speed, Kanaha Beach Park is dedicated to beginners in the morning hours, before the waves and wind really get roaring. After 11 am, the professionals choose from their quiver of sails the size and shape best suited for the day's demands. This beach tends to have smaller waves and forceful winds—sometimes sending sailors flying at 40 knots. ■TIP→ If you aren't ready to go pro, this is a great place for a picnic while you watch from the beach. To get here, use any of the three entrances on Amala Place, which runs along the shore just north of Kahului Airport. ✉ *Amala Pl., Kahului.*

EQUIPMENT AND LESSONS

Action Sports Maui. The quirky, friendly professionals here will meet you at Kanaha Beach Park on the North Shore, outfit you with your sail and board, and guide you through your first "jibe" or turn. They promise your learning time will be cut in half. Lessons begin at 9 am every day except Sunday and cost $89 for a 2½-hour class. Three- and five-day courses cost $240 and $395. ✉ *96 Amala Pl., Kahului* ☎ *808/871–5857* ⊕ *www.actionsportsmaui.com.*

Fodor's Choice ★ **Hawaiian Sailboarding Techniques.** Considered Maui's finest windsurfing school, Hawaiian Sailboarding Techniques brings you quality instruction by skilled sailors. Founded by Alan Cadiz, an accomplished World Cup Pro, the school sets high standards for a safe, quality windsurfing experience. Intro classes start at $89 for 2½ hours, gear included. The company is inside Hi-Tech Surf Sports, which offers excellent equipment rentals. ✉ *Hi-Tech Surf Sports, 425 Koloa St., Kahului* ☎ *808/871–5423* ⊕ *www.hstwindsurfing.com.*

Second Wind. Located in Kahului, this company rents boards with two sails for $55 per day. Additional sails are $10 each. Intro classes start at $89. ✉ *111 Hana Hwy., Kahului* ☎ *808/877–7467* ⊕ *www. secondwindmaui.com.*

5

GOLF, HIKING, AND
OUTDOOR ACTIVITIES

Updated by
Heidi Pool

We know how tempting it is to spend your entire vacation on the beach (we're tempted many days as well), but if you do, you'll miss out on the "other side of Maui"—the eerie, moonlike surface of Haleakala Crater, the lush rain forests of East Maui, and the geological wonder that is Iao Valley State Monument, to name just a few. Even playing a round of golf on one of the world-class courses provides breathtaking vistas, reminding you just why you chose to come to Maui in the first place.

Maui's exceptional climate affords year-round opportunities for outdoor adventures, whether it's exploring cascading waterfalls on a day hike, riding horseback through verdant valleys, soaring across vast gulches on a zipline, or taking an exhilarating bicycle ride down Haleakala. When you take time to get off the beaten path, you'll discover just why Maui *no ka oi* (is the best). But make sure not to overbook yourself—one or two activities per day is plenty. You're on vacation, remember?

For easy reference, activities are listed in alphabetical order.

AERIAL TOURS

Helicopter flight-seeing excursions can take you over the West Maui Mountains, Haleakala Crater, or the island of Molokai. This is a beautiful, thrilling way to see the island, and the *only* way to see some of its most dramatic areas and waterfalls. Tour prices usually include a DVD of your trip so you can relive the experience at home. Prices run from about $160 for a half-hour rain-forest tour, to more than $400 for a 90-minute experience that includes a midflight landing at an exclusive remote site where you can enjoy refreshments along with the view. Generally the 45- to 50-minute flights are the best value; discounts

may be available online or, if you're willing to chance it, by calling at the last minute.

Tour operators come under sharp scrutiny for passenger safety and equipment maintenance. Don't be shy; ask about a company's safety record, flight paths, age of equipment, and level of operator experience. Generally, though, if they're still in business, they're doing something right.

Air Maui Helicopters. Priding itself on a perfect safety record, this company provides 30- to 65-minute flights covering the waterfalls of the West Maui Mountains, Haleakala Crater, Hana, and the spectacular sea cliffs of Molokai. Prices range from $198 to $348, with considerable discounts available online. Charter flights are also available. ⌂ *Kahului Heliport, Hangar 110, Kahului Airport Rd. and Keolani Blvd., Kahului* ☎ *877/238–4942, 808/877–7005* ⊕ *www.airmaui.com.*

Blue Hawaiian Helicopters. Since 1985 this company has provided aerial adventures in Hawaii and has been integral in some of the filming Hollywood has done on Maui. Its A-Star and Eco-Star helicopters are air-conditioned and have Bose noise-blocking headsets for all passengers. Flights are 30 to 120 minutes and cost $169 to $563, with considerable discounts online. Charter flights are also available. ⌂ *Kahului Heliport, Hangar 105, Kahului Airport Rd. and Keolani Blvd., Kahului* ☎ *808/871–8844, 800/745–2583* ⊕ *www.bluehawaiian.com.*

Sunshine Helicopters. Sunshine offers tours of Maui in its FXStar or WhisperStar aircraft. A pilot-narrated DVD of your actual flight is available for purchase. Prices start at $190 for 30 to 65 minutes, with discounts available online. First-class seating is available for an additional fee. Charter flights can be arranged. ⌂ *Kahului Heliport, Hangar 107, Kahului Airport Rd. and Keolani Blvd., Kahului* ☎ *808/270–3999, 866/501–7738* ⊕ *www.sunshinehelicopters.com.*

BIKING

Long distances and mountainous terrain keep biking from being a practical mode of travel on Maui. Still, painted bike lanes enable cyclists to travel all the way from Makena to Kapalua, and you'll see hardy souls battling the trade winds under the hot Maui sun.

Several companies offer guided bike tours down Haleakala. This activity is a great way to enjoy an easy, gravity-induced bike ride, but isn't for those not confident on a bike. The ride is inherently dangerous due to the slope, sharp turns, and the fact that you're riding down an actual road with cars on it. That said, the guided bike companies take every safety precaution. A few companies offer unguided (or, as they like to say, "self-guided") tours where they provide you with the bike and transportation to the mountain and then you're free to descend at your own pace. Most companies offer discounts for Internet bookings.

Haleakala National Park no longer allows commercial downhill bicycle rides within the park's boundaries. As a result, tour amenities and routes differ by company. Ask about sunrise viewing from the Haleakala summit (be prepared to leave *very* early in the morning), if this is an important feature for you. Some lower-price tours begin at the 6,500-foot elevation just outside the national park boundaries, where you will be unable to view the sunrise over the crater. Weather conditions on Haleakala vary greatly, so a visible sunrise can never be guaranteed. Sunrise is downright cold at the summit, so be sure to dress in layers and wear closed-toe shoes.

Each company has age and weight restrictions, and pregnant women are discouraged from participating, although they are generally welcome in the escort van. Reconsider this activity if you have difficulty with high altitudes, have recently been scuba diving, or are taking medications that may cause drowsiness.

BEST SPOTS

At present there are few truly good spots to ride on Maui, though this is changing.

Makawao Forest Reserve. The Makawao Forest Reserve provides mountain bikers a 5.2-mile romp under a dense canopy of trees. To get here from Piiholo Road, turn left on Waiahiwi Road and then right on Kahakapao Road. ⊠ *Kahakapao Rd., Makawao.*

Polipoli Spring State Recreation Area. Mountain bikers have favored the remote Polipoli Spring State Recreation Area for its bumpy trail through an unlikely forest of conifers. ⊠ *End of Waipoli Rd., off Rte. 377, Kula.*

Thompson Road. Street bikers will want to head out to scenic Thompson Road. It's quiet, gently curvy, and flanked by gorgeous views on both sides. Because it's at a higher elevation, the air temperature is cooler and the wind lighter. The coast back down toward Kahului on the Kula Highway is worth the ride up. ⊠ *Kula Hwy., off Rte. 37, Keokea.*

EQUIPMENT AND TOURS

Fodor's Choice ★ **Bike It Maui.** Small and family-owned, this company offers two guided sunrise tours down Haleakala each day. The price of $144 ($134 if booked more than a week ahead) includes transfers from your hotel, a sunrise van tour of the summit, a guided 28-mile bicycle ride down the mountain, and a full sit-down breakfast at Cafe O'Lei at the Dunes in Kahului. Riders must be at least 12 and weigh no more than 260 pounds. ⊠ *Kula* ☎ *808/878–3364, 866/776–2453* ⊕ *www.bikeitmaui. com.*

Fodor's Choice ★ **Cruiser Phil's Volcano Riders.** Known as "Cruiser Phil," Phil Feliciano has been in the downhill bicycle industry since 1983. He offers sunrise tours ($150) and morning tours ($135) that include hotel transfers, Continental breakfast, a van tour of the summit, and a guided 28-mile ride down the mountain. Participants should be between 15 and 65, taller than 5 feet, weigh less than 250 pounds, and have ridden a bicycle in the past year. Feliciano also offers independent bike tours ($99) and van-only tours ($125). Discounts are available for online bookings. ⊠ *58-A Amala Pl., Kahului* ☎ *808/893–2332, 877/764–2453* ⊕ *www. cruiserphil.com.*

Go Cycling Maui. Serious cyclists can join an exhilarating group ride with Donnie Arnoult, a fixture on the Maui cycling scene since 1999. Routes include Haiku to Keanae, Kula to Kahikinui, and the ultimate Maui cycling challenge: Paia to the top of Haleakala Crater. Rides are $140 per person. You bring your own cycling shoes, pedals, and clothes, and Donnie provides the bicycle, helmet, gloves, water bottle, snacks, and energy drinks. His shop is also a full-service cycling store offering sales, rentals, and repairs. ⊠ *99 Hana Hwy., Unit A, Pahala* ☎ *808/579–9009* ⊕ *www.gocyclingmaui.com.*

Haleakala Bike Company. If you're thinking about an unguided Haleakala bike trip, consider this company. Meet at the Old Haiku Cannery and take the van shuttle to the summit. Along the way you can learn about the history of the island, the volcano, and other Hawaiiana. Food is not included, but there are several spots along the way down to stop, rest, and eat. The simple, mostly downhill route takes you right back to the cannery where you started. HBC also offers bike sales, rentals, and services, as well as van tours. Tour prices range from $70 to $120, with discounts available for online bookings. ⊠ *810 Haiku Rd., Suite 120, Haiku* ☎ *808/575–9575, 888/922–2453* ⊕ *www.bikemaui.com.*

Island Biker. Maui's premier bike shop for rentals, sales, and service, Island Biker offers standard front-shock bikes, road bikes, and full-suspension mountain bikes. Daily rental rates range from $50 to $75, and weekly rates are $200 to $280. The price includes a helmet, pump, water bottle, cages, tire-repair kit, and spare tube. Car racks are $5 per day (free with weekly rentals). The staff can suggest routes appropriate for mountain or road biking. ⊠ *415 Dairy Rd., Kahului* ☎ *808/877–7744* ⊕ *www.islandbikermaui.com.*

West Maui Cycles. Serving the island's west side, West Maui Cycles offers cruisers for $15 per day ($60 per week), hybrids for $30 per day ($120 per week), and performance road bikes for $60 per day ($220 per week). Tandems start at $30 per day ($120 per week). The shop also rents baby joggers and car racks. Sales and service are available. ⊠ *1087 Limahana Pl., No. 6, Lahaina* ☎ *808/661–9005* ⊕ *www. westmauicycles.com.*

GOLF

Maui's natural beauty and surroundings offer some of the most jaw-dropping vistas imaginable on a golf course; add a variety of challenging, well-designed courses and it's easy to explain the island's popularity with golfers. Holes run across small bays, past craggy lava outcrops, and up into cool, forested mountains. Most courses have mesmerizing ocean views, some close enough to feel the salt in the air. Although many of the courses are affiliated with resorts (and therefore a little pricier), the general-public courses are no less impressive. Playing on Lanai is another option.

Greens Fees: Golf can be costly on Maui. Greens fees listed here are the highest course rates per round on weekdays and weekends for U.S. residents. (Some courses charge non-U.S. residents higher prices.) Rental clubs may or may not be included with the greens fee. Discounts are often available for resort guests, for twilight tee times, and for those who book online.

■TIP→ Resort courses, in particular, offer more than the usual three sets of tees, so bite off as much or little challenge as you like. Tee it up from the tips and you can end up playing a few 600-yard par 5s and see a few 250-yard forced carries.

DISCOUNTS
AND DEALS

Maui Golf Shop. Near the airport in Kahului, Maui Golf Shop offers discounted tee times and club rentals. Ask about the resort delivery program. ⊠ *201 Dairy Rd., Kahului* ☎ *808/875–4653, 800/981–5512* ⊕ *www.golf-maui.com.*

MAUI GOLF
TOURNA-
MENTS

Maui has a number of golf tournaments, most of which are of professional caliber and worth watching. Many are also televised nationally.

Hyundai Tournament of Champions. Held in January, the Hyundai Tournament of Champions is an attention-getter. This is the first official PGA tour event, held on Kapalua's Plantation Course. ☎ *808/665–9160* ⊕ *www.kapalua.com/golf/hyundai-tournament-champions.*

Ka Lima O Maui Celebrity 100. Every May, self-proclaimed "lunatic" golfers play from sunrise to sunset in Wailea's annual Ka Lima O Maui Celebrity 100, a fund-raiser for a local charity. ☎ *808/875–7450* ⊕ *www.kalimaomaui.org.*

Kapalua Clambake Pro-Am. A clambake feast at the Ritz-Carlton tops off the Kapalua Clambake Pro-Am in June. ☎ *808/665–3759* ⊕ *www. kapaluamaui.com.*

WEST MAUI

Kaanapali Golf Resort. The Royal Kaanapali (North) Course (1962) is one of three in Hawaii designed by Robert Trent Jones Sr., the godfather of modern golf architecture. The greens average a whopping 10,000 square feet, necessary because of the often-severe undulation. The par-4 18th hole (into the prevailing trade breezes, with out-of-bounds on the left, and a lake on the right) is notoriously tough. Designed by Arthur Jack Snyder, the Kaanapali Kai (South) Course (1976) shares similar seaside-into-the-hills terrain, but is rated a couple of strokes easier, mostly because putts are less treacherous. ⊠ *2290 Kaanapali Pkwy., Lahaina* ☎ *808/661–3691, 866/454–4653* ⊕ *www.kaanapali-golf.com* ⚐ *North Course: 18 holes. 6500 yds. Par 71. Slope 126. Greens fee: $249. South Course: 18 holes. 6400 yds. Par 70. Slope 124. Greens fee: $205.* ☞ *Facilities: Driving range, putting green, golf carts, rental clubs, lessons, restaurant, bar.*

Fodor's Choice
★

Kapalua Resort. Perhaps Hawaii's best-known golf resort and the crown jewel of golf on Maui, Kapalua hosts the PGA Tour's first event each January: the Hyundai Tournament of Champions at the Plantation Course at Kapalua. Ben Crenshaw and Bill Coore (1991) tried to incorporate traditional shot values in a nontraditional site, taking into account slope, gravity, and the prevailing trade winds. The par-5 18th hole, for instance, plays 663 yards from the back tees (600 yards from the resort tees). The hole drops 170 feet in elevation, narrowing as it goes to a partially guarded green, and plays downwind and down-grain. Despite the longer-than-usual distance, the slope is great enough and the wind at your back usually brisk enough to reach the green with two

well-struck shots—a truly unbelievable finish to a course that will challenge, frustrate, and reward the patient golfer.

The Bay Course (Arnold Palmer and Francis Duane, 1975) is the more traditional of Kapalua's courses, with gentle rolling fairways and generous greens. The most memorable hole is the par-3 fifth hole, with a tee shot that must carry a turquoise finger of Onelua Bay. Each of the courses has a separate clubhouse. ⊠ *Kapalua* ⊕ *www.kapalua.com.*

Kapalua Golf Academy. Along with 23 acres of practice turf and 11 teeing areas, an 18-hole putting course, and 3-hole walking course, the Kapalua Golf Academy also has an instructional bay with video analysis. ⊠ *1000 Office Rd., Kapalua* ☎ *808/665–5455, 877/527–2582* ⊕ *www.kapalua.com/hawaii-golf*

Bay Course ⊠ *300 Kapalua Dr., Kapalua* ☎ *808/669–8044, 877/527–2582* ⊕ *www.kapalua.com/hawaii-golf* ⅄ *18 holes. 6600 yds. Par 72. Slope 133. Greens fee: $208* ⌁ *Facilities: Driving range, putting green, rental clubs, pro shop, lessons, restaurant, bar.*

Plantation Course ⊠ *2000 Plantation Club Dr., Kapalua* ☎ *808/669–8044, 877/527–2582* ⊕ *www.kapalua.com/hawaii-golf* ⅄ *18 holes. 7411 yds. Par 73. Slope 135. Greens fee: $268* ⌁ *Facilities: Driving range, putting green, golf carts, pull carts, rental clubs, pro shop, golf academy/lessons, restaurant, bar.*

THE SOUTH SHORE

elleair Maui Golf Club. Formerly known as Silversword (1987), elleair is an exacting test. Fairways tend to be narrow, especially in landing areas, and can be quite a challenge when the trade winds come up in the afternoon. The course is lined with enough coconut trees to make them a collective hazard, not just a nutty nuisance. ⊠ *1345 Piilani Hwy., Kihei* ☎ *808/874–0777* ⊕ *elleairmauigolfclub.com* ⅄ *18 holes. 6404 yds. Par 71. Slope 117. Greens fee: $120* ⌁ *Facilities: Driving range, putting green, golf carts, rental clubs, pro shop, lessons.*

Fodor's Choice ★ **Makena Beach & Golf Resort.** Robert Trent Jones Jr. designed Makena Golf Course (1994) in harmony with the existing landscape: Hawaiian rock walls still stand in their original locations, and natural gullies and stream beds were left in their natural states. Sculpted from the lava flows on the western flank of Haleakala, Makena offers quick greens with lots of breaks and plenty of scenic distractions. The fourth hole is one of Hawaii's most picturesque inland par 3s, with the green guarded on the right by a duck pond. The sixth is an excellent example of option golf: The fairway is sliced up the middle by a gaping ravine, which must sooner or later be crossed to reach the green. The last three holes are

TIPS FOR GOLFING ON MAUI

Golf is golf, and Hawaii is part of the United States, but island golf nevertheless has its own quirks. Here are a few tips to make your golf experience in the Islands more pleasant.

■ Sunscreen: Buy it, apply it (we're talking a minimum of 30 SPF). The subtropical rays of the sun are intense, even in December. Good advice is to apply sunscreen, at a minimum, on the 1st and 10th tees.

■ Stay hydrated. Spending four-plus hours in the sun and heat means you'll perspire away considerable fluids and energy.

■ All resort courses and many daily-fee courses provide rental clubs. In many cases, they're the latest lines from top manufacturers. This is true both for men and women, as well as for left-handers, which means you don't have to schlep clubs across the Pacific.

■ Pro shops at most courses are well stocked with balls, tees, and

other accouterments, so even if you bring your own bag, it needn't weigh a ton.

■ Come spikeless—few Hawaii courses still permit metal spikes. And most of the resort courses require a collared shirt.

■ Maui is notorious for its trade winds. Consider playing early if you want to avoid the breezes, and remember that although it will frustrate you at times and make club selection difficult, you may well see some of your longest drives ever.

■ In theory you can play golf in Hawaii 365 days a year, but there's a reason the Hawaiian Islands are so green. An umbrella and light jacket can come in handy.

■ Unless you play a muni or certain daily-fee courses, plan on taking a cart. Riding carts are mandatory at most courses and are included in the greens fee.

relatively short par 4s, but keen accuracy is required, as the tees wind through kiawe trees. ⊠ *5415 Makena Alanui, Makena* ☎ *808/891–4000* ⊕ *www.makenagolf.com* ⚑ *18 holes. 6567 yds. Par 72. Slope 135. Greens fee: $185* ⌒ *Facilities: Driving range, putting green, golf carts, rental clubs, pro shop, golf academy/lessons, restaurant, bar.*

Fodor's Choice ★   **Wailea.** This is the only Hawaii resort to offer three different courses: Gold, Emerald, and Old Blue. Designed by Robert Trent Jones Jr. (Gold and Emerald) and Arthur Jack Snyder (Old Blue), these courses share similar terrain, carved into the leeward slopes of Haleakala. Although the ocean does not come into play, its beauty is visible on almost every hole. ■TIP➡ Remember, putts break dramatically toward the ocean.

Jones refers to the Gold Course at Wailea (1993) as the "masculine" course. It's all trees and lava, and regarded as the hardest of the three courses. The trick here is to note even subtle changes in elevation. The par-3 8th, for example, plays from an elevated tee across a lava ravine to a large, well-bunkered green framed by palm trees, the blue sea, and tiny Molokini. The course demands strategy and careful club selection. The Emerald Course (1994) is the "feminine" layout with lots of flowers and bunkering away from greens. Although this may seem to render the bunker benign, the opposite is true. A bunker well in front of a green disguises the distance to the hole. Likewise, the Emerald's extensive flower beds are dangerous distractions because of their beauty. The Gold and Emerald share a clubhouse, practice facility, and 19th hole.

At Wailea's first course, the Old Blue Course (1971), judging elevation change is also key. Fairways and greens tend to be wider and more forgiving than on the Gold or Emerald, and run through colorful flora that includes hibiscus, wiliwili, bougainvillea, and plumeria. ⊠ *Wailea* ⊕ *www.waileagolf.com.*

Old Blue Course ⊠ *100 Wailea Golf Club Dr., Wailea* ☎ *808/875– 7450, 888/328–6284* ⊕ *www.waileagolf.com* ⚑ *18 holes. 6765 yds. Par 72. Slope 129. Greens fee: $225* ⚐ *Facilities: Driving range, putting green, golf carts, rental clubs, pro shop, golf academy/lessons, restaurant, bar.*

Gold and Emerald Courses ⊠ *100 Wailea Golf Club Dr., Wailea* ☎ *808/875–7450, 888/328–6284* ⊕ *www.waileagolf.com* ⚑ *Gold Course: 18 holes. 6653 yds. Par 72. Slope 132. Greens fee: $235. Emerald Course: 18 holes. 6407 yds. Par 72. Slope 130. Greens fee: $225.* ⚐ *Facilities: Driving range, putting green, golf carts, rental clubs, pro shop, golf academy/lessons, restaurant, bar.*

CENTRAL MAUI

Fodor's Choice ★ **The Dunes at Maui Lani.** Robin Nelson is at his minimalist best here, creating a bit of British links in the middle of the Pacific. Holes run through ancient, lightly wooded sand dunes, 5 miles inland from Kahului Harbor. Thanks to the natural humps and slopes of the dunes, Nelson had to move very little dirt and created a natural beauty. During the design phase he visited Ireland, and not so coincidentally the par-3 3rd looks a lot like the Dell at Lahinch: a white dune on the right sloping down into a deep bunker and partially obscuring the right side of the green—just one of several blind to semiblind shots here. Popular with residents, this course (1999) has won several awards including being named one of the "Five Best Kept Secret Golf Courses in America" by *Golf Digest.* ⊠ *1333 Maui Lani Pkwy., Kahului* ☎ *808/873–0422* ⊕ *www.dunesatmauilani.com* ⚑ *18 holes. 6841 yds. Par 72. Slope 136. Greens fee: $112* ⚐ *Facilities: Driving range, putting green, golf carts, rental clubs, pro shop, golf academy/lessons, restaurant, bar.*

Kahili Golf Course. The former Sandalwood Course (1991) was completely redone in 2005 by Robin Nelson and is now one of two 18-hole courses—one private (King Kamehameha) and one public (Kahili)—that make up the King Kamehameha Golf Club. Course holes run along the slopes of the West Maui Mountains, overlooking Maui's central plain, and feature panoramic ocean views of both the North and South shores. Consistent winds negate the course's shorter length. ⊠ *2500 Honoapiilani Hwy., Wailuku* ☎ *808/242–4653* ⊕ *www.kahiligolf.com* ⚑ *18 holes. 6570 yds. Par 72. Slope 124. Greens fee: $95* ⚐ *Facilities: Driving range, putting green, golf carts, rental clubs, pro shop, lessons, restaurant, bar.*

PLACES TO RELAX AFTER A ROUND

Among golf's great traditions is the so-called 19th hole. No matter how the first 18 go, the 19th is sure to offer comfort and cheer, not to mention a chilled beverage. Here's a look at some of the best.

Kapalua boasts three 19th holes with great fare and views: the **Plantation House** has a commanding view of the Plantation Course's 18th hole, the Pailolo Channel, and the island of Molokai beyond; the **Pineapple Grill** overlooks the Bay Course's 18th; and **Merriman's Kapalua** sits beside the ocean at Kapalua Bay.

At Wailea's Gold and Emerald courses, **Gannon's** overlooks the sea in a lovely garden setting and serves excellent food. The restaurant, with its elegant Red Bar, is owned and managed by famed chef Beverly Gannon of Haliimaile General Store and Joe's Bar & Grill in Wailea. Makena Golf Course's **Cafe on the Green** offers al fresco dining on the trellised veranda.

The **Kahili Restaurant**, a plantation-style clubhouse at the King Kamehameha Golf Club's Kahili Course, offers commanding views of the ocean on both sides of the island and of 10,000-foot Haleakala.

Café O'Lei at the Dunes at Maui Lani offers indoor and outdoor seating overlooking the golf course, as well as a stunning view of the West Maui Mountains. There is also a **Café O'Lei** restaurant at the Waiehu Golf Course.

And though not affiliated with elleair, golfers from this course frequent **Henry's** in the heart of Kihei.

Waiehu Golf Course. Maui's lone municipal course and undoubtedly the best bargain on the island, Waiehu is really two courses in one. The front 9, dating to 1930, feature authentic seaside links that run along Kahului Bay. The back 9, which climb up into the lower reaches of the West Maui Mountains through macadamia orchards, were designed by Arthur Jack Snyder and opened in 1963. ⊠ *200 Halewaiu Rd., Wailuku* ☎ *808/243–7400* ⊕ *www.co.maui.hi.us* ⚑ *18 holes. 6330 yds. Par 72. Slope 120. Greens fees: $55, plus $20 per cart* ☞ *Facilities: Driving range, putting green, golf carts, pull carts, rental clubs, pro shop, restaurant, bar.*

UPCOUNTRY

Pukalani Golf Course. At 1,110 feet above sea level, Pukalani (Bob E. Baldock and Robert L. Baldock, 1970) provides one of the finest vistas in all Hawaii. Holes run up, down, and across the slopes of Haleakala. The trade winds tend to come up in the late morning and afternoon. This, combined with frequent elevation change, makes club selection a test. The fairways tend to be wide, but greens are undulating and quick. ⊠ *360 Pukalani St., Pukalani* ☎ *808/572–1314* ⊕ *www.pukalanigolf. com* ⚑ *18 holes. 6962 yds. Par 72. Slope 127. Greens fee: $60* ☞ *Facilities: Driving range, putting green, golf carts, rental clubs, pro shop, restaurant, bar.*

LANAI

The island of Lanai features two championship-caliber golf courses—the **Challenge at Manele** and the **Experience at Koele**—that are rarely crowded due to the exclusivity of the island. Both courses require a ferry ride from Lahaina or Maalaea harbors on Maui.

Expeditions Ferry. Golf packages are available through Expeditions Ferry. ☎ *808/661–3756, 800/695–2624* ⊕ *www.go-lanai.com.*

For reviews of the two courses, see Chapter 11, Lanai.

HANG GLIDING AND PARAGLIDING

If you've always wanted to know what it feels like to fly, hang gliding or paragliding might be your perfect Maui adventure. You'll get open-air, bird's-eye views of the Valley Isle that you'll likely never forget. And you don't need to be a daredevil to participate.

Hang Gliding Maui. Armin Engert will take you on an instructional powered hang-gliding trip out of Hana Airport in East Maui. With more than 13,000 hours in the air and a perfect safety record, Armin flies you 1,000 feet over Maui's most beautiful coast. A 30-minute flight lesson costs $170, a 45-minute lesson costs $230, and a 60-minute lesson is $280. Snapshots of your flight from a wing-mounted camera cost an additional $40, and a 34-minute DVD of the flight is available for $80. Reservations are required. ⊠ *Hana Airport, Alalele Pl., off Hana Hwy., Hana* ☎ *808/572–6557* ⊕ *www.hangglidingmaui.com.*

Proflyght Paragliding. This is the only paragliding outfit on Maui to offer solo, tandem, and instruction at Polipoli Spring State Recreation Area. The leeward slope of Haleakala lends itself to paragliding with breathtaking scenery and air currents that increase during the day. Polipoli creates tremendous thermals that allow you to peacefully descend 3,000 feet to land. Prices are $95 to $185, with full certification available. ⊠ *Polipoli Spring State Recreation Area, Waipoli Rd., Kula* ☎ *808/874–5433* ⊕ *www.paraglidemaui.com.*

HIKING

Hikes on Maui include treks along coastal seashore, verdant rain forest, and alpine desert. Orchids, hibiscus, ginger, heliconia, and anthuriums grow wild on many trails, and exotic fruits like mountain apple, lilikoi (passion fruit), and strawberry guava provide refreshing snacks for hikers. Much of what you see in lower-altitude forests is alien, brought to Hawaii at one time or another by someone hoping to improve on nature. Plants like strawberry guava and ginger may be tasty, but they grow over native plants and have become problematic weeds.

The best hikes get you out of the imported landscaping and into the truly exotic wilderness. Hawaii possesses some of the world's rarest plants, insects, and birds. Pocket field guides are available at most grocery or drug stores and can really illuminate your walk. If you watch

Cinder cones, deposits formed around a volcanic vent, are a striking feature in Haleakala Crater.

the right branches quietly you can spot the same honeycreepers or happy-face spiders scientists have spent their lives studying.

BEST SPOTS

HALEAKALA NATIONAL PARK

Fodor'sChoice **Haleakala Crater.** Undoubtedly the best hiking on the island is at Hale-
★ akala Crater. If you're in shape, do a day hike descending from the
summit along **Keoneheehee Trail** (also known as Sliding Sands Trail)
to the crater floor. You might also consider spending several days here
amid the cinder cones, lava flows, and all that loud silence. Entering the crater is like landing on a different planet. In the early 1960s
NASA actually brought moon-suited astronauts here to practice what
it would be like to "walk on the moon." On the 30 miles of trails you
can traverse black sand and wild lava formations, follow the trail of
blooming *ahinahina* (silverswords), and witness tremendous views of
big sky and burned-red cliffs.

The best time to go into the crater is in the summer months, when
the conditions are generally more predictable. Be sure to bring layered
clothing—and plenty of warm clothes if you're staying overnight. It
may be scorching hot during the day, but it gets mighty chilly after
dark. Bring your own drinking water, as potable water is only available at the two visitor centers. Overnight visitors must get a permit
at park headquarters before entering the crater. *Moderate to difficult.
For detailed information on hikes in the crater, see Haleakala National
Park in Chapter 2, Exploring Maui.* ⊠ *Haleakala Crater Rd., Makawao*
☎ *808/572–4400* ⊕ *www.nps.gov/hale.*

OHEO GULCH

A branch of Haleakala National Park, Oheo Gulch is famous for its pools (the area is sometimes called the "Seven Sacred Pools"). Truth is, there are more than seven pools, and there's nothing sacred about them. A former owner of the Travaasa Hotel Hana started calling the area "Seven Sacred Pools" to attract the masses to sleepy old Hana. His plan worked and the name stuck, much to the chagrin of many Mauians.

The best time to visit the pools is in the morning, before the crowds and tour buses arrive. Start your day with a vigorous hike. Oheo has some fantastic trails to choose from, including our favorite, the Pipiwai Trail. When you're done, nothing could be better than going to the pools, lounging on the rocks, and cooling off in the freshwater reserves. (Keep in mind, however, that the park periodically closes the pools to swimming when the potential for flash flooding exists.)

You can find Oheo Gulch on Route 31, 10 miles past Hana town. All visitors must pay a $10 national park fee (per car, not per person), which is valid for three days and can be used at Haleakala's summit as well. Be sure to visit Haleakala National Park's Kipahulu Visitor Center, 10 miles past Hana, for information about scheduled orientations and cultural demonstrations. Note that there is no drinking water here.

Kahakai Trail. This quarter-mile hike (more like a walk) stretches between Kuloa Point and the Kipahulu campground. You'll see rugged shoreline views, and you can stop to gaze at the surging waves below. *Easy.* ⊠ *Trailhead: Kuloa Point, Hana.*

Kuloa Point Trail. A half-mile walk, this trail takes you from the Kipahulu Visitor Center down to the Pools of Oheo at Kuloa Point. On the trail you pass native trees and precontact Hawaiian sites. Don't forget to bring your swimsuit and a towel if you're planning a dip in the pools. Exercise extreme caution, as no lifeguards are on duty. Stick to the pools—don't even think about swimming in the ocean. The park periodically closes the pools when the potential for flash flooding exists. *Easy.* ⊠ *Trailhead: Kipahulu Visitor Center, Hana Hwy., Hana.*

FodorśChoice
★

Pipiwai Trail. This 2-mile trek upstream leads to the 400-foot Waimoku Falls, pounding down in all its power and glory. Following signs from the parking lot, head across the road and uphill into the forest. The trail borders a sensational gorge and passes onto a boardwalk through a mystifying forest of giant bamboo. This stomp through muddy and rocky terrain includes two stream crossings and takes around three hours to fully enjoy. Although this trail is never truly crowded, it's best done early in the morning before the tours arrive. Be sure to bring mosquito repellent. *Moderate.* ⊠ *Hana Hwy., near mile marker 42, Hana.*

POLIPOLI SPRING STATE RECREATION AREA

A hiking area with great trails for all levels—and something totally unexpected on a tropical island—is the Kula Forest Reserve at Polipoli Spring State Recreation Area in Upcountry Maui. During the Great Depression the government began a program to reforest the mountain, and soon cedar, pine, cypress, and even redwood took hold. The area, at an elevation of 6,200 feet, feels more like Vermont than Hawaii. It's cold and foggy, and often wet, but there's something about the enormity of the trees, quiet mist, and mysterious caves that makes you feel you've discovered an unspoken secret. Hikers should wear brightly colored clothing, as hunters may be in the area.

To reach the forest, take Route 37 all the way out to the far end of Kula. Then turn left at Route 377. After about ½ mile, turn right at Waipoli Road. You'll encounter switchbacks; after that the road is bad but passable. Four-wheel-drive vehicles are strongly recommended, although standard cars have been known to make it. Use your best judgment.

Boundary Trail. This 4-mile trail begins just past the Kula Forest Reserve boundary cattle guard on Polipoli Road and descends into the lower boundary southward, all the way to the ranger's cabin at the junction of the Redwood and Plum trails. Combine them and you've got a hearty 5-mile day hike. The trail crosses many scenic gulches, with an overhead of tall eucalyptus, pine, cedar, and plum trees. Peep through the trees for wide views of Kula and Central Maui. *Moderate.* ⊠ *Trailhead: Polipoli Campground, Polipoli Rd., Kula.*

Redwood Trail. This colorful hike winds through redwoods and conifers past the short Tie Trail down to the old ranger's cabin. Although the views are limited, groves of trees and flowering bushes abound. At the end of the trail is an old cabin site and three-way junction with the Plum Trail and the Boundary Trail. *Easy.* ⊠ *Trailhead: Near Polipoli Campground, Polipoli Rd., Kula.*

Fodor's Choice
★

IAO VALLEY STATE MONUMENT

In Hawaiian, *Iao* means "supreme cloud." When you enter this mystical valley in the middle of an unexpected rain forest near Wailuku in West Maui, you'll know why. At 750 feet above sea level, the 10-mile valley clings to the clouds as if it's trying to cover its naked beauty. One of Maui's great wonders, the valley is the site of a famous battle to unite the Hawaiian Islands. Out of the clouds, the **Iao Needle,** a tall chunk of volcanic rock, stands as a monument to the long-ago lookout for Maui warriors. Today, there's nothing warlike about it: the valley is a peaceful land of lush, tropical plants, clear pools and a running stream, and easy, enjoyable strolls.

To get to Iao Valley State Monument, head to the western end of Route 32. The road dead-ends into the parking lot ($5 per car). The park is open daily 7 am to 7 pm. Facilities are available, but there is no drinking water.

Iao Valley Trail. Anyone (including your grandparents) can handle this short walk from the parking lot at Iao Valley State Monument. On your choice of two paved walkways, you can cross the Iao Stream and

Continued on page 154

HAWAII'S PLANTS 101

Hawaii is a bounty of rainbow-colored flowers and plants. The evening air is scented with their fragrance. Just look at the front yard of almost any home, travel any road, or visit any local park and you'll see a spectacular array of colored blossoms and leaves. What most visitors don't know is that many of the plants they are seeing are not native to Hawaii; rather, they were introduced during the last two centuries as ornamental plants, or for timber, shade, or fruit.

Hawaii boasts nearly every climate on the planet, excluding the two most extreme: arctic tundra and arid desert. The Islands have wine-growing regions, cactus-speckled ranchlands, icy mountaintops, and the rainiest forests on earth.

Plants introduced from around the world thrive here. The lush lowland valleys along the windward coasts are predominantly populated by non-native trees including yellow- and red-fruited **guava**, silvery-leafed **kukui**, and orange-flowered **tulip trees**.

The colorful **plumeria flower**, very fragrant and commonly used in lei making, and

the giant multicolored **hibiscus flower** are both used by many women as hair adornments, and are two of the most common plants found around homes and hotels. The umbrella-like **monkeypod tree** from Central America provides shade in many of Hawaii's parks including Kapiolani Park in Honolulu. Hawaii's largest tree, found in Lahaina, Maui, is a giant **banyan tree.** Its canopy and massive support roots cover about two-thirds of an acre. The native **ohia tree**, with its brilliant red brush-like flowers, and the **hapuu**, a giant tree fern, are common in Hawaii's forests and are also used ornamentally in gardens.

Bougainvillea

Guava

Monkeypod

Banyan

Ohia Lehua*

Tulip Tree

Plumeria

Pandanus

Hibiscus

Anthurium

Kukui

Hapuu

*endemic to Hawaii

5

IN FOCUS HAWAII'S PLANTS 101

DID YOU KNOW?

More than 2,200 plant species are found in the Hawaiian Islands, but only about 1,000 are native. Of these, 270 are so rare, they are endangered. Hawaii's endemic plants evolved from ancestral seeds arriving in the Islands over thousands of years as baggage with birds, floating on ocean currents, or drifting on winds from continents thousands of miles away. Once here, these plants evolved in isolation, creating many new species known nowhere else in the world.

Sunrise on top of Haleakala can be memorable; start early and wear warm clothing.

explore the junglelike area. Ascend the stairs up to the Iao Needle for spectacular views of Central Maui. Be sure to stop at the lovely Kepaniwai Heritage Gardens, which commemorate the cultural contributions of various immigrant groups. *Easy.* ⊠ *Trailhead: Iao Valley State Monument parking lot, Rte. 32, Wailuku.*

HIKES ON THE SOUTH SHORE AND WEST MAUI

In addition to the trails listed below, the Kapalua Resort offers free access to 100 miles of self-guided hiking trails. Trail information and maps are available at the Kapalua Adventure Center.

Hoapili Trail. A challenging hike through eye-popping scenery in southwestern Maui is this 5.5-mile coastal trail beyond the Ahihi-Kinau Natural Area Reserve. Named after a bygone king, it follows the shoreline, threading through the remains of ancient villages. King Hoapili created an island-wide road, and this wide path of stacked lava rocks is a marvel to look at and walk on. (It's not the easiest surface for the ankles and feet, so wear sturdy shoes.) This is brutal territory with little shade and no facilities, and extra water is a must. To get here, follow Makena Road to La Pérouse Bay. The trail can be a challenge to find—walk south along the ocean through the kiawe trees, where you'll encounter numerous wild goats (don't worry—they're tame), and past a scenic little bay. The trail begins just around the corner to the left. *Difficult.* ⊠ *Trailhead: La Pérouse Bay, Makena Rd., Makena.*

Kapalua Resort. The resort offers free access to 100 miles of hiking trails to guests and visitors as a self-guided experience. Trail information and maps are available at the Kapalua Adventure Center. Access to most trails is via a complimentary resort shuttle, which must be reserved

TIPS FOR DAY HIKES

Hiking is a perfect way to see Maui. Just wear sturdy shoes to spare your ankles from a crash course in loose lava rock. At upper elevations the weather is guaranteed to be extreme—alternately chilly or blazing—so layers are good.

When hiking near streams or waterfalls, be cautious: Flash floods can occur at any time. Don't drink stream water or swim in streams if you have open cuts; bacteria and parasites are not the souvenir you want to take home with you.

Here's a checklist for what to take for a great hike.

■ Water (at least two quarts per person; drink even if you're not thirsty)

■ Food—fruit, trail mix, and lunch

■ Rain gear—especially if going into the crater

■ Sturdy hiking shoes

■ Layered clothing

■ Wide-brimmed hat and sunglasses

■ Sunscreen (SPF 30 or higher recommended)

■ Mosquito repellent (a must around waterfalls and pools)

in advance. Guided hiking tours are also available. ⊠ *2000 Village Rd., corner of Office Rd., Kapalua* ☎ *808/665–4386, 877/665–4386* ⊕ *www.kapalua.com.*

Waihee Ridge. This moderately strenuous 4¾-mile hike in West Maui offers a generous reward at the top: breathtaking panoramic views of the windward coast and the ridges that rise inland, as well as Mt. Lanilili, Puu Kukui, Eke Crater, and the remote village of Kahakuloa. A picnic table enables you to enjoy a comfortable lunch. In rainy conditions the trail can quickly turn into a muddy, slippery affair. To get here from Highway 340, turn left across the highway from Mendes Ranch and drive ¾ mile up a partially paved road to the signed trailhead. *Moderate.* ⊠ *Trailhead: Opposite Mendes Ranch, Hwy. 340, Wailuku.*

GOING WITH A GUIDE

Guided hikes can help you see more than you might on your own. If the company is driving you to the site, be sure to ask about drive times; they can be fairly lengthy for some hikes.

Fodor'sChoice ★ **Friends of Haleakala National Park.** This nonprofit offers day and overnight trips into the volcanic crater. The purpose of your trip, the service work itself, isn't too much—mostly native planting, removing invasive plants, and light cabin maintenance. An interpretive park ranger accompanies each trip, taking you to places you'd otherwise miss and teaching you about the native flora and fauna. ☎ *808/876–1673* ⊕ *www.fhnp.org.*

Fodor'sChoice ★ **Hike Maui.** Started in 1983, the area's oldest hiking company remains extremely well regarded for waterfall, rain forest, and crater hikes led by enthusiastic, highly trained guides who weave botany, geology,

These horses on the less-developed North Shore seem to be taking in the ocean view.

ethnobotany, culture, and history into the outdoor experience. Prices range from $80 to $170 for excursions lasting 3 to 11 hours (discounts for booking online). Hike Maui supplies day packs, rain gear, mosquito repellent, first-aid supplies, bottled water, snacks, lunch for the longer trips, and transportation to and from the site. Hotel transfers are available for most hikes (extra fee may apply). ⊠ *285 Hukilike St., Unit B-104, Kahului* ☎ *808/879–5270, 866/324–6284* ⊕ *www.hikemaui.com.*

Kipahulu Ohana. Native Hawaiian guides from this nonprofit organization lead cultural interpretive hikes and taro patch tours at Kipahulu near Hana through a cooperative agreement with Haleakala National Park. The two-hour hike ($49) takes you to scenic overlooks and past remnants from the sugarcane industry, culminating at an ancient taro farm that has been restored to active production. A three-hour hike ($79) includes a side trip to 400-foot Waimoku Falls. You can park at Kipahulu Visitor Center ($10 per car) and meet your guide at the Hale Kuai, the traditional thatched house near the center. ⊠ *Hana* ☎ *808/248–8558* ⊕ *www.kipahulu.org.*

Sierra Club. One great avenue into the island's untrammeled wilderness is Maui's chapter of the Sierra Club. Join one of the club's hikes into pristine forests, along ancient coastal paths, to historic sites, and to Haleakala Crater. Some outings require volunteer service, but most are just for fun. Bring your own food and water, rain gear, sunscreen, sturdy shoes, and a suggested donation of $5 for hikers over age 14. This is a true bargain. ☎ *808/573–4147* ⊕ *www.hi.sierraclub.org/maui.*

COWBOY FUN: RODEOS AND POLO

Paniolos (Hawaiian cowboys) show off their skills at three major annual events: the **Piiholo Cowboy Classic** in September; the **Oskie Rice Memorial Rodeo** in December; and Maui's biggest event, the **4th of July Rodeo**, which comes with a full parade in Makawao town and festivities that last for days.

Polo is popular with the Upcountry paniolos. From April through June, Haleakala Ranch hosts "indoor" or arena contests on a field flanked by side boards. The field is on Route 377, 1 mile from Route 37. During the "outdoor" polo season, September to mid-November, matches are held at Olinda Field, 1 mile above Makawao on Olinda Road. There's a $5 admission for most games, which start at 1:30 pm on Sunday.

Manduke Baldwin Memorial Tournament. Held over Memorial Day weekend, the Manduke Baldwin Memorial Tournament is a popular two-day polo event. It draws challengers from Argentina, England, South Africa, New Zealand, and Australia. ☎ 808/877-7744 ⊕ www.mauipoloclub.com.

HORSEBACK RIDING

Several companies on Maui offer horseback riding that's far more appealing than the typical hour-long trudge over a dull trail with 50 other horses.

GOING WITH A GUIDE

Fodor's Choice ★ **Maui Stables.** Hawaiian-owned and operated, this company provides a trip back in time to an era when life moved more slowly and reverently. Tours begin at the stable in remote Kipahulu and pass through several historic Hawaiian sites. Before heading up into the forest, your guide intones the words to a traditional oli, or chant, asking for permission to enter. Along the way, you can learn about the principles of Hawaiian culture, including a deep respect for the aina (land). By the time you reach the mountain pasture overlooking several waterfalls, including the 400-foot Waimoku Falls, you'll feel lucky to have been a part of the tradition. Rides begin at 9:45 am daily and cost $160 per rider—definitely well worth it. Maui Stables provides refreshments and bottled water only; bring a picnic lunch if you're a hearty eater. ⊠ Hwy. 37, between mile markers 40 and 41, Hana ☎ 808/248-7799 ⊕ www.mauistables.com.

Mendes Ranch. Family-owned and run, Mendes operates out of the beautiful ranchland of Kahakuloa on the windward slopes of the West Maui Mountains. Two-hour morning and afternoon trail rides ($99) are available. Cowboys take you cantering up rolling pastures into the lush rain forest, and then you'll descend all the way down to the ocean for a photo op with a dramatic backdrop. Don't expect a Hawaiian cultural experience here—it's all about the horses and the ride. Skip the optional barbecue lunch ($20); you'll do better in town. ⊠ 3530 Kahekili Hwy., Wailuku ☎ 808/244-7320, 800/871-5222 ⊕ www.mendesranch.com.

Piiholo Ranch. The local wranglers here lead you on a rousing ride through family ranchlands—up hillside pastures, beneath a eucalyptus canopy, and past many native trees. One-hour rides ($75) and two-hour rides ($120) are offered twice daily. Their well-groomed horses navigate the challenging terrain easily, but hold on when axis deer pass by! You must be at least eight years old and in good physical condition to participate. Small groups (no more than six riders) make it a more personal experience. ⊠ *End of Waiahiwi Rd., Makawao* ☎ *808/270-8750* ⊕ *www.piiholo.com.*

Pony Express Tours. This outfit offers horseback journeys into Haleakala Crater. The half-day ride, which descends into the crater floor for a picnic lunch, is a great way to experience the majesty of the volcano without having to hike. Prior riding experience is highly recommended, as you're on horseback for at least 4 hours. The company also offers 1½- and 2-hour rides on the slopes of the Haleakala Ranch. Prices range from $95 to $182. ⊠ *Kula* ☎ *808/667–2200* ⊕ *www. ponyexpresstours.com.*

TENNIS

Most courts charge by the hour but will let players continue after their initial hour for free, provided no one is waiting. Many hotels and condos charge a fee for nonguests.

BEST SPOTS

Kapalua Tennis Garden. Home to the Kapalua Tennis Club, this complex has 10 courts (four lighted for night play) and a pro shop. The fee is $10 per person per day. Each month the Kapalua Tennis Garden plays host to a special theme tournament for resort guests and residents. ⊠ *Kapalua Resort, 100 Kapalua Dr., Kapalua* ☎ *808/662–7730* ⊕ *www.kapalua.com.*

Lahaina Civic Center. The best free courts are the nine at the Lahaina Civic Center, near Wahikuli State Park. They all have overhead lighting for night play, and are available on a first-come, first-served basis. ⊠ *1840 Honoapiilani Hwy., Lahaina* ☎ *808/661–4685.*

Makena Tennis Club. This club features six Plexipave courts, two of which are lighted for night play. Private lessons, ball machines, racquet stringing, and daily clinics are available. Rates are $35 per hour. ⊠ *5415 Makena Alanui Dr., Makena* ☎ *808/891–4050* ⊕ *www. makenagolf.com.*

Wailea Tennis Club. Featuring 11 Plexipave courts (two lighted for night play), this club also offers lessons, rentals, and ball machines. Daily clinics help you improve ground strokes, serve, volley, or doubles strategy. The daily court fee, which guarantees one hour of reserved time for singles and 1.5 hours for doubles, is $15 per player. ⊠ *131 Wailea Ike Pl., Wailea* ☎ *808/879–1958* ⊕ *www.waileatennis.com.*

ZIPLINE TOURS

Ziplining on one of Maui's several courses lets you satisfy your inner Tarzan by soaring high above deep gulches and canyons—for a price that can seem steep. A harness keeps you fully supported on each ride. Each course has its own age minimums and weight restrictions but, generally, you must be at least 10 years old and weigh a minimum of 60–80 pounds and a maximum of 250–275 pounds. You should wear closed-toe athletic-type shoes and expect to get dirty. ■ TIP→ Reconsider this activity if you are pregnant, uncomfortable with heights, or have serious back or joint problems.

Fodor'sChoice ★ **Flyin' Hawaiian Zipline.** These guys have the longest line in the state (a staggering 3,600 feet), as well as the most unique course layout. You build confidence on the first line, then board a four-wheel-drive vehicle that takes you 1,500 feet above the town of Waikapu to seven more lines that carry you over 11 ridges and nine valleys. The total distance covered is more than 2½ miles, and the views are astonishing. The price of $185 includes water and snacks. You must be able to hike over steep, sometimes slippery terrain while carrying a 10-pound metal trolley. ⊠ *Waikapu* ☎ *808/463–5786* ⊕ *www.flyinhawaiianzipline.com.*

Fodor'sChoice ★ **Piiholo Ranch Zipline.** This complex, on a gorgeous 900-acre family ranch, has six ziplines—five parallel lines and one quadruple—plus a 12-person climbing tower. Access to the fifth and longest line is via a four-wheel-drive vehicle to the top of Piiholo Hill, where you are treated to stunning bicoastal views. Guides do a good job of weaving Hawaiian culture into the adventure. You must be able to climb three steep suspension bridges while hefting a 12-pound trolley over your shoulder. Prices range from $140 for four lines to $190 for five. The canopy tour keeps you in the trees the entire time ($90 to $165). Bring a lightweight jacket. ⊠ *Piiholo Rd., Makawao* ☎ *800/374-7050* ⊕ *www.piiholozipline.com.*

Skyline Eco Adventures. The first company to open a zipline course in the United States, Skyline operates in two locations on Maui: the original course on the slope of Haleakala (five lines ranging from 50 to 720 feet) and the newer venue at 1,000 feet above Kaanapali (eight lines ranging from 50 to 1,000 feet). Guides have you "zipping" confidently in no time. Dress in layers for the $95 Haleakala tour, as it can get chilly. The $150 Kaanapali tour includes breakfast or lunch. Advance reservations are suggested, and discounts are available for online bookings. ☎ *808/878–8400* ⊕ *www.zipline.com.*

6

SHOPS AND SPAS

Updated by
Eliza Escaño-
Vasquez

We hope you've saved room in your suitcase. With the help of our shopping guide, you can find the top shops for everything "Maui grown," from *lilikoi* (passion fruit) jams and fresh pineapples to koa wood bowls and swimwear. Style hunters can get their fill of bohemian-resort chic in Paia, luxury brands in Wailea, and *paniolo* (cowboy) threads in Upcountry's quiet Makawao town.

If you're seeking authentic Hawaiian artistry, check out handcrafted Mele Ukulele, Randy Jay Braun photography, and Maui Divers' jewelry designs. Splurge on an heirloom Niihau shell lei found in art galleries around the island or score some pretty puka charms from the Maui Swap Meet in Kahului. Maxed out on your luggage weight? No problem. There's Hello Makana, a subscription service that curates food and gift items from quality local artisans and ships to your doorstep. While the cost of basic goods might be higher on the Islands, keep in mind that the state has a much lower sales tax (4%) than the mainland.

Before packing up your plunder, conjure up some Zen by soaking in Maui's natural resources. Rejuvenate in a yoga class, then enter one of the island's world-class spas to unwind. Among the best are the Waihua Spa at the Ritz-Carlton in Kapalua, the Grand Wailea Resort's Spa Grande, and the Four Seasons Resort's spa in Wailea. Most treatments are infused with ingredients indigenous to the Valley Isle, like *kukui* nut, coconut, ginger, and eucalyptus. With coveted beauty lines like Eminence or Epicuren sharing the shelves with locally made Ola Hawaii, you're bound to find a spa product or two to bring home.

SHOPS

Whether you're searching for a dashboard hula dancer or an original Curtis Wilson Cost painting, you can find it on Front Street in Lahaina or at the Shops at Wailea. Art sales are huge in the resort areas, where artists regularly show up to promote their work. Alongside the flashy galleries are standards like Quicksilver and ABC store, where you can stock up on swim trunks, sunscreen, and flip-flops.

Beyond Lahaina and Wailea, don't miss the great boutiques lining the streets of small towns like Paia and Makawao. You can purchase boutique fashions and art while strolling through these charming, quieter communities. Notably, several local designers—Tamara Catz, Letarte, and Maui Girl—all produce top-quality island fashions. In neighboring galleries, local artisans turn out gorgeous work in a range of prices. Special souvenirs include rare hardwood bowls and boxes, prints of sea life, Hawaiian quilts, and blown glass.

Specialty food products—pineapples, coconuts, or Maui onions—and "Made in Maui" jams and jellies make great, less expensive souvenirs. Cook Kwee's Maui Cookies have gained a following, as have Maui Potato Chips. Coffee sellers now offer Maui-grown-and-roasted beans alongside the better-known Kona varieties. Remember that fresh fruit must be inspected by the U.S. Department of Agriculture before it can leave the state, so it's safest to buy a box that has already passed inspection.

Business hours for individual shops on the island are usually 9 to 5, seven days a week. Shops on Front Street and in shopping centers tend to stay open later (until 9 or 10 on weekends).

6

WEST MAUI

One of Maui's top resort areas, West Maui supports abundant shopping options both cheap and high-end, from weekend crafts fairs under Lahaina's historical banyan tree to golf apparel at Kapalua and the art galleries on Front Street. Souvenir tchotchkes can be found in local swap meets, and Hawaiian confectionery items are available in most grocery stores.

SHOPPING CENTERS

Lahaina Cannery Mall. This building, reminiscent of an old pineapple cannery, houses 50 shops. The mall hosts fabulous free events year-round like the Keiki Hula Festival and an annual ice-sculpting competition. Free ukulele lessons are available on Tuesday afternoons. Recommended stops include Na Hoku, purveyor of striking Hawaiian heirloom-quality jewelry and pearls, and Banana Wind, which carries island-inspired home decor. Whether you're searching for surf and skate threads or tropical resortwear, Crazy Shirt, Hawaiian Island Creations, Serendipity, and other retailers will give you ample selections. ⊠ *1221 Honoapiilani Hwy., Lahaina* ☎ *808/661–5304* ⊕ *www.lahainacannerymall.com.*

Lahaina Gateway. Besides reliable restaurants like Italian Delight and 100 Wines, this plaza includes Barnes & Noble, Maui Dive Shop, Lahaina Farms (a gourmet grocery store), and other stores featuring sporting goods and trendy apparel. ⊠ *305 Keawe St., Lahaina* ☎ *808/877–7073* ⊕ *www.lahainagateway.com.*

Fodor'sChoice
★
Whalers Village. Chic Whalers Village has a whaling museum and more than 50 restaurants and shops. Upscale haunts include Louis Vuitton and Coach, and beautyphiles can get their fix at Sephora. Peruse

some elegant koa home accessories and other local gifts at Martin and MacArthur. The complex also offers some interesting diversions: Hawaiian artisans display their crafts daily; hula dancers perform on an outdoor stage some nights from 7 to 8 pm; sunset jazz is featured every first Sunday of the month; and Polynesian rhythms resound on Saturday. If you find yourself there on the first Saturday of May, the Maui Onion Festival is a fun foodie event. ⊠ *2435 Kaanapali Pkwy., Kaanapali* ☎ *808/661–4567* ⊕ *www.whalersvillage.com.*

BOOKSTORES

Fodor's Choice ★   **Maui Friends of the Library Used Book Store.** Behind the Wharf Cinema Center, this shop lets you spend a few minutes (or hours) browsing shelves filled with mystery, sci-fi, fiction, military history, and "oddball" volumes. There's a nice section reserved for new Hawaiiana books. Finished with your vacation reading? You can donate it to benefit the island's public libraries. ⊠ *658 Front St., Lahaina* ☎ *808/667–2696* ⊕ *www.mfol.org.*

CLOTHING

Hilo Hattie Fashion Center. Hawaii's largest manufacturer of aloha shirts also carries brightly colored blouses, skirts, and children's clothing, along with gift items such as soaps and lotions. ⊠ *Lahaina Center, 900 Front St., Lahaina* ☎ *808/667–7911* ⊕ *www.hilohattie.com.*

Honolua Surf Company. If you're not in the mood for an aloha shirt, check out this surf shop—popular with young men and women for surf trunks, casual clothing, and accessories. ⊠ *845 Front St., Lahaina* ☎ *808/661–8848* ⊕ *www.honoluasurf.com.*

Hula Gypsy. This store is covered from top to bottom with delicate knits and white lace, both vintage and new. The style is less Victorian and more beachy bohemian. Prices range from $10 for a lace cape to $200 for the perfect beach wedding dress. Anna Jackson, the store's owner, scouts past collections from Free People and Anthropologie, and enlists her globe-trotting friends as unofficial buyers. ⊠ *505 Front St. Ste. 204A, Lahaina* ☎ *808/280–9914.*

Maggie Coulombe. This local designer's day-to-evening pieces add glam to resort wear. The printed silk caftans and kimono-style tunics are worth a look. ⊠ *2435 Kaanapali Pkwy., Lahaina* ☎ *808/344–6672* ⊕ *www.maggiecoulombe.com.*

Mahina. At this boutique you can work the latest styles without breaking the bank. A friendly staff, easy-breezy dresses, resort-perfect rompers

---

BEST MADE-ON-MAUI GIFTS

- *Koa* jewelry boxes from **Maui Hands.**

- Sushi platters and bamboo chopsticks from the **Maui Crafts Guild.**

- Black pearl pendant from **Maui Divers.**

- Handmade Hawaiian quilt from **Hana Coast Gallery.**

- Jellyfish paperweight from **Hot Island Glass.**

- Ukulele from **Mele Ukulele.**

- Hawaiian spice blends from **Volcano Spice Co.**

- Plumeria lei, made by you!

and loads of accessories await the smart shopper. There are branches in Kihei and Paia. ⊠ *335 Keawe St., Lahaina* ☎ *808/661–0383* ⊕ *www. mahinamaui.com.*

Maui Vintage. This vibrant clothing store champions locally made products from vintage aloha wear to embroidered hats. Owner Roy Wemyss personally makes earth-friendly Kula Herbs Excellent Soap, which he infuses with local flowers, herbs, and even red clay. The soaps are used in local resorts and spas. ⊠ *136 Dickenson St., Lahaina* ☎ *808/661– 0550* ⊕ *www.mauivintage.com.*

FLEA MARKETS

Lahaina Civic Center Craft Fair. An eclectic mix of vendors and artists set up shop here, offering the whole gamut of souvenir shopping, from towels to aloha prints. ⊠ *1840 Honoapiilani Hwy., Lahaina* ☒ *$1 suggested donation* ⊙ *Most Sun. 9–4.*

FOOD

Lahaina Square Shopping Center Foodland. This Foodland serves West Maui and is open daily from 6 am to midnight. ⊠ *878 Front St., Lahaina* ☎ *808/661–0975.*

Safeway. The chain has three stores on the island open 24 hours daily. ⊠ *Lahaina Cannery Mall, 1221 Honoapiilani Hwy., Lahaina* ☎ *808/667–4392.*

Take Home Maui. The folks at this colorful grocery and deli in West Maui will supply, pack, and deliver produce to the airport or your hotel. They can even ship the produce straight from the farm to your door. ⊠ *121 Dickenson St., Lahaina* ☎ *808/661–8067* ⊕ *www.takehomemaui.com.*

GALLERIES

Lahaina Galleries. Works of both national and international artists are displayed at this well-regarded gallery. Besides the space in Lahaina, there's a second location in the Shops at Wailea. Prices start at over $2,000 for originals. ⊠ *828 Front St., Lahaina* ☎ *808/661–6284* ⊕ *www.lahainagalleries.com.*

Lahaina Printsellers Ltd. Hawaii's largest selection of original antique maps and prints pertaining to Hawaii and the Pacific is available here. You can also buy museum-quality reproductions. ⊠ *Whalers Village, 2435 Kaanapali Pkwy., Kaanapali* ☎ *808/667–7617* ⊕ *www.printsellers.com.*

Fodor's Choice
★
Martin Lawrence Galleries. In business since 1975, Martin Lawrence displays the works of such world-renowned artists as Picasso, Erté, and Chagall in a bright and friendly gallery. Modern and pop-art enthusiasts will also find pieces by Miró, Haring, Warhol, and Japanese icon Takashi Murakami. ⊠ *Lahaina Market Place, 790 Front St., at Lahainaluna Rd., Lahaina* ☎ *808/661–1788* ⊕ *www.martinlawrence.com.*

Village Gallery. This gallery houses the landscape paintings of popular local artists Betty Hay Freeland, George Allan, Joseph Fletcher, Pamela Andelin, Fred KenKnight, and Macario Pascual. There's a second location in Kapalua at the Ritz-Carlton. ⊠ *120 Dickenson St., Lahaina* ☎ *808/661–4402* ⊕ *www.villagegalleriesmaui.com.*

Wyland Galleries. Robert Wyland is a globally celebrated artist known for his gigantic murals of whales, dolphins, and other marine life. Enjoy his artwork—along with some from other fine artists—at his namesake gallery in Lahaina. ✉ *711 Front St., Lahaina* ☎ *808/667–2285* ⊕ *www. wyland.com.*

HOME FURNISHINGS

Hale Zen. If you're shopping for gifts in West Maui, don't miss this store packed with beautiful island-inspired pieces for the home. Most of the teak furniture is imported from Bali, but local purveyors supply the inventory of clothing, accessories, beauty products, kitchenware, and food. ✉ *180 Dickenson St., Suite 111, Lahaina* ☎ *808/661–4802.*

JEWELRY

Jessica's Gems. Specializing in black pearls, Jessica's also has a good selection of Hawaiian heirloom jewelry and locally made sterling silver, including custom designs by David Welty, Dave Haake, and Cici Maui Designs. ✉ *Whalers Village, 2435 Kaanapali Pkwy., Kaanapali* ☎ *808/661–4223* ⊕ *www.jessicagemsmaui.com.*

Lahaina Scrimshaw. Here you can buy brooches, rings, pendants, cuff links, tie tacks, and collector's items adorned with intricately carved sailors' art. The store sells a few antiques, but most pieces are modern creations. ✉ *845A Front St., Lahaina* ☎ *808/661–8820* ⊕ *www. lahainascrimshawmaui.com* ✉ *Whalers Village, 2435 Kaanapali Pkwy., Kaanapali* ☎ *808/661–4034.*

Maui Divers. This company has been crafting pearls, coral, and traditional gemstones into jewelry for more than 50 years. ✉ *640 Front St., Lahaina* ☎ *808/661–0988* ⊕ *www.mauidivers.com.*

CENTRAL MAUI

Locals come here in droves for their monthly Costco run or to catch the latest flick at Queen Kaahumanu Center, but Central Maui can also be an ideal shopping destination for visiting families who are passing time on their way to or from the airport. Most of the stores here can be found on the mainland; however, some specialty shops are worth a peek for Hawaiiana or water-sports goods.

SHOPPING CENTERS

Maui Mall. Longs Drugs anchors the mall, which also has a Whole Foods where you can put together a great picnic lunch. There's a decent Chinese restaurant, Dragon Dragon, and the cult fave Tasaka Guri Guri Shop—it's been around for nearly a hundred years, selling an ice-cream–like confection called "guri guri." The mall also has a whimsically designed 12-screen megaplex. ✉ *70 E. Kaahumanu Ave., Kahului* ☎ *808/877–8952* ⊕ *www.mauimall.com.*

Maui Marketplace. On the busy stretch of Dairy Road, this behemoth mall near Kahului Airport couldn't be more conveniently located. The 20-acre complex houses several outlet stores and big retailers, such as Pier One Imports, Sports Authority, and Old Navy. Sample local and ethnic cuisines at the Kau Kau Corner food court. ✉ *270 Dairy Rd., Kahului* ☎ *808/873–0400.*

Continued on page 170

ALL ABOUT LEI

Lei brighten every occasion in Hawaii, from birthdays to bar mitzvahs to baptisms. Creative artisans weave nature's bounty—flowers, ferns, vines, and seeds—into gorgeous creations that convey an array of heartfelt messages: "Welcome," "Congratulations," "Good luck," "Farewell," "Thank you," "I love you." When it's difficult to find the right words, a lei expresses exactly the right sentiment.

WHERE TO BUY THE BEST LEI

These florists carry a nice variety of lei: **A Special Touch** (Emerald Plaza, 142 Kupuohi St., Ste. F-1, Lahaina, 808/661-3455); **Kahului Florist** (Maui Mall, 70 E. Kaahumanu Ave., Kahului, 808/877-3951); **Napili Florist** (5059 Napilihau St., Lahaina, 808/669-4861); and **Kihei-Wailea Flowers by Cora** (1280 S. Kihei Rd., Ste. 126, Kihei, 808/879-7249 or 800/339-0419). **Costco**, **Kmart**, **Wal-Mart**, and **Safeway** sell basic lei, such as orchid and plumeria.

LEI ETIQUETTE

■ To wear a closed lei, drape it over your shoulders, half in front and half in back. Open lei are worn around the neck, with the ends draped over the front in equal lengths.

■ Pikake, ginger, and other sweet, delicate blossoms are "feminine" lei. Men opt for cigar, crown flower, and ti leaf, which are sturdier and don't emit as much fragrance.

■ Lei are always presented with a kiss, a custom that supposedly dates back to World War II when a hula dancer fancied an officer at a U.S.O. show. Taking a dare from members of her troupe, she took off her lei, placed it around his neck, and kissed him on the cheek.

■ You shouldn't wear a lei before you give it to someone else. Hawaiians believe the lei absorbs your *mana* (spirit); if you give your lei away, you'll be giving away part of your essence.

ORCHID

Growing wild on every continent except Antarctica, orchids—which range in color from yellow to green to purple—comprise the largest family of plants in the world. There are more than 20,000 species of orchids, but only three are native to Hawaii—and they are very rare. The pretty lavender vanda you see hanging by the dozens at local lei stands has probably been imported from Thailand.

MAILE

Maile, an endemic twining vine with a heady aroma, is sacred to Laka, goddess of the hula. In ancient times, dancers wore maile and decorated hula altars with it to honor Laka. Today, "open" maile lei usually are given to men. Instead of ribbon, interwoven lengths of maile are used at dedications of new businesses. The maile is untied, never snipped, for doing so would symbolically "cut" the company's success.

ILIMA

Designated by Hawaii's Territorial Legislature in 1923 as the official flower of the island of Oahu, the golden ilima is so delicate it lasts for just a day. Five to seven hundred blossoms are needed to make one garland. Queen Emma, wife of King Kamehameha IV, preferred ilima over all other lei, which may have led to the incorrect belief that they were reserved only for royalty.

PLUMERIA

This ubiquitous flower is named after Charles Plumier, the noted French botanist who discovered it in Central America in the late 1600s. Plumeria ranks among the most popular lei in Hawaii because it's fragrant, hardy, plentiful, inexpensive, and requires very little care. Although yellow is the most common color, you'll also find plumeria lei in shades of pink, red, orange, and "rainbow" blends.

PIKAKE

Favored for its fragile beauty and sweet scent, pikake was introduced from India. In lieu of pearls, many brides in Hawaii adorn themselves with long, multiple strands of white pikake. Princess Kaiulani enjoyed showing guests her beloved pikake and peacocks at Ainahau, her Waikiki home. Interestingly, pikake is the Hawaiian word for both the bird and the blossom.

KUKUI

The kukui (candlenut) is Hawaii's state tree. Early Hawaiians strung kukui nuts (which are quite oily) together and burned them for light; mixed burned nuts with oil to make an indelible dye; and mashed roasted nuts to consume as a laxative. Kukui nut lei may not have been made until after Western contact, when the Hawaiians saw black beads from Europe and wanted to imitate them.

Queen Kaahumanu Center. Maui's largest mall has 75 stores, a movie theater, and a food court. The mall's interesting rooftop, composed of a series of manta ray–like umbrella shades, is easily spotted. Stop at Camellia Seeds for what locals call "crack seed," a snack made from dried fruits, nuts, and lots of sugar. Other stops include mall standards such as Macy's, Pacific Sunwear, and American Eagle Outfitters. ⊠ *275 W. Kaahumanu Ave., Kahului* ☎ *808/877–3369* ⊕ *www.queenkaahumanucenter.com.*

ARTS AND CRAFTS

Mele Ukulele. For those looking for a professional quality, authentically Maui ukulele, skip the souvenir shops. Mele's handcrafted beauties are made of koa or mahogany and strung and finished by the store's owner, Michael Rock. ⊠ *1750 Kaahumanu Ave., Wailuku* ☎ *808/244–3938* ⊕ *www.meleukulele.com.*

CLOTHING

Bohemia. Find upscale designer resale *and* new pieces by local designers, all at affordable prices at this consignment store. ⊠ *105 N. Market St., Wailuku* ☎ *808/244–9995.*

Hi-Tech. Stop here immediately after deplaning to stock up on surf trunks, windsurfing gear, bikinis, and sundresses. ⊠ *425 Koloa St., Kahului* ☎ *808/877–2111* ⊕ *www.surfmaui.com.*

FLEA MARKETS

Maui Swap Meet. Crafts, souvenirs, fruit, shells, and more make this flea market in a college parking lot the island's biggest bargain. ⊠ *Off Kahului Beach Rd., Kahului* ☎ *808/244–3100* ⊕ *www.mauiexposition. com* ⊴ *50¢* ☉ *Sat. 7 am–1 pm.*

FOOD

Maui Coffee Roasters. The best stop for Kona and island coffees on Maui is this café and roasting house near Kahului Airport. Salespeople give good advice and will ship items, and you even get a free cup of joe in a signature to-go cup when you buy a pound of coffee. ⊠ *444 Hana Hwy., Kahului* ☎ *808/877–2877* ⊕ *www.mauicoffeeroasters.com.*

Safeway. If you're coming from the airport, this grocery store (one of three on the island) may be a useful stop. It's open 24 hours daily. ⊠ *170 E. Kamehameha Ave., Kahului* ☎ *808/877–3377.*

SOUTH SHORE

The South Shore resort area is best known for expensive designer shopping, but you can find some cheaper, more local options. Browse ornate beaded accessories while listening to island rhythms at Kihei Kalama Village Marketplace, or splurge on high-end labels at the Shops at Wailea. Otherwise, stumble upon a strip mall—or seven—to fulfill your gifting needs.

SHOPPING CENTERS

Azeka Place Shopping Center. Azeka II, on the *mauka* (toward the mountains) side of South Kihei Road, has the Coffee Store (a great place for iced mochas) and the Nail Shop (for shaping, waxing, and tweezing).

Azeka I, the older half on the *makai* (toward the ocean) side of the street, has a decent Vietnamese restaurant, Ono Gelato, and Kihei's post office. ⊠ *1280 S. Kihei Rd., Kihei* ☎ *808/879–5000.*

Kihei Kalama Village Marketplace. Head to this fun place to investigate. Shaded outdoor stalls sell everything from printed and hand-painted T-shirts and sundresses to jewelry, pottery, wood carvings, fruit, and gaudily painted coconut husks—some, but not all, made by local craftspeople. ⊠ *1941 S. Kihei Rd., Kihei* ☎ *808/879–6610.*

Rainbow Mall. Condo guests can do some one-stop shopping at this mall—it offers spa treatments, Hawaiian gifts, plate lunches, snorkel rental, and a liquor store. ⊠ *2439 S. Kihei Rd., Kihei* ☎ *808/879–1145* ⊕ *www.rainbowmall-maui.com.*

The Shops at Wailea. Stylish, upscale, and close to most of the resorts, this mall brings high fashion to Wailea. Luxury boutiques such as Gucci, Cos Bar, and Tiffany & Co. are represented, as are less-expensive chains like Gap, Guess, and Tommy Bahama's. Several good restaurants face the ocean, and regular Wednesday-night events include live entertainment, art exhibits, and fashion shows. ⊠ *3750 Wailea Alanui Dr., Wailea* ☎ *808/891–6770* ⊕ *www.shopsatwailea.com.*

Wailea Gateway Center. While lunch at chef Peter Merriman's Monkeypod is enough reason to venture to Wailea Gateway Center, you might also be enticed by the artisanal confections from Sweet Paradise Chocolate, fine cheese and charcuterie from Guava, Gouda and Caviar, and a vast collection of vintage clothing from The Aloha Shirt Museum. ⊠ *34 Wailea Gateway Pl., Wailea.*

CLOTHING

Cruise. Sundresses, swimwear, sandals, bright beach towels, and a few nice pieces of resort wear fill this upscale resort boutique. ⊠ *Grand Wailea Resort, 3850 Wailea Alanui Dr., Wailea* ☎ *808/874–3998.*

Enchantress Boutique. Painted silk gowns and glittering tiaras command attention in the window of the Enchantress—the only boutique on the island where you can buy a fantasy wedding gown off the rack. Indulge the feminine whims with a woven leather handbag from Isabella Fiore, or Swarovski crystal–studded sandals. ⊠ *The Shops at Wailea, 3750 Wailea Alanui Dr., Wailea* ☎ *808/891–6360* ⊕ *www.mauienchantress.com.*

Hilo Hattie Fashion Center. Hawaii's largest manufacturer of aloha shirts also carries brightly colored blouses, skirts, and children's clothing. You can also pick up many local gift items here. ⊠ *297 Piikea Ave., Kihei* ☎ *808/875–4545* ⊕ *www.hilohattie.com.*

Honolua Surf Company. If you're in the mood for colorful print shirts and sundresses, check out this surf shop. It's popular with young women and men for surf trunks, casual clothing, and accessories. ⊠ *2411 S. Kihei Rd., Kihei* ☎ *808/874–0999* ⊕ *www.honoluasurf.com.*

Sisters & Company. Opened by four sisters, this little shop has a lot to offer: contemporary lines like True Religion, XCVI and Michael Stars, plus locally produced loungewear from Island Hunny. Sister No. 3, Rhonda, runs a tiny, ultrahip hair salon in back, while Caroline, Sister No. 2, offers mani-pedis and waxing. ✉ *The Shops at Wailea, 3750 Wailea Alanui Dr., Wailea* ☎ *808/874–0003* ⊕ *www.sistersandco.com.*

Tommy Bahama's. It's hard to find a man on Maui who *isn't* wearing a TB–logo aloha shirt. For better or worse, here's where you can get yours. And just to prove you're on vacation, grab a drink or dessert on the way out at the restaurant attached to the shop. ✉ *The Shops at Wailea, 3750 Wailea Alanui Dr., Wailea* ☎ *808/879–7828* ⊕ *www.tommybahamas.com.*

FOOD

Foodland. In Kihei town center, this is the most convenient supermarket for those staying in Wailea. It's open around the clock. ✉ *1881 S. Kihei Rd., Kihei* ☎ *808/879–9350.*

Safeway. Open 24 hours a day, this store is a convenient place to stock up for South Maui stays. ✉ *277 Piikea Ave., Kihei* ☎ *808/891–9120.*

Tutu's Pantry. In the middle of Kihei Kalama Village Marketplace is this humble nook with an extensive supply of coffees, teas, cookies, jams, and other specialty-food items made in Hawaii. You're encouraged to ask for samples. ✉ *1941 South Kihei Rd., Kihei* ☎ *808/874–6400* ⊕ *www.tutuspantry.com.*

> ## MAUI'S BEST OMIYAGE
>
> *Omiyage* is the Japanese term for food souvenirs.
>
> ■ Lavender-salt seasoning from **Alii Kula Lavender.**
>
> ■ Maui Gold Pineapple from **Take Home Maui.**
>
> ■ Peaberry beans from **Maui Coffee Company,** sold in food stores.
>
> ■ Nicky Beans from **Maui Coffee Roasters.**
>
> ■ Jeff's Jams and Jellies from **Ono Gelato.**

UPCOUNTRY

Beyond the resort areas and the airport retail strip you can find some of Maui's most distinctive shops. Discover Upcountry Maui's treasures like Alii Kula Lavender products (available only on Maui) and gourmet cheeses from Surfing Goat Dairy. Traipse around Makawao for fashion-forward tropical pieces and Hawaiian cowboy, or *paniolo*, gear.

ARTS AND CRAFTS

Hot Island Glass. With furnaces glowing bright orange and loads of mesmerizing sculptures on display, this glassworks is an exciting place to visit. The studio, set back from Makawao's main street in a little courtyard, is owned by a family of glassblowers. There's one day each week when the furnace is at rest, so call the studio if you're visiting to see the artists at work. ✉ *3620 Baldwin Ave. 101A, Makawao* ☎ *808/572–4527* ⊕ *www.hotislandglass.com.*

CLOTHING

Collections. This eclectic boutique is brimming with clothing, pretty jewelry, humorous gift cards, housewares, leather goods, yoga wear, Asian-inspired silk shirts, and local beauty products. ✉ *3677 Baldwin Ave., Makawao* ☎ *808/572–0781* ⊕ *www.collectionsmauiinc.com.*

Designing Wahine Emporium. At this Upcountry haven for Hawaiian merchandise and Balinese imports, you can find endless gift options like authentic aloha shirts, jams and jellies, bath and beauty products, and home decor crafted from wood. ⊠ *3640 Baldwin Ave., Makawao* ☎ *808/573–0990.*

Pink By Nature. Owner Desiree Martinez's dresses the modern bohemian as she keeps the rustic store stocked with local jewelry and pieces from Indah, Mother Denim, Jen's Pirate Booty, and Linea Pelle. ⊠ *3663 Baldwin Ave., Makawao* ☎ *808/572–9576.*

> **BEST BETS FOR SWIMWEAR**
>
> **Hi-Tech** ⊠ *425 Koloa St., Kahului* ☎ *808/877–2111.*
>
> **Honolua Surf Company** ⊠ *845 Front St., Lahaina* ☎ *808/661–8848* ⊠ *2411 S. Kihei Rd., Kihei* ☎ *808/874–0999.*
>
> **Maui Girl** ⊠ *12 Baldwin Ave., Paia* ☎ *808/579–9266.*

GALLERIES

Randy Jay Braun Gallery. Randy Jay Braun's black-and-white hula photographs, sepia *paniolo* (Hawaiian cowboy) images, and vivid landscapes are instant classics. His gallery features a slew of his own work, along with koa wood furniture, fused-glass collectibles, shell jewelry, and ceramics from local artists. ⊠ *1152 Makawao Ave., Makawao* ☎ *808/264-0054* ⊕ *www.randyjaybraun.com.*

Sherri Reeve Gallery and Gifts. Watercolor enthusiasts rave about Sherri Reeve's pastel expressions of Maui's landscapes, flora, and fauna. Her origami-like sculpted works are sublime, and her designs have been applied to houseware goods that make for ideal gifts. ⊠ *3669 Baldwin Ave., Makawao* ☎ *808/572–8931* ⊕ *www.sreeve.com.*

Viewpoints Gallery. This gallery is co-owned by six local artists and offers eclectic paintings, sculptures, photography, ceramics, and glass, along with locally made jewelry and quilts. In a courtyard across from Market Fresh Bistro, its monthly exhibits feature artists from various disciplines. ⊠ *3620 Baldwin Ave., Makawao* ☎ *808/572–5979* ⊕ *www. viewpointsgallerymaui.com.*

JEWELRY

Maui Master Jewelers. The shop's exterior is as rustic as all the old buildings of Makawao, so be prepared for the elegance of the handcrafted jewelry displayed within. The store has added a diamond collection to its designs. ⊠ *3655 Baldwin Ave., Makawao* ☎ *808/573–5400* ⊕ *www. mauimasterjewelers.com.*

NORTH SHORE

Shops in the North Shore's Paia are as diverse as the town's history and eclectic as its residents.

CLOTHING

Alice in Hulaland. While the store is famous for its vintage tees, it also carries a lovely mix of gift items and casual wear for the whole family. Best sellers include burnout band tees, Goorin Bros. hats, Havaianas slippers, and Cosabella lingerie. ⊠ *19 Baldwin Ave., Paia* ☎ *808/579–9922* ⊕ *www.aliceinhulaland.com.*

Biasa Rose. The whole family can shop at this boutique for stylish island threads. Charming items—including pillows, shoes, and earth-friendly bags—are on display along with comfy Splendid and James Perse cotton tees, airy tunics, Joie dresses, Mother Denim jeans, Frye boots, and locally made jewelry. At the women's consignment area in the back, you can score designer pieces on a dime. ⊠ *104 Hana Hwy., Paia* ☎ *808/579–8602.*

Hemp House. Shopping "green" is easy at this North Shore shop that stocks eco-friendly loungewear, hoodies, aloha shirts, accessories, books, and bath products. ⊠ *16 Baldwin Ave., Paia* ☎ *808/579–8880* ⊕ *www.hemphousemaui.com.*

Letarte. These sultry swimsuits and cover-ups have graced countless magazine covers and wowed celebrities. Letarte's eco-friendly flagship store carries cool gift items, including local jewelry by Maui Mari. The designer's daughter has inspired a girls' line, called Petite Letarte. ⊠ *24 Baldwin Ave., Paia* ☎ *808/579–6022* ⊕ *www.letarteswimwear.com.*

Moonbow Tropics. If you're looking for an aloha shirt that won't look out of place on the mainland, make a stop at this store, which sells great quality shirts by Nat Nast. The women's store across the street carries work-friendly casual wear in luxurious and breatheable fabrics. ⊠ *27 Baldwin Ave., Paia* ☎ *808/579–3131.*

Nuage Bleu. Los Angeles meets Maui at Nuage Bleu, a good spot for the coveted resort collections of Mara Hoffman and Rory Beca, the downtown flair of Rebecca Minkoff and J Brand, and beachy Joie A La Plage sandals and stylish children's clothing. The entrance emanates exotic scents from Comptoir Sud Pacifique, a fragrance line from Paris. ⊠ *76 Hana Hwy., Paia* ☎ *808/579–9792* ⊕ *www.nuagebleu.com.*

Fodor's Choice ★ **Tamara Catz.** This Maui designer has a worldwide following, and her superstylish sarongs and beachwear have appeared in many fashion magazines. If you're looking for sequined tunics, delicately embroidered sundresses, or beaded wedge sandals, this is the place. Catz also has a bridal line that is elegant and beach-appropriate. Her pieces cost a pretty penny, but if you visit around May or December, you might luck out on one of her sample sales. ⊠ *83 Hana Hwy., Paia* ☎ *808/579–9184* ⊕ *www.tamaracatz.com.*

FOOD

Fodor's Choice ★ **Mana Foods.** At this bustling health-food store you can stock up on local fish and grass-fed beef for your barbecue. You'll find the best selection of organic produce on the island, as well as a great bakery and deli. ⊠ *49 Baldwin Ave., Paia* ☎ *808/579–8078* ⊕ *www. manafoodsmaui.com.*

Ono Gelato. Fresh gelato made with organic fruit is the drawing card here. You'll also find jams, jellies, and dressings from Jeff Gomes; coffees from Maui Oma Roasters; and treats from the Maui Culinary Academy. There's a second location on Front Street in Lahaina, which carries TOMS shoes and locally made jewelry. ⊠ *115 Hana Hwy., Paia* ☎ *808/579–9201* ⊕ *www.onogelatocompany.com.*

GALLERIES

Fodor's Choice ★ **Maui Crafts Guild.** Set in a bright yellow plantation building alongside the highway, Maui Crafts Guild is the island's only artist cooperative, and it is crammed with treasures. Resident artists produce lead-glazed pottery, basketry, glass and feather art, photography, ceramics, and pressed-flower art. The prices are surprisingly low. ⊠ *69 Hana Hwy., Paia* ☎ *808/579–9697* ⊕ *www.mauicraftsguild.com.*

Maui Hands. This gallery shows work by hundreds of local artists, including exquisite woodwork, lovely ceramics, authentic Niihau shell lei, and famous wave photography by Clark Little. There are locations in Lahaina and Makawao and at the Hyatt Regency in Kaanapali. ⊠ *84 Hana Hwy., Paia* ☎ *808/579–9245* ⊕ *www.mauihands.com.*

SWIMWEAR

Fodor's Choice ★ **Maui Girl.** This is *the* place on Maui for swimwear, cover-ups, beach hats, and sandals. Maui Girl designs its own suits, which have been spotted in *Sports Illustrated* fashion shoots, and imports teenier versions from Brazil as well. Tops and bottoms can be purchased separately, greatly increasing your chances of finding the perfect fit. ⊠ *12 Baldwin Ave., Paia* ☎ *808/579–9266* ⊕ *www.maui-girl.com.*

Pakaloha Bikinis. These Maui-designed bikinis are manufactured in Brazil and come in itty-bitty cuts that stay put during surfing or beach volleyball sessions. ⊠ *151 Hana Hwy, Paia* ☎ *808/579-8882* ⊕ *www.pakalohamaui.com.*

ROAD TO HANA

Hana's shopping scene consists mainly of flower and fruit stands, but you won't want to miss the fine art collection of Hana Coast Gallery.

ARTS AND CRAFTS

Hana Cultural Center. The center sells distinctive island quilts and other Hawaiian crafts. ⊠ *4974 Uakea Rd., Hana* ☎ *808/248–8622* ⊕ *www.hanaculturalcenter.org.*

GALLERIES

Fodor's Choice ★ **Hana Coast Gallery.** One of the best-curated galleries on the island, this 3,000-square-foot facility has fine art, handcrafted koa furniture, marble sculptures, and jewelry on consignment from local artists. ⊠ *Travaasa Hana, Hana Hwy., Hana* ☎ *808/248–8636, 800/637–0188* ⊕ *www.hanacoast.com.*

SPAS

Traditional Swedish massage and European facials anchor most spa menus on the island, though you can also find shiatsu, ayurveda, aromatherapy, and other body treatments drawn from cultures across the globe. It can be fun to try some more local treatments or ingredients, though. *Lomilomi,* traditional Hawaiian massage involving powerful strokes down the length of the body, is a regional specialty passed down through generations. Many treatments incorporate local plants and flowers. *Awapuhi,* or Hawaiian ginger, and *noni,* a pungent-smelling fruit, are regularly used for their therapeutic benefits. *Limu,* or seaweed, and even coffee are employed in rousing salt scrubs and soaks.

WEST MAUI

Heavenly Spa by Westin at the Westin Maui. Pamper yourself with the exquisite 80-minute Island Indulgence treatment that combines a body scrub and a warm coconut milk bath in a hydrotherapy tub. Other options include cabana massage (for couples, too) and sunburn relief with a lavender-aloe blend. Facials use high-end lines like Priori and Eminence, while body treatments feature eco-friendly Pure Fiji products. The facility is serene and flawless. While you wait for your treatment, sip on citrusy tropical juice in the posh, ocean-view waiting room. ⊠ *Westin Maui, 2365 Kaanapali Pkwy., Kaanapali* ☎ *808/661–2588* ⊕ *www.westin maui.com* ☞ *$145 50-min massage, $275 day spa packages. Hair salon, sauna, steam room. Gym with: Cardiovascular machines, free weights, weight-training equipment. Services: aromatherapy, body wraps, facials, hydrotherapy, massage, Vichy shower. Classes and programs: Aquaerobics, Pilates, Spinning, yoga.*

SPA TIPS
■ Arrive early for your treatment so you can enjoy the amenities.
■ Bring a comfortable change of clothing and remove your jewelry.
■ Most spas are clothing-optional. If a swimsuit is required, you will be notified.
■ If you're pregnant, or have allergies, say so before you book a treatment.
■ Your therapist should be able to explain the ingredients of products being used in your treatment. If anything stings or burns, say so.
■ Gratuities of 15%–20% are suggested.

Fodor's Choice ★ **Kapalua Spa.** The spa's nondescript entrance opens onto an airy, modern beach house with a panoramic view of Kapalua Bay. With amenities including a gym, an infinity pool, and outdoor hydrotherapy circuits, you can easily spend a day meandering about the spa's three floors without feeling cooped up. The menu includes some ancient Hawaiian healing practices. The *lomi* wrap, designed by Big Island resident and healer Darrell Lapulapu, begins with a special cava tea for instant relaxation, is followed by a body wrap of cacao and kukui oil, and finishes with *lomilomi* (a traditional Hawaiian massage involving strokes down the length of the body). Men can enjoy a therapeutic beer bath, or a hot shave at the newly opened barbershop. The cafe and juice bar serve health potions that combine pure fruits and juiced veggies with natural additives like yogurt. Lunch can be served poolside or in the waiting areas. ⊠ *100 Bay Dr., Kapalua* ☎ *808/665–8282* ⊕ *www.kapalua.com* ☞ *$160 50-min massage, $246 half-day spa package. Saline infinity pool, hair salon, 1960's-style barber shop, nail salon, sauna, Eucalyptus* steam room, movement studio. Gym with: Cardiovascular and Kinesis machines, free weights, weight-training equipment. Services: Aromatherapy, body wraps, hydrotherapy, facials, massage. Classes and programs: Cycling, Zumba, Pilates, yoga, free Sunday beach walk.

Spa Helani, a Heavenly Spa by the Westin Kaanapali Ocean Resort Villas. Find tranquility at this stellar spa near Kaanapali's Airport Beach. The decor is modern and Asian-inspired, and treatments incorporate Hawaiian elements. Try the Signature Heavenly Ritual body treatment, which infuses cane sugar in a gentle exfoliation, pineapple and green papaya in a mask, and then finishes with a cream application, plus a scalp and foot massage. Couples can opt for tandem *lomilomi* massages (traditional Hawaiian massage involving powerful strokes down the length of the body) in the privacy of a beautiful tropical suite. Although access to the gym next door is reserved for resort guests only, other amenities such as the steam room and nail salon more than suffice. ⊠ *Westin Kaanapali Ocean Resort Villas, 6 Kai Ala Dr., Kaanapali* ☎ *808/662–2644* ⊕ *www.westin.com* ☞ *$135 50-min massage, $270 spa package. Steam room. Services: Aromatherapy, body wraps, facials, massage, nail services.*

Spa Moana, Hyatt Regency Maui. The spa's oceanfront salon has a million-dollar view. It's a perfect place to beautify before a wedding or special anniversary, and it's a convenient beach stroll from its adjacent parking lot. The facility is spacious and well-appointed, offering traditional Swedish and deep tissue massage, and shiatsu, in addition to innovative treatments such as the hydrating vitamin C facial for sun lovers, the detoxifying volcanic clay body wrap, and the back-walk massage that's followed by stretching therapy. The coed waiting area has light snacks: banana bread, pineapple slices, coconut macaroons, and coffee and tea. Fitness buffs can take advantage of its state-of-the-art gym and complimentary fitness classes. ⊠ *Hyatt Regency Maui, 200 Nohea Kai Dr., Lahaina* ☎ *808/661–1234, 800/233–1234* ⊕ *www.maui.hyatt. com* ☞ *$145 50-min massage, $275 spa packages. Hair salon, hot tub, sauna, steam room. Gym with: Cardiovascular machines, free weights, weight-training equipment. Services: Aromatherapy, body wraps, facials, massage, Vichy shower. Classes and programs: hydrofit, Pilates, yoga, beach boot camp.*

Fodor'sChoice **Waihua Spa, Ritz-Carlton, Kapalua.** At this gorgeous 17,500-square-foot
★ spa, you enter a blissful maze where floor-to-ceiling riverbed stones lead to serene treatment rooms, couples' *hales* (cabanas), and a rain forest–like grotto with a Jacuzzi, dry cedar sauna, and eucalyptus steam rooms. Hang out in the co-ed waiting area, where sliding-glass doors open to a whirlpool overlooking a taro patch garden. Exfoliate any rough spots with a pineapple-papaya or coffee scrub; then wash off in a private outdoor shower garden before indulging in a *lomilomi* massage (traditional Hawaiian massage involving powerful strokes down the length of the body). High-end beauty treatments include advanced oxygen technology to tighten and nourish mature skin. The boutique has a well-curated display of organic, local, and high-end beauty products, fitness wear, and Maui-made jewelry. ⊠ *Ritz-Carlton, Kapalua, 1 Ritz-Carlton Dr., Kapalua* ☎ *808/669–6200, 800/262–8440* ⊕ *www.*

6

Spa Grande, Grand Wailea Resort

The Spa at the Four Seasons Resort Maui

Spa Grande, Grand Wailea Resort

The Westin Maui Resort & Spa, Kaanapali

Ritz-Carlton, Kapalua

ritzcarlton.com ☞ *$155 50-min massage, $395 half-day spa packages. Hair salon, hot tubs (outdoor and indoor), sauna, steam room. Gym with: Cardiovascular machines, free weights, weight-training equipment. Services: Aromatherapy, body wraps, facials, massage. Classes and programs: cycling, Pilates, yoga.*

Zensations Spa. This spa is for the budget-conscious visitor who wants professional pampering but can do away with extra resort amenities. The humble oasis is tucked between a few casual lunch spots, and its highly skilled aestheticians and massage therapists provide a wide array of facial and body treatments, including waxing services. ⊠ *3600 Lower Honoapiilani Rd. Ste. E, Lahaina* ☎ *808/669-0100* ⊕ *www. zensationsspa.com.*

SOUTH SHORE

Fodor'sChoice
★
The Spa at Four Seasons Resort Maui. The resort's hawk-like attention to detail is reflected here. Thoughtful gestures like fresh flowers beneath the massage table, organic ginger tea in the relaxation room, and your choice of music eases your mind and muscles before the treatment even begins. The spa is romantic yet modern, and the therapists are superb. Thanks to an exclusive partnership, the spa offers excellent treatments created by skin guru Kate Somerville. The Lomi Mohala massage uses muscle-relaxing oils blended exclusively for the treatment. Shop for sustainable and organic beauty products like ISUN and Ola Hawaii from the Big Island, or book an appointment at the Ajne blending bar to customize a scent according to your body chemistry. For the ultimate indulgence, reserve one of the seaside open-air *hale hau* (traditional thatch-roof houses). You can have two therapists realign your body and spirit with a *lomilomi* massage (traditional Hawaiian massage involving powerful strokes down the length of the body). ⊠ *Four Seasons Resort Maui, 3900 Wailea Alanui Dr., Wailea* ☎ *808/874–8000, 800/334–6284* ⊕ *www.fourseasons.com/maui* ☞ *$165 50-min massage. Hair salon, steam room. Gym with: Cardiovascular machines, free weights, weight-training equipment. Services: Aromatherapy, body wraps, facials, massage. Classes and programs: Aquaerobics, meditation, personal training, Pilates, Spinning, tai chi, yoga.*

Fodor'sChoice
★
Spa Grande, Grand Wailea Resort. This 50,000-square-foot spa makes others seem like well-appointed closets. Slathered in honey and wrapped up in the steam room (if you go for the honey steam wrap), you'll feel like royalty. All treatments include a loofah scrub and a trip to the *termé*, a hydrotherapy circuit including five therapeutic baths with Hawaii-grown esssences. The circuit includes a Japanese Furo bath, waterfall massage, cold plunge pool, jet showers, and a large Roman hot tub. To fully enjoy the baths, plan to arrive an hour before your treatment. Free with any treatment, the *termé* is also available separately for $55 for two hours. At times—especially during the holidays—this wonderland can be crowded. When it isn't, it is quite difficult to pry yourself away. ⊠ *Grand Wailea Resort, 3850 Wailea Alanui Dr., Wailea* ☎ *808/875–1234, 800/888–6100* ⊕ *www.grandwailea.com* ☞ *$150 50-min massage, $318 day-spa packages. Hair salon, hot tub, sauna, steam room.*

Gym with: Cardiovascular machines, free weights, weight-training equipment. Services: Aromatherapy, body wraps, facials, hydrotherapy, massage, Vichy shower. Classes and programs: Aquaerobics, cycling, Pilates, Spinning, yoga.

ROAD TO HANA

The Spa at Travaasa Hana. A bamboo gate opens into an outdoor sanctuary with a lava-rock basking pool and hot tub. At first glimpse, this spa seems to have been organically grown, not built. The decor can hardly be called decor—it's an abundant, living garden that overlooks Hana Bay. Ferns still wet from Hana's frequent downpours nourish the spirit as you rest with a cup of Hawaiian herbal tea, or take an invigorating dip in the cold plunge pool, or have a therapist stretch your limbs as you soak in the warm waters of the aquatic therapy pool. Luxurious skin-care teatments feature organic products from Amala and essential oils from locally produced Maui Excellent. ⊠ *Travaasa Hana, 5031 Hana Hwy., Hana* ☎ *808/270–5290* ⊕ *www.travaasa.com/ hana* ☞ *$130 60-min massage, $200 spa package. Outdoor hot tub, steam room. Gym with: Cardiovascular machines, free weights, weight-training equipment. Services: Aromatherapy, body wraps, facials, massage. Classes and programs: Meditation, Pilates, yoga.*

ENTERTAINMENT
AND NIGHTLIFE

Updated by
Eliza Escaño-
Vasquez

Looking for wild island nightlife? We can't promise you'll always find it here—and sometimes you'll just have to be the party. This island has little of Waikiki's after-hours decadence, and the club scene can be quirky, depending on the season and day of the week. But Maui will surprise you with a big-name concert or world-class DJ. Outdoor music festivals are usually held at the Maui Arts & Cultural Center, or even a randomly scouted performance space in Hana.

Block parties in each town happen on Fridays, with Wailuku leading the pack. Main streets are blocked for local bands, food vendors, and street performers, and it's a family-friendly affair. Lahaina, Paia, and Kihei are your best bets for action. Lahaina tries to uphold its reputation as a party town, and succeeds every Halloween when thousands of masqueraders converge for a Mardi Gras–style party on Front Street. Good music isn't too hard to find on this side of the island. In addition to its local acts, Lahaina regularly attracts mainland and global DJs for an intimate set. Kihei seems to have more venues for live bands but can have something of a rough-and-rowdy crowd in parts. On the right night both towns stir with activity, and if you don't like one scene, there's always next door.

Outside Lahaina and Kihei, you might be able to hit an "on" night in Paia (North Shore) or Makawao (Upcountry), especially on weekend nights. But, generally, these towns are on the mellow side. Your best option? Pick up the free *Maui Time Weekly,* or Thursday's edition of the *Maui News,* where you can find a listing of all your after-dark options, island-wide.

Slack-Key Guitars and Ukuleles

You may not think about Hawaii's music until you step off a plane on the Islands, and then there's no escaping it. It's a unique blend of the strings and percussion favored by the early settlers and the chants and rituals of the ancient Hawaiians.

Hawaiian music today includes island-devised variations on acoustic guitar—slack-key and steel guitar—along with the ukulele (a four-string guitar about the size of a violin), and vocals that have evolved from ritual chants to more melodic compositions.

This is one of the few folk-music traditions in the United States that is fully embraced by the younger generation, with no prodding from their parents or grandparents. Many of the radio stations on Maui play plenty of Hawaiian music, and concerts performed by island favorites fill with fans of all ages.

One don't-miss opportunity to hear Hawaiian music on Maui is the outstanding George Kahumoku Jr.'s Slack Key Show: Masters of Hawaiian Music (☎ 888/669–3858 ⊕ www.slackkey. com), a weekly concert held at the Napili Kai Beach Resort. You can catch Grammy-winning slack-key legends in an intimate setting. The mellow *ki hoalu* (slack key) music will show you a bit of Hawaii's *paniolo* (cowboy) history and knee-slapping banter among the musicians as they tune their guitars.

Check ads and listings in local papers, and the Maui Arts & Cultural Center, for information on island concerts, which take place in indoor and outdoor theaters, hotel ballrooms, and cozy nightclubs.

ENTERTAINMENT

Before 10 pm there's a lot to offer by way of luau shows, dinner cruises, and tiki-lighted cocktail hours. Aside from that, you should at least be able to find some down-home DJ-spinning or the strum of acoustic guitars at your nearest watering hole or restaurant.

DINNER CRUISES AND SHOWS

There's no better place to see the sun set on the Pacific than from one of Maui's many boat tours. You can find a tour to fit your mood, as the options range from a quiet, sit-down dinner to a festive, beer-swigging booze cruise. Note, however, that many cocktail cruises have put a cap on the number of free drinks offered with open bars, instead including a limited number of drinks per ticket.

Tours leave from Maalaea or Lahaina harbors. Be sure to arrive at least 15 minutes early (count in the time it will take to park). The dinner cruises typically feature music and are generally packed—which is great if you're feeling social, but you might have to fight for a good seat. You can usually get a much better meal at one of the local restaurants, and opt instead for a different type of tour. Most nondinner cruises offer *pupu* (appetizers) and sometimes a chocolate-and-champagne toast.

Winds are consistent in summer but variable in winter—sometimes making for a rocky ride. If you're worried about seasickness, you might consider a catamaran, which is much more stable than a monohull. Keep in mind that the boat crews are experienced in dealing with such matters. A Dramamine before the trip should keep you in tip-top shape, but if you feel seasick you should sit in the shade, place a cold rag or ice on the back of your neck, and *breathe* as you look at the horizon.

FAMILY

Fodor's Choice

★

Hula Girl Dinner Cruise. This custom catamaran is one of the slickest and best-equipped boats on the island, complete with a VIP lounge for 12 people by the captain's fly bridge. Trips are on the pricier side, mainly because the initial cost doesn't include the cooked-to-order meals. But if you're willing to splurge a little for live music, an onboard chef, and upscale service, it's absolutely worth it. From mid-December to early April the cruise focuses on whale-watching. Check-in is in front of Leilani's restaurant at Whalers Village. ⊠ *2435 Kaanapali Pkwy., Kaanapali* ☎ *808/665–0344, 808/667–5980* ⊕ *www.sailingmaui.com* 🖘 *$78* ⊗ *Tues., Thurs., and Sat. 4:30–7.*

Kaulana Cocktail Cruise. Live music and a festive atmosphere are the calling cards of this two-hour sunset cruise. Accommodating up to 140 people, the cruise generally attracts a younger, more boisterous crowd. Vegetable and cheese platters are served, and two drinks from the full bar are included. ⊠ *Lahaina Harbor, Front St., Lahaina* ☎ *877/500–6284, 808/667–6165* ⊕ *www.mauiprincess.com* 🖘 *$59.95* ⊗ *Mon., Wed., and Fri. 5–7 pm.*

Maui Princess Dinner Cruise. This 118-foot yacht is set up with a dance floor, open-air deck, snack bar, and cocktail lounge. Unlike other sunset dinner cruises, there's no need to rush to get a good seat—the upper-deck tables are reserved. Dinner is prepared fresh daily by the onboard staff, which also provides table-side service. You have a choice of roasted chicken with sesame sauce, a 12-ounce prime rib au jus and horseradish, macadamia-crusted mahimahi, or a vegetarian couscous pocket with tomato, mushroom, and herb sauce. ⊠ *Lahaina Harbor, Front St., Lahaina* ☎ *877/500–6284, 808/667–6165* ⊕ *www.mauiprincess. com* 🖘 *$74.95* ⊗ *Daily 5–8.*

Pacific Whale Foundation Island Rhythms. If you're going out on a Friday, opt for a relaxing cocktail cruise with local reggae artist Marty Dread. You can fill up on barbecued pulled-pork sandwiches and chicken satay while you enjoy live music. Marty's classic reggae covers and original tunes will have you dancing your way back to the harbor. ⊠ *Maalaea Harbor, 101 Maalaea Boat Harbor Rd., Maalaea* ☎ *808/249–8811* ⊕ *www.pacificwhale.org* 🖘 *$59.95* ⊗ *Friday; call for check-in times.*

Paragon Champagne Sunset Sail. You can spread out on deck and enjoy the gentle trade winds on this 47-foot catamaran. Cruises are limited

7

Hula, music, and traditional foods are all part of the popular Old Lahaina Luau.

to groups of 24, and children three and under are free. An easygoing, attentive crew will serve you hot and cold *pupu,* such as grilled chicken skewers, spring rolls, and a fruit platter, along with beer, wine, mai tais, and champagne at sunset. ⊠ *Lahaina Harbor, Front St., Lahaina* ☎ *808/244–2087* ⊕ *www.sailmaui.com* ☒ *$59* ☉ *Mon., Wed., Fri.; call for check-in times.*

Pride of Maui Charters. A 65-foot catamaran built specifically for Maui's waters, the *Pride of Maui* has a spacious cabin with live entertainment, dance floor, and large upper deck for unobstructed viewing. Evening cruises include top-shelf cocktails and an impressive spread of baby back ribs, grilled chicken, warm artichoke dip, Maui onion tartlets, and seasonal desserts. ⊠ *Maalaea Harbor, 101 Maalaea Boat Harbor Rd., Maalaea* ☎ *877/867-7433* ⊕ *www.prideofmaui.com* ☒ *$69.65* ☉ *Tues., Thurs., and Sat. 5–7.*

Teralani Sailing Charters. These catamarans are modern, spotless, and laid out nicely for dining and lounging. They head back shortly after sunset, which means there's plenty of light to savor dinner and the view. During whale-watching season, the best seats are the corner booths by the stern of the boat. Catered by local fave Pizza Paradiso, the meal outdoes most dinner-cruise spreads, with ratatouille, chipotle-citrus rotisserie chicken, and potato gratin and sun-dried tomatoes. The trip departs from Kaaanapali's Dig Me Beach in front of Leilani's at Whalers Village. ⊠ *2435 Kaanapali Pkwy., Kaanapali* ☎ *808/661-1230* ⊕ *www. teralani.net* ☒ *$93.95* ☉ *Daily, hrs vary.*

LUAU

A trip to Hawaii isn't complete without a good luau. With the beat of drums and the sway of hula, luau give you a snippet of Hawaiian culture left over from a long-standing tradition. Early Hawaiians celebrated many occasions with luau—weddings, births, battles, and more. The feasts originally brought people together as an offering to the gods, and to practice *hookipa,* the act of welcoming guests. The word *luau* itself refers to the taro root, a staple of the Hawaiian diet, which, when pounded, makes a gray, puddinglike substance called *poi.* You'll find *poi* at all the best feasts, along with platters of salty fish, fresh fruit, and *kalua* (baked underground) pork. *For more information about Hawaiian food and luau, see the Luau: A Taste of Hawaii feature in Chapter 8, Where to Eat.*

Locals still hold luau to mark milestones or as informal, family-style gatherings. For tourists, luau are a major attraction and, for that reason, have become big business. Keep in mind—some are watered-down tourist traps just trying to make a buck; others offer a night you'll never forget. As the saying goes, you get what you pay for.

■ TIP➔ Many of the best luau book weeks or months in advance, so reserve early. Plan your luau night early on in your trip to help you get into the Hawaiian spirit.

Feast at Lele. This feast redefines the luau by crossing it with island-style fine dining in an intimate beach setting. Each course of this succulent sit-down meal expresses the spirit of specific island cultures—Hawaiian, Samoan, Aotearoan, Tahitian. Don't pass up the delicious desserts. Lahaina's gorgeous sunset serves as the backdrop to the accompanying show, which forgoes gimmicks and pageantry for an authentic cultural presentation of Polynesian chants and dances. "Lele," by the way, is a more traditional name for Lahaina. ⊠ *505 Front St., Lahaina* ☎ *808/667–5353* ⊕ *www.feastatlele.com* ✉ *$115* ⌂ *Reservations essential* ⊙ *Oct.–Jan., daily 5:30 pm; Feb.–Apr. and Sept., daily 6 pm; May–Aug., daily 6:30 pm.*

Grand Luau at Honuaula. At the Grand Wailea Resort and Spa, this show captivates with a contemporary interpretation of Hawaiian mythology and folklore. Indulge in pre-luau fun with Hawaiian games, lei making, and photo-ops with the cast, then witness the unearthing of the *kalua* pig from the underground oven. Traditional dances share a vision of the first Polynesian voyage to the island, and there are also dancers on stilts, an iridescent aerialist suspended by silk, and many elaborate costumes. As a finale, champion fire-knife dancer Ifi Soo brings the house down with a fiery display. ⊠ *Grand Wailea Resort and Spa, 3850 Wailea Alanui Dr., Wailea* ☎ *808/875–7710* ⊕ *www.honuaula-luau.com* ✉ *$100 standard, $110 premium* ⊙ *Mon., Thurs., Fri. and Sat. 5 pm–8 pm.*

Fodor's Choice ★ **Hyatt Regency Maui Drums of the Pacific Luau.** By Kaanapali Beach, this luau excels in every category—breathtaking location, well-made food, smooth-flowing buffet lines, and a nicely paced program that touches on Hawaiian, Samoan, Tahitian, Fijian, Tongan, and Maori cultures. The finale features a solo fire-knife dancer. You'll feast on delicious

7

WAILUKU FIRST FRIDAY

Wailuku sheds its reputation as a quiet, sleepy town for First Friday, a lively block party that shuts down all of Market Street between 5:30 and 10 pm on the first Friday of each month. At last count about 4,000 people were turning out for good eats, local music, and a bit of retail therapy. Businesses hold wine-and-cheese receptions and other special events while performers appear on multiple stages set up along the charming block. Arrive early, as the nearby parking lot gets full by 6 pm. First Friday's success prompted other towns to hold their own. The party is on Front Street in Lahaina on second Fridays, Baldwin Avenue in Makawao on third Fridays, and fourth Fridays bring the festivities to Paia.

Hawaiian delicacies like shoyu chicken, *lomilomi* (rubbed with onions and herbs) salmon, and Pacific ahi *poke* (pickled raw tuna, tossed with herbs and seasonings). The dessert spread consists of various chocolate, pineapple, and coconut indulgences. An open bar offers beer, wine, and the usual tropical concoctions. ⊠ *Hyatt Regency Maui, 200 Nohea Kai Dr., Kaanapali* ☎ *808/667–4727* ⊕ *www.maui.hyatt.com* ☎ *$95 standard, $130 premium* ☉ *Tues., Wed., Fri., and Sat. 5–8.*

FAMILY
Fodor's Choice
★

Old Lahaina Luau. Considered the best luau on Maui, the Old Lahaina Luau is certainly the most traditional. Immerse yourself in making *kapa* (bark cloth), weaving *lauhala* (coconut palm fronds), and pounding *poi* at the various interactive stations. Sitting either at a table or on a *lauhala* mat, you can dine on Hawaiian cuisine such as pork *laulau* (wrapped with taro sprouts in *ti* leaves), ahi *poke* (pickled raw tuna tossed with herbs and seasonings), *lomilomi* salmon (rubbed with onions and herbs), and *haupia* (coconut pudding). At sunset, the historical journey touches on the arrival of the Polynesians, the influence of missionaries, and, later, the advent of tourism. Talented performers will charm you with beautiful music, powerful chanting, and variety of hula styles from *kahiko*, the ancient way of communicating with the gods, to *auana*, the modern hula. You won't see fire dancers here, as they aren't considered traditional. ■TIP→ This luau sells out regularly, so make reservations before your trip to Maui. ⊠ *1251 Front St., near Lahaina Cannery Mall, Lahaina* ☎ *808/667–1998* ⊕ *www.oldlahainaluau.com* ☎ *$99* ⚑ *Reservations essential* ☉ *Oct.–Mar., daily 5:15 pm; Apr.–Sept., daly 5:45 pm.*

Wailea Beach Marriott Te Au Moana. Te Au Moana means "ocean tide," which is all you need to know about the simply gorgeous backdrop for this south Maui luau. The evening begins with lei making, local crafts, and an *imu* (underground oven) ceremony. The tasty buffet serves local staples, including a plethora of desserts like carrot cake, macadamia-nut brownies, and key lime squares. The performance seamlessly intertwines ancient Hawaiian stories and contemporary songs with traditional hula and Polynesian dances, concluding with a jaw-dropping solo fire-knife dance. ⊠ *Wailea Beach Marriott, 3700 Wailea Alanui*

Dr., Wailea ☎ *808/879–1922* ⊕ *www.marriotthawaii.com* ⊠ *$100* ⌂ *Reservations essential* ◷ *Mon. and Thurs.–Sat. 4:30–8.*

Westin Maui Resort and Spa Wailele Polynesian Luau. The Westin Maui Resort and Spa's oceanfront Aloha Pavilion provides a picturesque setting for this Polynesian feast. Seating is family-style. A buffet of traditional dishes such as pickled ahi tuna, fire-roasted teriyaki beef, and Molokai sweet potato with coconut precede the dessert spread. The performances originate from the islands of Hawaii, Tahiti, New Zealand, and Samoa, and although the costumes may not be as elaborate as elsewhere, the pulse-raising five-member fire-knife dance is a thrilling highlight. Tickets can be pricey for some. ⊠ *Westin Maui Resort and Spa, 2365 Kaanapali Pkwy., Kaanapali* ☎ *808/661–2992* ⊕ *www. westinmaui.com* ⊠ *$105* ◷ *Sat., Tues., and Thurs. 5:30.*

STARGAZING

Tour of the Stars. For nightlife of a different sort, children and astronomy buffs can try Tour of the Stars, a one-hour stargazing program on the roof or patio of the Hyatt Regency Maui. Romance of the Stars, with champagne and chocolate-covered strawberries, is held on Friday and Saturday at 11 pm. Check-in at the hotel lobby 15 minutes prior to starting time. ⊠ *Lahaina Tower, Hyatt Regency Maui Resort & Spa, 200 Nohea Kai Dr., Kaanapali* ☎ *808/661–1234* ⊕ *www.maui.hyatt.com* ⊠ *$25–$30* ◷ *Sun.–Thurs. 8, 9, and 10; Fri. and Sat. 8, 9, 10, and 11.*

ARTS CENTER

Maui Arts & Cultural Center (MACC). This hub of all highbrow arts features everything from hip-hop and reggae performances to Hawaiian slack-key guitar shows to international dance and circus troupes—you name it. On selected evenings, the MACC hosts movie selections from the Maui Film Festival. The complex includes the 350-seat McCoy Theater, the 1,200-seat Castle Theater, a 4,000-seat amphitheater for outdoor concerts, and a courtyard café for preshow dining and drinks. For upcoming events, check the *Maui News.* ⊠ *1 Cameron Way, Kahului* ☎ *808/242–7469* ⊕ *www.mauiarts.org.*

FILM

In the heat of the afternoon a theater may feel like paradise. There are megaplexes showing first-run movies in Kukui Mall (Kihei), Lahaina Center, Maui Mall (Kahului), and Kaahumanu Shopping Center (Kahului).

Maui Film Festival. In summer, this weeklong international festival attracts big-name celebrities to Maui for cinema and soirees under the stars. Throughout the year, the Maui Arts & Cultural Center presents art-house films on selected evenings, often accompanied by live music, cocktails, and wine. ☎ *808/579–9244* ⊕ *www.mauifilmfestival.com.*

THEATER

For live theater, check local papers for events and showtimes.

Maui Academy of Performing Arts. Founded in 1974, this nonprofit performing-arts group offers fine productions, as well as dance and drama classes for children and teens. Recent shows have included *Macbeth,*

Continued on page 194

HULA: MORE THAN A FOLK DANCE

Hula has been called "the heartbeat of the Hawaiian people" and also "the world's best-known, most misunderstood dance." Both are true. Hula isn't just dance. It is storytelling.

Chanter Edith McKinzie calls it "an extension of a piece of poetry." In its adornments, implements, and customs, hula integrates every important Hawaiian cultural practice: poetry, history, genealogy, craft, plant cultivation, martial arts, religion, protocol. So when 19th-century Christian missionaries sought to eradicate a practice they considered depraved, they threatened more than just a folk dance.

With public performance outlawed and private hula practice discouraged, hula went underground for a generation, to rural villages. The fragile verbal link by which culture was transmitted from teacher to student hung by a thread. Even increasing literacy did not help because hula's practitioners were a secretive and protected circle.

As if that weren't bad enough, vaudeville, Broadway, and Hollywood got hold of the hula, giving it the glitz treatment in an unbroken line from "Oh, How She Could Wicky Wacky Woo" to "Rock-A-Hula Baby." Hula became shorthand for paradise: fragrant flowers, lazy hours. Ironically, this development assured that hundreds of Hawaiians could make a living performing and teaching hula. Many danced *auana* (modern form) in performance; but taught *kahiko* (traditional), quietly, at home or in hula schools.

Today, 30 years after the cultural revival known as the Hawaiian Renaissance, language immersion programs have assured a new generation of proficient—and even eloquent—chanters, songwriters, and translators. Visitors can see more, and more authentic, traditional hula than at any other time in the last 200 years.

Like the culture of which it is the beating heart, hula has survived.

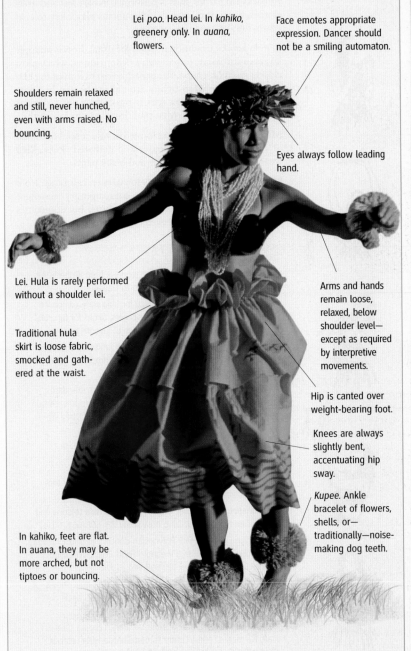

Lei *poo*. Head lei. In *kahiko*, greenery only. In *auana*, flowers.

Face emotes appropriate expression. Dancer should not be a smiling automaton.

Shoulders remain relaxed and still, never hunched, even with arms raised. No bouncing.

Eyes always follow leading hand.

Lei. Hula is rarely performed without a shoulder lei.

Arms and hands remain loose, relaxed, below shoulder level— except as required by interpretive movements.

Traditional hula skirt is loose fabric, smocked and gathered at the waist.

Hip is canted over weight-bearing foot.

Knees are always slightly bent, accentuating hip sway.

Kupee. Ankle bracelet of flowers, shells, or— traditionally—noise-making dog teeth.

In kahiko, feet are flat. In auana, they may be more arched, but not tiptoes or bouncing.

BASIC MOTIONS

Speak or Sing

Moon or Sun

Grass Shack or House

Mountains or Heights

Love or Caress

At backyard parties, hula is performed in bare feet and street clothes, but in performance, adornments play a key role, as do rhythm-keeping implements.

In hula *kahiko* (traditional style), the usual dress is multiple layers of stiff fabric (often with a pellom lining, which most closely resembles *kapa*, the paperlike bark cloth of the Hawaiians). These wrap tightly around the bosom but flare below the waist to form a skirt. In pre-contact times, dancers wore only kapa skirts. Men traditionally wear loincloths.

Monarchy-period hula is performed in voluminous muumuu or high-necked muslin blouses and gathered skirts. Men wear white or gingham shirts and black pants.

In hula *auana* (modern), dress for women can range from grass skirts and strapless tops to contemporary tea-length dresses. Men generally wear aloha shirts, but sometimes grass skirts over pants or even everyday gear.

SURPRISING HULA FACTS

■ Grass skirts are not traditional; workers from Kiribati (the Gilbert Islands) brought this custom to Hawaii.

■ In olden-day Hawaii, *mele* (songs) for hula were composed for every occasion—name songs for babies, dirges for funerals, welcome songs for visitors, celebrations of favorite pursuits.

■ Hula *mai* is a traditional hula form in praise of a noble's genitals; the power of the *alii* (royalty) to procreate gave *mana* (spiritual power) to the entire culture.

■ Hula students in old Hawaii adhered to high standards: scrupulous cleanliness, no sex, daily cleansing rituals, certain food prohibitions, and no contact with the dead. They were fined if they broke the rules.

WHERE TO WATCH

■ Feast at Lele: Nightly beachside luau includes show that strives for authenticity. ☎ 866/244–5353.

■ Kaanapali Beach Hotel: Employees teach hula lessons and staff a free nightly hour-long hula show. ☎ 808/661–0011.

■ Lahaina Cannery Mall: Polynesian dancers perform Tuesday and Thursday at 7 PM by Pineapple Food Court. Weekend children's hula is at 1 PM. ☎ 808/661–5304.

■ Whalers Village: Three weekly free evening hula shows (usually Monday, Wednesday, and Saturday, but check schedule). ☎ 808/661–4567.

■ Hula festivals: Festival of Hula, January, Lahaina Cannery Mall; Na Mele O Maui/Emma Farden Sharpe Hula Festival, December, Kaanapali Resort (call to check month).

The ukulele, a small, four-string guitar, is part of Hawaiian music's unique sound.

Nutcracker Sweets, and *Les Miserables*. ⊠ *81 N. Church St., Wailuku* ☎ *808/244–8760* ⊕ *www.mauiacademy.org* ✉ *$10–$35*.

Maui OnStage. Located at the Historic Iao Theater, this nonprofit theater group stages five shows each season. Productions include shows such as *The Wizard of Oz, Rent,* and *SHOUT! The Mod Musical*. Each October, it holds a haunted-theater experience in honor of Halloween. The audience is mostly locals, but visitors are warmly welcomed. ⊠ *Iao Theater, 68 N. Market St., Wailuku* ☎ *808/242–6969* ⊕ *www. mauionstage.com* ✉ *$15–$20*.

FAMILY
Fodor's Choice
★
Ulalena at Maui Theatre. One of Maui's hottest tickets, *Ulalena* is a musical extravaganza that has received accolades from audiences and Hawaiian culture experts. The powerful ensemble (20 singer-dancers and five musicians) uses creative stage wizardry to give an enchanting portrayal of island history and mythology. Native rhythms from authentic and rare instruments are blended with heart-wrenching chants and aerialist precision, making the 75-minute production seem like a whirlwind. Beer and wine are for sale at the concession stand. ■ TIP➔ Check out dinner-theater packages in conjunction with local restaurants. ⊠ *Maui Theatre, 878 Front St., Lahaina* ☎ *808/661–9913, 877/688–4800* ⊕ *www.mauitheatre.com* ✉ *$59.50–$129.50 for dinner package* ⌂ *Reservations essential* ☉ *Mon. to Fri. 6:30, check in at 6 pm.*

Warren & Annabelle's. This is a hearty comedy with amazing sleight of hand. Magician Warren Gibson entices guests into his swank nightclub with a gleaming mahogany bar, a grand piano, and a resident ghost named Annabelle who tickles the ivories. Servers efficiently ply you with appetizers (coconut shrimp, crab cakes), desserts (chocolate pots de crème, assorted pies and cheesecakes, crème brûlée), and cocktails, while obliging a few impromptu song requests. Then, guests are ushered into a small theater where magic hilariously ensues. Since this is a nightclub act, no one under 21 is allowed. ⊠ *Lahaina Center, 900 Front St., Lahaina* ☎ *808/667–6244* ⊕ *www.warrenandannabelles.com* ☜ *$59 or $99.50, including food and drinks* ⌂ *Reservations essential* ⊘ *Mon.–Sat. 5 and 7:30.*

NIGHTLIFE

Your best bet when it comes to bars on Maui? If you walk by and it sounds like it's happening, go in. If you want to scope out your options in advance, be sure to check the free *Maui Time Weekly,* found at most stores and restaurants, to find out who's playing where. Don't overlook the resorts and their bars and restaurants. *Maui News* also publishes an entertainment schedule in its Thursday edition of the "Maui Scene." With an open mind (and a little luck), you can usually find some fun.

WEST MAUI

West Maui's Lahaina offers the best nightlife on the island. From local musicians to contemporary DJs, hop around town to find your choice of scene.

BARS AND RESTAURANTS

Alaloa Lounge. When ambience weighs heavy on the priority list, this spot at the Ritz-Carlton might just be the ticket. Nightly performances range from jazz to island rhythms. The menu includes such dishes as a fantastic seared filet mignon on a pretzel roll. Step onto the lanai for that plumeria-tinged Hawaiian air and gaze at the deep blue of the Pacific. ⊠ *Ritz-Carlton, Kapalua, 1 Ritz-Carlton Dr., Kapalua* ☎ *808/669–6200* ⊕ *www.ritzcarlton.com.*

Cheeseburger in Paradise. A chain joint on Front Street, this place is known for—what else?—big beefy cheeseburgers, not to mention a great spinach-nut burger. It's a casual place to start your evening, as they have live music (usually classic or contemporary rock) until 10:30 pm and big, fruity cocktails for happy hour. The second-floor balcony gives you a bird's-eye view of Lahaina's Front Street action. ⊠ *811 Front St., Lahaina* ☎ *808/661–4855* ⊕ *www.cheeseburgerland.com.*

Cool Cat Café. You could easily miss this casual 1950s-style diner while strolling through Lahaina. Tucked in the second floor of the Wharf Cinema Center, its semi-outdoor area plays host to rockin' local music nightly until 10 pm. The entertainment lineup covers jazz, contemporary Hawaiian, and traditional island rhythms. It doesn't hurt that the kitchen dishes out specialty burgers, fish that's fresh from the harbor, and delicious homemade sauces from the owner's family recipes. ⊠ *658 Front St., Lahaina* ☎ *808/667–0908* ⊕ *www.coolcatcafe.com.*

George Kahumoku Jr.'s Slack Key Show: Masters of Hawaiian Music at the Napili Kai Beach Resort. Beloved musician George Kahumoku Jr. hosts this weekly program, which features the Islands' most renowned slack-key artists as well as other traditional forms of Hawaiian music. The set-up at Aloha Pavilion is humble, but you get to enjoy Grammy-winning, legendary musicians from the genre. ⊠ *5900, Lower Honoapiilani Road, Lahaina* ☎ *808/669–3858* ⊕ *www.slackkeyshow.com.*

FAMILY **Kupanaha Magic Dinner Theater at Kaanapali Beach Hotel.** While the food might not wow the discerning palate, your eyes will be perplexed by the illusions performed by Jody and Kathleen Baran. From levitation to sawing a body in half, this astonishing show is an homage to the legendary magicians who have spread awe on Hawaiian shores. Hula and table-side magic round out the evening. ⊠ *2525 Kaanapali Parkway, Lahaina* ☎ *808/667–0128* ⊕ *www.kupanaha.com.*

Sansei Seafood Restaurant and Sushi Bar. Sansei has stayed a favorite among locals and visitors for years. The atmosphere is always spirited. If you're more prone to doing the entertaining yourself, why not indulge in some mai tai–induced karaoke Thursday to Saturday and get half-off fresh sushi at the same time? ⊠ *600 Office Rd., Kapalua* ☎ *808/669–6286* ⊕ *www.sanseihawaii.com* ☾ *5:30 pm–2 am.*

Spanky's Riptide. Spanky's draws the casual sports-bar crowd for *pau hana* (after work get-together). The bottle shop offers more than 30 beers and at least 6 on tap. There's no cover, the televisions stream sports nonstop, and you can help yourself to the condiment stand when you order a dawg. ⊠ *505 Front St., Lahaina* ☎ *808/667–2337* ⊕ *www.spankysriptide.com.*

CLUBS

Moose McGillycuddy's. The Moose offers live or DJ music on most nights, drawing a young, mostly single crowd who come for the burgers, beer, and dance-floor beats. Tuesday and Saturday dollar nights are highly popular, offering dollar domestic and well drinks with your dollar admission. Local bands play Sunday, Wednesday, and Thursday nights. ⊠ *844 Front St., Lahaina* ☎ *808/667–7758.*

THE SOUTH SHORE

If you're staying on the South Shore, you can find some great intimate venues for live music but only a few options for dancing.

BARS AND RESTAURANTS

Fodor'sChoice **Ambrosia Martini Lounge.** A South Maui favorite, Ambrosia is a lively
★ hangout for house music and old school jams, as well as the occasional absinthe drink. The art of mixology is taken more seriously here than other venues. ⊠ *1913 S. Kihei Rd., Kihei* ☎ *808/891–1011* ⊕ *www.ambrosiamaui.com* ☾ *5 pm–2 am.*

MAI TAI

Don't let your sweet tooth fool you. Maui's favorite drink—the mai tai—can be as lethal as it is sweet. The Original Trader Vic's recipe calls for two ounces of aged dark rum, mixed with almond syrup, orange curaçao, the juice of one lime, and (wouldn't you know it) rock-candy syrup.

Kahale's Beach Club. A friendly, festive dive bar, Kahale's offers live music until 11 pm (including funk, country, and rock) and burgers until 2 in the morning. If the place is empty, try the Tiki Lounge or Ambrosia. ⊠ *36 Keala Pl., Kihei* ☎ *808/875–7711.*

Life's a Beach. This place brings in a young bunch looking to par-tay. Thursday, Friday, and Saturday nights feature reggae or classic rock; Sunday, Monday, and Tuesday nights are for karaoke; and Wednesdays are open-mic nights when aspiring local musicians come to jam. ⊠ *1913 S. Kihei Rd., Kihei* ☎ *808/891–8010.*

> **WHAT'S A LAVA FLOW?**
>
> Can't decide between a piña colada and strawberry daiquiri? Go with a Lava Flow—a mix of light rum, coconut and pineapple juice, and a banana, with a swirl of strawberry purée. Add a wedge of fresh pineapple and a paper umbrella, and mmm . . . good.

Lobby Lounge at the Four Seasons Resort Maui at Wailea. This lofty resort's lobby lounge is perfect when you want live Hawaiian music, a bit of hula, freshly prepared sushi, and artisanal cocktails all in one sitting. Gorgeous orange ceilings, stark-white stone columns, and modern wicker furnishing pull off understated look quite well. The colorful sunset over Lanai isn't too shabby either. ⊠ *Four Seasons Resort Maui at Wailea, 3900 Wailea Alanui Dr., Wailea* ☎ *808/874–8000* ⊕ *www.fourseasons.com.*

Mulligan's on the Blue. Frothy pints of Guinness and late-night fish-and-chips—who could ask for more? Sunday nights feature foot-stomping Irish jams that will have you dancing a jig, and singing something about "a whiskey for me-Johnny." Local favorite Willie K performs most Wednesdays. Other nights bring in various local bands. ⊠ *Blue Golf Course, 100 Kaukahi St., Wailea* ☎ *808/874–1131* ⊕ *www.mulligansontheblue.com.*

South Shore Tiki Lounge. Good eats are paired with cool tunes in this breezy, tropical tavern. Local acts and DJs are featured most evenings; if you're craving some old-school hip-hop, Monday is your night. Thursday is a mix of old-school and top 40's hits. Happy hour specials run from 11 am to 6 pm. ⊠ *1913 S. Kihei Rd., Kihei* ☎ *808/874–6444* ⊕ *www.southshoretikilounge.com.*

UPCOUNTRY

This part of Maui is quite mellow and more of a local scene.

BARS AND RESTAURANTS

Casanova Italian Restaurant & Deli. Casanova brings in some big acts, including Kool and the Gang, Los Lobos, Taj Majal, and electro DJs from the mainland. Most Friday and Saturday nights attract a hip, local scene with live bands and eclectic DJs spinning house, funk, and world music. Wednesday is for Wild Wahine (code for ladies get in free), which can be on the smarmy side, but hey, a vacation is a "no judgment" zone. There's a $5 to $25 cover. ⊠ *1188 Makawao Ave., Makawao* ☎ *808/572–0220* ⊕ *www.casanovamaui.com.*

Stopwatch Bar & Grill. This friendly dive bar books favorite local bands on Friday and charges only $5. ✉ *1127 Makawao Ave., Makawao* ☎ *808/572–1380.*

NORTH SHORE

On the North Shore, Paia gets a bit more action and a vibrant crowd.

BARS AND RESTAURANTS

Charley's. The closest thing to country Maui has to offer, Charley's is a down-home dive bar in the heart of Paia that is also known for its great breakfasts. It hosts reggae, house, Latin soul, and jazz nights, as well as one-off events with visiting DJs. Live bands are featured on Friday and Saturday. ✉ *142 Hana Hwy., Paia* ☎ *808/579–9453* ⊕ *www.charleysmaui.com.*

8

WHERE TO EAT

By Bonnie Friedman

"Mischievous, marvelous, magical Maui," sings Israel Kamakawiwoole in *Maui Hawaiian Sup'pa Man*, his ode to the demigod. The island is all those things and more, and its restaurants try to keep up with the sophisticated palates and discriminating tastes of locals and visitors. For a place the size of Maui, there's a lot going on, from ethnic holes-in-the-wall to stunningly appointed hotel dining rooms, and from seafood trucks to oceanfront fish houses with panoramic views. Much of the food is excellent, but some of it is overpriced and touristy. If you're coming from a "food destination" city, you may have to adjust your expectations.

Follow the locavore trend, and at casual and fine-dining restaurants choose menu items made with products that are abundant on the island, including local fish, onions, avocados, cabbage, broccoli, asparagus, hydroponic tomatoes, myriad herbs, salad greens, *kalo* (taro), bananas, papaya, guava, *lilikoi* (passion fruit), coconut, mangoes, strawberries, and Maui pineapple. You can also look for treats grown on neighboring islands, such as mushrooms, purple sweet potatoes, and watermelon.

"Local food," a specific and official cuisine designated as such in the 1920s, is an amalgam of foods brought by the ethnic groups that have come here since the mid-1800s and also blended with the foods native Hawaiians have enjoyed for centuries. Dishes to try include *lomilomi* salmon, *laulau*, poi, Portuguese bean soup, *kalbi* ribs, chicken *katsu*, chow fun, hamburger steak, and macaroni salad. For a food adventure, take a drive into Central Maui and have lunch or dinner at one of the "local" spots recommended here. Or get even more adventurous and take a drive around Wailuku or Kahului and find your own hidden gem. There are plenty out there.

MAUI DINING PLANNER

EATING OUT STRATEGY

"Where should we eat?" With scores of restaurants competing for your appetite—not to mention your dollars—the very idea of having to choose may seem daunting. But our expert writers and editors have done most of the legwork—the dozens of selections here represent the best eating experiences Maui has to offer. Search "Best Bets" for top recommendations by price, cuisine, and experience. Or find a restaurant quickly; reviews are ordered alphabetically within their geographic area.

WITH KIDS

Hawaii is an extremely kid-friendly place. The vibe is casual, and even the fancy restaurants have a *keiki*, or children's, menu, and usually a box of crayons or other diversion tucked away somewhere. Some of the hotel restaurants feature cute-as-a-button "knee-high buffets" for the kids. Take advantage of local treats and experiences such as shave ice and a luau.

SMOKING

Smoking is prohibited in all Hawaii restaurants and bars, including on patios and other outdoor dining areas.

RESERVATIONS

Maui is one of the most popular vacation destinations in the world. It's always best to make reservations in advance, especially if you're traveling in a group of four or more. If you're determined to go to places like Mama's Fish House or the Old Lahaina Luau, you should make reservations as far in advance as possible. Most other places will do their best to accommodate you, even at the last minute.

WHAT TO WEAR

Casual clothing works for just about every restaurant on Maui. For dinner at hotels and other upscale restaurants, it's nice to see men in shirts with collars and women in evening resort wear, but nothing dressier is required anywhere. Bring a sweater or cover-up in winter months—many restaurants are open-air and can be breezy.

HOURS AND PRICES

Many restaurants on Maui are busiest from 5 pm to 7 pm, the early-bird-special hours and sunset time. By 8:30 many dining rooms are quiet, and by 10 most are closed. Places with popular bars and karaoke usually keep the kitchens open, too, but serve a limited menu. Unfortunately, many hotel restaurants are expensive and not very good; the best are listed here. To dine well on the cheap, look for coupons in the *Maui News*, found mostly in the *Maui Scene* section on Thursday, or check online for coupons at sites such as ⊕ *www.originalcouponbook. com*. Or go into Central Maui and enjoy the great ethnic restaurants where locals eat. Many upscale restaurants offer discounts of up to 50% during slow months (September through November). As for tipping, 18% to 20% is considered standard for quality service.

Prices in the reviews are the average cost of a main course at dinner or, if dinner is not served, at lunch.

WEST MAUI

Beautiful West Maui encompasses the area from tiny Olowalu, with its famous mom-and-pop Olowalu General Store, full of local-style *bentos* (box lunches), all the way north to the ritzy Kapalua Resort, with its glitzy (some say tired) annual wine-and-food festival. In between are Lahaina, the historic former capital of Hawaii, with its myriad restaurants on and off Front Street, and the resort area of Kaanapali. Have some fun checking out restaurants in the nooks and crannies of Kahana, Honokowai, and Napili, north of Kaanapali. All over the west side you'll find a rainbow of cuisines in just about every price category.

OLOWALU

$ ✕ **Leoda's Kitchen and Pie Shop.** Slow down as you drive through the little
AMERICAN roadside village of Olowalu, about 15 minutes before Lahaina town if you're coming from the airport, so you don't miss this adorable farmhouse-chic restaurant and pie shop where everything is prepared with care. Old photos of the area, distressed wood, and muted colors set the mood. Have a sandwich or a burger with Kula onions. All the breads are home baked and excellent, and most ingredients are sourced locally. Don't get too full: you must try the pie. The banana cream is out of this world, or dig into the yuzu-lemon tart. ⑤ *Average main: $13* ⊠ *820 Olowalu Village Rd.* ☎ *808/662–3600* ⊕ *www. leodas.com.*

$ ✕ **Olowalu General Store.** A Maui landmark for almost seven decades,
HAWAIIAN one of the island's last true mom-and-pops is best known for its hot dogs, homemade Spam *musubi* (a slice of Spam on top of a block of rice, all wrapped in nori), and boiled peanuts. Don't overlook the plate lunches—Kalua pork, *mochiko* chicken, and breaded teriyaki beef are best sellers—and the burgers. Full, local-style, hearty breakfast plates are just $5.99, including a soda or juice. There are also smoothies and shave ices in so many flavor choices, you'll have to go more than once to try them all. ⑤ *Average main: $8* ⊠ *820 Olowalu Village Rd.* ☎ *808/667–2883* ⊗ *No dinner.*

LAHAINA

$ ✕ **Aloha Mixed Plate.** From the wonderful folks who bring you Maui's
HAWAIIAN best luau—the Old Lahaina Luau—comes this extremely casual, multi-award-winning, oceanfront eatery. If you've yet to indulge in a "plate lunch" (a protein—usually in an Asian-style preparation—two scoops of rice, and a scoop of potato-macaroni salad), this is a good place to try one. New on the menu are fresh, local fish preparations, lots of local produce, and such favorites as dry mein, saimin, Asian-style pickle platters, and poi beef stew made with poi from the restaurant's own farm. Take your plate to a table so close to the ocean you just might get wet. Oh, and don't forget the mai tai! ⑤ *Average main: $10* ⊠ *1285 Front St.* ☎ *808/661–3322* ⊕ *www.AlohaMixedPlate.com.*

BEST BETS FOR MAUI DINING

Looking for the best? Fodor's writers and editors have selected their favorite restaurants by price, cuisine, and experience in the lists here. In the first column, the Fodor's Choice properties represent the "best of the best" across price categories. You can also search by area for excellent eats—just peruse our complete reviews on the following pages.

Fodor's Choice ★

Ba-Le Sandwiches & Plate Lunch, $, p. 226

Café des Amis, $, p. 229

Colleen's at the Cannery, $$, p. 228

Mala Ocean Tavern, $$$, p. 207

Paia Fishmarket, $, p. 230

Pita Paradise Mediterranean Bistro, $$, p. 221

Roy's Kaanapali, $$$$, p. 213

Sam Sato's, $, p. 226

Sansei Seafood Restaurant & Sushi Bar, $$, p. 215

Star Noodle, $, p. 207

Tokyo Tei, $, p. 226

Tommy Bahama, $$$, p. 223

Tropica Restaurant & Bar, $$$$, p. 214

By Price

$

Ba-Le Sandwiches & Plate Lunch, p. 226

Café des Amis, p. 229

Cilantro, p. 204

Da Kitchen, p. 223

Kihei Caffe, p. 216

Paia Fishmarket, p. 230

Sam Sato's, p. 226

Star Noodle, p. 207

Tokyo Tei, p. 226

$$

Asian Star, p. 225

Colleen's at the Cannery, p. 228

Sansei Seafood Restaurant & Sushi Bar, p. 215

Tiki Terrace, p. 213

$$$

Mala Ocean Tavern, p. 207

Market Fresh Bistro, p. 228

Tommy Bahama, p. 223

$$$$

Pineapple Grill, p. 215

Roy's Kaanapali, p. 213

Spago, p. 222

Tropica Restaurant & Bar, p. 214

By Cuisine

MODERN HAWAIIAN

Mala Ocean Tavern, $$$, p. 207

Market Fresh Bistro, $$$, p. 228

Pineapple Grill, $$$$, p. 215

Roy's Kaanapali, $$$$, p. 213

PLATE LUNCH

Aloha Mixed Plate, $, p. 202

Ba-Le Sandwiches & Plate Lunch, $, p. 226

Da Kitchen, $, p. 223

SUSHI

Japengo, $$$$, p. 208

Makawao Sushi & Deli, $$, p. 227

Sansei Seafood Restaurant & Sushi Bar, $$, p. 215

Tokyo Tei, $, p. 226

By Experience

MOST KID-FRIENDLY

Da Kitchen, $, p. 223

Flatbread Company, $$, p. 229

Koho Grill and Bar, $, p. 225

Seascape Maalaea, $, p. 220

Zippy's, $, 225

MOST ROMANTIC

Humuhumunukunukuapuaa, $$$, p. 221

Son'z at Swan Court, $$$$, p. 213

Tropica Restaurant & Bar, $$$$, p. 214

BEST VIEW

Gannon's, $$$$, p. 220

Mala Ocean Tavern, $$$, p. 207

PacificO, $$$$, p. 207

Plantation House Restaurant, $$$, p. 215

Sea House Restaurant, $$$, p. 215

8

MAUI'S FOOD TRUCKS: MOVABLE FEASTS

As in so many other places, the food-truck culture is taking hold on Maui, but don't expect to find well-equipped, customized trucks like the ones you see on the Food Network. And none (or almost none) have websites, Twitter accounts, or Facebook pages; some don't even have phones. So just take a chance and consider it an adventure.

A group of trucks has formed a sort of food-truck food court by the harbor on Kahului Beach Road opposite the Maui Arts & Cultural Center (⊠ 1 Cameron Way, Kahului).

The best of the trucks is the **Geste Shrimp Truck**, which serves four different preparations of shrimp with sides of crab, mac salad, and rice. Hours are generally Tuesday through Saturday, from 10:30 am to 5:30 pm.

The **$6 Plate Lunches** truck— simple steak, chicken, or pork plates with green salad and rice—sells out fast Tuesday through Saturday. It's open from approximately 9:30 am until everything sells out. (☎ 808/283–8544).

On Saturday, there are usually additional trucks here.

Another great truck, called **Like Poke?**, is parked in front of Kahului Trucking & Storage on Hobron Lane near Matson (Kahului) on weekdays from 8:30 am to 2:30 pm. It serves breakfast, *poke* (raw fish salad), and plates. Ahi katsu is the signature plate item. Everything is delicious and sells out early, so if you want something specific, you can call ahead (☎ 808/757–2239).

$ ✕ **Cilantro.** The flavors of Old Mexico are given new life here, where a dozen chilis are used to create the salsas. The owner, a former high-end food and beverage pro, spent three years visiting authentic eateries in 40 Mexican cities before opening this place. Tucked into an older and unfancy mall, this restaurant requires you to order at the counter and fill your own disposable beverage cup at the soda fountain. But as soon as you bite into a chipotle-citrus rotisserie chicken plate or, really, anything on the menu, you'll forget all about the plastic cutlery and lack of a view. The brilliantly colored, clever decor—a collection of worn-from-duty tortilla presses, now hand-painted—coupled with consistently excellent food at affordable prices more than makes up for the lack of fine-dining amenities. $ *Average main: $12* ⊠ *Old Lahaina Center, 170 Papalaua Ave.* ☎ *808/667–5444* ⊕ *www.cilantrogrill.com.*

MEXICAN

$$$$ ✕ **Gerard's.** For nearly three decades, classically trained French chef Gerard Reversade—he started as an apprentice in acclaimed Paris restaurants when he was just 14—has remained true to his Gascony roots. His exacting standards—in the dining room as well as in the kitchen—have always been the hallmarks of his charming eponymous restaurant. He cooks *his* way, utilizing island ingredients in such classic dishes as Hamakua mushrooms in puff pastry, escargots *forestière*, Molokai shrimp consommé, terrine of foie gras, and confit of duck. The wine list is first-class. Floral fabrics and white tablecloths echo the look of a French country inn. $ *Average main: $45* ⊠ *Plantation Inn, 174 Lahainaluna Rd.* ☎ *808/661–8939* ⊕ *www.gerardsmaui.com* ⊙ No lunch.

FRENCH

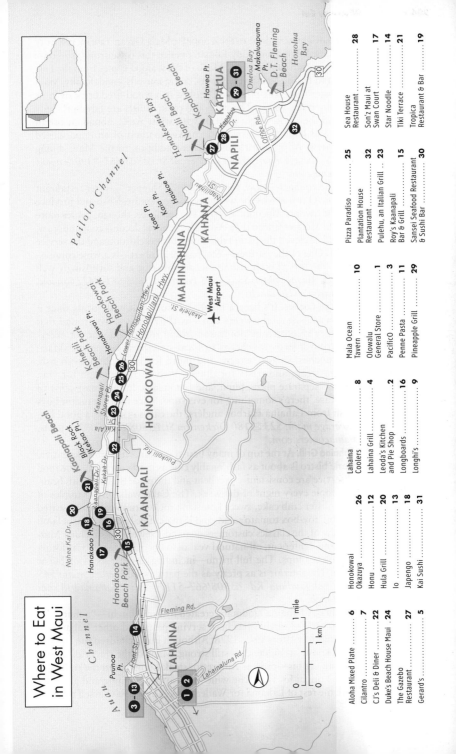

Where to Eat in West Maui

$$$$ ✕ **Honu.** Right next door to their popular Mala Ocean Tavern, celebrity
ECLECTIC   chef Mark Ellman and Judy Ellman opened this oceanfront fish house
and pizza restaurant in 2011. Much of the seafood comes from the East
Coast and Pacific Northwest: clams, crabs, mussels—and, finally, Maui
has lobster rolls. The pizzas are cooked in a wood-fired brick oven (is
there any other way?). The wine and cocktail lists are fabulous. Judy
designed the sleek, bright interior with white walls, abundant use of
wood, and large windows: Honu makes the best of an unparalleled
ocean view. All in all, it's an excellent addition to the Maui dining
scene. $ *Average main: $36* ✉ *1295 Front St.* ☎ *808/667–9390* ⊕ *www.
honumaui.com.*

$$$$ ✕ **Io.** The younger—okay, some would say "hipper"—sister restaurant
MODERN   of Pacific'O just across the walkway, focuses on fresh fish and produce
HAWAIIAN   from the owners' Upcountry farm. The influence, though, comes more
from the Mediterranean than Asia. The nautical decor is contemporary,
the menu is clever, the patio tables are truly beachfront, and the service
is good. One of the partners—Stephan Bel Robert—is a wine connois-
seur, so the lists at both restaurants are fantastic and surprisingly well
priced. $ *Average main: $36* ✉ *505 Front St.* ☎ *808/661–8422* ⊕ *www.
iomaui.com* ☾ *No lunch.*

$$ ✕ **Lahaina Coolers.** It's been a popular, casual spot with locals since it
AMERICAN   first opened—several owners ago—in 1989. And to be around that
long, they've got to be doing something right. You can get every-
thing from huevos rancheros to local-style fried rice at breakfast;
plate lunches, salads, wraps, and more for lunch; and fresh fish,
chicken, steak, and pasta for dinner. If that's not enough for you,
there are separate pizza, pupu, and bar menus. In the truest sense of
the phrase, there's something for everyone. Since this restaurant buys
its fish from Lahaina Harbor anglers, the catch is always a good bet.
$ *Average main: $23* ✉ *180 Dickenson St.* ☎ *808/661–7082* ⊕ *www.
lahainacoolers.com.*

$$$$ ✕ **Lahaina Grill.** At the top of many best-restaurants lists, this expensive,
AMERICAN   upscale bistro is about as fashionably chic as it gets on Maui. The food
and service are consistently excellent and the place is abuzz with beau-
tiful people every night of the week. The Cake Walk (little samples of
Kona lobster crab cake, sweet Louisiana rock-shrimp cake, and seared
ahi cake), toy-box tomato salad, and Kona-coffee-roasted rack of lamb
are a few of the classics customers demand. Newer items include Mar-
cho Farms center-cut, all-natural veal osso buco and seared California
lion-paw scallops. The full menu—including dessert—is available at
the bar. The interior is as pretty as the patrons. $ *Average main: $45*
✉ *127 Lahainaluna Rd.* ☎ *808/667–5117* ⊕ *www.lahainagrill.com*
☾ *No lunch.*

$$$ ✕ **Longhi's.** A Lahaina landmark created by Bob Longhi—"a man who
ITALIAN   loves to eat"—Longhi's has been serving pasta and other Italian fare
to throngs of visitors since 1976. Although Bob's children run the restaurants now, his influence is still strong. Many of the classic dishes on
the menu are his—prawns Amaretto, steak Longhi, and the signature
lobster Longhi for two. The wine list is award winning and gigantic.
Before the rest of Lahaina (or Wailea) wakes up, have yourself a cup of

freshly squeezed orange juice, a fluffy frittata, and some good, strong coffee to start the day. The in-house bakery shines with outstanding breakfast pastries. There are two spacious, open-air dining levels; and there's a second Maui restaurant at the Shops at Wailea. $ *Average main: $34* ✉ *888 Front St.* ☎ *808/667–2288* ⊕ *www.longhis.com.*

$$$
MODERN
HAWAIIAN
Fodor's Choice
★

✕ **Mala Ocean Tavern.** Chef-owner Mark Ellman started Maui's culinary revolution of the late '80s with his restaurant Avalon, but Mala is a more than satisfactory successor. The place is adorable; the best tables are on the lanai, which actually juts out over the water. The menu reflects Mark's and his wife Judy's world travels with dishes influenced by the Middle East, the Mediterranean, Italy, Bali, and Thailand. Every item on the menu is delicious, and there's a focus on ingredients that promote local sustainability. The cocktails and wine list are great, too. Another location of Mala is at the Wailea Beach Marriott Resort, but the Lahaina original is highly recommended. $ *Average main: $30* ✉ *1307 Front St.* ☎ *808/667–9394* ⊕ *www.malaoceantavern.com.*

$$$$
MODERN
HAWAIIAN

✕ **PacificO.** Sophisticated outdoor dining on the beach (no, really *on* the beach) and creative island cuisine using local, fresh-caught fish and greens and veggies grown in the restaurant's own Upcountry O'o Farm (and, quite possibly, picked that very morning)—this is the Maui dining experience you've been dreaming about. Start with the award-winning appetizer of prawn and basil wontons, move on to any of the fantastic fresh fish dishes, and for dessert, finish with the banana pineapple *lumpia* served hot with homemade banana ice cream. $ *Average main: $36* ✉ *505 Front St.* ☎ *808/667–4341* ⊕ *www.pacificomaui.com.*

$
ITALIAN

✕ **Penne Pasta.** A couple of blocks off Front Street in Lahaina, this small restaurant packs a powerhouse of a menu with pizza, pastas, salads, and sandwiches. Heaping plates of reasonably priced, flavorful food make this low-key place a perfect alternative to an expensive night at the resort. House favorites include the cheesy baked penne in tomato cream sauce, and the linguine in clam sauce with lemon butter. There are nightly specials like the osso buco on Wednesday, made with lamb instead of veal and served with fettuccine and salad. Two can easily split a salad and entrée and leave completely sated. $ *Average main: $12* ✉ *180 Dickenson St.* ☎ *808/661–6633* ⊕ *www.pennepastacafe.com.*

$
ASIAN
Fodor's Choice
★

✕ **Star Noodle.** In a very short time this wonderful spot has become one of Maui's best restaurants. It's way up above the highway in a light industrial park, but don't be discouraged by the location. Take the drive and you'll find a hip place and a welcoming staff that knows the meaning of "aloha." There's a communal table in the center of the room, smaller tables around the perimeter, and comfortable stools for those who like to eat at a bar. Menu musts include the Ahi Avo, pan-roasted brussels sprouts with bacon and kim chee purée, and really any of the noodle dishes, especially the Lahaina fried soup (fat chow fun, pork, bean sprouts). The cocktail list is fabulous and the lychee martinis served here may be the best on Maui. $ *Average main: $12* ✉ *286 Kupuohi St.* ☎ *808/667–5400* ⊕ *www.starnoodle.com.*

8

KAANAPALI

$ ✕ **CJ's Deli & Diner.** Chef Christian Jorgensen left fancy hotel kitchens
AMERICAN behind to open a casual place serving simple, delicious food at reasonable prices. The mango-glazed ribs, burgers, and classic Reuben sandwich are good choices, and the pineapple fried rice is *ono* (delicious);
just order and pick up at the counter, and take your food to a table. If
you're traveling to Hana or the Haleakala Crater, buy a box lunch and
you're set. If you're staying in a condo, the "Chefs to Go" service is a
great alternative to picking up (run of the mill and usually lousy) fast
food. Everything is prepped and comes with easy cooking instructions.
And if you decide, even on the spur of the moment, that Maui is a nice
place for a wedding, CJ's can cater it. $ *Average main: $10* ⊠ *Fairway
Shops, 2580 Kekaa Dr.* ☎ *808/667–0968* ⊕ *www.cjsmaui.com.*

$$$ ✕ **Duke's Beach House Maui.** The spot's the thing—the view is amazing—
MODERN at this casual eatery just steps from the beach on the grounds of the
HAWAIIAN Honua Kai Resort & Spa. The food is reliable, the decor all surfer-
dudes and little grass shacks, and the signature cocktails big and
umbrella-garnished. The fresh fish is a good bet, and you'll know from
the aroma when you enter that there are burgers on the grill. Kimo's
original hula pie is reason enough to come. You can buy the cool
retro plate on which it's served for 20 bucks. $ *Average main: $28*
⊠ *Honua Kai Resort & Spa, 130 Kai Malina Pkwy.* ☎ *808/662–2900*
⊕ *www.dukesmaui.com.*

$$$ ✕ **Hula Grill.** A bustling and family-oriented spot on Kaanapali Beach
MODERN at Whalers Village shopping center, this restaurant designed to look
HAWAIIAN like a sprawling '30s beach house represents a partnership between
FAMILY TS Restaurants group and Hawaii Regional Cuisine pioneer chef Peter
Merriman. They serve up large dinner portions with an emphasis on
fresh local fish—try the macadamia nut–crusted catch, fire-grilled ahi
steak, or coconut seafood chowder. Just in the mood for an umbrella-
adorned cocktail and some pupu? Go to the Barefoot Bar, where you
can wiggle your toes in the sand while you sip. The beach is called
"Dig Me"—you'll understand why after just a few moments. $ *Average
main: $29* ⊠ *Whalers Village, 2435 Kaanapali Pkwy.* ☎ *808/667–6636*
⊕ *www.hulagrill.com.*

$$$$ ✕ **Japengo.** This nicely appointed open-air restaurant gives hotel din-
ASIAN ing a better name. The ocean views are stunning, and the gentle trade
winds cool the night air. The glassed-in sushi bar is gorgeous. But it's
the food that makes Japengo worth a visit. The award-winning sashimi-
style hamachi and watermelon is delicious, while the fresh local fish is
well prepared and perfectly accompanied. Many dishes are offered in
half portions at half price, the better to taste more of the creative menu.
Perhaps most surprising are the desserts, which are crazy good. Even if
dessert translates for you to "chocolate," the flaming piña colada crème
here will change your mind forever. $ *Average main: $38* ⊠ *Hyatt
Regency Maui Resort & Spa, 200 Nohea Kai Dr.* ☎ *808/661–1234*
⊕ *www.maui.hyatt.com/hyatt/hotels-maui/entertainment/dining_detail.
jsp?itemDesc=fboutlet&itemId=1003060* ⊗ *No lunch.*

Continued on page 213

LUAU: A TASTE OF HAWAII

The best place to sample Hawaiian food is at a backyard luau. Aunts and uncles are cooking, the pig is from a cousin's farm, and the fish is from a brother's boat.

8

But even locals have to angle for invitations to those rare occasions. So your choice is most likely between a commercial luau and a Hawaiian restaurant.

Some commercial luau are less authentic; they offer little of the traditional diet and are more about umbrella drinks, spectacle, and fun.

For greater authenticity, folksy experiences, and rock-bottom prices, visit a Hawaiian restaurant (most are in anonymous storefronts in residential neighborhoods). Expect rough edges and some effort negotiating the menu.

In either case, much of what is known today as Hawaiian food would be as foreign to a 16th-century Hawaiian as risotto or chow mien. The pre-contact diet was simple and healthy—mainly raw and steamed seafood and vegetables. Early Hawaiians used earth ovens and heated stones to cook seafood, taro, sweet potatoes, and breadfruit and seasoned their food with sea salt and ground kukui nuts. Seaweed, fern shoots, sweet potato vines, coconut, banana, sugarcane, and select greens and roots rounded out the diet.

Successive waves of immigrants added their favorites to the ti leaf–lined table. So it is that foods as disparate as salt salmon and chicken long rice are now Hawaiian—even though there is no salmon in Hawaiian waters and long rice (cellophane noodles) is Chinese.

AT THE LUAU: KALUA PORK

The heart of any luau is the *imu*, the earth oven in which a whole pig is roasted. The preparation of an imu is an arduous affair for most families, who tackle it only once a year or so, for a baby's first birthday or at Thanksgiving, when many Islanders prefer to imu their turkeys. Commercial luau operations have it down to a science, however.

THE ART OF THE STONE

The key to a proper imu is the *pohaku*, the stones. Imu cook by means of long, slow, moist heat released by special stones that can withstand a hot fire without exploding. Many Hawaiian families treasure their imu stones, keeping them in a pile in the backyard and passing them on through generations.

PIT COOKING

The imu makers first dig a pit about the size of a refrigerator, then lay down *kiawe* (mesquite) wood and stones, and build a white-hot fire that is allowed to burn itself out. The ashes are raked away, and the hot stones covered with banana and ti leaves. Well-wrapped in ti or banana leaves and a net of chicken wire, the pig is lowered onto the leaf-covered stones. *Laulau* (leaf-wrapped bundles of meats, fish, and taro leaves) may also be placed inside. Leaves—ti, banana, even ginger—cover the pig followed by wet burlap sacks (to create steam). The whole is topped with a canvas tarp and left to steam for the better part of a day.

OPENING THE IMU

This is the moment everyone waits for: The imu is unwrapped like a giant present and the imu keepers gingerly wrestle out the steaming pig. When it's unwrapped, the meat falls moist and smoky-flavored from the bone, looking just like Southern-style pulled pork, but without the barbecue sauce.

WHICH LUAU?

The Feast at Lele. Technically not a luau, but a top-notch (and top-price) evening of Pacific Islands food and entertainment.

Old Lahaina Luau. The best on Maui: a perennial sell-out, so book as far in advance as possible.

Wailea Beach Marriott Te Au Moana. Imu ceremony and buffet.

MEA AI ONO:
GOOD THINGS TO EAT.

LAULAU

Steamed meats, fish, and taro leaf in ti-leaf bundles: fork-tender, a medley of flavors; the taro resembles spinach.

LOMI LOMI SALMON

Salt salmon in a piquant salad or relish with onions, tomatoes.

POI

Poi, a paste made of pounded taro root, may be an acquired taste, but it's a must-try during your visit.

Consider: The Hawaiian Adam is descended from *kalo* (taro). Young taro plants are called "keiki"–children. Poi is the first food after mother's milk for many Islanders. Ai, the word for food, is synonymous with poi in many contexts.

Not only that, we love it. "There is no meat that doesn't taste good with poi," the old Hawaiians said.

But you have to know how to eat it: with something rich or powerfully flavored. "It is salt that makes the poi go in," is another adage. When you're served poi, try it with a mouthful of smoky kalua pork or salty lomi lomi salmon. Its slightly sour blandness cleanses the palate. And if you don't like it, smile and say something polite. (And slide that bowl over to a local.)

Laulau

Lomi Lomi Salmon

Poi

8

E HELE MAI AI! COME AND EAT!

Hawaiian restaurants tend to be inconveniently located in well-worn storefronts with little or no parking, outfitted with battered tables and clattering Melmac dishes, but they personify aloha, invariably run by local families who welcome tourists who take the trouble to find them.

Many are cash-only operations and combination plates are a standard feature: one or two entrées, a side such as chicken long rice, choice of poi or steamed rice and—if the place is really old-style—a tiny portion of coarse Hawaiian salt and some raw onions for relish.

Most serve some foods that aren't, strictly speaking, Hawaiian, but are beloved of kamaaina, such as salt meat with watercress (preserved meat in a tasty broth), or *akubone*

(skipjack tuna fried in a tangy vinegar sauce).

A favorite local spot on Maui: **Aloha Mixed Plate**.

MENU GUIDE

Much of the Hawaiian language encountered during a stay in the Islands will appear on restaurant menus and lists of luau fare. Here's a quick primer.

ahi: *yellowfin tuna.*

aku: *skipjack, bonito tuna.*

amaama: *mullet; it's hard to get but tasty.*

bento: *a box lunch.*

chicken luau: *a stew made from chicken, taro leaves, and coconut milk.*

haupia: *a light, pudding-like sweet made from coconut.*

imu: *the underground oven in which pigs are roasted for luau.*

kalua: *to bake underground.*

kau kau: *food. The word comes from Chinese but is used in the Islands.*

kimchee: *Korean dish of pickled cabbage made with garlic and hot peppers.*

Kona coffee: *coffee grown in the Kona district of the Big Island.*

laulau: *literally, a bundle. Laulau are morsels of pork, chicken, butterfish, or other ingredients wrapped with young taro leaves and then bundled in ti leaves for steaming.*

lilikoi: *passion fruit, a tart, seedy yellow fruit that makes delicious desserts, juice, and jellies.*

lomi lomi: *to rub or massage; also a massage. Lomi lomi salmon is fish that has been rubbed with onions and herbs; commonly served with minced onions and tomatoes.*

luau: *a Hawaiian feast; also the leaf of the taro plant used in preparing such a feast.*

luau leaves: *cooked taro tops with a taste similar to spinach.*

mahimahi: *mild-flavored dolphinfish, not the marine mammal.*

mai tai: *potent rum drink with orange liqueurs and pineapple juice, from the Tahitian word for "good."*

malasada: *a Portuguese deep-fried doughnut without a hole, dipped in sugar.*

manapua: *steamed chinese buns filled with pork, chicken, or other fillings.*

mano: *shark.*

niu: *coconut.*

onaga: *pink or red snapper.*

ono: *a long, slender mackerel-like fish; also called wahoo.*

ono: *delicious; also hungry.*

opihi: *a tiny shellfish, or mollusk, found on rocks; also called limpets.*

papio: *a young ulua or jack fish.*

poha: *Cape gooseberry. Tasting a bit like honey, the poha berry is often used in jams and desserts.*

poi: *a paste made from pounded taro root, a staple of the Hawaiian diet.*

poke: *cubed raw tuna or other fish, tossed with seaweed and seasonings.*

pupu: *appetizers or small plates.*

saimin: *long thin noodles and vegetables in broth, often garnished with small pieces of fish cake, scrambled egg, luncheon meat, and green onion.*

sashimi: *raw fish thinly sliced and usually eaten with soy sauce.*

ti leaves: *a member of the agave family. The leaves are used to wrap food while cooking and removed before eating.*

uku: *deep-sea snapper.*

ulua: *a member of the jack family that also includes pompano and amberjack. Also called crevalle, jack fish, and jack crevalle.*

$$$
MODERN
HAWAIIAN

✕ **Longboards.** This casual open-air restaurant set right on the Kaanapali beach walk is a good, reasonably priced dinner choice for anyone staying within the resort area. The signature calamari and coconut shrimp pupu are delicious and everything is artfully plated. Besides fresh local fish prepared four ways, choices include chicken, ribs, teriyaki beef, and fish tacos. Would you like fries with that? Try the *ono*-licious sweet-potato fries for a change of pace. The sunset views are great, the decor is, well, surf-y, and the service is pleasant. ⑤ *Average main: $30* ✉ *Marriott's Maui Ocean Club, 100 Nohea Kai Dr.* ☎ *808/667–1200* ⊕ *www.marriott.com* ⊗ *No lunch.*

$$$
ITALIAN

✕ **Pulehu, an Italian Grill.** If you need proof that Italian plays in paradise, you'll find it here. Chef Wesley Holder and his merry band of kitchen innovators are using 80% local Maui products to do what the Italians do best: craft simple, delicious food that lets the ingredients shine. Must-haves include the local vine-ripened Caprese salad, the award-winning tortellini en brodo, and Chianti-braised short ribs. The wine list is excellent. As if great food and drink weren't enough, the service is stellar, and the glassed-in exhibition kitchen provides an eyeful of culinary entertainment. ⑤ *Average main: $32* ✉ *The Westin Kaanapali Ocean Resort Villas, 6 Kai Ala Dr.* ☎ *808/667–3254* ⊕ *www.westinkaanapali.com/dining/pulehu* ⊗ *Closed Tues. and Wed.*

$$$$
MODERN
HAWAIIAN
Fodor'sChoice
★

✕ **Roy's Kaanapali.** Roy Yamaguchi is a James Beard award-winning chef and the granddaddy of East-meets-West cuisine. He has restaurants all over the world, but his eponymous Maui restaurant was one of the first, and it's still one of the best. It's loud and brassy with a young vibe, but come for the great food, even if the atmosphere isn't quite your thing. Signatures like fire-grilled, Szechuan-spiced, baby back pork ribs, Roy's original blackened ahi tuna, hibachi-style grilled salmon, and the to-die-for hot chocolate soufflé have been on the menu from the beginning, and with good reason. Roy's wine list is exceptionally user-friendly. The service here is welcoming and professional. ⑤ *Average main: $36* ✉ *2990 Kaanapali Pkwy.* ☎ *808/669–6999* ⊕ *www.roysrestaurant.com.*

$$$$
MEDITERRANEAN

✕ **Son'z at Swan Court.** If you're celebrating a special occasion and want to splurge, this just might be the place for you. You'll descend a grand staircase into an amber-lighted dining room with soaring ceilings and a massive artificial lagoon complete with swans, waterfalls, and tropical gardens. Must-haves on Chef Geno Sarmiento's contemporary, Mediterranean-influenced menu include ahi saltimbocca; goat-cheese ravioli with Kula corn, edamame, and Hamakua mushrooms; and grilled beef tenderloin marinated in coffee and served with Parmesan-garlic fries. The restaurant claims the largest wine cellar in Hawaii with 3,000 bottles. ⑤ *Average main: $38* ✉ *Hyatt Regency Maui, 200 Nohea Kai Dr.* ☎ *808/667–4506* ⊕ *www.sonzmaui.com* ⊗ *No lunch.*

$$
MODERN
HAWAIIAN

✕ **Tiki Terrace.** Executive chef Tom Muromoto is a local boy who loves to cook modern, upscale Hawaiian food. He augments the various fresh fish dishes on his menu with items influenced by Hawaii's ethnic mix. This casual, open-air restaurant is the only place on Maui—maybe in Hawaii—where you can have a Native Hawaiian combination plate that is as healthful as it is authentic. Sunday brunch,

8

complete with strolling Hawaiian musicians and hula dancers, is renowned here; and if you're around for any holiday, chow down at the amazing holiday brunch buffets. $ *Average main: $26 ⊠ Kaanapali Beach Hotel, 2525 Kaanapali Pkwy.* ☎ *808/667–0124* ⊕ *www. kbhmaui.com* ☾ *No lunch.*

$$$$ ✕ **Tropica Restaurant & Bar.** As far as hotel dining goes, this beautifully
MODERN   appointed, oceanfront restaurant serving fare infused with European,
HAWAIIAN Pacific, and Hawaiian influences is as cool, calm, comfortable, and
Fodor'sChoice delicious as it gets. Start with an exceptionally creative cocktail—the
★   martinis are superb—or a glass of wine from a long, excellent list. Then, indulge in the chili-grilled *tako* (octopus), Hamakua mushroom stone-baked flatbread, and one of the delectable fresh fish preparations. As a sweet way to end your meal, try the "Study in Chocolate." This is a perfect spot for that special Maui dinner. $ *Average main: $36 ⊠ The Westin Maui Resort & Spa, 2365 Kaanapali Pkwy.* ☎ *808/667–2525* ⊕ *www.westinmaui.com* ☾ *Closed Mon. and Tues. No lunch.*

KAPALUA AND VICINITY

$ ✕ **The Gazebo Restaurant.** Breakfast is the reason to seek out this res-
DINER   taurant located poolside at the Napili Shores Resort. The ambience is a little funky but the oceanfront setting and views are spectacular—including the turtle, spinner dolphin, and, in winter, humpback-whale sightings. The food is standard diner fare and portions are big. Many folks think the Gazebo serves the best pancakes on West Maui. Have them with pineapple, bananas, macadamia nuts, or chocolate chips, or make up your own combination. You will almost certainly have to wait for a table, sometimes for quite a while, but at least it's a pleasant place to do so. $ *Average main: $11 ⊠ Napili Shores Resort, 5315 Lower Honoapiilani Hwy., Napili* ☎ *808/669–5621* ☾ *No dinner.*

$ ✕ **Honokowai Okazuya.** Sandwiched between a dive shop and a salon
ECLECTIC in a nondescript mini strip mall, this small place has only a few stools and a couple of tables outside, but it's fast and the food is consistently good—all it takes to keep the place filled with locals. The mahimahi with lemon capers, and beef black bean chow fun are the top-selling favorites. There's plenty more including vegetarian and lighter fare such as Grandma's spicy tofu, egg fu young, and even a veggie burger. The fresh chow fun noodles sell out quickly. $ *Average main: $12* ⊠ *3600-D Lower Honoapiilani Hwy., Honokowai* ☎ *808/665–0512* ⊟ *No credit cards* ☾ *Closed all day Sunday and every day between 2:30 and 4:30.*

$$$ ✕ **Kai Sushi.** For a quiet, light dinner, or to meet friends for a cock-
JAPANESE tail and some ultrafresh sushi, head to this handsome restaurant on the lobby level of the Ritz-Carlton Kapalua. You have your choice of sushi, sashimi, and a list of rolls. The especially good Kai special roll combines spicy tuna, yellowtail, and green onion. In keeping with the hotel's commitment to the culture, the restaurant's design was inspired by the story of Native Hawaiians' arrival by sea; the hand-carved ceiling beams resemble outrigger canoes. $ *Average main: $30 ⊠ Ritz-Carlton, Kapalua, 1 Ritz-Carlton Dr., Kapalua* ☎ *808/669–7385* ⊕ *www. ritzcarlton.com/kapalua* ☾ *Closed Tues. and Wed. No lunch.*

$$$$
MODERN
HAWAIIAN

✕ **Pineapple Grill.** High on the hill overlooking the Kapalua resort, this restaurant exudes casual elegance. Executive Chef Isaac Bancaco makes good use of the island's bounty, with dishes featuring Maui pineapple, Roselani ice cream, Maui Cattle Company beef, greens and vegetables from Waipoli and Nalo farms, and local, sustainable fish. If you've had enough of the gorgeous ocean, mountain, or

WORD OF MOUTH

"Start your day having breakfast at the gorgeous Plantation House at Kapalua golf course. The food for breakfast is excellent and super reasonable with great views and no lines! Ahi Benedict with a wasabi hollandaise is our fave with a Bloody Mary." —ksucat

resort views, you can watch the chef and his crew in the shiny exhibition kitchen as they assemble their specialties like lemongrass and macadamia-nut-crusted mahimahi and Asian braised Wagyu beef short ribs. $ *Average main: $38* ✉ *200 Kapalua Dr., Kapalua* ☎ *808/669–9600* ⊕ *www.pineapplekapalua.com.*

$
ITALIAN

✕ **Pizza Paradiso.** When it opened in 1995, this was an over-the-counter pizza place. It has evolved over the years into a local favorite serving Italian, Mediterranean, and Middle Eastern comfort food as well as pizza. The pies are so popular because of the top ingredients—100% pure Italian olive oil, Maui produce whenever possible, and Maui Cattle Company beef. The menu also features gyros, falafel, grilled fish, rotisserie chicken, and tiramisu. $ *Average main: $12* ✉ *Honokowai Marketplace, 3350 Lower Honoapiilani Rd., Honokowai* ☎ *808/667–2929* ⊕ *www.pizzaparadiso.com.*

$$$
MODERN
HAWAIIAN

✕ **Plantation House Restaurant.** It's a bit of a drive, but when you get there you'll find a beautiful and comfortable restaurant with expansive views of the ocean below and the majestic mountains above. At this writing, Chef JoJo Vasquez was turning the menu upside down and infusing his own particular style. He calls his cuisine "Hawaiian Eclectic," and is renowned for sourcing as many local ingredients as possible. You won't be taking much of a chance if you choose Plantation House for dinner—Vasquez is a very talented chef. $ *Average main: $35* ✉ *Plantation Course Clubhouse, 2000 Plantation Club Dr., Kapalua* ☎ *808/669–6299* ⊕ *www.theplantationhouse.com.*

$$
ASIAN
Fodor's Choice
★

✕ **Sansei Seafood Restaurant & Sushi Bar.** If you are a fish or shellfish lover, then this is the place for you. One of the most wildly popular restaurants in Hawaii with locations on three islands, Sansei takes sushi, sashimi, and contemporary Japanese food to a new level. Favorite dishes include the mango-and-crab-salad hand roll, panko-crusted, sashimi-grade ahi roll, Asian shrimp cake, Japanese calamari salad, and Dungeness crab ramen with Asian-truffle broth. There are great deals on sushi and small plates for early birds and night owls. This busy restaurant has several separate dining areas, a sushi bar, and a bar area, but the focus is squarely on excellent food and not the ambience. $ *Average main: $26* ✉ *600 Office Rd., Kapalua* ☎ *808/669–6286* ⊕ *www.sanseihawaii.com* ☾ *No lunch.*

$$$
MODERN
HAWAIIAN

✕ **Sea House Restaurant.** Built in the 1960s at the Napili Kai Beach Resort before there were laws forbidding construction so close to the beach,

8

this restaurant is, literally, just footsteps away from gorgeous Napili Bay. Wear your beach wrap to breakfast and enjoy the signature oven-baked pancakes or Molokai sweet potato egg frittata. For dinner, start with the award-winning *poke* (raw fish) nachos and move on to the taro-crusted sea bass. Several entrées are offered in both "lite" and regular-size portions. Folks who are gluten-intolerant will find excellent choices here. $ *Average main: $32* ✉ *Napili Kai Beach Resort, 5900 Lower Honoapiilani Rd., Napili* ☎ *808/669–1500* ⊕ *www.seahousemaui.com.com.*

SOUTH SHORE

South Maui's dining scene begins at Maalaea Harbor and wends its way through the beach towns of Kihei and Wailea. There are plenty of casual, relatively inexpensive eateries along the way—until you reach Wailea, where most of the dining is pricey. Some of it, fortunately, is worth it.

Besides restaurants listed below, you can find branches of Mala Ocean Tavern (here called Mala Wailea), and Longhi's in this area. For reviews of these establishments, see the West Maui section.

KIHEI AND NORTH (MAALAEA)

KIHEI

$$　✕**Cuatro.** Chef-owner Eric Arbogast has admirably turned this tiny
ECLECTIC　space tucked into a corner of a strip mall into a comfortable restaurant serving well-prepared, delicious food. Signature dishes include spicy tuna nachos, Togarashi seared ahi, fresh local fish (prepared nightly in at least four different ways), Asian marinated grilled steak, and South of the Border marinated pork. The wine list is user-friendly, and the service is welcoming. $ *Average main: $25* ✉ *Kihei Town Center, 1881 S. Kihei Rd.* ☎ *808/879–1110* ⊕ *www.cuatromaui.com* ☾ *No lunch.*

$　✕**Eskimo Candy.** Eskimo Candy has been one of Maui's best fresh fish
AMERICAN　purveyors for many years. Their casual little restaurant/takeout place/fish market allows visitors and residents to enjoy the same fresh fish cooked in many of Maui's best restaurants. Everything on the menu is delicious. Signatures include Davey Jones' fish-n-chips, the big kahuna fish platter, and Captain Charlie Butterfly's famous fish burger. They make several varieties of *poke* (Hawaiian ceviche) fresh daily. If you're staying somewhere with kitchen/grilling facilities, get your fresh fish here. Be sure to look at their fabulous T-shirt designs and cool packaging. $ *Average main: $12* ✉ *2665 Wai Wai Place* ☎ *808/891–8898* ⊕ *www.eskimocandy.com* ☾ *Closed weekends.*

$　✕**Kihei Caffe.** This small, unassuming place across the street from Kal-
AMERICAN　ama Beach Park has a breakfast menu that runs the gamut from healthy yogurt-filled papaya to the local classic, *loco moco*—two eggs, ground beef patty, rice, and brown gravy—and everything in between. And the best thing about it is that the breakfast menu is served all day long. Prices are extremely reasonable and it's a good spot for people-watching.

This is a popular place with locals, so you may have to wait for a table, depending on the time and day. $\boxed{\$}$ *Average main: $8* ✉ *1945 S. Kihei Rd.* ☎ *808/879–2230* ⊕ *www.kiheicaffe.com* ☾ *No dinner.*

$$ ✕ **Monsoon India.** Here you can enjoy a lovely ocean view while feast-
INDIAN ing on authentic Indian cuisine. Appetizers like *papadum* chips and *samosas* are served with homemade chutneys. There are 10 breads—naan and more—that come hot from the tandoori oven, along with six mix-and-match curries, lots of vegetarian selections, kebabs, and biryanis. There's live music on Saturday evenings and popular buffets on Friday nights and for Sunday brunch. A second restaurant is located in Lahaina at the Wharf Cinema Center. $\boxed{\$}$ *Average main: $20* ✉ *Menehune Shores, 760 S. Kihei Rd.* ☎ *808/875–6666* ⊕ *www. monsoonindiamaui.com.*

$$$$ ✕ **Sarento's on the Beach.** This upscale Italian restaurant's setting right
ITALIAN on spectacular Keawakapu Beach, with views of Molokini and Kahoolawe, is irresistible. After years of serving dinner only, it now offers breakfast service so diners can enjoy the extraordinary view in the morning, too. The breakfast menu offers all the regular fare; dinner has a decidedly Italian bent, with dishes like linguine with clams, penne Bolognese, and portobello napoleon with local eggplant, mozzarella, tomatoes, and arugula pesto. The food is very good, if a bit old-fashioned, and the portions may be too big for some. $\boxed{\$}$ *Average main: $36* ✉ *2980 S. Kihei Rd.* ☎ *808/875–7555* ⊕ *www. sarentosonthebeach.com* ☾ *No lunch.*

$ ✕ **South Shore Tiki Lounge.** Come on, how can you come to Hawaii and
AMERICAN *not* go to a tiki bar? And this one—tucked into Kihei Kalama Village—is consistently voted "Best Bar" by the readers of *Maui Time Weekly.* During the day, sit on the shaded lanai to enjoy a burger, sandwich, or, better yet, one of their delicious specialty pizzas, crafted from scratch with sauces made from fresh Roma tomatoes and Maui herbs. Their pies have been voted "Best Local Pizza" by those same *Maui Time Weekly* readers for three years running. Seven nights a week, the tiny bar area lights up with a lively crowd, as DJs spin dance tunes under the glowing red eyes of the lounge's namesake tiki. And you can order food right up until midnight. $\boxed{\$}$ *Average main: $15* ✉ *Kihei Kalama Village, 1913-J S. Kihei Rd.* ☎ *808/874–6444* ⊕ *www. southshoretikilounge.com.*

$ ✕ **Thailand Cuisine.** Fragrant tea and coconut-ginger chicken soup begin
THAI a satisfying meal at this excellent Thai restaurant, set unassumingly in the middle of a shopping mall. The care and expense that goes into the decor—glittering Buddhist shrines, elaborate hardwood facades, fancy napkin folds, and matching blue china—also applies to the cuisine. Take an exotic journey with the fantastic pad Thai, special house noodles, curries, and crispy fried chicken. Can't decide? Try the family dinners for two or four. The fried bananas with ice cream are wonderful. There's a second location in Kahului's Maui Mall, a perfect choice before or after a movie at the megaplex. $\boxed{\$}$ *Average main: $15* ✉ *Kukui Mall, 1819 S. Kihei Rd.* ☎ *808/875–0839* ⊕ *www.thailandcuisinemaui. com* ☾ *No lunch Sun.*

8

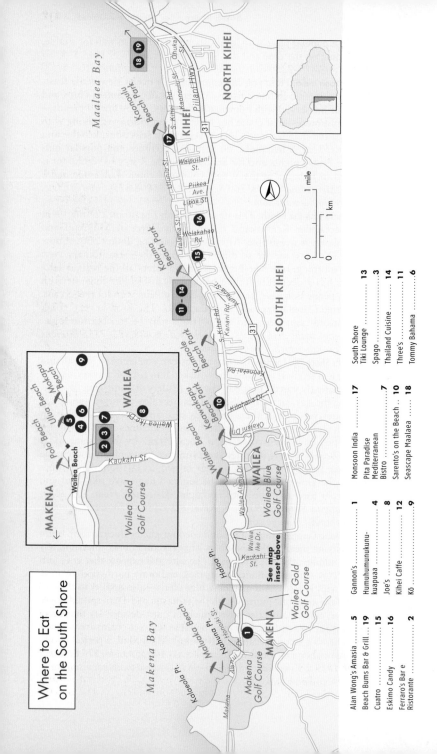

Where to Eat on the South Shore

Alan Wong's Amasia **5**
Beach Bums Bar & Grill ... **19**
Cuatro **15**
Eskimo Candy **16**
Ferraro's Bar e
Ristorante **2**

Gannon's **1**
Humuhumunukunu-
kuapuaa **4**
Joe's **8**
Kihei Caffe **12**
Kō **9**

Monsoon India **17**
Pita Paradise
Mediterranean
Bistro **7**
Sarento's on the Beach .. **10**
Seascape Maalaea **18**

South Shore
Tiki Lounge **13**
Spago **3**
Thailand Cuisine **14**
Three's **11**
Tommy Bahama **6**

The Plate Lunch Tradition

To experience island history firsthand, take a seat at one of Hawaii's ubiquitous "plate lunch" eateries, where you'll be served a segmented Styrofoam plate piled with a protein—usually in an Asian-style preparation like beef teriyaki—two scoops of rice, a scoop of macaroni salad, and maybe a pickled vegetable condiment. On the sugar plantations, immigrant workers from many different countries ate together in the fields, sharing food from their *kaukau* tins, the utilitarian version of the Japanese *bento* (Japanese divided box filled with savory items) lunchbox. From this stir-fry of people came the vibrant language of pidgin and its equivalent in food: the plate lunch.

At beaches and public parks you will probably see locals eating plate lunches from nearby restaurants, stands, or trucks. Favorite combos include deep-fried chicken *katsu* (rolled in Japanese panko flour and spices), marinated beef teriyaki, and miso butterfish. *Saimin*, a noodle soup with Japanese fish stock and Chinese red-tinted barbecue pork, is a distinctly local medley. Koreans have contributed spicy barbecue *kalbi* ribs, often served with chili-laden *kimchi* (pickled cabbage). Portuguese bean soup and tangy Filipino *pinakbet* (a mixed-vegetable dish with eggplant, okra, and bitter melons in fish sauce) are also favorites. The most popular contribution to this genre is the Hawaiian plate, featuring *laulau*, a mix of meat and fish and young taro leaves, wrapped in ti leaves and steamed.

$$
ASIAN

✕ **Three's.** The name of the restaurant comes from the three young chefs who met working at a Wailea restaurant, only to decide in 2010 to strike out on their own. Each has a distinctive style (Hawaiian, Southwestern, and Pacific Rim), but somehow it all works. The food is good, with a large selection of salads, burgers, and flatbreads for lunch; fresh fish and steaks are served at dinner. There's also a raw bar, sushi, ceviche, and poke. The space is as big as the menu with three separate dining areas, plus an outdoor patio. ⑤ *Average main: $25* ⊠ *1945-G S. Kihei Rd.* ☎ *808/879–3133* ⊕ *www.threesbarandgrill.com.* ⊙ *Closed for breakfast Mondays and Tuesdays.*

MAALAEA

$
AMERICAN

✕ **Beach Bums Bar & Grill.** Its proximity to the harbor and a good surf spot means that this joint is always jumping. The decor is funky, beach-y, and kitschy. There's a major cocktail list, and drinks are prepared by experienced, excellent bartenders. But the draw here is definitely the barbecue—ribs, chicken, and prime rib, all smoked on-site. Try the Tuesday night lobster fest or the Wednesday night ribs fest for big portions at low prices. The sweet-potato fries drizzled with honey are an obvious must. There's a new "express" location at the Maui Marketplace food court. ⑤ *Average main: $16* ⊠ *300 Maalaea Rd.* ☎ *808/243–2286.*

$
MEDITERRANEAN

✕ **Porto Mediterranean Grill and Pizzeria.** The best thing about Porto— besides the delicious, fresh food—is that 100% of the profits go to the

Pacific Whale Foundation, which owns the restaurant. The menu is short and manageable. The house-made chicken meatballs rise to the top of the appetizer list. There are plenty of panini and pastas, but the flame-fired artisan pizzas may be the best reason to come. The toppings make good use of Maui's bounty. The short wine list is excellent. Try the luscious strawberry shortcake for dessert. [$] *Average main: $15* ✉ *Maalaea Harbor Shops, 300 Maalaea Rd., Suite 106* ☎ *808/856–8337* ⊕ *www.portomaui.com.*

$ ✕**Seascape Maalaea.** A good choice for a seafood lunch, the Maui Ocean
SEAFOOD Center's signature restaurant (aquarium admission is not required to
FAMILY dine here) offers harbor views from its open-air perch. The restaurant promotes heart-healthy cuisine, using sustainable seafood and trans-fat-free items. Lunch-size salads, sandwiches, burgers, fish tacos, teriyaki tofu, fish-and-chips, chicken, ribs, and a full kids' menu are on offer. There's something for everyone here, and the view isn't bad either. [$] *Average main: $15* ✉ *Maui Ocean Center, 192 Maalaea Rd.* ☎ *808/270–7068* ⊕ *www.mauioceancenter.com* ☾ *No dinner.*

WAILEA

$$$$ ✕**Alan Wong's Amasia.** This big, labyrinthine restaurant offers a slew of
INTERNATIONAL seating and menu options. There's a sushi bar, a *robata* (Japanese grill) bar, tatami rooms, private dining rooms, and regular restaurant tables. On first visit, it can be a little confusing. But Alan Wong is definitely Hawaii's biggest culinary name, and Maui has wanted him to open a restaurant here for years. Small plates are the way to go, and you can choose from local ingredients prepared in many ways—fried, griddled or baked, steamed, grilled, and, of course, raw. Szechuan chicken wings, pork adobo empanadas, shoyu duck bao buns, and soy-braised short ribs are just a few of the internationally flavored offerings. [$] *Average main: $40* ✉ *Grand Wailea, 3850 Wailea Alanui* ☎ *808/891–3954* ⊕ *www.alanwongamasia.com* ☾ *No lunch.*

$$$$ ✕**Ferraro's Bar e Ristorante.** Overlooking the ocean from a bluff above
ITALIAN Wailea Beach, this outdoor Italian restaurant at the Four Seasons Resort Maui at Wailea is beautiful both day and night. For lunch, indulge in a lobster sandwich or a variety of stone-baked pizzas. At dinner, try the arugula and endive salad and a house-made pasta. If chef Nicholas Porreca is offering one of his tasting menus, you should order it. Not surprisingly, the wine list includes excellent Italian choices. Live classical music often adds to the atmosphere, and occasionally you can spot celebrities at the bar. [$] *Average main: $40* ✉ *Four Seasons Resort Maui at Wailea, 3900 Wailea Alanui Dr.* ☎ *808/874–8000* ⊕ *www. fourseasons.com/maui.*

$$$$ ✕**Gannon's.** You'll love the amazing ocean and mountain views at this
MODERN outpost of acclaimed chef Beverly Gannon, as well as the splashy Red
HAWAIIAN Bar. Here you'll find Beverly's style of food, which consists of local products prepared with international flavors. For a starter, try the warm goat cheese Maui onion tart with roasted pears, and follow that with fennel-chili-crusted ahi with lemon beurre blanc. Breakfast is especially nice here. The outdoor lanai seating is cool in the morning and overlooks the parade of boats heading out to Molokini.

$ *Average main: $38 ⊠ 100 Golf Club Dr. ☏ 808/875–8080 ⊕ www. gannonsrestaurant.com.*

$$$
MODERN
HAWAIIAN

✕ **Humuhumunukunukuapuaa.** You don't have to wrestle with the restaurant's formidable name (it's Hawaii's state fish); simply tell the valet or concierge you're going to Hoo-moo-hoo-moo. The Polynesian-style thatch-roofed, open-air restaurant "floats" atop a saltwater lagoon. It's exotic, romantic, and well suited for special occasions. Dinner is accompanied nightly by heavenly sunsets. Obviously, fresh fish dominates the menu here, but there's also Kobe beef, lamb, and even a vegetarian plate. Order the "Growing Future Farmers Salad"—$1 of each one sold goes to the Maui County Farm Bureau program of the same name. For dessert, try an over-the-top coconut rice pudding tower or Humu hula pie. **$** *Average main: $35 ⊠ Grand Wailea, 3850 Wailea Alanui Dr. ☏ 808/875–1234 ⊕ www.grandwailea. com ⊘ No lunch.*

$$$$
AMERICAN

✕ **Joe's.** Chef–restaurateur Beverly Gannon's second restaurant—named for her husband, Joe—serves up classy comfort food alongside island-inspired dishes (think ahi carpaccio, Joe's favorite meat loaf, and pumpkin seed–crusted fresh catch). Don't miss Joe's pastry chef daughter Cheech Shurilla's chocolate bread pudding. The wine list is user-friendly and features selections from both well-known and boutique vineyards. The restaurant overlooks the Wailea Tennis Center and is adorned with lots of fun memorabilia from Joe's days in show biz. **$** *Average main: $36 ⊠ 131 Wailea Ike Pl. ☏ 808/875–7767 ⊕ www. bevgannonrestaurants.com ⊘ No lunch.*

$$$$
MODERN
HAWAIIAN

✕ **Ko.** The renovations took a long time (almost nine months) and cost a lot of money (more than $5 million), but the result is spectacular. While the setting is anything but humble, the menu at Ko—which means "sugarcane" in Hawaiian—borrows treasured family recipes from plantation days. Executive Chef Tylun Pang adds modern, innovative twists to Hawaiian, Chinese, Filipino, Portuguese, Korean, and Japanese dishes. The cocktail and wine lists arrive via iPad. Take note of the tabletops—glassware, cutlery, plates, bowls, serving pieces. They are among the most handsome you'll see anywhere. **$** *Average main: $45 ⊠ The Fairmont Kea Lani, Maui, 4100 Wailea Alanui Dr. ☏ 808/875–2210 ⊕ www.ko.kealani@fairmont.com.*

$$
MEDITERRANEAN
Fodor'sChoice
★

✕ **Pita Paradise Mediterranean Bistro.** This is the more upscale and newer outpost of the very casual Pita Paradise location in Kihei Kalama Village. The room is beautiful and welcoming, and the staff is knowledgeable and friendly; but it's the food that is the main event here.

BEST BETS FOR BREAKFAST

Colleen's (North Shore). Eavesdrop on surfers here, while munching on a scone or breakfast burrito.

Gazebo Restaurant (West Maui). It's worth the wait if you're a sucker for macadamia-nut pancakes and a Pacific view.

Kihei Caffe (South Shore). Hearty portions prepare you for surfing.

Plantation House (West Maui). Which is better, the crab-cake Benedict or the view of Molokai? Breakfast is served until 3 pm.

8

SHAVE ICE AND ICE CREAM

The two most critical components in the making of the Islands' favorite frosty treat—shave ice—are the fineness of the "shave" and the quality of the syrup. The shave should be almost powdery like snow. Top that ice with tropical flavors like mango, *lilikoi* (passion fruit), or guava. For a multipart taste sensation, start with a scoop of vanilla ice cream in the bottom (and maybe some Japanese adzuki beans), add shave ice and flavoring, and then top it with a drizzle of cream or a sprinkle of *mochi* (rice cracker) crunch. **Tom's Mini Mart** (⊠ *372 Waiehu Beach Rd., Wailuku* ☎ *808/244-2323*) boasts the largest selection of toppings. **Ululani's** (⊠ *333 Dairy Rd.* ☎ *360/606-2745*) in Kahului, two locations in Lahaina (⊠ *790 and 819 Front St.* ☎ *360/606-2745*), and the newest in Kihei (⊠ *61 S. Kihei Rd.*

☎ *360/606-2745*) makes "gourmet" shave ice.

Prefer ice cream on its own? Maui's Own Roselani has been made from scratch in Wailuku since 1932. Look for the brand's line of Tropics flavors, available at all Maui supermarkets. *Haupia* (coconut pudding) is the best-selling flavor. Some of the best ice-cream parlors are **Hula Cookies & Ice Cream** in Maalaea (⊠ *300 Maalaea Rd., No. 207* ☎ *808/243-2271*) and Lahaina (⊠ *655 Front St.* ☎ *808/661-5854*), **Royal Scoops** (⊠ *2780 Kekaa Dr., Kaanapali* ☎ *808/661-3611*) at the Royal Lahaina Resort, **Peggy Sue's** (⊠ *1279 S. Kihei Rd., No. 303* ☎ *808/875-8944*) in Kihei, and **Makawao Sushi & Deli** (⊠ *3647 Baldwin Ave., Makawao* ☎ *808/573-9044*).

Lunch features affordable and delicious Greek/Mediterranean appetizers, fresh salads, and, of course, the signature pita sandwiches. The spicy falafel and Greek burgers are standouts. In the evening the restaurant is transformed into an Italian/Greek bistro with entrées like chicken fettucine and moussaka. Although you'll be tempted to fill up on the scrumptious food, save room for the award-winning baklava ice-cream pie—yes, you read that right!—made with Maui's own Roselani Hawaiian vanilla-bean ice cream. $ *Average main: $20* ⊠ *Wailea Gateway Center, 34 Wailea Gateway Center* ☎ *808/879-7177* ⊕ *www.pitaparadisehawaii.com.*

$$$$ ✕ **Spago.** It's a marriage made in Hawaii heaven. The California cuisine of celebrity-chef Wolfgang Puck is combined with Maui flavors and served lobby level and oceanfront at the luxurious Four Seasons Resort. Try the spicy ahi tuna *poke* in sesame-miso cones to start, and then see what the chefs-in-residence can do with some of Maui's fantastic local fishes. Finish with a little wild *lilikoi* (passion fruit) crème brûlée with white chocolate–macadamia nut biscotti. Oh, it'll cost you, but the service is spot-on and the smooth, Asian-inspired decor allows the food to claim the spotlight. $ *Average main: $42* ⊠ *Four Seasons Resort Maui at Wailea, 3900 Wailea Alanui Dr.* ☎ *808/879-2999* ☻ *No lunch.*

ASIAN

$$$
ASIAN
Fodor'sChoice
★

✕**Tommy Bahama.** It's more "island-style" than Hawaii, and yes, it's a chain, but the food is consistently great, the service is filled with aloha, and the ambience is just so island refined. Try the ahi *poke* napoleon (with capers, sesame, guacamole, and flatbread), the Kalua pork or blackened-fish sandwich, any of the generous salads, or the local fish preparations. The crab bisque is worthy of a cross-island drive, as are the desserts. The cocktails are among the best and most creative on the island. ⑤ *Average main: $35* ⊠ *The Shops at Wailea, 3750 Wailea Alanui Dr.* ☏ *808/875–9983* ⊕ *www.tommybahama.com.*

CENTRAL MAUI

Central Maui is where the locals live, and the area where you can find just about every ethnic cuisine in the Islands. Savory *saimin* (noodle soup) shops and small joints dishing up *loco moco*—hamburger patties set on top of two scoops of rice with rich brown gravy—are plentiful. Be sure to check out Wailuku; drive along Lower Main Street and take a chance on any of the numerous mom-and-pop eateries. It's truly a culinary adventure. If you walk along historic Market Street, you can shop for antiques between bites.

Kahului offers more variety, because it's in the main traffic corridor and near the big-box stores; you can even find potatoes instead of rice on a few menus. If you want to eat like a local and, more important, at local prices, don't miss Central Maui.

KAHULUI

8

$$
THAI

✕**Bangkok Cuisine.** It's easy to miss Bangkok Cuisine, nestled in the center of a strip of nondescript shops and offices on Dairy Road, but keep your eyes peeled. This little place, with just a few tables and lots of burgundy linen and gilt trim, turns out what is arguably the best pad thai on Maui. You can also expect to find curries, satays, and hot-and-spicy soups. The stuffed chicken wings are particularly good, as is the Cornish game hen. If you're coming from or going to the airport, this is a good place to stop. ⑤ *Average main: $20* ⊠ *395 Dairy Rd.* ☏ *808/893–0026* ⊕ *www.bangkokcuisinemaui.com.*

$$
MEDITERRANEAN

✕**Bistro Casanova.** The location of this Mediterranean restaurant is smack-dab in the middle of Kahului, making it a convenient choice for lunch or dinner. The menu features everything from salads and crepes (both savory and sweet) to pastas and simple fish and meat preparations. A tapas menu—available after 3 pm—changes weekly and always has an excellent selection of dishes. If you're flying out on a red-eye, this is a perfect place for dinner before heading to the airport. ⑤ *Average main: $26* ⊠ *33 Lono Ave.* ☏ *808/873–3650* ⊕ *www.bistrocasanova. com* ⊙ *Closed Sun.*

$
ECLECTIC
FAMILY

✕**Da Kitchen.** There's an "express" location in Kihei, but try the happy, always-crowded Kahului location of Da Kitchen for the mahimahi tempura, the loco moco, Hawaiian plate, and chicken katsu. Everything on the lengthy menu is delicious and the portions are gigantic. The upbeat ambience is reflected in the service as well as the food. ⑤ *Average*

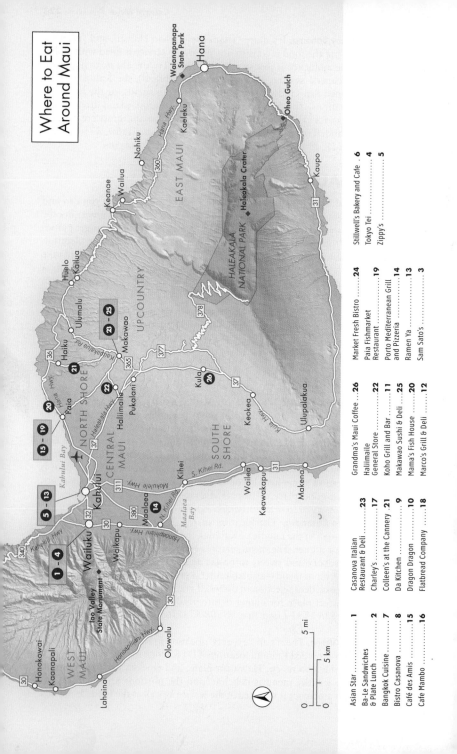

Where to Eat Around Maui

main: $14 ✉ *425 Koloa St.* ☎ *808/871–7782* ⊕ *www.da-kitchen.com* ⊘ *Closed Sun.*

$
CHINESE
✕**Dragon Dragon.** Whether you're a party of 10 or 2, this is the place to stop for what is arguably the best Chinese food on Maui. Dim sum is available only during lunch, but for a real treat, try some of the house specialties like the honey walnut prawns, spicy crab Singapore-style, and the sizzling platter of fish with basil leaves. Top it all off with Maui's own Roselani lychee sherbet. $ *Average main: $16* ✉ *Maui Mall, 70 E. Kaahumanu Ave.* ☎ *808/893–1628.*

$
AMERICAN
FAMILY
✕**Koho Grill and Bar.** Year after year, Koho proves itself as a casual, family-friendly restaurant still worth recommending. If Hawaii had city-style diners, this would be Maui's version. For those looking for a hearty breakfast, a business lunch, or a quick, simple dinner, this is a great choice. Burgers, sandwiches, salads, sizzling fajitas, and pastas are all menu staples. $ *Average main: $12* ✉ *Queen Kaahumanu Center, 275 W. Kaahumanu Ave.* ☎ *808/877–5588.*

$$
ITALIAN
✕**Marco's Grill & Deli.** One of the go-to places for airport comers and goers, this popular Italian restaurant also draws a steady crowd of local residents, mostly for business lunches. Meatballs, sausages, and sauces are all made in-house; the owner was a butcher in his former life. There's a long list of sandwiches that are available all day, and the salads are big enough to share. Note that food substitutions or special requests are not appreciated here. $ *Average main: $18* ✉ *444 Hana Hwy.* ☎ *808/877–4446.*

$
JAPANESE
✕**Ramen Ya.** Part of a Japanese chain, this outpost in a mall is the first and only location in Maui. All of the ramen combinations are slurp-worthy, and the *gyoza* (dumplings) and local-style curries are reason enough to dine here. The portions are gigantic—seriously gigantic—so if you're not that hungry or just have a small appetite, you can order kid-size portions. The service is quick and friendly, and the prices are right. $ *Average main: $9* ✉ *Queen Kaahumanu Center, 275 W. Kaahumanu Ave.* ☎ *808/873–9688.*

$
ECLECTIC
FAMILY
✕**Zippy's.** Hawaii's favorite casual, eat-in, or takeout restaurant, Zippy's was founded more than 45 years ago. Today Oahu has more than two-dozen locations from which to choose, and Maui waited a long time to get one. It's a 24-hour-a-day (takeout only, after midnight Sunday–Thursday), diner-type place with a big menu. Spaghetti with chili, oxtail soup, Korean chicken, chicken katsu, noodles, burgers, and burritos are just a few of the tasty menu options. Napoleon's Bakery counter up front serves its only-in-Hawaii-style turnovers, pies, cakes, and pastries, as well as made-to-order malasadas and andagi. $ *Average main: $10* ✉ *15 Hookele St.* ☎ *808/856–7599* ⊕ *www.zippys.com.*

WAILUKU

$$
VIETNAMESE
✕**Asian Star.** This restaurant in Wailuku's Millyard (a light industrial area) is the best choice for Vietnamese food on Maui. Owner Jason Chau grows his own Hawaiian chili peppers, mint, basil, chives, lemongrass, and green onions around the perimeter of the parking lot, and these seasonings add robust and concentrated flavors to his dishes. Try the lemongrass chicken or tofu, the garlic beef or green papaya salad,

8

the crispy sesame or orange beef, the clay pots with crunchy, charred rice bits on the bottom, and the *bun,* bowls brimming with cold vermicelli noodles and topped with chicken, beef, or pork. $ *Average main: $18* ⊠ *The Millyard, 1764 Wili Pa Loop* ☎ *808/244–1833.*

$ × **Ba-Le Sandwiches & Plate Lunch.** It began as a French-Vietnamese bakery
VIETNAMESE   on Oahu and has branched into popular small restaurants sprinkled
Fodor's Choice   throughout the Islands. Some are kiosks in malls; others are stand-
★   alones with some picnic tables out front, as is the case at this location, which is one of four on Maui. Vietnamese *pho* (the famous soups laden with seafood or rare beef, fresh basil, bean sprouts, and lime) share menu space with local-style *saimin* and plates of barbecue or spicy chicken, beef, pork, or local fish served with jasmine rice. The delicious sandwiches—*banh mi* in Vietnamese—are perfect for lunch to stay or to go. There are a slew of tapioca flavors for dessert. $ *Average main: $8* ⊠ *1824 Oihana St.* ☎ *808/249–8833* ⊕ *www.ba-le.com.*

$ × **Sam Sato's.** Every island has its noodle shrine, and this is Maui's.
HAWAIIAN   Dry mein, *saimin,* chow fun—they all come in different-size portions
Fodor's Choice   and with add-ins to satisfy every noodle craving. While you wait
★   for your bowl, be sure to try a teriyaki beef stick or two. Save room for the popular turnovers—pineapple, coconut, apple, or peach—and traditional Japanese manju filled with either lima or azuki beans. At busy times, which is almost always, you will likely have to wait for a table or a stool at the counter. Be sure to write your name on the little yellow pad at the takeout window. $ *Average main: $8* ⊠ *The Millyard, 1750 Wili Pa Loop* ☎ *808/244–7124* ▭ *No credit cards* ☺ *No dinner. Closed Sun.*

$ × **Stillwell's Bakery & Cafe.** Roy Stillwell has been around Maui for a
BAKERY   long time, and is unquestionably one of the best pastry chefs on the island. So this is the place to come for coffee and an outrageously good macadamia-nut muffin or a renowned cream horn. At lunchtime you'll rub elbows with local folks who work in the area; they come for the fresh sandwiches served, of course, on homemade breads (try the crab-cake sandwich), and for the Chinese chicken, tofu, and shrimp and crab salads. Be sure to order a macoco roll on the side. The desserts on display will surely make you drool. Oh, go ahead! You're on vacation. And if you're celebrating a birthday—or any other special occasion— Roy is the guy you want to bake your cake. $ *Average main: $12* ⊠ *1740 Kaahumanu Ave.* ☎ *808/243–2243* ⊕ *www.stillwellsbakery. com* ☺ *No dinner.*

$ × **Tokyo Tei.** Getting there is half—well, maybe a quarter—of the fun.
JAPANESE   Tucked in the back corner of a covered parking garage, Tokyo Tei is
Fodor's Choice   worth seeking out for wonderful Japanese food. At lunch you'll rub
★   elbows with bankers and construction workers; at dinner, three generations might be celebrating *Tutu's* (Grandma's) birthday at the next table. This is a bona fide local institution where for more than six decades people have come for the food and the comfort of familiarity. You'll find the freshest sashimi, feather-light yet crispy shrimp and vegetable tempura, and local-style bentos and plate lunches. $ *Average main: $12* ⊠ *1063 Lower Main St.* ☎ *808/242–9630* ⊕ *www.tokyotei.com* ☺ *No lunch Sun.*

UPCOUNTRY

Take the drive up the slopes of magnificent Mt. Haleakala and you can find an abundance of restaurants catering to both locals and visitors. Haliimaile General Store is a landmark in the middle of a soon-to-disappear pineapple field, and in the *paniolo* (cowboy) town of Makawao you can sidle up to everything from an Italian restaurant to a Mexican cantina. Upcountry also encompasses cool Kula with a few mom-and-pops. Many visitors opt to check out nearby farm tours between meals.

$$$
ITALIAN

✕ **Casanova Italian Restaurant & Deli.** An authentic Italian dinner house and nightclub, this place is smack in the middle of Maui's *paniolo* (cowboy) town of Makawao. The brick wood-burning oven, imported from Italy, has been turning out perfect pies and steaming hot focaccia for more than 20 years. You can pair a pie with a salad (they're all big enough to share) and a couple of glasses of wine without breaking the bank. The daytime deli is fabulous for breakfast, cappuccino, croissants, and people-watching. The place turns positively raucous—in a good way—on Wednesday, Friday, and Saturday nights. ⑤ *Average main: $28* ✉ *1188 Makawao Ave., Makawao* ☎ *808/572–0220* ⊕ *www.casanovamaui.com.*

$
AMERICAN

✕ **Grandma's Maui Coffee.** If you're taking a drive through gorgeous Upcountry Maui, this is a great place to stop for a truly homegrown cup of coffee and snack. All the coffee is grown right on the slopes of Haleakala and roasted on the premises in a 100-year-old roaster proudly on display. The baked goods are fabulous—particularly the lemon bars—and the variety of menu items for breakfast and lunch is vast. Eggs, omelets, crepes, and fantastic home fries are served for breakfast; salads, sandwiches, lasagna, and more can be ordered at lunch. Enjoy your coffee and goodies on the lovely deck; sometimes a Hawaiian musician is there playing a tune. ⑤ *Average main: $9* ✉ *9232 Kula Hwy., Kula* ☎ *808/878–2140* ⊕ *www.grandmascoffee.com* ⊘ *No dinner.*

$$$$
MODERN HAWAIIAN

✕ **Haliimaile General Store.** Chef-restaurateur Beverly Gannon's first restaurant remains a culinary destination after more than two decades. The big, rambling former plantation store has two dining rooms: sit in the front to be seen and heard; head on back for some quiet and privacy. Classic dishes like crab boboli, Asian duck tostada, grilled lamb chops, and many more are complemented with daily and nightly specials. To get here, take the exit on the left halfway up Haleakala Highway. ⑤ *Average main: $38* ✉ *900 Haliimaile Rd., Haliimaile* ☎ *808/572–2666* ⊕ *www.bevgannonrestaurants.com.*

$$
ECLECTIC

✕ **Makawao Sushi & Deli.** It may seem an odd mix: sushi and deli. But this is a cute place on Makawao's main drag, with a lovely patio out back where you can sip an espresso and snack on pastries, sandwiches, or any of the sushi rolls. The menu is much longer than you might expect, and the fish is always fresh. The most popular rolls are the 007, a spicy tuna roll topped with ebi, avocado, and unagi sauce, and the Rockin' Roll, a traditional California roll wrapped with tuna and covered with baked scallops. The baked mussels are divine and so is their version of ahi *poke.* $ *Average main: $25* ✉ *3647 Baldwin Ave., Makawao* ☎ *808/573–9044.*

$$$
MODERN
HAWAIIAN

✕ **Market Fresh Bistro.** This hard-to-find restaurant tucked into a courtyard serves excellent food by chef Justin Pardo, formerly of Union Square Café in New York City. He uses locally grown and produced ingredients, and in a nod to healthful eating, prefers reductions and infused oils rather than butter. Representative dishes include the Upcountry vegetable salad and the slow-cooked Maui Cattle Company short ribs, which are downright dreamy. Fresh fish preparations are always good choices. $ *Average main: $30* ✉ *3620 Baldwin Ave., Makawao* ☎ *808/572–4877* ⊕ *www.marketfreshbistro.com* ☉ *Closed Mon.; closed for dinner Sat.–Wed.*

WORD OF MOUTH

"For some local flavor, try Paia Fish Market in Paia (best for lunch) or Hula Grill in Kaanapali (good lunch or dinner). More on the gourmet side, but still with local flavor, is Haliimaile General Store between Kahului and Kula. Try the Gazebo at Napili Shores for breakfast or lunch." —voyager61

NORTH SHORE

The North Shore sets the dramatic stage for Maui's most famous—and most expensive—restaurant, Mama's Fish House in Kuau. The area also encompasses the great food town of Paia and the up-and-coming restaurant town of Haiku. Be sure to bring your bathing suit for a dip in the ocean at one of the nearby beaches.

HAIKU

$$
AMERICAN
Fodor's Choice
★

✕ **Colleen's at the Cannery.** From the nondescript exterior and the location in an old pineapple cannery-cum–strip mall, you'd never anticipate what's inside. Colleen's is one of the most overlooked restaurants on Maui. It's popular with locals for breakfast and lunch, but try it at dinner when the candles come out and it's time for martinis and fresh fish. The food is excellent, in particular the huge salads made with Upcountry's best produce; the fish specials; the burgers; and the simple roast chicken. When eating here, you'll feel like you're at a hip, urban eatery. $ *Average main: $20* ✉ *Haiku Cannery Marketplace, 810 Haiku Rd.* ☎ *808/575–9211* ⊕ *www.colleensinhaiku.com.*

KUAU

$$$$
SEAFOOD

✕ **Mama's Fish House.** For almost four decades, Mama's has been *the* Maui destination for special occasions. A path of gecko-shaped stones leads through the coconut grove past the giant clamshell and under the banyan arch to an ever-changing fantasyland of Hawaiiana kitsch. True, the setting couldn't be more spectacular, and yes, the menu names the angler that reeled in your fresh catch (do we know he *really* caught it?), but the dishes are decidedly dated in terms of preparation and presentation—and the prices are off the charts. But if you're looking for an overall experience, make a reservation and celebrate your special occasion here. $ *Average main: $50* ✉ *799 Poho Pl.* ☎ *808/579–8488* ⊕ *www.mamasfishhouse.com* ⌂ *Reservations essential.*

PAIA

$
ECLECTIC
Fodor'sChoice
★

✕**Café des Amis.** The menu is a little neurotic—in a good way—featuring Mediterranean and Indian dishes, but the food is fresh and tasty. This budget-friendly café offers flavors and preparations not easily obtainable at other island eateries, with a nice selection of sweet and savory crepes, Indian wraps, and salads. Now, you can have a cocktail, too. All in all, you get delicious, good-value food, as well as excellent people-watching from the umbrella-shaded tables outside. $ *Average main: $16* ✉ *42 Baldwin Ave.* ☎ *808/579–6323* ⊕ *www.cdamaui.com* ▬ *No credit cards.*

$
ECLECTIC

✕**Cafe Mambo.** Paia is one of Maui's most interesting food towns, and this Mediterranean-inspired joint is right in the thick of things. It's kind of frenetic in every way, from the menu to the decor and the service. But the food is good and well priced, and the people-watching is fascinating. The husband-and-wife owners, from England and Spain respectively, decorated the place with Moroccan clay pieces; teak and coconut-wood tables are set in the middle of benches with Middle Eastern pillows. The menu goes all over the place, too, with all-American burgers, island fish, falafel and hummus, Spanish tapas, and paella. $ *Average main: $15* ✉ *30 Baldwin Ave.* ☎ *808/579–8021* ⊕ *www.cafemambomaui.com.*

$$
AMERICAN

✕**Charley's.** A Maui institution, this is the place to take your cowboy-size breakfast appetite. Omelets, pancakes, sausage biscuits with country gravy, and giant-size French toast slices lure the customers in. Charley's also serves hearty portions for lunch and dinner, including handmade pizzas and awesome burgers made from local beef. The saloon is open until 1 am every night, so you can rack 'em up on the pool tables and enjoy a beer or two. If you're lucky, Willie Nelson may just wander in and tune up. $ *Average main: $19* ✉ *142 Hana Highway* ☎ *808/579–8085* ⊕ *www.charleysmaui.com.*

$$
PIZZA
FAMILY

✕**Flatbread Company.** Vermont-based Flatbread Company marched right in to Paia in 2007 and instantly became a popular restaurant and a valued addition to the community. As part of the company's mission, they started "giving back" to local nonprofits immediately. Happily, along with the altruism, the food is fantastic. There's a big, primitive-looking, earthen, wood-fired oven from which emerge utterly delicious flatbread pizzas. They use organic, local, sustainable products, including 100% organically grown wheat for the made-fresh-daily products. The place is a good spot to take the kids. There's a no-reservations policy but they do have "call ahead seating"—you can put your name on the wait list before you arrive. $ *Average main: $22* ✉ *89 Hana Hwy.* ☎ *808/579–8989* ⊕ *www.flatbreadcompany.com* ⌂ *Reservations not accepted.*

8

$ ✕ **Paia Fishmarket Restaurant.** If you're okay with communal picnic tables,
SEAFOOD   or taking your meal to a nearby beach, this place in funky Paia town
Fodor's Choice   serves, arguably, the best fresh fish for the best prices on this side of the
★   island. Four preparations are offered and, on any given day, there are
at least four fresh fishes from which to choose. For the non-fish fans,
there are burgers, chicken, and pasta. The side dishes—Cajun rice, home
fries, and the amazing hand-cut crunchy cole slaw—are all as delectable
as the main event. You can have a beer or a glass of wine, too, as long
as you stay inside, of course. ⑤ *Average main: $15* ⊠ *100 Hana Hwy.*
☎ *808/579–8030* ⊕ *www.paiafishmarket.com.*

WHERE TO STAY

Updated
by Bonnie
Friedman

Maui's accommodations run the gamut from rural B&Bs to superopulent megaresorts. In between the extremes, there's something for every vacation style and budget. The large resorts, hotels, and condominiums for which Maui is noted are on the sunny leeward southern and western shores. They bustle with activity and are near plenty of restaurants, shopping, golf, and water sports. Those seeking a different experience can try the inns, bed-and-breakfasts, and rentals in the small towns and quieter areas along the North Shore and Upcountry on the verdant slopes of Haleakala.

If the latest and greatest is your style, be prepared to spend a small fortune. Properties like the Ritz-Carlton, Kapalua, the Four Seasons Resort Maui at Wailea, and newer condo complexes such as the Wailea Beach Villas may set you back at least $600 a night, though the weaker economy has brought more discounts.

Although there aren't many of them, small bed-and-breakfasts are charming. They tend to be in residential or rural neighborhoods around the island, sometimes beyond the resort areas of West Maui and the South Shore. The B&Bs offer both a personalized experience and a window onto authentic local life. The prices tend to be the lowest available on Maui, sometimes less than $200 per night.

Apartment and condo rentals are perfect for modest budgets, for two or more couples traveling together, and for families. Not only are the nightly rates lower than hotel rooms, but "eating in" (all have kitchens of some description) is substantially less expensive than dining out. There are literally hundreds of these units, ranging in size from studios to luxurious four-bedrooms with multiple baths, all over the island. The vast majority are along the sunny coasts—from Makena to Kihei on the South Shore and Lahaina up to Kapalua in West Maui. Prices depend on the size of the unit and its proximity to the beach, as well as the amenities and services offered. For about $250 a night, you can get a lovely one-bedroom apartment without many frills or flourishes, close to but probably not on the beach. Many rentals have minimum stays (usually three to five nights).

Most of Maui's resorts—several are megaresorts—have opulent gardens, fantasy swimming pools, championship golf courses, and full-service fitness centers and spas. Expect to spend at least $350 a night at the resort hotels; they are all in the Wailea and Makena resort area on the South Shore and Kaanapali and Kapalua in West Maui. At all lodgings, ask about discounts and deals (free nights with longer stays, for example), which have proliferated.

MAUI LODGING PLANNER

LODGING STRATEGY

With resorts, condos, and bed-and-breakfasts all over the island, there's a lodging option for anyone. Our team of expert writers and editors has compiled its top recommendations, organized by geographical area.

PROPERTY TYPES

HOTELS AND RESORTS

Maui's resorts are clustered along the island's leeward (West and South) shores, so they offer near-perfect weather year-round. Kaanapali, in West Maui, has the most action. Kapalua, farther north, is more private and serene. Among the South Shore resort communities, posh Wailea has excellent beaches and golf courses. Most resorts charge parking and facility fees—a "resort fee." In Hawaii room prices can rise dramatically if a room has an ocean view. To save money, ask for a garden or mountain view.

CONDOS AND RENTALS

If you compromise on luxury, you can find convenient condos in West Maui in Napili, Honokowai, or Kahana, and on the South Shore in Kihei. Many are oceanfront and offer the amenities of a hotel without the cost, though central air-conditioning is rare. Be sure to ask about minimum stays. Besides the condos listed here, Maui has condos rented through central agents. (See the Vacation Rental Companies box in this chapter for recommended companies.)

B&BS AND INNS

Maui County has updated its policies regarding the licensing of B&Bs and what are technically called TVRs (transient vacation rentals). New rules and permitting policies have been enacted and, as of this writing, many new permits have been issued. In the past, glorious inns were lumped together—for the county's legal purposes—with what may have been nothing more than a bed set up in someone's garage. To avoid disappointment (some places have closed), the best advice is to ask whether the property is licensed by the county. You might even ask for the permit number, which should be posted on the property's website. Contact Bed & Breakfast Hawaii or Hawaii's Best Bed & Breakfasts for additional B&Bs on Maui.

BEST BETS FOR MAUI LODGING

Fodor's writers and editors have selected their favorite hotels, resorts, condos, vacation rentals, and B&Bs by price and experience. Fodor's Choice properties represent the "best of the best" across price categories. You can also search by area for excellent places to stay—check out our complete reviews on the following pages.

Fodor's Choice ★

Four Seasons Resort Maui at Wailea, $$$$, p. 249

Grand Wailea Resort Hotel & Spa, $$$$, p. 249

Hale Hookipa Inn, $, p. 254

Hana Kai-Maui Resort Condominiums, $$$, p. 258

Hooilo House, $$$, p. 236

Kaanapali Beach Hotel, $$$, p. 239

Luana Kai, $, p. 246

The Old Wailuku Inn at Ulupono, $, p. 252

Outrigger Maui Eldorado Kaanapali, $$$, p. 239

The Ritz-Carlton, Kapalua, $$$$, p. 244

The Westin Maui Resort & Spa, $$$$, p. 240

By Price

$

The Banyan Tree House, p. 254

Hale Hookipa Inn, p. 254

Luana Kai, p. 246

Plantation Inn, p. 238

Puu Koa Maui Rentals, p. 257

The Old Wailuku Inn at Ulupono, p. 252

$$

Hale Hui Kai, p. 244

Kamaole Sands, p. 246

Paia Inn Hotel, p. 257

Royal Lahaina Resort, p. 239

$$$

Hana Kai-Maui Resort Condominiums, p. 258

Hooilo House, p. 236

Kaanapali Beach Hotel, p. 239

Outrigger Maui Eldorado Kaanapali, p. 239

$$$$

Four Seasons Resort Maui at Wailea, p. 249

Grand Wailea Resort Hotel & Spa, p. 249

Makena Surf, p. 251

Polo Beach Club, p. 251

Ritz-Carlton, Kapalua, p. 244

Wailea Beach Villas, p. 251

The Westin Maui Resort & Spa, p. 240

By Experience

BEST BEACH

Kaanapali Alii, $$$$, p. 239

Mana Kai Maui, $$$$, p. 246

Napili Kai Beach Resort, $$$, p. 243

Polo Beach Club, $$$$, p. 251

BEST B&BS AND INNS

Hale Hookipa Inn, $, p. 254

The Old Wailuku Inn at Ulupono, $, p. 252

BEST SPA

Four Seasons Resort Maui at Wailea, $$$$, p. 249

The Ritz-Carton, Kapalua, $$$$, p. 244

Wailea Beach Marriott Resort & Spa, $$$$, p. 251

The Westin Maui Resort & Spa, $$$$, p. 240

MOST KID-FRIENDLY

The Banyan Tree House, $, p. 254

Fairmont Kea Lani Maui, $$$$, p. 249

Kamaole Sands, $$, p. 246

Mana Kai Maui, $$$$, p. 246

Napili Kai Beach Resort, $$$, p. 243

MOST ROMANTIC

Four Seasons Resort Maui at Wailea, $$$$, p. 249

Hale Hookipa Inn, $, p. 254

Hooilo House, $$$, p. 236

The Old Wailuku Inn at Ulupono, $, p. 252

The Ritz-Carlton, Kapalua, $$$$, p. 244

WHERE TO STAY IN MAUI

	Local Vibe	Pros	Cons
West Maui	Popular and busy, West Maui includes the picturesque, touristy town of Lahaina and the upscale resort areas of Kaanapali and Kapalua.	A wide variety of shops, water sports, and historic sites provide plenty to do. To relax, there are great beaches and brilliant sunsets.	Traffic is usually congested; parking is hard to find; beaches can be crowded.
South Shore	The protected South Shore of Maui offers diverse experiences and accommodations, from comfortable condos to luxurious resorts—and golf, golf, golf.	Many beautiful beaches; sunny weather; great snorkeling.	Numerous strip malls; crowded with condos; there can be lots of traffic.
Upcountry	Country and chic come together in farms, ranches, and trendy towns on the cool, green slopes of Haleakala.	Cooler weather at higher elevations; panoramic views of nearby islands; distinctive shops, boutiques, galleries, and restaurants.	Fewer restaurants; no nightlife; can be very dark at night and difficult to drive for those unfamiliar with roads and conditions.
North Shore	The North Shore is a mecca for surfing, windsurfing, and kite sailing. When the surf's not up, the focus is on shopping: Paia is full of galleries, shops, and hip eateries.	Wind and waves are terrific for water sports; colorful small towns to explore without the intrusion of big resorts.	Weather may not be as sunny as other parts of the island; no nightlife; most stores in Paia close early, around 6 pm.
Road to Hana and East Maui	Remote and rural, laid-back and tropical Hana and East Maui are special places to unwind.	Natural experience; rugged coastline and lush tropical scenery; lots of waterfalls.	Accessed by a long and winding road; no nightlife; few places to eat or shop.

Contacts Bed & Breakfast Hawaii ☎ *808/822–7771, 800/733–1632* ⊕ *www. bandb-hawaii.com.* **Hawaii's Best Bed & Breakfasts** ☎ *808/263–3100, 800/262–9912* ⊕ *www.bestbnb.com.*

RESERVATIONS

The farther in advance you book, the more likely you are to get the room you want. This is especially true at the big resort hotels for December 20 through April, and again during July and August, Maui's busiest times. At these times, booking a year in advance is not uncommon.

PRICES

There's no denying that Maui's lodging prices can be steep, but rates run the full range. Many hotels slash their rates significantly for promotions and Web-only deals. Note that prices exclude 13.42% sales tax.

Prices shown in the reviews are the lowest cost of a standard double room in high season. Prices for rentals are the lowest per-night cost for a one-bedroom unit in high season. For expanded hotel reviews, visit Fodors.com.

WEST MAUI

LAHAINA

Lahaina doesn't have a huge range of accommodations, but it does make a great headquarters for active families, or those who want to avoid spending a bundle on resorts. One major advantage is the proximity of restaurants, shops, and activities—everything is within walking distance. It's a business district, however, and won't provide the same peace and quiet as resorts or secluded vacation rentals. Still, Lahaina has a nostalgic charm, especially early in the morning before the streets have filled with visitors and vendors.

$
HOTEL
Best Western Pioneer Inn. Built in 1901 when Lahaina was the bawdy heart of the Pacific's whaling industry, this small, right-in-town hotel has been substantially remodeled, updated, and rebranded as a Best Western; rooms are clean and basic, but the price is certainly right. **Pros:** Lahaina town shops and restaurants are within easy walking distance; proximity to Lahaina Harbor makes for easy access to oceangoing activities; children under 12 stay free. **Cons:** few in-room amenities; can be noisy, with Front Street on one side and the busy harbor on the other; two floors, no elevator. $ *Rooms from: $160* ⊠ *658 Wharf St.* ☎ *808/661–3636, 800/457–5457* ⊕ *www.pioneerinnmaui.com* ➾ *34 rooms* ⦿| *No meals.*

$
B&B/INN
Garden Gate Bed & Breakfast Inn. A few minutes outside busy Lahaina town, behind brightly colored walls, past a garden gate, and across a bridge lies a quiet place that welcomes you with light and airy rooms that have pleasant tropical furnishings and private entrances. **Pros:** free use of chairs, coolers, boogie boards, and other beach toys; knowledgeable hosts; Maui Bus stops at the corner. **Cons:** not a secluded location; no resort amenities; beach is a short drive away. $ *Rooms from: $159* ⊠ *67 Kaniau Rd.* ☎ *808/661–8800, 800/939–3217* ⊕ *www.gardengatebb.com* ➾ *5 rooms* ⦿| *Breakfast.*

$$$
B&B/INN
Fodor's Choice
★
Hooilo House. If you want to treat yourself to a luxurious but intimate getaway and don't require resort facilities, spend a few nights at this Bali-inspired B&B; in the foothills of the West Maui Mountains, just south of Lahaina town, the stunning property exemplifies quiet perfection. **Pros:** friendly on-site hosts Amy and Dan Martin are an asset; beautiful furnishings. **Cons:** not good for families with younger children; three-night minimum; beaches are a short drive away. $ *Rooms from: $309* ⊠ *138 Awaiku St.* ☎ *808/667–6669* ⊕ *www.hooilohouse.com* ➾ *6 rooms* ⦿| *Breakfast.*

$
B&B/INN
Lahaina Inn. An antique jewel in the heart of town, this two-story wooden building is classic Lahaina and will transport romantics back to the turn of the 20th century; the small rooms shine with authentic period furnishings, including antique bureaus and headboards. **Pros:** a half block off Front Street, the location is within easy walking distance of shops, restaurants, and attractions; lovely antiques. **Cons:** rooms are small, bathrooms particularly so; some street noise; two stories, no elevator. $ *Rooms from: $125* ⊠ *127 Lahainaluna Rd.* ☎ *808/661–*

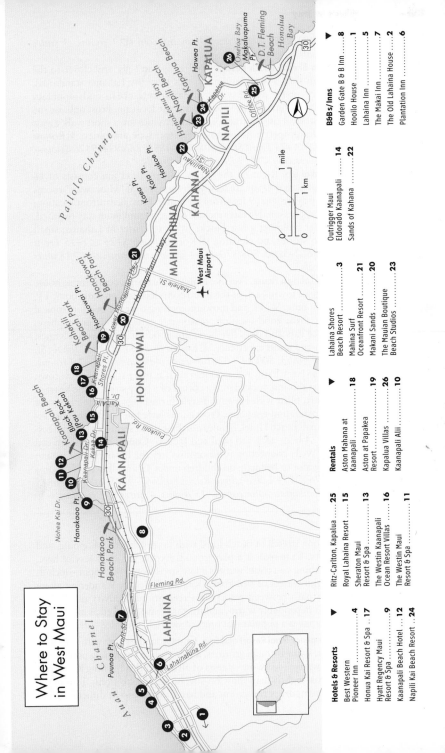

Where to Stay in West Maui

Hotels & Resorts ▶

Best Western
Pioneer Inn 4
Honua Kai Resort & Spa .. 17
Hyatt Regency Maui
Resort & Spa 9
Kaanapali Beach Hotel ... 12
Napili Kai Beach Resort .. 24

Ritz-Carlton, Kapalua 25
Royal Lahaina Resort 15
Sheraton Maui
Resort & Spa 13
The Westin Kaanapali
Ocean Resort Villas 16
The Westin Maui
Resort & Spa 11

Rentals

Aston Mahana at
Kaanapali 18
Aston at Papakea
Resort 19
Kapalua Villas 26
Kaanapali Alii 10

Lahaina Shores
Beach Resort 3
Mahina Surf
Oceanfront Resort 21
Makani Sands 20
The Mauian Boutique
Beach Studios 23

Outrigger Maui
Eldorado Kaanapali 14
Sands of Kahana 22

B&Bs/Inns

Garden Gate B & B Inn 8
Hoolio House 1
Lahaina Inn 5
The Makai Inn 7
The Old Lahaina House 2
Plantation Inn 6

0577, 800/222–5642 ⊕ *www.lahainainn.com* ⤴ *9 rooms, 3 suites* ⊙❙ *No meals.*

$
RENTAL
⊞ **Lahaina Shores Beach Resort.** You really can't get any closer to the beach than this: a local landmark, this lofty (by Lahaina standards), seven-story rental property offers panoramic ocean and mountain views for a reasonable price considering the location. **Pros:** right on the beach; historical sites, attractions, and activities are a short walk away. **Cons:** older property; no up-to-date resort-type amenities. ⑤ *Rooms from: $169* ⊠ *475 Front St.* ☎ *808/661–4835, 866/934–9176* ⊕ *www. lahainashores.com* ⤴ *199 rooms* ⊙❙ *No meals.*

$
B&B/INN
⊞ **The Makai Inn.** Right on the ocean, this pleasant inn consists of 18 units, all at least 400 square feet, with four special "Hideaway" rooms featuring private lanai 9 feet from the water. **Pros:** oceanfront location; full kitchens; reasonable rates include taxes; no minimum stay required. **Cons:** older building; a few blocks' walk to center of Lahaina; small units; two stories, no elevator. ⑤ *Rooms from: $125* ⊠ *1415 Front St.* ☎ *808/662–3200, 808/870–9004* ⊕ *www.makaiinn.net* ⤴ *18 units* ⊙❙ *No meals.*

$
B&B/INN
⊞ **The Old Lahaina House.** Feel like family in this large, comfortable house at the edge of town; each of the four rooms has its own bathroom, TV, air conditioning, Wi-Fi, and mosquito netting over the bed for tropical ambience. **Pros:** good location; reasonable rates; family atmosphere. **Cons:** since cats and dogs live here, not good for those with allergies; not a high-end resort experience. ⑤ *Rooms from: $139* ⊠ *407 Ilikahi St.* ☎ *808/667–4663, 800/847–0761* ⊕ *www.oldlahaina.com* ⤴ *4 rooms.*

$
B&B/INN
⊞ **Plantation Inn.** Charm and amenities such as free parking in downtown Lahaina set this inn, tucked into a corner of a busy street in the heart of town, apart; filled with Hawaiian-style furnishings, it's reminiscent of an island plantation-era home. **Pros:** guests have full privileges at the sister Kaanapali Beach Hotel, 3 miles north; walk to shops, sights, and restaurants; 24-hour access to pool and Jacuzzi. **Cons:** Lahaina town can be noisy; Wi-Fi connection is hit-or-miss (try the lanai); two-story inn has no elevator or bellman; no children under 13 are allowed. ⑤ *Rooms from: $176* ⊠ *174 Lahainaluna Rd.* ☎ *808/667–9225, 800/433–6815* ⊕ *www.theplantationinn.com* ⤴ *15 rooms, 4 suites* ⊙❙ *Breakfast.*

KAANAPALI

With its long stretch of beach lined with luxury resorts, shopping, and restaurants, Kaanapali is a playground. Expect top-class service here, and everything you could want is a few steps from your room—including the calm waters of sun-kissed Kaanapali Beach. Wandering along the beach path between resorts is a recreational activity unto itself. Weather is dependably warm, and for that reason as well as all the others, Kaanapali is a popular—at times, downright crowded—destination.

$$$$
RESORT
⊞ **Hyatt Regency Maui Resort and Spa.** Fantasy landscaping with splashing waterfalls, swim-through grottoes, a lagoon-like swimming pool, and a 130-foot waterslide "wow" guests of all ages at this bustling Kaanapali resort. **Pros:** nightly luau show on-site; home of Astronomy Tour of the Stars; contemporary restaurant and bar. **Cons:** it can be difficult to find

a space in self-parking; service can be uneven. $ *Rooms from: $399* ✉ *200 Nohea Kai Dr.* ☎ *808/661–1234, 800/233–1234* ⊕ *www.maui. hyatt.com* ⌁ *806 rooms* ⦿ *No meals.*

$$$$
RENTAL

⊞ **Kaanapali Alii.** It's the best of both worlds: homelike condo living with hotel amenities—daily maid service, an activities desk, small store with complimentary DVDs for guests to borrow, and 24-hour front-desk service. **Pros:** large, comfortable units on the beach; good location in the heart of the action in Kaanapali Resort. **Cons:** elevators are notoriously slow; crowded parking; no on-site restaurant. $ *Rooms from: $480* ✉ *50 Nohea Kai Dr.* ☎ *808/667–1400, 800/642–6284* ⊕ *www. kaanapalialii.com* ⌁ *264 units* ⦿ *No meals.*

$$
HOTEL
Fodor'sChoice
★

⊞ **Kaanapali Beach Hotel.** Older but still attractive, this charming hotel is full of aloha—locals say that it's one of the few resorts on the island where you can get a true Hawaiian experience. **Pros:** exceptional Hawaiian culture program; friendly staff; Tiki Terrace restaurant serves delicious dinners and one of the most bountiful Sunday brunches on the island. **Cons:** a bit run-down; fewer amenities than other places along this beach. $ *Rooms from: $258* ✉ *2525 Kaanapali Pkwy.* ☎ *808/661–0011, 800/262–8450* ⊕ *www.kbhmaui.com* ⌁ *432 rooms* ⦿ *No meals.*

$$$
RENTAL
Fodor'sChoice
★

⊞ **Outriggger Maui Eldorado Kaanapali.** The Kaanapali Golf Course's fairways wrap around this fine, good-value condo complex that offers several perks, most notably access to a fully outfitted beach cabana on a semiprivate beach. **Pros:** privileges at the Kaanapali Golf Courses; Wi-Fi available in all units; friendly staff. **Cons:** not right on beach; some distance from attractions of the Kaanapali Resort; two-story buildings have no elevator. $ *Rooms from: $310* ✉ *2661 Kekaa Dr.* ☎ *808/661–0021* ⊕ *www.mauieldorado.com* ⌁ *204 units* ⦿ *No meals.*

$$
RESORT

⊞ **Royal Lahaina Resort.** Built in 1962 as the first hotel in the Kaanapali Resort, this grand property toward the northern end of Kaanapali has hosted millionaires and Hollywood stars; major room upgrades in the 12-story Lahaina Kai Tower include dark teak furnishings set against light-color walls, plush beds with Egyptian-cotton linens, sound systems with an iPod and MP3 docking station, and 32-inch flat-screen TVs. **Pros:** on-site luau nightly; variety of accommodation types and rates; tennis ranch with 11 courts and a pro shop. **Cons:** older property still in need of updating. $ *Rooms from: $199* ✉ *2780 Kekaa Dr.* ☎ *808/661–3611, 800/447–6925* ⊕ *www.hawaiihotels.com* ⌁ *511 rooms* ⦿ *No meals.*

$$$$
RESORT

⊞ **Sheraton Maui Resort & Spa.** Set among dense gardens on Kaanapali's best stretch of beach, the Sheraton offers a quieter, more low-key atmosphere than its neighboring resorts; it sits next to and on top of the 80-foot-high Puu Kekaa, from which divers leap in a nightly torch-lighting and cliff-diving ritual. **Pros:** luxury resort with terrific beach location; great snorkeling right off the beach. **Cons:** extensive property can mean a long walk from your room to the lobby, restaurants, and beach. $ *Rooms from: $619* ✉ *2605 Kaanapali Pkwy.* ☎ *808/661–0031, 866/500–8313* ⊕ *www.sheraton-maui.com* ⌁ *464 rooms, 44 suites* ⦿ *No meals.*

$$$$
RESORT

⊞ **The Westin Kaanapali Ocean Resort Villas.** Farther up the beach from its sister property, the Westin Maui, these villas are available for vacation ownership and hotel accommodations; the abundant resort amenities and pools are notable. **Pros:** just about anything you could ever want inside and out; notable pools. **Cons:** large complex could be overwhelming; not technically within the boundaries of the Kaanapali Resort; expensive. ⑤ *Rooms from: $650* ✉ *6 Kai Ala Dr., Lahaina* ☎ *808/667–3200, 886/716–8112* ⊕ *www.westinkaanapali.com* ⇨ *500 studios, 521 1-bedroom units* ❢◎❢ *No meals.*

$$$$
RESORT
FAMILY
Fodor's Choice
★

▥ **The Westin Maui Resort & Spa.** The cascading waterfall in the lobby of this hotel gives way to an "aquatic playground" with five heated swimming pools, abundant waterfalls (15 at last count), lagoons complete with pink flamingos and swans, and a premier beach; the water features combined with a spa and fitness center and privileges at two 18-hole golf courses make this an active resort—great for families. **Pros:** complimentary shuttle to Westin Kaanapali Ocean Resort Villas and to Lahaina, where parking can be difficult; activity programs for all ages; one pool just for adults. **Cons:** you could end up with fantasy overload; can seem a bit stuffy at times. ⑤ *Rooms from: $560* ✉ *2365 Kaanapali Pkwy.* ☎ *808/667–2525, 866/716–8112* ⊕ *www.westinmaui. com* ⇨ *731 rooms, 28 suites* ❢◎❢ *No meals.*

KAPALUA AND VICINITY

The neighborhoods north of Kaanapali—Honokowai, Mahinahina, Kahana, Napili, and finally, Kapalua—blend almost seamlessly into one another along Lower Honoapiilani Highway. Each has a few shops and restaurants and a secluded bay or two to call its own. Many visitors have found a second home here, at one of the condominiums nestled between beach-access roads and groves of mango trees. You won't get the stellar service of a resort (except at Kapalua), but you'll be among the locals here, in a relatively quiet part of the island. Be prepared for a long commute, though, if you're planning to do much exploring elsewhere on the island. Kapalua is the area farthest north, but well worth all the driving to stay at the elegant Ritz-Carlton, which is surrounded by misty greenery and overlooks beautiful D.T. Fleming Beach.

HONOKOWAI

$$$
RENTAL
FAMILY

▥ **Aston at Papakea Resort.** All studios and one- and two-bedroom units at this casual, oceanfront condominium complex face the ocean and, because its units are spread out among 11 low-rise buildings on about 13 acres of land, Papakea has built-in privacy. **Pros:** units have large rooms; lovely garden landscaping; complimentary swimersize, yoga, and tennis lessons. **Cons:** no beach in front of property; pool can get crowded. ⑤ *Rooms from: $269* ✉ *3543 Lower Honoapiilani Hwy.* ☎ *808/669–4848, 866/774–2924* ⊕ *www.astonhotels.com* ⇨ *364 units* ❢◎❢ *No meals.*

$$$$
RENTAL
FAMILY

▥ **Aston Mahana at Kaanapali.** Though the address claims Kaanapali, this older 12-story condominium complex is really in quiet, neighboring Honokowai; all the studio, one-, and two-bedroom units in this building are oceanfront, with unobstructed panoramic views of the ocean and nearby islands. **Pros:** the private lanai and floor-to-ceiling windows are great for watching Maui's spectacular sunsets; daily maid

VACATION RENTAL COMPANIES

There are many real-estate companies that specialize in short-term vacation rentals. They may represent an entire resort property, most of the units at one property, or even individually owned units. The companies listed here have a long history of excellent service to Maui visitors.

AA Oceanfront Rentals and Sales. As the name suggests, the specialty is "oceanfront." With rental units in more than 25 condominium complexes on the South Shore from the northernmost reaches of Kihei all the way to Wailea, there's something for everyone at prices that range from $120 to $395 a night. ✉ *1279 S. Kihei Rd., #107, Kihei* ☎ *808/879–7288, 800/488-6004* ⊕ *www. aaoceanfront.com.*

Bello Maui Vacations. The Bellos are Maui real-estate experts and have a full range of vacation rentals in 20 South Shore condominium complexes. They also have gorgeous houses for rent. Condos start at right around $100 per night (most are $200 or less); a beautiful oceanfront villa rents for $1,950 per night. ✉ *95 E. Lipoa, No. 201, Kihei* ☎ *808/879-3328, 800/541-3060* ⊕ *www.bellomauivacations.com.*

Chase 'n Rainbows. Family-owned and -operated, this is the largest property management company on West Maui, with the largest selection of rentals from studios to three bedrooms. Rentals are everywhere from Lahaina town up to Kapalua. Prices range from about $100 to $1,500 per night. The company has been in business since 1980, and is good at what it does. ✉ *118 Kupuohi St., Lahaina* ☎ *808/667-7088, 800/367-6092* ⊕ *www.chasenrainbows.com.*

Destination Resorts Hawaii. If it's the South Shore luxury of Wailea and Makena you seek, look no further. This company has dozens of condominiums and villas ranging in size from studios to three bedrooms, and in price from $260 a night for a studio at Wailea Ekahi, an older property, to more than $3,000 for the new Wailea Beach Villas. The company offers excellent personalized service and is known for particularly fine housekeeping services. ✉ *34 Wailea Gateway Pl., Suite A102, Wailea* ☎ *808/891–6249, 800/367-5246* ⊕ *www.drhmaui.com.*

Maalaea Bay Realty and Rentals. A little strip of condominiums within the isthmus that links Central and West Maui, Maalaea is often overlooked, but it shouldn't be. This company has more than 100 one- and two-bedroom units from $100 to $300 per night. The wind is usually strong here, but there's a nice beach, a harbor, and some good shopping and decent restaurants. ✉ *280 Hauoli St., Maalaea* ☎ *808/244-5627, 800/367-6084* ⊕ *www.maalaeabay.com.*

Maui Condo & Home Vacations. This Maui-based agency, part of Interval Acquisition Corporation, manages more than 3,000 individually owned condos. Most of the units are near the beach or golf courses, and are located throughout Maui. Studios to three-bedroom units range in price from $100 to $450 per night. ✉ *1819 S. Kihei Rd., Suite D103, Kihei* ☎ *808/879-5445, 800/822-4409* ⊕ *www.mauicondo.com.*

9

Westin Maui Resort & Spa

Outrigger Maui Eldorado Kaanapali

Hooilo House

service. **Cons:** furnishings in some units may need updating; no shops or restaurants on property. $ *Rooms from: $349* ✉ *110 Kaanapali Shores Pl.* ☎ *808/661–8751, 866/774–2924* ⊕ *www.themahana.com* ⇆ *215 units* ⦾ *No meals.*

$$$$
RENTAL
 🏨 **Honua Kai Resort & Spa.** Situated in two high-rise towers, these individually owned units offer the conveniences of a condo with the full service of a hotel, such as daily housekeeping, valet, concierge, room service, and an on-site restaurant and gourmet food market. **Pros:** large units; upscale appliances and furnishings. **Cons:** property can be windy; spa not yet open; very expensive. $ *Rooms from: $779* ✉ *130 Kai Malina Pkwy.* ☎ *808/662–2800, 855/718–5789* ⊕ *www.honuakai.com* ⇆ *628.*

$
RENTAL
 🏨 **Makani Sands.** Set right on a thin strip of sandy beach, this slightly older but well-maintained complex offers an economical way to stay on West Maui. **Pros:** beachfront; reasonable rates; friendly staff; walking distance to farmers' market. **Cons:** older buildings; few amenities; back bedrooms are close to the road and may be noisy at night. $ *Rooms from: $180* ✉ *3765 Lower Honoapiilani Hwy.* ☎ *808/669–8223, 800/227–8223* ⊕ *www.makanisands.com* ⇆ *20 units* ⦾ *No meals.*

MAHINAHINA

$
RENTAL
 🏨 **Mahina Surf Oceanfront Resort.** One of the many condo complexes lining the ocean-side stretch of Honoapiilani Highway offers affordable accommodations; you won't be charged fees for parking or local phone use, and discount car rentals are available. **Pros:** oceanfront barbecues; no "hidden" fees. **Cons:** units need updating; oceanfront but with rocky shoreline rather than a beach. $ *Rooms from: $170* ✉ *4057 Lower Honoapiilani Hwy., Mahinahina* ☎ *808/669–6068, 800/367–6068* ⊕ *www.mahina-surf.com* ⇆ *56 units* ⦾ *No meals.*

KAHANA

$$$$
RENTAL
 🏨 **Sands of Kahana.** Meandering gardens, spacious rooms, and an on-site restaurant distinguish this large condominium complex that's primarily a time-share property; a few units are available as vacation rentals and are managed by Sullivan Properties. **Pros:** spacious units at reasonable prices; restaurant on the premises. **Cons:** you may be approached about buying a unit; street-facing units may get a bit noisy. $ *Rooms from: $445* ✉ *4299 Lower Honoapiilani Hwy.* ☎ *808/669–0400 property phone, 808/669–0423, 800/332–1137 Sullivan Properties for vacation rentals* ⊕ *www.mauiresorts.com* ⇆ *196 units* ⦾ *No meals.*

NAPILI

$$
RENTAL
 🏨 **The Mauian Boutique Beach Studios.** If you're looking for a quiet place to stay, this small, delightful property way out in Napili may be for you; the renovated and redecorated rooms have neither TVs nor phones—such noisy devices are relegated to the Ohana (Family) Room, where a Continental breakfast is served daily. **Pros:** reasonable rates; friendly staff. **Cons:** older building; few amenities. $ *Rooms from: $196* ✉ *5441 Lower Honoapiilani Hwy.* ☎ *808/669–6205, 800/367–5034* ⊕ *www.mauian.com* ⇆ *44 rooms* ⦾ *Breakfast.*

$$$
RESORT
FAMILY
 🏨 **Napili Kai Beach Resort.** On 10 beautiful beachfront acres—the beach here is one of the best on West Maui for swimming and snorkeling—the Napili Kai draws a loyal following to its Hawaiian-style rooms

9

that open onto private lanai. **Pros:** kids' hula performance and Hawaiian slack-key guitar concert every week; fantastic swimming and sunning beach; old-Hawaii feel; no resort fees. **Cons:** older property; some might call it "unhip." $ *Rooms from: $315* ⊠ *5900 Lower Honoapiilani Hwy.* ☎ *808/669–6271, 800/367–5030* ⊕ *www.napilikai.com* ⤳ *163 units* ⦿ *No meals.*

KAPALUA

$$$$ ⊡ **Kapalua Villas.** Set among the 22,000 sprawling acres of the Kapalua
RENTAL Resort, these condominiums are named for their locations: the Golf Villas line the fairways of Kapalua's championship Bay Golf Course; the Ridge Villas are perched along a cliff overlooking the ocean; and the Bay Villas are at the water's edge. **Pros:** large, well-appointed condos; amazing views. **Cons:** you may hear noise from neighboring condos; units do not have direct beach access; Kapalua can be windy. $ *Rooms from: $480* ⊠ *2000 Village Rd.* ☎ *808/665–5400, 800/545–0018* ⊕ *www. outrigger.com* ⤳ *564 rooms* ⦿ *No meals.*

$$$$ ⊡ **The Ritz-Carlton, Kapalua.** One of Maui's most notable resorts, this
RESORT elegant hillside property features luxurious service, upscale accommo-
Fodor's Choice dations, a spa, restaurants, and pool, along with an education center
★ and an enhanced Hawaiian sense of place. **Pros:** luxury and service you'd expect from a Ritz; many cultural and recreational programs. **Cons:** expensive; can be windy on the grounds and at the pool; the hotel is not on the beach and is far from major attractions such as Haleakala. $ *Rooms from: $629* ⊠ *1 Ritz-Carlton Dr.* ☎ *808/669–6200, 800/262–8440* ⊕ *www.ritzcarlton.com* ⤳ *463 rooms* ⦿ *No meals.*

SOUTH SHORE

The South Shore is composed of two main communities: resort-filled Wailea and down-to-earth Kihei. In general, the farther south you go, the fancier the accommodations get. ■ **TIP→ North Kihei tends to have great prices, but it also has some windy beaches scattered with seaweed. (This isn't a problem if you don't mind driving to another beach.)** As you travel down South Kihei Road, you can find condos both fronting and across the street from inviting beach parks and close to shops and restaurants. Once you hit Wailea, the opulence quotient takes a giant leap—this is the land of perfectly groomed resorts. Wailea and West Maui's Kaanapali continuously compete over which is more exclusive and which has better weather—in our opinion, it's a draw.

KIHEI

If you're a beach lover, you won't find many disadvantages to staying in Kihei. A string of welcoming beaches stretches from tip to tip. Snorkeling, boogie boarding, and barbecuing find their ultimate expression here. Affordable condos line South Kihei Road; however, some find the busy traffic and the strip-mall shopping distinctly un-Maui and prefer quieter hideaways.

$$ ⊡ **Hale Hui Kai.** Bargain hunters who stumble across this small three-
RENTAL story condo complex of mostly two-bedroom units will think they've

Ritz Carlton Kapalua

Grand Wailea Resort & Spa

Luana Kai

died and gone to heaven; the beachfront units are older, but most of them have been renovated. **Pros:** far enough from the noise and tumult of "central" Kihei; close enough to all the conveniences; guest discounts at neighboring restaurants. **Cons:** nondescript 1970s architecture; a private home next door blocks the ocean view from some units. $ *Rooms from: $185 ⊠2994 S. Kihei Rd. ☎808/879–1219, 800/809–6284 ⊕ www.halehuikaimaui.com ⇴40 units* ⍩ *No meals.*

$$
RENTAL
FAMILY

🏠 **Kamaole Sands.** At this South Kihei property, a good choice for active families, there are tennis courts for a friendly game, and the ideal family beach (Kamaole III) is just across the street. **Pros:** in the seemingly endless strip of Kihei condos, this stands out for its pleasant grounds and well-cared-for units. **Cons:** the complex of buildings may seem a bit too "citylike"; all buildings look the same, so remember a landmark to help you find your unit. $ *Rooms from: $259 ⊠2695 S. Kihei Rd. ☎808/874–8700, 800/367–5004 ⊕ www.castleresorts.com ⇴205 units managed by Castle Resorts* ⍩ *No meals.*

$
RENTAL
Fodor'sChoice
★

🏠 **Luana Kai.** If you don't need everything to be totally modern, consider setting up house at this North Kihei condominium-by-the-sea with individually owned units offered in two categories: standard and deluxe. **Pros:** great value; meticulously landscaped grounds; excellent management team. **Cons:** three stories with no elevator; no maid service. $ *Rooms from: $139 ⊠940 S. Kihei Rd. ☎808/879–1268, 800/669–1127 ⊕ www.luanakai.com ⇴113 units* ⍩ *No meals.*

$$$$
RENTAL
FAMILY

🏠 **Mana Kai Maui.** An unsung hero of South Shore hotels, this place with both hotel rooms and condos may be older than its competitors, but you simply cannot get any closer to gorgeous Keawakapu Beach than this. **Pros:** arguably the best beach on the South Shore; great value; Maui Yoga Path is on property and offers classes at an additional cost. **Cons:** older property; the decor is a little rough around the edges. $ *Rooms from: $370 ⊠2960 S. Kihei Rd. ☎808/879–2778, 800/367–5242 ⊕ www.crhmaui.com ⇴98 units* ⍩ *No meals.*

$$$
HOTEL

🏠 **Maui Coast Hotel.** You may never notice this lovely hotel because it's set back off the street, but it's worth a look; although the refurbished standard rooms are fine—clean and modern—the best deal is to pay a little more for one of the suites so you'll get more space to relax. **Pros:** closest thing to a boutique hotel on the South Shore; Spices restaurant on property is open for breakfast, lunch, and dinner; free use of bicycles. **Cons:** right in the center of Kihei, so traffic and some street noise are issues. $ *Rooms from: $295 ⊠2259 S. Kihei Rd. ☎808/874–6284, 800/895–6284 ⊕ www.mauicoasthotel.com ⇴151 rooms, 114 suites* ⍩ *No meals.*

$$
RENTAL

🏠 **Maui Kamaole.** Across the street from one of Maui's best beach parks, Kamaole III, these one- and two-bedroom condos each have two bathrooms, fully equipped kitchens, air conditioning, Wi-Fi, cable TV, and washers and dryers. **Pros:** great location in sunny Kihei; nice grounds and pool. **Cons:** two-story buildings have no elevators. $ *Rooms from: $225 ⊠2777 S. Kihei Rd. ☎808/879–2778, 866/975–1864 ⊕ www. crhmaui.com ⇴310 units.*

$
RENTAL

🏠 **Maui Sunseeker Resort.** Particularly popular with a gay and lesbian clientele, this small, private, and relaxed North Kihei property is a great

CONDO COMFORTS

Condo renters in search of food and take-out meals should try these great places around Maui.

WEST MAUI

Foodland Farms. This large supermarket combines the best of gourmet selections with all the familiar staples you need to stock your vacation kitchen. ⊠ *Lahaina Gateway Shopping Center, 345 Keawe St., Lahaina* ☎ *808/662–7088.*

The Maui Fish Market. It's worth stopping by this little fish market for oysters or a cup of fresh fish chowder. You can also get live lobsters and marinated fish fillets for your barbecue. ⊠ *3600 Lower Honoapiilani Hwy., Honokowai* ☎ *808/665–9895* ⊕ *www.fishmarketmaui.com.*

SOUTH SHORE

Guava, Gouda & Caviar. This shop, formerly called Who Cut the Cheese, continues to offer a wide selection of cheeses, wines, and gourmet items in its new location. ⊠ *10 Wailea Gateway Pl., Suite B-106, Wailea* ☎ *808/874–3930* ⊕ *www.guavagoudaandcaviar.com.*

Safeway. Find everything you could possibly need at this huge supermarket. ⊠ *277 Piikea Ave., Kihei* ☎ *808/891–9120.*

CENTRAL MAUI

Safeway. This supermarket has a deli, prepared-foods section, and bakery that are all fantastic. There's a good wine selection, tons of produce, and a flower shop where you can treat yourself to a fresh lei. ⊠ *170 E. Kaahumanu Ave., Kahului* ☎ *808/877–3377.*

UPCOUNTRY

Pukalani Terrace Center. Come here if you're looking for pizza, a bank, post office, hardware store, Laundromat, or Starbucks. ⊠ *55 Pukalani St., Pukalani.*

Foodland. This member of a local supermarket chain is at Pukalani Terrace Center; it has fresh sushi and a good seafood section in addition to the usual fare. ⊠ *55 Pukalani St., Pukalani* ☎ *808/572–0674*

NORTH SHORE

Haiku Cannery. This marketplace is home to the Haiku Grocery, a Laundromat, and a few other small stores. The post office is across the street. ⊠ *810 Haiku Rd., Haiku.*

Haiku Grocery. You can find the basics, such as veggies, meats, wine, snacks, and ice cream, at this local store in the Haiku Cannery. ⊠ *810 Haiku Rd., Haiku* ☎ *808/575–9291*

value for the area. **Pros:** impeccably maintained; webcam on building videos panoramic ocean views and whales in winter months. **Cons:** no frills. ⑤ *Rooms from: $175* ⊠ *551 S. Kihei Rd.* ☎ *808/879–1261, 800/532–6284* ⊕ *www.mauisunseeker.com* ⤵ *23 units* ⦿ *No meals.*

$

B&B/INN

⌂ **Pineapple Inn.** After successful careers in the hospitality industry, hosts Mark Warner and Steve Much realized their dreams of owning a place that offers the amenities of a fine hotel with the peace and quiet of a small inn at a reasonable price. **Pros:** no resort fees; recycling available; free off-street parking. **Cons:** although you don't see it from the inn, the rest of the neighborhood is not as well maintained; short drive to the beach. ⑤ *Rooms from: $169* ⊠ *3170 Akala Dr.* ☎ *808/298–4403,*

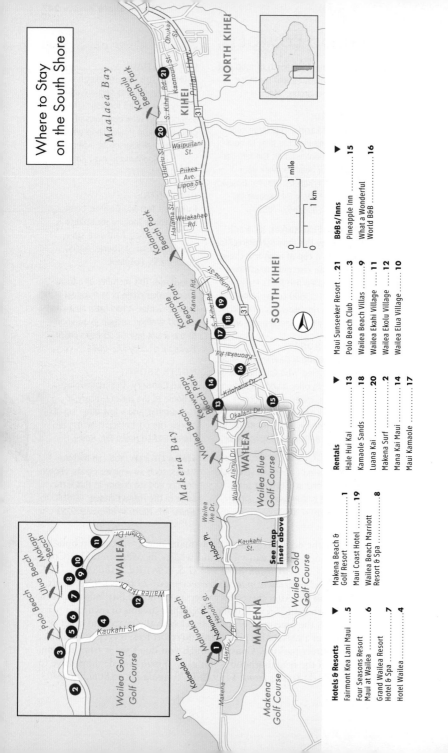

Where to Stay on the South Shore

Hotels & Resorts ▶
Fairmont Kea Lani Maui **5**
Four Seasons Resort
Maui at Wailea **6**
Grand Wailea Resort
Hotel & Spa **7**
Hotel Wailea **4**
Makena Beach &
Golf Resort **1**
Maui Coast Hotel **19**
Wailea Beach Marriott
Resort & Spa **8**

Rentals ▶
Hale Hui Kai **13**
Kamaole Sands **18**
Luana Kai **20**
Makena Surf **2**
Mana Kai Maui **14**
Maui Kamaole **17**

Maui Sunseeker Resort ... **21**
Polo Beach Club **3**
Wailea Beach Villas **9**
Wailea Ekahi Village **11**
Wailea Ekolu Village **12**
Wailea Elua Village **10**

B&Bs/Inns ▶
Pineapple Inn **15**
What a Wonderful
World B&B **16**

877/212-6284 ⊕ www.pineappleinnmaui.com ⇄ 4 rooms, 1 cottage ⊟ No credit cards ⊙ No meals.

$ ⊡ **What a Wonderful World B&B.** Convenient, comfortable, and afford-
B&B/INN able, this B&B provides a good base for exploring the island; in a residential neighborhood, it's only a half mile from beaches, five minutes
from golf courses, and close to restaurants and shopping. **Pros:** the
host, Eva, is knowledgeable about the island; affordable rates. **Cons:**
owner's dogs live here so if you don't like dogs, this is not the place
for you; a little hard to find in the neighborhood; no resort amenities.
⑤ *Rooms from: $130 ⊠ 2828 Umalu Pl. ☎ 800/943–5804 ⊕ www.
amauibedandbreakfast.com ⇄ 4 suites ⊙ Breakfast.*

WAILEA AND MAKENA

Warm, serene, and luxurious, Wailea properties offer less "action" than
West Maui resorts. The properties here tend to focus on ambience—
thoughtful details and natural scenery. Nightlife is pretty much nil, save
for a few swanky bars and a boisterous Irish pub. However, you have
your choice of sandy beaches with good snorkeling. Farther south,
Makena is a little less developed. Expect everything—even bottled
water—to double in price when you cross the line from Kihei to Wailea.

$$$$ ⊡ **Fairmont Kea Lani Maui.** Gleaming white spires and tiled archways are
RESORT the hallmark of this stunning resort that's particularly good for fami-
FAMILY lies; the spacious suites have comfortable furnishings and come with
microwaves, stereos, and marble bathrooms. **Pros:** for families, this is
the best of the South Shore luxury resorts; on-site deli good for picnic
fare; no resort fee. **Cons:** some feel the architecture and design scream
anything *but* Hawaii; great villas but price puts them out of range
for many. ⑤ *Rooms from: $499 ⊠ 4100 Wailea Alanui Dr., Wailea
☎ 808/875–4100, 866/540–4456 ⊕ www.fairmont.com/kealani ⇄ 413
suites, 37 villas ⊙ No meals.*

$$$$ ⊡ **Four Seasons Resort Maui at Wailea.** Impeccably stylish, subdued, and
RESORT relaxing describe most Four Seasons properties, and this one fronting
Fodor'sChoice award-winning Wailea Beach is no exception; thoughtful luxuries—
★ like Evian spritzers poolside and twice-daily housekeeping—earned this
Maui favorite its reputation. **Pros:** no resort fee; children's program,
poolside cabanas, tennis, and other activities are complimentary; the
most low-key elegance on Maui; known for exceptional service. **Cons:**
expensive; a bit pretentious for some. ⑤ *Rooms from: $495 ⊠ 3900
Wailea Alanui Dr., Wailea ☎ 808/874–8000, 800/332–3442 ⊕ www.
fourseasons.com/maui ⇄ 305 rooms, 75 suites ⊙ No meals.*

$$$$ ⊡ **Grand Wailea Resort Hotel & Spa.** "Grand" is no exaggeration for this
RESORT opulent, sunny, 40-acre resort with elaborate water features such as a
Fodor'sChoice "canyon riverpool" with slides, caves, a Tarzan swing, and a water ele-
★ vator. **Pros:** you can meet every vacation need without ever leaving the
property; many shops. **Cons:** at these prices, service should be extraordi-
nary, and it isn't; room prices don't include a resort fee, parking fee, and
more; sometimes too much is too much. ⑤ *Rooms from: $399 ⊠ 3850
Wailea Alanui Dr., Wailea ☎ 808/875–1234, 800/888–6100 ⊕ www.
grandwailea.com ⇄ 728 rooms, 52 suites ⊙ No meals.*

9

Four Seasons Resort Maui at Wailea

Old Wailuku Inn at Ulupono

$$$
HOTEL

🏨 **Hotel Wailea.** This small, boutique hotel offers romance at a good value: perched on a quiet hillside above the Wailea Resort, the property has spectacular views of the ocean, sunsets, and stars from just about every suite, garden nook, and spacious public area. **Pros:** spectacular views; beautiful grounds; good for whale-watching (in season). **Cons:** not on the beach; spa needs updating; no elevator; few utensils provided in units with kitchenettes. ⓢ *Rooms from: $279* ⊠ *555 Kaukahi St., Wailea* ☎ *808/874–0500, 800/800–0720* ⊕ *www.hotelwailea.com* ↩ *72 suites* ⦿ *Breakfast.*

$$$$
RESORT

🏨 **Makena Beach & Golf Resort.** Renovated and upgraded, this resort (formerly the Maui Prince) has a superb location just south of Makena, on a secluded piece of land surrounded by a magnificent golf course and abutting a beautiful, near-private beach. **Pros:** new fitness center; for quiet and a great beach, the location is ideal. **Cons:** not as luxurious as nearby properties in Wailea; the property is far from attractions. ⓢ *Rooms from: $360* ⊠ *5400 Makena Alanui Rd., Makena* ☎ *808/874–1111, 800/321–6284* ⊕ *www.makenaresortmaui.com* ↩ *290 rooms, 20 suites* ⦿ *No meals.*

$$$$
RENTAL

🏨 **Makena Surf.** For travelers who've done all there is to do on Maui and just want simple but luxurious relaxation at a rental, this is the spot. **Pros:** away from it all, yet still close enough to "civilization"; laundry facilities in every unit. **Cons:** too secluded and "locked-up" for some; Hawaiian legend has it that spirits may have been disturbed here. ⓢ *Rooms from: $435* ⊠ *34 Wailea Gateway Pl., Suite A102, Wailea* ☎ *808/801–6249, 800/367–5246* ⊕ *www.drhmaui.com* ↩ *107 units* ⦿ *No meals.*

$$$$
RENTAL

🏨 **Polo Beach Club.** Lording over a hidden section of Polo Beach, this wonderful, older, eight-story rental property somehow manages to stay under the radar. **Pros:** you can pick fresh herbs for dinner out of the garden; beach fronting the building is a beautiful, private crescent of sand. **Cons:** some may feel isolated. ⓢ *Rooms from: $650* ⊠ *3750 Wailea Alanui Dr., Wailea* ☎ *808/891–6249, 800/367–5246* ⊕ *www.drhmaui. com* ↩ *71 units* ⦿ *No meals.*

$$$$
RESORT

🏨 **Wailea Beach Marriott Resort & Spa.** The Marriott was built before current construction laws, so rooms sit much closer to the crashing surf than at most resorts; Wailea Beach is a few steps away, as are the Shops at Wailea. **Pros:** spa is one of the best in Hawaii; near good shopping; luau four nights a week. **Cons:** it's not quite beachfront and has a rocky shore, so you must walk left or right to sit on the sand; there can be a lot of foot traffic on the beach walk along the coast. ⓢ *Rooms from: $519* ⊠ *3700 Wailea Alanui Dr., Wailea* ☎ *808/879–1922* ⊕ *www. waileamarriott.com* ↩ *497 rooms, 47 suites* ⦿ *No meals.*

$$$$
RENTAL

🏨 **Wailea Beach Villas.** These überluxurious vacation rentals include units that are bigger than many houses—about 3,000 square feet—and the furnishings and accessories are gorgeous. **Pros:** steps away from the Shops at Wailea; near several excellent restaurants; no resort fee; pool cabanas, valet parking, and twice-daily housekeeping are included in the rates. **Cons:** certainly not in most visitors' budgets. ⓢ *Rooms from: $1,200* ⊠ *3800 Wailea Alanui Dr., Wailea* ☎ *808/891–6249, 800/367–5246* ⊕ *www.waileabeachvillas.com* ↩ *98 units* ⦿ *No meals.*

9

$$$$ ⊞ **Wailea Ekahi Village.** Overlooking Keawakapu Beach, this family-friendly vacation resort features studios and one- and two-bedroom suites in low-rise buildings that span 34 acres of tropical gardens. **Pros:** convenient access to a great beach; kitchen and laundry facilities in-suite. **Cons:** the large complex can be tricky to find your way around. ⑤ *Rooms from: $350 ⊠ 34 Gateway Plaza, Suite A102, Wailea* ☎ *808/891–6249, 800/357–5246* ⊕ *www.drhmaui.com* ⇆ *294 suites* ⦾ *No meals.*
RESORT

$$$$ a ⊞ **Wailea Elua Village.** Located on Ulua Beach, one of the island's most beloved snorkeling spots, these upscale one-, two-, and three-bedroom condo suites have spectacular views and 24 acres of manicured lawns and gardens. **Pros:** easy access to the designer boutiques and upscale restaurants at the Shops at Wailea; for a nominal fee, the concierge will stock your refrigerator with groceries, even hard-to-find items for those with dietary restrictions. **Cons:** large complex; hard to find your way around. ⑤ *Rooms from: $550 ⊠ 34 Gateway Plaza, Suite A102, Wailea* ☎ *808/891–6249, 800/367–5246* ⊕ *www.drhmaui.com* ⇆ *152 units* ⦾ *No meals.*
RESORT

> **LANAI**
>
> Islanders love their porches, balconies, and verandas, all wrapped up in the single Hawaiian word *lanai*. When booking your lodging, ask about the lanai and be sure to specify the view (understanding that top views command top dollars). Also, check that the lanai is not merely a step-out or Juliet balcony, with just enough room to lean against a railing. You want a lanai that is big enough for patio seating.

CENTRAL MAUI

Kahului and Wailuku, the commercial, residential, and government centers that make up Central Maui, are not known for their lavish accommodations, but there are options that meet some travelers' needs perfectly.

$$ ⊞ **Courtyard Marriott.** Opened in June 2012, this hotel is conveniently located near Kahului Airport and offers many amenities for business travelers as well as tourists. **Pros:** newly constructed; central location; no resort fee. **Cons:** not on—or even really near—any good beaches; some construction nearby. ⑤ *Rooms from: $209 ⊠ 532 Keolani Place, Kahului* ☎ *808/871–1800, 877/852–1880* ⊕ *www.marriotthawaii.com* ⇆ *138 rooms.*
HOTEL

$ ⊞ **The Old Wailuku Inn at Ulupono.** Built in 1924 and listed on the State of Hawaii Register of Historic Places, this home may be the ultimate Hawaiian B&B; each room is decorated with the theme of a Hawaiian flower, and the flower motif appears in the heirloom Hawaiian quilt on each bed. **Pros:** the charm of old Hawaii; knowledgeable innkeepers; walking distance to Maui's best ethnic restaurants; free Wi-Fi; free parking; no resort fees. **Cons:** closest beach is a 20-minute drive away; you may hear some traffic at certain times. ⑤ *Rooms from: $165 ⊠ 2199 Kahookele St., Wailuku* ☎ *808/244–5897, 800/305–4899* ⊕ *www.mauiinn.com* ⇆ *10 rooms* ⦾ *Breakfast.*
B&B/INN
Fodor's Choice
★

Hale Ho okipa Inn

Hana Kai Maui Resort Condominiums

UPCOUNTRY

Upcountry accommodations (those in Kula, Makawao, and Haliimaile) are generally on country properties and, with the exception of Kula Lodge, are privately owned vacation rentals. At high elevation, these lodgings offer splendid views of the island, temperate weather, and a "getting away from it all" feeling—which is actually the case, as most shops and restaurants are a fair drive away, and beaches even farther. You'll definitely need a car here.

$
B&B/INN
FAMILY

The Banyan Tree House. If a taste of rural Hawaii life in plantation days is what you crave, you can find it at this pastoral spot—the 2-acre property is lush with tropical foliage, has an expansive lawn, and is fringed with huge monkeypod and banyan trees. **Pros:** two cottages and the pool are outfitted for travelers with disabilities; you can walk to Makawao town for dining and shopping. **Cons:** the furniture in the cottages is pretty basic; few amenities. $ *Rooms from: $155* ✉ *3265 Baldwin Ave., Makawao* ☎ *808/572–9021* ⊕ *www.bed-breakfast-maui.com* ⤵ *7 rooms* ¶⊘ *Breakfast.*

$
B&B/INN
Fodor'sChoice
★

Hale Hookipa Inn. A handsome 1924 Craftsman-style house in the heart of Makawao town, this inn on both the Hawaii and the National Historic Registers provides a great base for excursions to Haleakala or to Hana. **Pros:** genteel rural setting; price includes buffet breakfast with organic fruit from the garden. **Cons:** a 20-minute drive to the nearest beach; this is not the sun, sand, and surf surroundings of travel posters. $ *Rooms from: $138* ✉ *32 Pakani Pl., Makawao* ☎ *808/572–6698, 877/572-6698* ⊕ *www.maui-bed-and-breakfast.com* ⤵ *3 rooms, 1 suite* ¶⊘ *Breakfast.*

$$
B&B/INN

Ke Kihapai Bed & Breakfast. Loosely translated as "small farm," this charming Kula cottage surrounded by flowering plants and fruit trees is a wonderful getaway for honeymooners; families can enjoy it, too, as it can easily accommodate six guests. **Pros:** great family vacation spot; knowledgeable hosts; great views. **Cons:** can be cool in the evenings, the beach is a 20-minute drive away. $ *Rooms from: $250* ✉ *44 Pea Pl., Kula* ☎ *808/283–7733* ⊕ *www.kekihapai.com* ⤵ *1 cottage* ¶⊘ *Breakfast.*

$
HOTEL

Kula Lodge. Don't expect a local look despite being out in the country; this lodge inexplicably resembles a chalet in the Swiss Alps, and two units even have electric fireplaces. **Pros:** a quiet and peaceful place in the country; excellent shopping right next door. **Cons:** it's a long, long way to the beach; in winter, it can get downright cold; furniture looks worn. $ *Rooms from: $155* ✉ *1520 Haleakala Hwy., Rte. 377, Kula* ☎ *808/878–1535, 800/233–1535* ⊕ *www.kulalodge.com* ⤵ *5 units* ¶⊘ *No meals.*

$$$$
B&B/INN

Lumeria Maui. Peace, tranquillity, and a healthful experience are what you will find at this beautifully restored historic property. **Pros:** organic and healthy; peaceful and restful setting; **Cons:** bathrooms have shower only; not near the beach $ *Rooms from: $349* ✉ *1813 Baldwin Ave., Makawao* ☎ *808/579–8877, 855/579-8877* ⊕ *www.lumeriamaui.com* ⤵ *24 rooms* ¶⊘ *Breakfast.*

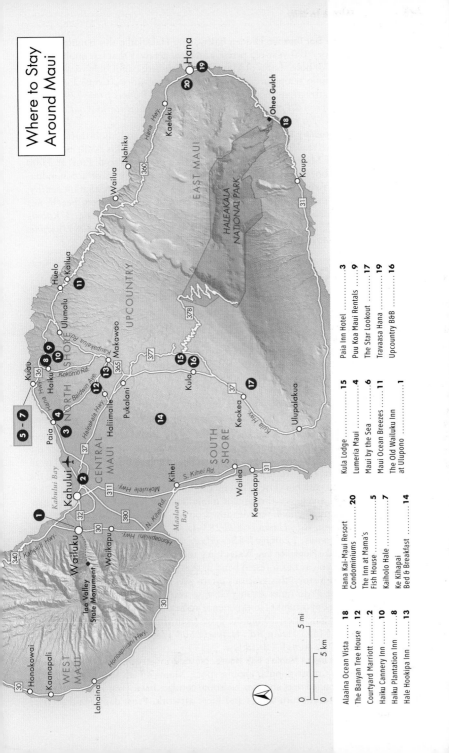

Where to Stay Around Maui

Alaaina Ocean Vista **18**
The Banyan Tree House .. **12**
Courtyard Marriott **2**
Haiku Cannery Inn **10**
Haiku Plantation Inn **8**
Hale Hookipa Inn **13**

Hana Kai-Maui Resort
Condominiums **20**
The Inn at Mama's
Fish House **5**
Kaiholo Hale **7**
Ke Kihapai
Bed & Breakfast **14**

Kula Lodge **15**
Lumeria Maui **4**
Maui by the Sea **6**
Maui Ocean Breezes **11**
The Old Wailuku Inn
at Ulupono **1**

Paia Inn Hotel **3**
Puu Koa Maui Rentals **9**
The Star Lookout **17**
Travaasa Hana **19**
Upcountry B&B **16**

$$ ⛫ **The Star Lookout.** Hidden halfway up Haleakala, this remote, serene,
RENTAL   and cozy 100-year-old perch is an ideal getaway that has unobstructed
views of both shores of Maui. **Pros:** secluded; panoramic views; cooler
nighttime temperatures at this higher elevation. **Cons:** long drive
from attractions, beaches, and shopping. ⑤ *Rooms from: $200* ⊠ *622
Thompson Rd., Keokea* ☎ *907/250–2364* ⊕ *www.starlookout.com* ⇆ *1
unit* �’❑ *No meals.*

$ ⛫ **Upcountry Bed & Breakfast.** Spacious rooms and unobstructed views
B&B/INN   are two reasons to experience Upcountry Maui at this B&B, into which
owner Michael Sullivan has put a lot of heart and soul. **Pros:** at 3,000
feet above sea level, it's closer to Haleakala than most accommoda-
tions; two rooms are ADA accessible; local store and restaurant nearby;
rates include taxes. **Cons:** can be cool in Kula; far from beach; not
everyone may enjoy the mellow and friendly resident dog. ⑤ *Rooms
from: $150* ⊠ *4925 Lower Kula Rd., Kula* ☎ *808/878–8083* ⊕ *www.
upcountrybandb.com* ⇆ *4 rooms* �’❑ *Breakfast.*

NORTH SHORE

You won't find any large resorts or condominium complexes along
the North Shore, yet there are a variety of accommodations along the
coastline from the surf town of Paia, through tiny Kuau, and along
the rain-forested Hana Highway through Haiku. Some are oceanfront
but not necessarily beachfront (with sand); instead, look for tropical
gardens overflowing with ginger, bananas, papayas, and nightly bug
symphonies. Some have breathtaking views or the type of solitude that
seeps in, easing your tension before you know it. You may encounter
brief, powerful downpours, but that's what makes this part of Maui
green and lush. You'll need a car to enjoy staying on the North Shore.

$ ⛫ **Haiku Cannery Inn.** Hidden down a long driveway that winds through
B&B/INN   tall trees and hanging vines is this stately house-turned-B&B, once the
residence of pineapple cannery managers and now listed on the Hawaii
Register of Historic Places. **Pros:** Hawaii born-and-raised hostess; off the
beaten path but close to restaurants and beaches. **Cons:** no pool or other
resort amenities; three-night minimum stay in B&B rooms, and five-
night minimum in the Meadow Cottage. ⑤ *Rooms from: $125* ⊠ *1061
Kokomo Rd., Haiku* ☎ *808/283–1274* ⊕ *www.haikucanneryinn.com*
⇆ *3 rooms, 1 cottage* �’❑ *Breakfast.*

$ ⛫ **Haiku Plantation Inn.** Water lilies and a shade tree bedecked in orchids
B&B/INN   greet you at this forested bend in the road; a remnant of Haiku's plan-
tation history, this gracious estate was built in 1870 for the company
doctor. **Pros:** quiet setting; close to restaurants, gas station, and post
office; opportunities to experience authentic Hawaiian culture. **Cons:** no
resort amenities; 10-minute drive from closest beach. ⑤ *Rooms from:
$119* ⊠ *555 Haiku Rd., Haiku* ☎ *808/575–7500* ⊕ *www.haikuleana.
net* ⇆ *4 rooms* �’❑ *Breakfast.*

$$ ⛫ **The Inn at Mama's Fish House.** Nestled in gardens adjacent to one of
B&B/INN   Maui's most popular dining spots, Mama's Fish House, these well-
maintained one- and two-bedroom cottages have a retro-Hawaiian style
with rattan furnishings and local artwork. **Pros:** daily maid service;

free parking; next to Hookipa Beach. **Cons:** three-night minimum stay; Mama's Fish House is popular, so there can be many people around in the evenings (it's more mellow during the day). $ *Rooms from: $250* ✉ *799 Poho Pl., Kauu* ☎ *808/579–9764, 800/860–4852* ⊕ *www. mamasfishhouse.com* ⤵ *12 units* ⌑ *No meals.*

$ ⌑ **Kaiholo Hale.** Set in a residential area, this well-maintained vacation

RENTAL house has large, light, and airy rooms with comfortable contemporary

FAMILY furnishings; there are four spacious suites decorated in muted colors of cream and cocoa with Mission-style teak furniture. **Pros:** big rooms; lots of kitchen equipment and beach gear; surfboard racks. **Cons:** no views; it's a 100-yard walk to the beach. $ *Rooms from: $175* ✉ *25 Kaiholo Pl., Kauu* ☎ *808/870–3481* ⊕ *www.northshoremauivacations. com* ⤵ *4 suites.*

$$ ⌑ **Maui by the Sea.** Just past Paia, on the other side of a stucco wall

RENTAL from Hana Highway, this cute, small but clean, one-bedroom apartment decorated with tropical prints is bright and airy. **Pros:** free interisland, mainland, and Canada phone calls; lots of fruit trees on property for guests' enjoyment; large flat-screen TV. **Cons:** road noise from Hana Highway; another house is right next door; no resort amenities. $ *Rooms from: $225* ✉ *523 Hana Hwy., Paia* ☎ *808/579–9865* ⊕ *www.mauibythesea.com* ⤵ *1 unit* ⌑ *No meals.*

$ ⌑ **Maui Ocean Breezes.** The warm ocean breeze rolls through these pretty

RENTAL eco-friendly rentals, making this a perfect spot to relax and enjoy the gorgeous scenery. **Pros:** one of few licensed rentals in area; expansive lawn with ocean views; meditation hut. **Cons:** 15 minutes from closest beach; the owner prefers stays of seven nights or longer, though will negotiate depending on availability. $ *Rooms from: $155* ✉ *240 N. Holokai Rd., Haiku* ☎ *808/283–8526* ⊕ *www.mauivacationhideaway. com* ⤵ *3 units* ⌑ *No meals.*

$$ ⌑ **Paia Inn Hotel.** Reopened as an inn in 2008, the original part of the

B&B/INN property was built in 1927 as a boarding house when Paia was a bustling plantation town; two more buildings between the street and the beach have been added and offer oceanfront and ocean-view accommodations. **Pros:** friendly and knowledgeable staff; no minimum stay required; guests receive a complimentary membership at Upcountry Fitness in Haiku. **Cons:** no elevator; guest rooms are extraordinarily small and have no closets. $ *Rooms from: $189* ✉ *93 Hana Hwy., Paia* ☎ *808/579–6000, 800/721–4000* ⊕ *www.paiainn.com* ⤵ *15 rooms* ⌑ *No meals.*

$ ⌑ **Puu Koa Maui Rentals.** Off a peaceful cul-de-sac in a residential area,

RENTAL these two well-maintained and immaculately clean homes offer studio and one-bedroom accommodations. **Pros:** very clean; reasonable rates; good spot for a group. **Cons:** 10-minute drive to the beach; set in quiet residential area. $ *Rooms from: $90* ✉ *66 Puu Koa Pl., Haiku* ☎ *808/573–2884* ⊕ *www.puukoa.com* ⤵ *7 rooms* ⌑ *No meals.*

THE ROAD TO HANA

Why stay in Hana when it's so far from everything? In a world where everything moves at high speed, Hana still travels on horseback, ambling along slowly enough to smell the flowers. But old-fashioned and remote do not mean tame—this is a wild coast, known for heart-stopping scenery and frequent downpours. Leave city expectations behind: The single grocery may run out of milk, and the only videos to rent may be several years old. Be advised that dining options are slim. ■ TIP→ If you're staying for several days or at a vacation rental, stock up on groceries before you head out to Hana. Even with these inconveniences, Hana is a place you'll remember for a lifetime.

$$

RENTAL

Fodor's Choice
★

Hana Kai-Maui Resort Condominiums. Perfectly situated on Hana Bay, this resort complex has a long history (it opened in 1970) and an excellent reputation for visitor hospitality. **Pros:** it's a stone's throw to Hana Bay, where you can take a swim or have a Roselani mac-nut ice-cream cone at Tutu's; one-night rentals are accepted; daily housekeeping. **Cons:** early to bed and early to rise—no nightlife or excitement here; no elevator. $ *Rooms from: $205* ✉ *4865 Uakea Rd., Hana* ☎ *808/248–8426, 800/346–2772* ⊕ *www.hanakaimaui.com* ⟿ *18 units* ⎮⊚⎮ *No meals.*

$$$$

RESORT

Travaasa Hana. Formerly the Hotel Hana-Maui, this property has a new name but remains secluded and quietly luxurious, with unobstructed views of the Pacific. **Pros:** if you want to get away from it all, there's no better or more beautiful place; spa is incredibly relaxing. **Cons:** everything moves slowly; if you can't live without your BlackBerry, this is not the place for you; it's oceanfront but does not have a sandy beach (red- and black-sand beaches are nearby). $ *Rooms from: $950* ✉ *5031 Hana Hwy., Hana* ☎ *808/248–8211, 855/868–7282* ⊕ *www.travaasa.com/hana* ⟿ *47 cottages, 23 garden suites, 4 Waikoloa Family Suites* ⎮⊚⎮ *Multiple meal plans.*

EAST MAUI

$$

B&B/INN

Alaaina Ocean Vista. This B&B is on the grounds of an old banana plantation past Oheo Gulch (about a 40-minute drive past Hana town). **Pros:** quiet and secluded; no pesticides or chemicals used on property. **Cons:** travel time from Kahului Airport is quite long; remote location with no restaurants nearby. $ *Rooms from: $195* ✉ *Off Hwy. 31, 10 miles past Hana, Kipahulu* ☎ *808/248–7824* ⊕ *www.hanabandb.com* ⟿ *1 room* ⎮⊚⎮ *Breakfast.*

MOLOKAI

WELCOME TO MOLOKAI

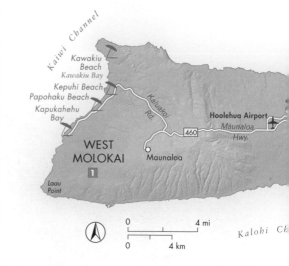

TOP REASONS TO GO

★ **Kalaupapa Peninsula:**
Hike or take a mule ride
down the world's tallest
sea cliffs to a fascinating,
historic community that
still houses a few former
Hansen's disease patients.

★ **A waterful hike in
Halawa:** A fascinating
guided hike through
private property takes
you past ancient ruins,
restored taro patches, and
a sparkling cascade.

★ **Deep-sea fishing:** Sport
fish are plentiful in these
waters, as are gorgeous
views of several islands.
Fishing is one of the
island's great adventures.

★ **Closeness to nature:**
Deep valleys, sheer cliffs,
and the untamed ocean
are the main attractions on Molokai.

★ **Papohaku Beach:** This
3-mile stretch of golden
sand is one of the most
sensational beaches in all
of Hawaii. Sunsets and
barbecues are perfect here.

1 **West Molokai.** The
most arid part of the island,
known as the west end,
has two inhabited areas:
the coastal stretch includes
a few condos and luxury
homes and the largest
beaches on the island.
Nearby is the fading hilltop
hamlet of Maunaloa.

2 **Central Molokai.** The
island's only true town,
Kaunakakai, with its mile-
long wharf, is here. Nearly
all the island's eateries and
stores are in or close to
Kaunakakai. Highway 470
crosses the center of the
island, rising to the top of
the sea cliffs and the Kalaupapa overlook. At the base
of the cliffs is Kalaupapa
National Historical Park, a
top attraction.

PACIFIC OCEAN

Kalaupapa
Airfield

KALAUPAPA
PENINSULA

Kalaupapa

Kalaupapa National
Historical Park

Hoolehua

Halawa
Beach

Halawa

Moaula Falls ◆

Kualapuu

470

MOKUHOONIKI
ISLAND

**CENTRAL
MOLOKAI**

Kamakou
Preserve

3 **EAST
MOLOKAI**

450

Waialua

Waialua
Beach Park

2

450

Pauwalu

Kaunakakai

Kamiloloa
Heights

Kawela

Pukoo

One Alii
Beach Park

Kamehameha V Hwy

Kaluaaha

Ualapue

Pailolo Channel

nnel

3 **East Molokai.** The scenic drive on Route 450 around this undeveloped area, also called the east end, passes through the green pastures of Puu O Hoku Ranch and climaxes with a descent into Halawa Valley. As you continue east, the road becomes increasingly narrow and the island ever more lush.

GETTING ORIENTED

Shaped like a long bone, Molokai is about 10 miles wide on average and four times that long. The north shore thrusts up from the sea to form the tallest sea cliffs on Earth, while the south shore slides almost flat into the water, then fans out to form the largest shallow-water reef system in the United States. Kaunakaki, the island's main town, has most of the stores and restaurants. Surprisingly, the highest point on Molokai rises to only 4,970 feet.

10

Updated by
Heidi Pool

Molokai is generally thought of as the last bit of "real" Hawaii. Tourism has been held at bay by the island's unique history and the pride of its predominantly native Hawaiian population. Exploring the great outdoors and visiting the historic Kalaupapa Peninsula, where St. Damien helped people with leprosy, are attractions for visitors.

With sandy beaches to the west, sheer sea cliffs to the north, and a rainy, lush eastern coast, Molokai offers a bit of everything, including a peek at what the Islands were like 50 years ago. Large tracts of land from Hawaiian Homeland grants have allowed the people to retain much of their traditional lifestyle. A favorite expression is "Slow down, you're on Molokai." Only 38 miles long and 10 miles wide at its widest point, Molokai is the fifth-largest island in the Hawaiian archipelago. Eight thousand residents call Molokai home, nearly 60% of whom are Hawaiian.

Molokai is a great place to be outdoors. There are no tall buildings, no traffic lights, no streetlights, no stores bearing the names of national chains, and nothing at all like a resort. You will, however, find 15 parks, and more than 100 miles of shoreline to play on. At night the whole island grows dark, creating a velvety blackness and a wonderful, rare thing called silence.

GEOLOGY

Roughly 1½ million years ago, two large volcanoes—Kamakou in the east and Mauna Loa in the west—broke the surface of the Pacific Ocean and created the island of Molokai. Shortly thereafter a third and much smaller caldera, Kauhako, popped up to form the Makanalua Peninsula on the north side. After hundreds of thousands of years of rain, surf, and wind, an enormous landslide on the north end sent much of the mountain into the sea, leaving behind the sheer sea cliffs that make Molokai's north shore so spectacularly beautiful.

HISTORY

Molokai is named in chants as the child of the moon goddess Hina. For centuries the island was occupied by native people who took advantage of the reef fishing and ideal conditions for growing taro. When leprosy broke out in the Hawaiian Islands in the 1840s, the Makanalua Peninsula, surrounded on three sides by the Pacific and accessible only by a steep trail, was selected as the place to exile people suffering from the disease. The first patients were thrown into the sea to swim ashore as best they could, and left with no facilities, shelter, or supplies. In 1873 a missionary named Father Damien arrived and began to serve the peninsula's suffering inhabitants. He died in 1889 from leprosy and was canonized as a saint by the Catholic Church in 2009. Though leprosy, now known as Hansen's disease, is no longer contagious and can be remitted, the buildings and infrastructure created by those who were exiled here still exist, and some longtime residents have chosen to stay in their homes. Today the area is Kalaupapa National Historical Park. Visitors are welcome but must prebook a tour operated by Damien Tours of Kalaupapa. You can reach the park by plane or by hiking or taking a mule ride down the steep Kalaupapa Trail.

THE BIRTHPLACE OF HULA

Tradition has it that centuries ago Lailai came to Molokai and lived on Puu Nana at Kaana. She brought the art of hula and taught it to the people, who kept it secret for her descendants, making sure the sacred dances were performed only at Kaana. Five generations later, Laka was born into the family and learned hula from an older sister. She chose to share the art and traveled throughout the Islands teaching the dance, though she did so without her family's consent. The yearly Ka Hula Piko Festival, held on Molokai in May, celebrates the birth of hula at Kaana.

PLANNING

WHEN TO GO

If you're keen to explore Molokai's beaches, coral beds, or fishponds, summer is your best bet for nonstop calm seas and sunny skies. The weather mimics that of the other Islands: low to mid-80s year-round, slightly rainier in winter. As you travel up the mountainside, the weather changes with bursts of downpours. The strongest storms occur in winter, when winds and rain shift to come in from the south.

For a taste of Hawaiian culture, plan your visit around a festival. In January, islanders and visitors compete in ancient Hawaiian games at the Ka Molokai Makahiki Festival. The Molokai Ka Hula Piko, an annual daylong event in May, draws premier hula troupes, musicians, and storytellers. Long-distance canoe races from Molokai to Oahu are in late September and early October. Although never crowded, the island is busier during these events—book accommodations and transportation six months in advance.

10

GETTING HERE AND AROUND
AIR TRAVEL

If you're flying in from the mainland United States or one of the Neighbor Islands, you must first make a stop in Honolulu. From there, it's a 25-minute trip to Molokai. Molokai's transportation hub is Hoolehua Airport, a tiny airstrip 8 miles west of Kaunakakai and about 18 miles east of Maunaloa. An even smaller airstrip serves the little community of Kalaupapa on the north shore.

From Hoolehua Airport it takes about 10 minutes to reach Kaunakakai and 25 minutes to reach the west end of the island by car. There's no public bus. A taxi will cost about $27 from the airport to Kaunakakai with Hele Mai Taxi. Shuttle service costs about $28 per person from Hoolehua Airport to Kaunakakai. For shuttle service, call Molokai Outdoors. Keep in mind, however, that it's difficult to visit the island without a rental car.

Contacts Hele Mai Taxi ☎ 808/336–0967, 808/646–9060 ⊕ www.molokaitaxi. com. **Molokai Outdoors** ☎ 808/553–4477, 877/553–4477 ⊕ www.molokai-outdoors.com.

CAR TRAVEL

If you want to explore Molokai from one end to the other, you must rent a car. With just a few main roads to choose from, it's a snap to drive around here. The gas stations are in Kaunakakai. Ask your rental agent for a free *Molokai Drive Guide*.

Alamo maintains a counter at Hoolehua Airport, and will pick you up at Kaunakakai Harbor. Make arrangements in advance, because the number of rental cars on Molokai is limited. Be sure to check the vehicle to make sure the four-wheel drive is working before departing from the agency. There is a $75 surcharge for taking a four-wheel-drive vehicle off-road. *See Travel Smart Maui for more information on renting a car and driving.*

Contact Alamo. ☎ 877/222–9075 ⊕ www.alamo.com.

FERRY TRAVEL

The Molokai Ferry crosses the channel every day between Lahaina (Maui) and Kaunakakai. Boats depart from Lahaina daily at 6 pm and Monday to Saturday at 7:15 am, and from Kauanakakai daily at 4 pm and Monday to Saturday at 5:15 am. The 1½-hour trip takes passengers but not cars, so arrange ahead of time for a car rental or tour at the arrival point.

Contact Molokai Ferry ☎ 808/661–3392, 866/307–6524 ⊕ www.molokaiferry. com.

RESTAURANTS

Dining on Molokai is more a matter of eating. There are no fancy restaurants, just pleasant low-key places to eat out. Paddlers' Inn has the best dinner offerings. Other options include burgers, plate lunches, pizza, coffee shop–style sandwiches, and make-it-yourself fixings.

HOTELS

Molokai appeals most to travelers who appreciate genuine Hawaiian ambience rather than swanky digs. Most hotel and condominium properties range from adequate to funky. Visitors who want to lollygag on the beach should choose one of the condos or home rentals in West Molokai. Travelers who want to immerse themselves in the spirit of the island should seek out a condo or cottage, the closer to East Molokai the better.

Molokai Visitors Association. Ask about a brochure with up-to-date listings of vacation rentals operated by this company's members. ☎ 808/553–3876.

Molokai Vacation Properties. This company handles condo rentals and can act as an informal concierge, including arranging for a rental car, during your stay. There is a three-night minimum on all properties. The company also handles private rental properties from beach cottages to large estates. ☎ 800/367–2984, 808/553–8334 ⊕ *www.molokai-vacation-rental.net*.

COMMUNICATIONS

There are many locations on the island where cell-phone reception is difficult, if not impossible, to obtain. Your best bet for finding service is in Kaunakakai.

VISITOR INFORMATION

Contacts Maui Visitors Bureau ☎ 808/244–3530, 800/525–6284 ⊕ *www. visitmaui.com*. **Molokai Visitors Association** ⊠ *12 Kamoi St., Suite 200, Kaunakakai* ☎ 808/553–3876, 800/800–6367 ⊕ *www.gohawaii.com/molokai*.

EXPLORING MOLOKAI

The first thing to do on Molokai is to drive everywhere. It's a feat you can accomplish comfortably in two days. Depending on where you stay, spend one day exploring the west end and the other day exploring the east end. Basically you have one 40-mile west–east highway (two lanes, no stoplights) with three side trips: the nearly deserted little west-end town of Maunaloa; the Highway 470 drive (just a few miles) to the top of the north shore and the overlook of Kalaupapa Peninsula; and the short stretch of shops in Kaunakakai town. After you learn the general lay of the land, you can return to the places that interest you most. ■TIP→ Directions on the island are often given as mauka (toward the mountains) and makai (toward the ocean).

10

WEST MOLOKAI

Papohaku Beach is 17 miles west of the airport; Maunaloa is 10 miles west of the airport.

The remote beaches and rolling pastures on Molokai's west end are presided over by Mauna Loa, a dormant volcano, and a sleepy little former plantation town of the same name. Papohaku Beach, the Hawaiian Islands' second-longest white-sand beach, is one of the area's biggest draws. *For information about Papohaku Beach, see Beaches.*

Kapuaiwa Coconut Grove in central Molokai is a survivor of royal plantings from the 19th century.

GETTING HERE AND AROUND

The sometimes winding paved road through West Molokai begins at Highway 460 and ends at Kapukahehu Bay. The drive from Kaunakakai to Maunaloa is about 30 minutes.

EXPLORING

Kaluakoi. Although the late-1960s Kaluakoi Hotel and Golf Club is closed and forlorn, some nice condos and a gift shop are operating nearby. Kepuhi Beach, the white-sand beach along the coast, is still worth a visit. ⊠ *Kaluakoi Rd.*

Maunaloa. Built in 1923, this quiet community at the western end of the highway once housed workers for the island's pineapple plantation. Many businesses have closed, but it's the last place to buy supplies when you're exploring the nearby beaches. If you're in the neighborhood, stop at Maunaloa's Big Wind Kite Factory. You'll want to talk story with Uncle Jonathan, who has been making and flying kites here for more than three decades. ⊠ *Maunaloa Hwy.*

CENTRAL MOLOKAI

Kaunakakai is 8 miles southeast of the airport.

Most residents live centrally, near the island's one and only true town, Kaunakakai. It's just about the only place on the island to get food and supplies. It *is* Molokai. Go into the shops along and around Ala Malama Street. Buy stuff. Talk with people. Take your time, and you'll really enjoy being a visitor. Also in this area, on the north side, are Coffees of Hawaii, a 500-acre coffee plantation, and the Kalaupapa

National Historical Park, one of the island's most notable sights.

GETTING HERE AND AROUND

Central Molokai is the hub of the island's road system, and Kaunakakai is the commercial center. Watch for kids, dogs, and people crossing the street in downtown Kaunakakai.

EXPLORING

TOP ATTRACTIONS

Coffees of Hawaii. Visit the headquarters of a 500-acre Molokai coffee plantation, where the espresso bar serves freshly made sandwiches, *lilikoi* (passion fruit) cheesecake, and java in artful ways. The "Mocha Mama" is a special Molokai treat. This is the place to pick up additions to your picnic lunch if you're headed to Kalaupapa. The Blue Monkey gift shop offers a wide range of Molokai handicrafts, memorabilia, and, of course, coffee. Live music is performed on the covered lanai every Sunday from 4 to 6 pm. ⊠ *1630 Farrington Hwy., off Rte. 470, Kualapuu* ☎ 877/322–3276, 808/567–9490 ⊕ *www.coffeesofhawaii.com* ⊙ *Café and gift shop weekdays 6 am–5 pm, Sat. 8–8, Sun. 8–5.*

MOLOKAI VIBES

Molokai is one of the last places in Hawaii where most of the residents are living an authentic rural lifestyle and wish to retain it. Many oppose developing the island for visitors or outsiders, so you won't find much to cater to your needs, but if you take time and talk to the locals, you will find them hospitable and friendly. Some may even invite you home with them. It's a safe place, but don't interrupt private parties on the beach or trespass on private property. Consider yourself a guest in someone's house, rather than a customer.

Fodor's Choice ★ **Kalaupapa.** *See photo feature, Kalaupapa Peninsula: A Tale of Tragedy and Triumph.*

Fodor's Choice ★ **Kalaupapa Guided Mule Tour.** Mount a friendly, well-trained mule and wind along a thrilling 3-mile, 26-switchback trail to reach the town of Kalaupapa, which was once home to patients with leprosy who were exiled to this remote spot. The path was built in 1886 as a supply route for the settlement below. Once in Kalaupapa, you take a guided tour of the town and enjoy a light picnic lunch. The trail traverses some of the highest sea cliffs in the world, and views are spectacular. ■ TIP→ Only those in good shape should attempt the ride, as two hours each way on a mule can take its toll. You must be at least 16 years old and weigh no more than 249 pounds; pregnant women are not allowed. The entire event takes seven hours. Make reservations ahead of time, as space is limited. The same outfit can arrange for you to hike down or fly in. No one is allowed in the park or on the trail without booking a tour; hikers must be down in the park by 10 am. *See Kalaupapa Peninsula: A Tale of Tragedy and Triumph photo feature for more information.* ⊠ *100 Kalae Hwy., Kualapuu* ☎ 808/567–6088, 800/567–7550 ⊕ *www.muleride.com* ⊠ *$199* ⊙ *Mon.–Sat. 8–3.*

Kaunakakai. Central Molokai's main town looks like a classic 1940s movie set. Along the one-block main drag is a cultural grab bag of restaurants and shops. Many people are friendly and willing to supply

10

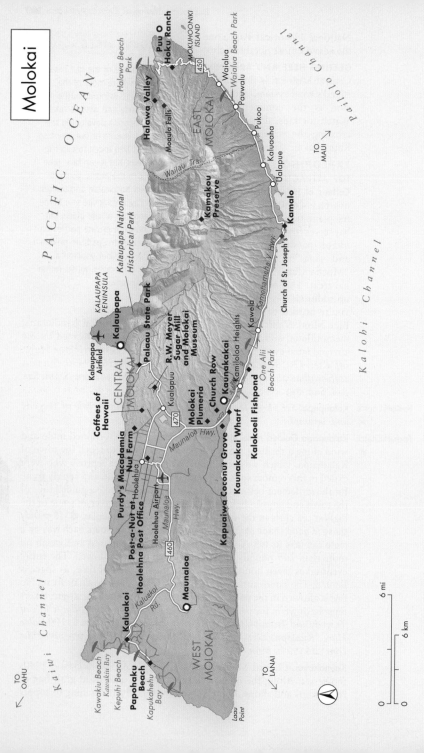

directions. The preferred dress is shorts and a tank top, and no one wears anything fancier than a cotton skirt or aloha shirt. ☒ *Rte. 460, 3 blocks north of Kaunakakai Wharf.*

Kamoi Snack-n-Go. Stop for some of Dave's Hawaiian Ice Cream at the Kamoi Snack-n-Go. Sit in the refreshing breeze on one of the benches outside for a Molokai rest stop. Snacks, crack seed, cold drinks, and water are also available. ☒ *28 Kamoi St.* ☎ *808/553-3742.*

Molokai Plumerias. The sweet smell of plumeria surrounds you at this ten-acre orchard containing thousands of these fragrant trees. Purchase a lei to go, or, for $25, owner Dick Wheeler will give you a basket, set you free to pick your own blossoms, and then teach you how to string your own lei. ☒ *1342 Maunaloa Hwy., Kaunakakai* ☎ *808/553-3391* ⊕ *www.molokaiplumerias.com* ☉ *Mon.–Fri. 9:30–12.*

HAWAII'S FIRST SAINT

A long-revered figure on Molokai and in Hawaii, Father Damien, who cared for the desperate patients at Kalaupapa, was elevated to sainthood in 2009. Plans call for a small museum and bookstore in his honor in Kaunakakai, and refurbishment of the three churches in the Catholic parish is currently underway. Visitors who cannot visit Kalaupapa can find information on St. Damien at the Damien Center in Kaunakakai, and may worship at Our Lady of Seven Sorrows (just west of Kaunakakai) or at St. Vincent Ferrer in Maunaloa.

Palaau State Park. One of the island's few formal recreation areas, this 233-acre retreat sits at a 1,000-foot elevation. A short path through an ironwood forest leads to **Kalaupapa Lookout,** a magnificent overlook with views of the town of Kalaupapa and the 1,664-foot-high sea cliffs protecting it. Informative plaques have facts about leprosy, Saint Damien, and the colony. The park is also the site of **Kaule O Nanahoa** (the phallus of Nanahoa)—where women in old Hawaii would come to the rock to enhance their fertility, and it is said some still do. It is a sacred site, so be respectful and don't deface the boulders. The park is well maintained, with trails, camping facilities, restrooms, and picnic tables. To get here, take Highway 460 west from Kaunakakai and then head *mauka* (toward the mountains) on Highway 470, which ends at the park. ☒ *Rte. 470* ☎ *Free* ☉ *Daily dawn–dusk.*

Post-A-Nut at Hoolehua Post Office. At this small, rural post office you can mail a coconut to anywhere in the world. Postmaster Gary Lam provides the coconuts and colored markers. You decorate and address your coconut, and Gary affixes eye-catching stamps on it from his extensive collection. Costs vary according to destination, but for domestic addresses they start around $10. The office is open Monday–Friday 8:30 to 4 pm; closed 12 to 12:30 for lunch. ☒ *69–2 Puupeelua Ave., Hoolehua* ☎ *808/567–6144.*

Purdy's Macadamia Nut Farm. Molokai's only working macadamia-nut farm is open for educational tours hosted by the knowledgeable and entertaining owner. A family business in Hoolehua, the farm takes up

10

1½ acres with a flourishing grove of 50 original trees that are more than 90 years old, as well as several hundred younger trees. The nuts taste delicious right out of the shell, home roasted, or dipped in macadamia-blossom honey. Look for Purdy's sign behind Molokai High School. ⊠ *Lihi Pali Ave., Hoolehua* ☎ *808/567–6601* ⊕ *www.molokai-aloha.com/ macnuts* ☎ *Free* ☉ *Mon.–Fri. 9:30–3:30, Sat. 10–2.*

R.W. Meyer Sugar Mill and Molokai Museum. Built in 1877, the three-room, fully restored R.W. Meyer Sugar Mill has been reconstructed as a testament to Molokai's agricultural history. It is located next to the Molokai Museum and is usually included in the museum tour. Several interesting machines from the past are on display, including a mule-driven cane crusher and a steam engine. The museum contains changing exhibits on the island's early history as well as a gift shop. ⊠ *Rte. 470, 2 miles southwest of Palaau State Park, Kualapuu* ☎ *808/567–6436* ☎ *$5* ☉ *Mon.–Sat. 10–2.*

WORTH NOTING

Church Row. Standing together along the highway are several houses of worship with primarily native-Hawaiian congregations. Notice the unadorned, boxlike architecture so similar to missionary homes. ⊠ *Rte. 460, 5½ miles south of airport.*

Kapuaiwa Coconut Grove. From far away this spot looks like a sea of coconut trees. Closer up you can see that the tall, stately palms are planted in long rows leading down to the sea. This is a remnant of one of the last surviving royal groves planted for Prince Lot, who ruled Hawaii as King Kamehameha V from 1863 until his death in 1872. Watch for falling coconuts. ⊠ *Rte. 460, 5½ miles south of airport.*

Kaunakakai Wharf. Once bustling with barges exporting pineapples, these docks now host visiting boats, the ferry from Lahaina, and the twice-weekly barge from Oahu. The wharf is also the starting point for fishing, sailing, snorkeling, whale-watching, and scuba diving excursions. It's a nice place at sunset to watch fish rippling on the water. To get here, take Kaunakakai Place, which dead-ends at the wharf. ⊠ *Rte. 450, at Ala Malama St.*

10

EAST MOLOKAI

Halawa Valley is 36 miles northeast of the airport.

On the beautifully undeveloped east end of Molokai you can find ancient fishponds, a magnificent coastline, splendid ocean views, and a fertile valley that's been inhabited for 14 centuries. The eastern uplands are flanked by Mt. Kamakou, the island's highest point at 4,961 feet and home to the Nature Conservancy's Kamakou Preserve. Mist hangs over

DID YOU KNOW?

Taro, grown in engineered
ponds called *loi*, is a Hawaiian food staple; the pounded
root is used to make *poi*.
The taro plant is revered as
an ancestor of the Hawaiian
people.

waterfall-filled valleys, and ancient lava cliffs jut out into the sea.

GETTING HERE AND AROUND

Driving the east end is a scenic adventure, but the road narrows and becomes curvy after the 20-mile marker. Take your time, especially in the seaside lane, and watch for oncoming traffic. Driving at night is not recommended.

EXPLORING

Fodor's Choice ★ **Halawa Valley.** Hawaiians lived in this valley as far back as AD 650, making it the oldest recorded habitation on Molokai. Inhabitants grew taro and fished until the 1960s, when an enormous flood wiped out the taro patches and forced old-timers to abandon their traditional lifestyle. Now, a new generation of Hawaiians has begun the challenging task of restoring the taro fields. Much of this work involves rerouting streams to flow through carefully engineered level ponds called *loi*. The taro plants with their big, dancing leaves grow in the submerged mud of the *loi*, where the water is always cool and flowing. Hawaiians believe that the taro plant is their ancestor and revere it both as sustenance and as a spiritual necessity. The Halawa Valley Cooperative leads hikes through the valley, which is home to two sacrificial temples, many historic sites, and the trail to **Moaula Falls**, a 250-foot cascade; contact Molokai Fish and Drive for information. The $75 fee supports the restoration efforts. The 4.2-mile round-trip hike is rated intermediate to advanced and includes two moderate river crossings. ⊠ *Eastern end of Rte. 450* ☎ *808/553–5926* ⊕ *www.molokaifishanddive.com.*

Kalokoeli Fishpond. With its narrow rock walls arching out from the shoreline, Kalokoeli is typical of the numerous fishponds that define southern Molokai. Many were built around the 13th century under the direction of powerful chiefs. This early type of aquaculture, particular to Hawaii, exemplifies the ingenuity of native Hawaiians. One or more openings were left in the wall, where gates called *makaha* were installed. These gates allowed seawater and tiny fish to enter the enclosed pond but kept larger predators out. The tiny fish would then grow too big to get out. At one time there were 62 fishponds around Molokai's coast. ⊠ *Rte. 450, 6 miles east of Kaunakakai.*

10

OFF THE BEATEN PATH

Kamakou Preserve. Tucked away on the slopes of Mt. Kamakou, Molokai's highest peak, this 2,774-acre rain-forest preserve is a dazzling wonderland full of wet *ohia* (hardwood trees of the myrtle family, with red blossoms called *lehua* flowers) forests, rare bogs, and native trees and wildlife. Guided hikes, costing $25 and limited to eight people, are held one Saturday each month between March and October. Reserve well in advance. You can visit the park without a tour, but you need a good four-wheel-drive vehicle (hard to find on the island). The Nature Conservancy requests that you sign in at the office and get directions first. The office is at Molokai Industrial Park, about 3 miles west of

Kaunakakai. ✉*23 Pueo Pl., Kualapuu* ☎*808/553–5236* ⊕*www. nature.org* ⌨*Free. $25 guided hike.*

Kamalo. A natural harbor used by small cargo ships during the 19th century and a favorite fishing spot for locals, Kamalo is also the location of the **Church of St. Joseph's,** a tiny white church built by Saint Damien of the Kalaupapa colony in the 1880s. It's a state historic site and place of pilgrimage. The door is often open; if it is, slip inside and sign the guest book. The congregation keeps the church in beautiful condition. ✉*Rte. 450, 11 miles east of Kaunakakai.*

QUICK BITES **Manae Goods & Grindz.** The best place to grab a snack or picnic supplies is Manae Goods & Grindz, 16 miles east of Kaunakakai. It's the only place on the east end where you can find essentials such as ice and bread, and not-so-essentials such as seafood plate lunches, bentos, burgers, and shakes. Try a refreshing smoothie while here. ✉ *Rte. 450* ☎ *808/558–8498, 808/558–8186.*

Puu O Hoku Ranch. A 14,000-acre private ranch in the highlands of East Molokai, Puu O Hoku was developed in the 1930s by wealthy industrialist Paul Fagan. Route 450 ambles right through this rural treasure with its pastures and grazing horses and cattle. As you drive slowly along, enjoy the splendid views of Maui and Lanai. The small island off the coast is Mokuhooniki, a favorite spot among visiting humpback whales, and a nesting seabird sanctuary. The ranch has limited accommodations, too. ✉*Rte. 450, 25 miles east of Kaunakakai* ☎*808/558–8109* ⊕*www.puuohoku.com.*

BEACHES

Molokai's unique geography gives the island plenty of drama and spectacle along the shorelines but not so many places for seaside basking and bathing. The long north shore consists mostly of towering cliffs that plunge directly into the sea and is inaccessible except by boat, and even then only in summer. Much of the south shore is enclosed by a huge reef that stands as far as a mile offshore and blunts the action of the waves. Within this reef you can find a thin strip of sand, but the water here is flat, shallow, and at times clouded with silt. This reef area is best suited to wading, pole fishing, kayaking, or learning how to windsurf.

The big, fat, sandy beaches lie along the west end. The largest of these—the second largest in the Islands—is Papohaku Beach, which fronts a grassy park shaded by a grove of *keawe* (mesquite) trees. These stretches of west-end sand are generally unpopulated. At the east end, where the road hugs the sinuous shoreline, you encounter a number of pocket-size beaches in rocky coves, good for snorkeling. Don't venture too far out, however, or you can find yourself caught in dangerous currents. The island's east-end road ends at Halawa Valley with its unique double bay, which is not recommended for swimming.

Continued on page 279

Father Damien's Church, St. Philomena

KALAUPAPA PENINSULA: TRAGEDY & TRIUMPH

For those who crave drama, there is no better destination than Molokai's Kalaupapa Peninsula—but it wasn't always so. For 100 years this remote strip of land was "the loneliest place on earth," a feared place of exile for those suffering from leprosy (now known as Hansen's Disease).

The world's tallest sea cliffs, rain-chiseled valleys, and tiny islets dropped like exclamation points along the coast emphasize the passionate history of the Kalaupapa Peninsula. Today, it's impossible to visit this stunning National Historical Park and view the evidence of human ignorance and heroism with-out responding. You'll be tugged by emotions—awe and disbelief for starters. But you'll also glimpse humorous facets of everyday life in a small town. Whatever your experience here may be, chances are you'll return home feeling that the journey to present-day Kalaupapa is one you'll never forget.

THE SETTLEMENT'S EARLY DAYS

Father Damien with patients outside St. Philomena church.

IN 1865, PRESSURED BY FOREIGN RESIDENTS, the Hawaiian Kingdom passed "An Act to Prevent the Spread of Leprosy." Anyone showing symptoms of the disease was to be permanently exiled to Kalawao, the north end of Kalaupapa Peninsula—a spot walled in on three sides by nearly impassable cliffs. The peninsula had been home to a fishing community for 900 years, but those inhabitants were evicted and the entire peninsula declared settlement land.

The first 12 patients were arrested and sent to Kalawao in 1866. People of all ages and many nationalities followed, taken from their homes and dumped on the isolated shore. Officials thought the patients could become self-sufficient, fishing and farming sweet potatoes in the stream-fed valleys. That was not the case. Settlement conditions were deplorable.

Belgian missionary Father Damien was one of four priests who volunteered to serve the leprosy settlement at Kalawao on a rotating basis. There were 600 patients at the time. His turn came in 1873; when it was up, he refused to leave. Father Damien is credited with turning the settlement from a merciless exile to a place where hope could be heard in the voices of his recruited choir. He organized the building of the St. Philomena church (and other churches on the island), nearly 300 houses, and a home for boys. A vocal advocate for his adopted community, he pestered the church for supplies, administered medicine, and oversaw the nearly daily funerals. Sixteen years after his arrival, in 1889, he died from the effects of leprosy, having contracted the disease during his service. Known around the world for his sacrifice, Father Damien was beatified by the Catholic Church in 1995, and canonized in 2009.

Mother Marianne heard of the mission while working at a hospital in Syracuse, New York. Along with six other Franciscan Sisters, she volunteered to work with those with leprosy in the Islands. They sailed to the Kalaupapa Peninsula in 1888. Like the Father, the Sisters were considered saints for their work. Mother Marianne stayed at Kalaupapa until her death in 1918; she was beatified by the Catholic Church in 2005, and canonized in 2012.

VISITING KALAUPAPA TODAY

Kalaupapa Peninsula

FROZEN IN TIME, Kalaupapa's one-horse town has bittersweet charm. Signs posted here and there remind residents when the bankers will be there (once monthly), when to place annual barge orders for nonperishable items, and what's happening around town. It has the nostalgic, almost naive ambience expected from a place almost wholly segregated from modern life.

About 13 former patients remain at Kalaupapa (by choice, as the disease is controlled by drugs and the patients are no longer carriers), but many have traveled to other parts of the world and all are over the age of 70. They never lost their chutzpah, however. Having survived a lifetime of prejudice and misunderstanding, Kalaupapa's residents haven't been willing to be pushed around any longer—in past years, several made the journey to Honolulu from time to time to testify before the state legislature about matters concerning them.

To get a feel for what residents' lives were like, visit the National Park Service Web site (⊕ *www.nps.gov/kala/history culture/*) or buy one of several heartbreaking memoirs at the park's library-turned-bookstore.

THE TRUTH ABOUT HANSEN'S DISEASE

■ A cure for leprosy has been available since 1941. Multidrug therapy, a rapid cure, has been available since 1981.

■ With treatment, none of the disabilities traditionally associated with leprosy need occur.

■ Most people have a natural immunity to leprosy. Only 5% of the world's population is even susceptible to the disease.

■ There are still about 228,000 new cases of leprosy each year; the majority are in India.

■ All new cases of leprosy are treated on an outpatient basis.

■ The term "leper" is offensive and should not be used. It is appropriate to say "a person is affected by leprosy" or "by Hansen's Disease."

GETTING HERE

The Kalaupapa Trail and Peninsula are all part of Kalaupapa National Historical Park (☎ *808/567–6802* ⊕ *www.nps. gov/kala/*), which is open every day but Sunday for tours only. Keep in mind, there are no public facilities (except an occasional restroom) anywhere in the park. Pack your own food and water, as well as light rain gear, sunscreen, and bug repellent.

TO HIKE OR TO RIDE?

There are two ways to get down the Kalaupapa Trail: in your hiking boots, or on a mule.

Hiking: Hiking allows you to travel at your own pace and stop frequently for photos—not an option on the mule ride. The hike takes about 1 hour down and 1½ hours up. You must book a tour in order to access the trail. **Damien Tours** ☎ *808/567–6171*.

Kalaupapa Beach & Peninsula

THE KALAUPAPA TRAIL

Unless you fly (flights are available through Pacific Wings [☎ *808/873–0877* or *888/575–4546* ⊕ *www.pacificwings. com*]), the only way into Kalaupapa National Historical Park is on a dizzying switchback trail. The switchbacks are numbered—26 in all—and descend 1,700 feet to sea level in just under 3 miles. The steep trail is more of a staircase, and most of the trail is shaded. Keep in mind, however, that footing is uneven and there is little to keep you from pitching over the side. If you don't mind heights, you can stare straight down to the ocean for most of the way. *Access Kalaupapa Trail off Hwy. 470 near the Kalaupapa Overlook. There is ample parking near end of Hwy. 470.*

Mule-Skinning: You'll be amazed as your mule trots up to the edge of the switchback, swivels on two legs, and completes a sharp-angled turn—26 times. The guides tell you the mules can do this in their sleep, but that doesn't take the fear out of the first few switchbacks. Make reservations well in advance. **Kalaupapa Guided Mule Tour** ☎ *808/567–6088 or 808/567–7550* ⊕ *www.muleride.com.*

IMPORTANT INFORMATION

Daily tours are offered Monday through Saturday through Damien Tours or the Kalaupapa Guided Mule Tour. Be sure to reserve in advance. Visitors ages 16 and under are not allowed at Kalaupapa, and photographing patients without their written permission is forbidden.

If you need beach gear, head to Molokai Fish and Dive at the west end of Kaunakakai's only commercial strip, or rent kayaks from Molokai Outdoors at Kaunakakai Wharf.

Department of Land and Natural Resources. All of Hawaii's beaches are free and public. None of the beaches on Molokai have telephones or lifeguards, and they're all under the jurisdiction of the Department of Land and Natural Resources. ☎ *808/587–0300* ⊕ *www.hawaiistateparks.org.*

WEST MOLOKAI

Molokai's west end looks across a wide channel to the island of Oahu. Crescent-shaped, this cup of coastline holds the island's best sandy beaches as well as the sunniest weather. Remember: all beaches are public property, even those that front developments, and most have public access roads. *Beaches below are listed from north to south.*

Kawakiu Beach. Seclusion is yours at this remote beach, accessible by four-wheel-drive vehicle (through a gate that is sometimes locked) or a 45-minute walk. The white-sand beach is beautiful. To get here, drive to Paniolo Hale off Kaluakoi Road and look for a dirt road off to the right. Park here and hike in or, with a four-wheel-drive vehicle, drive along the dirt road to beach.

> **BEACH SAFETY**
>
> Unlike protected shorelines such as Kaanapali on Maui, the coasts of Molokai are exposed to rough sea channels and dangerous rip currents. The ocean tends to be calmer in the morning and in summer. No matter what the time, however, always study the sea before entering. Unless the water is placid and the wave action minimal, it's best to stay on shore, even though locals may be in the water. Don't underestimate the power of the ocean. Protect yourself with sunblock. Cool breezes make it easy to underestimate the power of the sun as well.

⚠ Rocks and undertow make swimming extremely dangerous at times, so use caution. **Amenities:** none. **Best for:** solitude. ⊠ *Off Kaluakoi Rd., Maunaloa.*

Kepuhi Beach. The Kaluakoi Hotel is closed, but its half mile of ivory sand is still accessible. The beach shines against the turquoise sea, black outcroppings of lava, and magenta bougainvillea blossoms. When the sea is perfectly calm, lava ridges in the water make good snorkeling spots. With any surf at all, however, the water around these rocky places churns and foams, wiping out visibility and making it difficult to avoid being slammed into the jagged rocks. **Amenities:** showers; toilets. **Best for:** snorkeling; walking. ⊠ *Kaluakoi Rd., Maunaloa.*

Fodor's Choice ★ **Papohaku Beach.** One of the most sensational beaches in Hawaii, Papohaku is a 3-mile-long strip of light golden sand, the longest of its kind on the island. ■ TIP→ **Swimming is not recommended, as there's a dangerous undertow except on exceptionally calm summer days.** There's so much sand here that Honolulu once purchased barge loads of the stuff to replenish Waikiki Beach. A shady beach park just inland is the site of the Ka Hula Piko Festival, held each year in May. The park is also a great sunset-facing spot for a rustic afternoon barbecue. A park ranger

10

Lava ridges make Kepuhi Beach beautiful, but swimming is hard unless the water is calm.

patrols the area periodically. **Amenities:** showers; toilets. **Best for:** sunset; walking. ⊠ *Kaluakoi Rd., 2 miles south of the former Kaluakoi Hotel, Maunaloa.*

Kapukahehu Bay. The sandy, protected cove is usually completely deserted on weekdays but can fill up when the surf is up. The water in the cove is clear and shallow with plenty of well-worn rocky areas. These conditions make for excellent snorkeling, swimming, and boogie boarding on calm days. Locals like to surf in a break called Dixie's or Dixie Maru. **Amenities:** None. **Best for:** snorkeling; surfing; swimming. ⊠ *End of Kaluakoi Rd., 3½ miles south of Papohaku Beach, Maunaloa.*

CENTRAL MOLOKAI

The south shore is mostly a huge, reef-walled expanse of flat saltwater edged with a thin strip of gritty sand and stones, mangrove swamps, and the amazing system of fishponds constructed by the chiefs of ancient Molokai. From this shore you can look out across glassy water to see people standing on top of the sea—actually, way out on top of the reef—casting fishing lines into the distant waves. This is not a great area for beaches but is a good place to snorkel or wade in the shallows.

One Alii Beach Park. Clear, close views of Maui and Lanai across the Pailolo Channel dominate One Alii Beach Park (*One* is pronounced *o-nay*, not *won*), the only well-maintained beach park on the island's south-central shore. Molokai folks gather here for family reunions and community celebrations; the park's tightly trimmed expanse of lawn could almost accommodate the entire island's population. Swimming within the reef is perfectly safe, but don't expect to catch any waves. Nearby is the restored One Alii fishpond. **Amenities:** showers; toilets. **Best for:** partiers; swimming. ⊠ *Rte. 450, east of Hotel Molokai, Kaunakakai.*

EAST MOLOKAI

The east end unfolds as a coastal drive with turnouts for tiny cove beaches—good places for snorkeling, shore fishing, or scuba exploring. Rocky little Mokuhooniki Island marks the eastern point of the island and serves as a nursery for humpback whales in winter and nesting seabirds in spring. The road loops around the east end, then descends and ends at Halawa Valley.

Waialua Beach Park. Also known as Twenty Mile Beach, this arched stretch of sand leads to one of the most popular snorkeling spots on the island. The water here, protected by the flanks of the little bay, is often so clear and shallow that even from land you can watch fish swimming among the coral heads. Watch out for traffic when you enter the highway. ■ TIP➔ This is a pleasant place to stop on the drive around the east end. **Amenities:** none. **Best for:** snorkeling; swimming. ⊠ *Rte. 450, near mile marker 20.*

Halawa Beach Park. The vigorous water that gouged the steep, spectacular Halawa Valley also carved out two adjacent bays. Accumulations of coarse sand and river rock have created some protected pools that are good for wading or floating around. You might see surfers, but it's not wise to entrust your safety to the turbulent open ocean along this coast. Most people come here to hang out and absorb the beauty of Halawa Valley. The valley itself is private property, so do not wander without a guide. **Amenities:** toilets. **Best for:** solitude. ⊠ *End of Rte. 450, Kaunakakai.*

WATER SPORTS AND TOURS

10

Molokai's shoreline topography limits opportunities for water sports. Sea cliffs dominate the north shore; the south shore is largely encased by a huge, taming reef. ⚠ Open-sea access at west-end and east-end beaches should be used only by experienced ocean swimmers, and then with caution, because seas are rough, especially in winter. Generally speaking, there's no one around—certainly not lifeguards—if you get into trouble. For this reason alone, guided excursions are recommended. At least be sure to ask for advice from outfitters or residents. Two kinds of water activities predominate: kayaking within the reef area, and open-sea excursions on charter boats, most of which tie up at Kaunakakai Wharf.

BODY BOARDING AND BODYSURFING

You rarely see people body boarding or bodysurfing on Molokai, and the only surfing is for advanced wave riders. The best spots for body boarding, when conditions are safe (occasional summer mornings), are

the west-end beaches. Another option is to seek out waves at the east end around mile marker 20.

DEEP-SEA FISHING

For Molokai people, as in days of yore, the ocean is more of a larder than a playground. It's common to see residents fishing along the shoreline or atop South Shore Reef, using poles or lines. Deep-sea fishing by charter boat is a great Molokai adventure. The sea channels here, though often rough and windy, provide gorgeous views of several islands. Big fish are plentiful in these waters, especially mahimahi, marlin, and various kinds of tuna. Generally speaking, boat captains will customize the outing to your interests, share a lot of information about the island, and let you keep some or all of your catch.

EQUIPMENT

Molokai Fish and Dive. If you'd like to try your hand at fishing, you can rent or buy equipment and ask for advice at Molokai Fish and Dive. ⊠ *61 Ala Malama St., Kaunakakai* ☎ *808/553–5926* ⊕ *molokaifishanddive.com.*

BOATS AND CHARTERS

Alyce C. This 31-foot cruiser runs excellent sportfishing excursions in the capable hands of Captain Joe. The cost for the six-passenger boat is $550 for a full-day trip, $450 for four to five hours. Gear is provided. It's a rare day when you don't snag at least one memorable fish. ⊠ *Kaunakakai Wharf, Kaunakakai Pl., Kaunakakai* ☎ *808/558–8377* ⊕ *www.alycecsportfishing.com.*

Fun Hogs Sportfishing. Trim and speedy, the 27-foot flybridge boat named *Ahi* offers four-hour ($450), six-hour ($550), and eight-hour ($600) sportfishing excursions. Skipper Mike Holmes also provides one-way or round-trip fishing expeditions to Lanai, as well as sunset cruises and whale-watching trips in winter. ⊠ *Kaunakakai Wharf, Kaunakakai Pl., Kaunakakai* ☎ *808/567–6789, 808/336-0047* ⊕ *www.molokaifishing.com.*

Molokai Action Adventures. Walter Naki has traveled (and fished) all over the globe. He will create customized fishing expeditions and gladly share his wealth of experience. He will also take you to remote beaches for a day of swimming. If you want to explore the north side under the great sea cliffs, this is the way to go. His 21-foot *Boston Whaler* is usually seen in the east end at the mouth of Halawa Valley. ⊠ *Kaunakakai* ☎ *808/558–8184.*

10

KAYAKING

Molokai's south shore is enclosed by the largest reef system in the United States—an area of shallow, protected sea that stretches over 30 miles. This reef gives inexperienced kayakers an unusually safe, calm environment for shoreline exploring. ⚠ **Outside the reef, Molokai waters are often rough, and strong winds can blow you out to sea. Kayakers out here should be strong, experienced, and cautious.**

BEST SPOTS

South Shore Reef. Inside the South Shore Reef area is superb for flat-water kayaking any day of the year. It's best to rent a kayak from Molokai Outdoors in Kaunakakai and slide into the water from Kaunakakai Wharf. Get out in the morning before the wind picks up and paddle east, exploring the ancient Hawaiian fishponds. When you turn around to return, the wind will usually give you a push home. ⊠ *Kaunakakai.*

EQUIPMENT, LESSONS, AND TOURS

Molokai Fish and Dive. At the west end of Kaunakakai's commercial strip, this all-around outfitter offers guided kayak excursions inside the South Shore Reef. One excursion paddles through a mangrove forest and explores a hidden ancient fishpond. If the wind starts blowing hard, the company will tow you back with its boat. The fee is $69 for the half-day trip, which includes sodas and water. ⊠ *61 Ala Malama St., Kaunakakai* ☎ *808/553–5926* ⊕ *molokaifishanddive.com.*

Molokai Outdoors. This is the place to rent a kayak for exploring on your own. Kayaks rent for $42 per day or $210 per week, and extra paddles are available. ⊠ *Kaunakakai Wharf, Kaunakakai Pl., Kaunakai* ☎ *808/553–4477, 877/553–4477* ⊕ *www.molokai-outdoors.com.*

SAILING

Molokai is a place of strong, usually predictable winds that make for good and sometimes rowdy sailing. The island views in every direction are stunning. Kaunakakai Wharf is the home base for all of the island's charter sailboats.

SCUBA DIVING

Molokai Fish and Dive is the only PADI-certified dive company on Molokai. Shoreline access for divers is extremely limited, even nonexistent in winter. Boat diving is the way to go. Without guidance, visiting divers can easily find themselves in risky situations with wicked currents. Proper guidance, though, opens an undersea world rarely seen.

Molokai Fish and Dive. Owners Tim and Susan Forsberg can fill you in on local dive sites, rent you the gear, or hook you up with one of their PADI-certified guides to take you to the island's best underwater spots. Their 32-foot dive boat, the *Ama Lua*, can take eight divers and their gear. Two-tank dives lasting about five hours cost $145. Three-tank dives lasting around six hours cost $295. They know the best blue holes and underwater-cave systems, and can take you swimming with hammerhead sharks. ⊠ *61 Ala Malama St., Kaunakakai* ☎ *808/553–5926* ⊕ *molokaifishanddive.com.*

SNORKELING

During the times when swimming is safe—mainly in summer—just about every beach on Molokai offers good snorkeling along the lava outcroppings in the island's clean and pristine waters. Rough in winter,

Kepuhi Beach is a prime spot in summer. Certain spots inside the South Shore Reef are also worth checking out.

BEST SPOTS

Kepuhi Beach. In winter, the sea here is rough and deadly. But in summer, this ½-mile-long west-end beach offers plenty of rocky nooks that swirl with sea life. The presence of outdoor showers is a bonus. Take Kaluakoi Road all the way to the west end. Park at the now-closed Kaluakoi Resort and walk to the beach. ⊠ *Kaluakoi Rd., Maunaloa.*

Waialua Beach Park. A thin curve of sand rims a sheltered little bay loaded with coral heads and aquatic life. The water here is shallow—sometimes so shallow that you bump into the underwater landscape—and it's crystal clear. Head to the east end on Route 450, and pull off near mile marker 20. When the sea is calm, you can find several other good snorkeling spots along this stretch of road. ⊠ *Rte. 450, Kaunakakai.*

EQUIPMENT AND TOURS

Rent snorkel sets from either Molokai Outdoors or Molokai Fish and Dive in Kaunakakai. Rental fees are nominal—$7 to $10 a day. All the charter boats carry snorkel gear and include dive stops.

Fun Hogs Sportfishing. Mike Holmes, captain of the 27-foot *Ahi,* knows the island waters intimately, likes to have fun, and is willing to arrange any type of excursion—for example, one dedicated entirely to snorkeling. His two-hour snorkel trips leave early in the morning and explore rarely seen fish and turtle sites outside the reef. Bring your own food and drinks; the trips cost $70 per person. ⊠ *Kaunakakai Wharf, Kaunakakai Pl., Kaunakakai* ☎ *808/567–6789, 808/336–0047* ⊕ *www.molokaifishing.com.*

Molokai Fish and Dive. Climb aboard a 31-foot twin-hull Power Cat for a snorkeling trip to Molokai's pristine barrier reef. Trips cost $79 per person and include equipment, water, and soft drinks. ⊠ *61 Ala Malama St., Kaunakakai* ☎ *808/553–5926* ⊕ *www.molokaifishanddive.com.*

WHALE-WATCHING

Although Maui gets all the credit for the local wintering humpback-whale population, the big cetaceans also come to Molokai from December to April. Mokuhooniki Island at the east end serves as a whale nursery and courting ground, and the whales pass back and forth along the south shore. This being Molokai, whale-watching here will never involve floating amid a group of boats all ogling the same whale.

BOATS AND CHARTERS

Alyce C. Although this six-passenger sportfishing boat is usually busy hooking mahimahi and marlin, the captain will gladly take you on a three-hour excursion to admire the humpback whales. The price, around $75 per person, is based on the number of people in your group. ⊠ *Kaunakakai Wharf, Kaunakakai Pl., Kaunakakai* ☎ *808/558–8377* ⊕ *www.alycecsportfishing.com.*

Ama Lua. The crew of this 32-foot dive boat, which holds up to 18 passengers, is respectful of the whales and the laws that protect them. A 2-hour whale-watching trip is $79 per person; it departs from

Bikers on Molokai can explore the north-shore sea cliffs overlooking the Kalaupapa Peninsula.

Kaunakakai Wharf at 7 am from December to April. Call Molokai Fish and Dive for reservations. ✉ *61 Ala Malama St., Kaunakakai* ☎ *808/553–5926, 808/552–0184* ⊕ *molokaifishanddive.com.*

Fun Hogs Sportfishing. The *Ahi,* a flybridge sportfishing boat, takes you on 2½-hour whale-watching trips in the morning from December to April. The cost is $70 per person. Bring your own snacks and drinks. ✉ *Kaunakakai Wharf, Kaunakakai Pl., Kaunakakai* ☎ *808/567–6789, 808/336-0047* ⊕ *www.molokaifishing.com.*

GOLF, HIKING, AND OUTDOOR ACTIVITIES

Activity vendors in Kauanakakai are a good source of information on outdoor adventures on Molokai. For a mellow round of golf, head to the island's only golf course, Ironwood Hills, where you'll likely share the green with local residents. Molokai's steep and uncultivated terrain offers excellent hikes and some stellar views. Although the island is largely wild, all land is owned, so get permission before hiking.

BIKING

Cyclists who like to eat up the miles love Molokai, since its few roads are long, straight, and extremely rural. You can really go for it—there are no traffic lights and most of the time no traffic.

Molokai Bicycle. You can rent a bike from Molokai Bicycle in Kaunaka-kai. ✉ *80 Mohala St., Kaunakakai* ☎ *808/553–5740, 800/709-2453* ⊕ *www.mauimolokaibicycle.com.*

GOLF

Molokai is not a prime golf destination, but the single 9-hole course makes for a pleasant afternoon.

Ironwood Hills Golf Course. Like other 9-hole plantation-era courses, Ironwood Hills in is in a prime spot, with basic fairways and not always manicured greens. It helps if you like to play laid-back golf with locals and can handle occasionally rugged conditions. On the plus side, most holes offer ocean views. Fairways are *kukuya* grass and run through pine, ironwood, and eucalyptus trees. Carts and clubs are rented on the honor system; there's not always someone there to assist you. Bring your own water. Access is via a bumpy, unpaved road. ⊠ *Kalae Hwy., Kualapuu* ☎ *808/567–6000* ⊕ *www.molokaigolfcourse.com* ⅃ *9 holes. 3088 yds. Par 34. Greens fee: $18 for 9 holes, $24 for 18 holes* ☞ *Facilities: golf carts, pull carts, rental clubs.*

HIKING

Rural and rugged, Molokai is an excellent place for hiking. Roads and developments are few. The island is steep, so hikes often combine spectacular views with hearty physical exertion. Because the island is small, you can come away with the feeling of really knowing the place. And you won't see many other people around. Much of what may look like deserted land is private property, so be careful not to trespass without permission or an authorized guide.

BEST SPOTS

Kalaupapa Trail. You can hike down to the Kalaupapa Peninsula and back via this 3-mile, 26-switchback route. The trail is often nearly vertical, traversing the face of the high sea cliffs. You can reach Kalaupapa Trail off Highway 470 near Kalaupapa Overlook. Only those in excellent condition should attempt it. You can also arrange a guided hike with Molokai Outdoors. ⊠ *Off Hwy. 470, Kualapuu.*

Kamakou Preserve. A four-wheel-drive vehicle is essential for this half-day journey into the Molokai highlands. The Nature Conservancy of Hawaii manages the 2,774-acre Kamakou Preserve, one of the last stands of Hawaii's native plants and birds. A long rough dirt road, which begins not far from Kaunakakai, leads to the preserve.

On your way up to the preserve, be sure to stop at Waikolu Overlook, which gazes into a precipitous canyon. Once inside the preserve, various trails are clearly marked. The trail of choice—and you can drive right to it—is the 1.5-mile boardwalk trail through Pepeopae Bog, an ecological treasure. Be aware that incoming fog can blot out your trail and obscure markers. This is the landscape of prediscovery Hawaii and can be a mean trek. The road to the Kamakou Preserve is not marked, so you must check in with the Nature Conservancy. Let the staff know that you plan to visit the preserve, and pick up the informative 24-page brochure with trail maps. ⊠ *Molokai Industrial Park, 23 Pueo Pl., 3 miles west of Kaunakakai, Kaunakakai* ⊕ *www.nature.org.*

10

GOING WITH A GUIDE

Fodor'sChoice **Halawa Valley Cultural Waterfall Hike.** This gorgeous, steep-walled val-
★ ley was carved by two rivers and is rich in history. Site of the earliest
Polynesian settlement on Molokai, Halawa is a sustained island culture
with its ingeniously designed *loi,* or taro fields. Because of a tsunami
in 1948 and changing cultural conditions in the 1960s, the valley was
largely abandoned. Hawaiian families are restoring the *loi* and taking
visitors on guided hikes through the valley, which includes two of Molokai's *luakini heiau* (sacred temples), many historic sites, and the trail to
Moaula Falls, a 250-foot cascade. Bring water, food, and insect repellent, and wear sturdy shoes that can get wet. The 4.2-mile, round-trip
hike is rated intermediate to advanced and includes two moderate river
crossings. ☎ 808/553–5926 ⊕ *www.molokaifishanddive.com* 🖃 *$75.*

Molokai Outdoors. This company can arrange guided hikes that fit your
schedule and physical condition. The staff will take you down into
Kalaupapa and arrange for a plane to pick you up. ⊠ *Kaunakakai
Wharf, Kaunakakai Pl., Kaunakakai* ☎ *808/553–4477, 877/553–4477*
⊕ *www.molokai-outdoors.com.*

SHOPPING

Molokai has one main commercial area: Ala Malama Street in Kaunakakai. There are no department stores or shopping malls, and the clothing is typical island wear. Local shopping is friendly, and you may find
hidden treasures. A very few family-run businesses define the main drag
of Maunaloa, a rural former plantation town. Most stores in Kaunakakai are open Monday through Saturday between 9 and 6.

CENTRAL MOLOKAI

ARTS AND CRAFTS

Molokai Art From the Heart. A small downtown shop, this arts and crafts
co-op has locally made folk art like dolls, clay flowers, silk sarongs,
and children's items. The shop also carries original art by Molokai artists and Giclée prints, jewelry, locally produced music, and St. Damien
keepsakes. Store hours are Monday to Friday 10 to 4:30 and Saturday
9:30 to 2. ⊠ *64 Ala Malama St., Kaunakakai* ☎ *808/553–8018* ⊕ *www.
molokaigallery.com.*

CLOTHING AND SHOES

Imports Gift Shop. Across from Kanemitsu Bakery, this one-stop shop
offers fancy and casual island-style wear, including Roxy and Quicksilver for men, women, and children. The store is open Monday to
Saturday 9 to 6 and Sunday 9 to 1. ⊠ *82 Ala Malama St., Kaunakakai*
☎ *808/553–5734.*

FOOD

Friendly Market Center. The best-stocked supermarket on the island has a
slogan—"Your family store on Molokai"—that is truly credible. Sun-
and-surf essentials keep company with fresh produce, meat, groceries,
and liquor. Locals say the food is fresher here than at the other major

10

No traffic lights here: Molokai's rural, uncrowded roads have wide-open views.

supermarket. It's open weekdays 8:30 am to 8:30 pm and Saturday 8:30 am to 6:30 pm. ✉ *90 Ala Malama St., Kaunakakai* ☎ *808/553–5595.*

Home Town Groceries & Drygoods. For those staying at a condo in Molokai, this store will come in handy. It carries bulk items, and is like a mini-Costco. ✉ *93, Ala Malama, St., Kaunakakai* ☎ *808/553–3858.*

Kumu Farms. This is the most diverse working farm on Molokai, and *the* place to purchase fresh produce, herbs, and gourmet farm products. They're open Tuesday–Friday from 9 to 4. ✉ *Hua Ai, Rd., Kaunakakai* ☎ *808/567–6480* ⊕ *www.kumufarms.com.*

JEWELRY

Imports Gift Shop. You'll find soaps and lotions, a small collection of 14-karat-gold chains, rings, earrings, and bracelets, and a jumble of Hawaiian quilts, pillows, books, and postcards at this local favorite. The shop also special orders (takes approximately one week) Hawaiian heirloom jewelry, inspired by popular Victorian pieces and crafted here since the late 1800s. ✉ *82 Ala Malama St., Kaunakakai* ☎ *808/553–5734.*

WEST MOLOKAI

ARTS AND CRAFTS

Big Wind Kite Factory and Plantation Gallery. The factory has custom-made kites you can fly or display. Designs range from Hawaiian petroglyphs to *pueo* (owls). Also in stock are paper kites, minikites, and wind socks. Ask to go on the factory tour, or take a free kite-flying lesson. The adjacent gallery carries an eclectic collection of merchandise, including locally made crafts, Hawaiian books and CDs, jewelry, handmade batik sarongs, and an elegant line of women's linen clothing. ✉ *120 Maunaloa Hwy., Maunaloa* ☎ *808/552–2364* ⊕ *www.bigwindkites.com.*

FOOD

Maunaloa General Store. Stocking meat, produce, beverages, and dry goods, this shop is a convenient stop if you're planning a picnic at one of the west-end beaches. It's open Monday through Saturday 9 am to 6 pm and Sunday 9 am to noon. ✉ *200 Maunaloa Hwy., Maunaloa* ☎ *808/552–2346.*

ENTERTAINMENT AND NIGHTLIFE

Local nightlife consists mainly of gathering with friends and family, sipping a few cold ones, strumming ukuleles and guitars, singing old songs, and talking story. Still, there are a few ways to kick up your heels. Pick up a copy of the weekly Molokai *Dispatch* and see if there's a concert, church supper, or dance.

The bar at the Hotel Molokai is always a good place to drink. The "Aloha Friday" weekly gathering here from 4 to 6 pm is a must-see event, featuring Na Kapuna, a group of accomplished *kupuna* (old-timers) with guitars and ukuleles.

For something truly casual, stop in at Kanemitsu Bakery on Ala Malama Street in Kaunakakai for the nightly hot bread sale (Tuesday through Sunday beginning at 8 pm). You'll meet everyone in town, and you can take some hot bread home for a late-night treat.

SPAS

Molokai Acupuncture & Massage. This relaxing retreat offers acupuncture, massage, herbal remedies, wellness treatments, and private yoga sessions by appointment only. The professional staff also services the spa at the Hotel Molokai. ✉ *40 Ala Malama St., Kaunakakai* ☎ *808/553–3930* ⊕ *www.molokai-wellness.com.*

10

Molokai Lomi Massage. Allana Noury of Molokai Lomi Massage has studied natural medicine for more than 35 years and is a licensed massage therapist, master herbalist, and master iridologist. She will come to your hotel or condo by appointment. ☎ *808/553–8034* ⊕ *www.molokaimassage.com.*

WHERE TO EAT

During a week's stay, you might easily hit all the dining spots worth a visit and then return to your favorites for a second round. The dining scene is fun because it's a microcosm of Hawaii's diverse cultures. You can find locally grown vegetarian foods, spicy Filipino cuisine, and Hawaiian fish with a Japanese influence—such as tuna, mullet, and moonfish that's grilled, sautéed, or mixed with seaweed to make *poke* (salted and seasoned raw fish).

Most eating establishments are on Ala Malama Street in Kaunakakai. If you're heading to West Molokai for the day be sure to stock up on provisions, as there is no place to eat here. If you are on the east end, stop by Manae Goods & Grindz (☎ 808/558–8186) near mile marker 16 for good local seafood plates, burgers, and ice cream.

Prices in the reviews are the average cost of a main course at dinner or, if dinner is not served, at lunch.

CENTRAL MOLOKAI

Central Molokai offers most of the island's dining options.

$
CAFÉ
Fodor's Choice
★

✕ **Kanemitsu Bakery and Restaurant.** Stop at this Molokai institution for morning coffee and some of the the round Molokai bread—a sweet, pan-style white loaf that makes excellent cinnamon toast. Take a few loaves with you for a picnic or a condo breakfast. You can aalso try a taste of *lavosh,* a pricey flat bread flavored with sesame, taro, Maui onion, Parmesan cheese, or jalapeño. ⑤ *Average main: $6 ⊠ 79 Ala Malama St., Kaunakakai* ☎ 808/553–5855 ▭ *No credit cards* ⊘ *Closed Tues.*

$
HAWAIIAN

✕ **Kualapuu Cookhouse.** The only restaurant in rural Kualapuu, this local favorite is a classic, refurbished, green-and-white plantation house with a shady lanai. Inside, local photography and artwork enhance the simple furnishings. Typical fare is an inexpensive plate of chicken or pork served with rice, but at dinner there's also the more expensive spicy crusted ahi. This laid-back diner sits across the street from the Kualapuu Market. ⑤ *Average main: $10 ⊠ Farrington Hwy., 1 block west of Rte. 470, Kualapuu* ☎ 808/567–9655 ▭ *No credit cards* ⊘ *No dinner Sun. and Mon.*

$
BURGER

✕ **Molokai Burger.** Clean and cheery, Molokai Burger offers both drive-through and eat-in options. Burgers may be ordered on a whole wheat bun. Healthier items include breakfast sandwiches without cheese and mayonnaise, and salads featuring Kumu Farms-certified organic veggies. ⑤ *Average main: $6 ⊠ 20 Kamehameha V Hwy., Kaunakakai* ☎ 808/553–3533 ⊕ *www.molokaiburger.com* ⊘ *Closed Sun.*

$
HAWAIIAN

✕ **Molokai Drive Inn.** Fast food Molokai-style is served at this walk-up counter. Burgers, fries, and sundaes are on the menu, but residents usually choose the foods they grew up on, such as *saimin* (thin noodles and vegetables in broth), plate lunches, shave ice, and the beloved *loco moco* (rice topped with a hamburger and a fried egg and covered in gravy). ⑤ *Average main: $7 ⊠ 15 Kamoi St., Kaunakakai* ☎ 808/553–5655 ▭ *No credit cards.*

$
AMERICAN

✕ **Molokai Pizza Cafe.** Cheerful and busy, Molokai Pizza is a popular gathering spot for local families and a good place to pick up food for a picnic. Pizza, sandwiches, salads, pasta, and fresh fish are simply prepared and served without fuss. Kids keep busy at the nearby arcade, and art by local artists decorates the lavender walls. ⑤ *Average main: $12 ⊠ Kaunakakai Pl., at Wharf Rd., Kaunakakai* ☎ 808/553–3288 ▭ *No credit cards.*

$
AMERICAN

✕ **Paddlers' Inn.** There aren't many dinner options on Molokai, but this popular spot is a great place to grab a decent meal while rubbing elbows with locals. Hearty portions of ribs, pork chops, and chicken-fried steak come with two side dishes at a reasonable price. Fish options include salmon and mahimahi. There is live music on Tuesday, Thursday, and Saturday at 6:30 pm. Don't be surprised if the bass player is also a teacher at the local elementary school. ⑤ *Average main: $14* ✉ *10 N. Mohala St., Kaunakakai* ☎ *808/553–3300* ⊕ *www.molokaipaddlersinn. com.*

$ ✕ **Sundown Deli.** Small and clean, this deli focuses on freshly made take-
DELI out food. Sandwiches come on a half-dozen types of bread, and the Portuguese bean soup and chowders are rich and filling. It's open weekdays from 10:30 am to 2 pm. ⑤ *Average main: $8* ✉ *145 Ala Malama St., Kaunakakai* ☎ *808/553–3713* ▭ *No credit cards* ☉ *Closed weekends. No dinner.*

WHERE TO STAY

For expanded hotel reviews, visit Fodors.com.

The coastline along Molokai's west end has ocean-view condominium units and luxury homes available as vacation rentals. Central Molokai offers seaside condominiums. The only lodgings on the east end are some guest cottages in magical settings and the ranch house at Puu O Hoku. Note that room rates do not include 13.42% sales tax.

Note: Maui County has regulations concerning vacation rentals; to avoid disappointment, always contact the property manager or the owner and ask if the accommodation has the proper permits and is in compliance with local ordinances.

Prices in the reviews are the lowest price of a standard double room in high season. Prices for rentals are the lowest per-night cost for a one-bedroom unit in high season.

WEST MOLOKAI

If you want to stay in West Molokai so you'll have access to unspoiled beaches, your only choices are condos or vacation homes. Keep in mind that units fronting the abandoned Kaula Koi golf course present a bit of a dismal view.

10

$ ▦ **Ke Nani Kai.** These pleasant, spacious, one- and two-bedroom condos
RENTAL have ocean views and nicely maintained tropical landscaping. **Pros:** on island's secluded west end; uncrowded pool. **Cons:** amenities vary from unit to unit; far from commercial center; some units overlook abandoned golf course. ⑤ *Rooms from: $105* ✉ *50 Keuphi Beach Rd., Maunaloa* ☎ *808/553–8334, 800/367–2984* ⊕ *www.molokai-vacation-rental.net* ⇆ *120 units* ⫿◯⫿ *No meals.*

$ ▦ **Paniolo Hale.** Perched high on a ridge overlooking a favorite local
RENTAL surfing spot, this is Molokai's best condominium property. **Pros:** close to beach; quiet surroundings; perfect if you are an expert surfer. **Cons:** amenities vary; far from shopping; golf course units front abandoned course. ⑤ *Rooms from: $125* ✉ *100 Lio Pl., Kaunakakai* ☎ *808/553–8334, 800/367–2984* ⊕ *www.molokai-vacation-rental.net* ⇆ *77 units* ⫿◯⫿ *No meals.*

CENTRAL MOLOKAI

There are two condo properties in this area, one close to shopping and dining in Kaunakakai, and the other on the way to the east end.

$ | **Molokai Shores.** Many of the units in this three-story condominium
RENTAL | complex have a view of the ocean. **Pros:** convenient location; some units upgraded; near water. **Cons:** older accommodations; units close to highway can be noisy. $ *Rooms from: $105* ⊠ *1000 Kamehameha V Hwy., Kaunakakai* ☎ *808/553–5954, 800/535–0085* ⊕ *www.molokai-vacation-rental.net* ⤳ *100 units* ⫟*No meals.*

$ | **Wavecrest.** This oceanfront condominium complex is convenient if
RENTAL | you want to explore the east side of the island—it's 13 miles east of Kaunakakai. **Pros:** convenient location for divers; good value; nicely maintained grounds. **Cons:** amenities vary; far from shopping; area sometimes gets windy. $ *Rooms from: $105* ⊠ *Rte. 450, near mile marker 13, Kaunakakai* ☎ *800/367–2984, 808/553–8334* ⊕ *www. molokai-vacation-rental.net* ⤳ *126 units* ⫟*No meals.*

EAST MOLOKAI

Puu O Hoku Ranch, a rental facility on East Molokai, is the main lodging option on this side of the island. The ranch is quite far from the center of the island.

$$ | **Puu O Hoku Ranch.** At the east end of Molokai, you'll discover these
B&B/INN | ocean-view accommodations on 14,000 isolated acres of pasture and forest. **Pros:** ideal for large groups; authentic working ranch; great hiking. **Cons:** on remote east end of island; road to property is narrow and winding. $ *Rooms from: $200* ⊠ *Rte. 450, near mile marker 25, Kaunakakai* ☎ *808/558–8109* ⊕ *www.puuohoku.com* ⤳ *3 cottages, 11 rooms* ⫟*No meals.*

LANAI

WELCOME TO LANAI

TOP REASONS TO GO

★ **Seclusion and serenity:** Lanai is small: local motion is slow motion. Get into the spirit and go home rested instead of exhausted.

★ **Garden of the Gods:** Walk amid the eerie red-rock spires that Hawaiians still believe to be a sacred spot. The ocean views are magnificent, too; sunset is a good time to visit.

★ **A dive at Cathedrals:** Explore underwater pinnacle formations and mysterious caverns illuminated by shimmering rays of light.

★ **Dole Park:** Hang out in the shade of the Cook pines in Lanai City and talk story with the locals for a taste of old-time Hawaii.

★ **Hit the water at Hulopoe Beach:** This beach may have it all: good swimming, a shady park for perfect picnicking, great reefs for snorkeling, and sometimes schools of spinner dolphins.

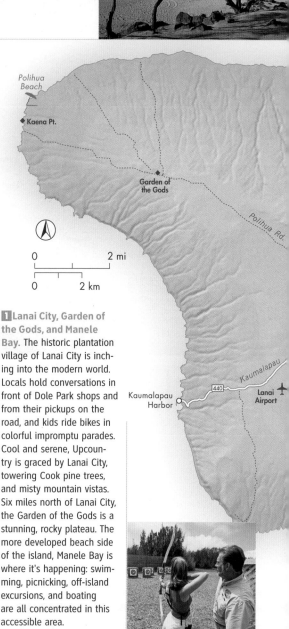

1 **Lanai City, Garden of the Gods, and Manele Bay.** The historic plantation village of Lanai City is inching into the modern world. Locals hold conversations in front of Dole Park shops and from their pickups on the road, and kids ride bikes in colorful impromptu parades. Cool and serene, Upcountry is graced by Lanai City, towering Cook pine trees, and misty mountain vistas. Six miles north of Lanai City, the Garden of the Gods is a stunning, rocky plateau. The more developed beach side of the island, Manele Bay is where it's happening: swimming, picnicking, off-island excursions, and boating are all concentrated in this accessible area.

GETTING ORIENTED

Unlike the other Hawaiian Islands with their tropical splendors, Lanai looks like a desert: kiawe trees right out of Africa, red-dirt roads, and a deep blue sea. Lanaihale (house of Lanai), the mountain that bisects the island, is carved into deep canyons by rain and wind on the windward side, and the drier leeward side slopes gently to the sea, where waves pound against surf-carved cliffs. The town of Lanai City is in the center of the island, Upcountry. Manele Bay, on the south side of the island, is popular for swimming and boating.

Shipwreck Beach

WINDWARD LANAI

Keomuku Beach

Halepalaoa

Four Seasons Resort Lodge at Koele

Lanai City

Mt. Lanaihale ▲ 3,370 ft.

UPCOUNTRY

Lopa Beach

Palawai Basin 440

Manele Rd.

Naha Beach

Four Seasons Resort Lanai at Manele Bay

Manele Bay

Hulopoe Beach

2 **Windward Lanai.** This area is the long white-sand beach at the base of Lanaihale. Now uninhabited, it was once occupied by thriving Hawaiian fishing villages and a sugarcane plantation.

By Joana
Varawa

With no traffic or traffic lights and miles of open space, Lanai seems suspended in time, and that can be a good thing. Small (141 square miles) and sparsely populated, it is the smallest inhabited Hawaiian Island and has just 3,500 residents, most of them living Upcountry.

Though it may seem a world away, Lanai is separated from Maui and Molokai by two narrow channels, and is easily accessed by commercial ferry from Maui. The two resorts on the island are run by Four Seasons. If you yearn for a beach with amenities, a luxury resort, and golf course, the Four Seasons Resort Lanai at Manele Bay beckons from the shoreline. Upcountry, the luxurious Four Seasons Resort Lodge at Koele provides cooler pleasures. This leaves the rest of the 100,000-acre island to explore. An afternoon strolling around Dole Park in historic Lanai City offers shopping, dining, and the opportunity to mingle with locals.

FLORA AND FAUNA
Lanai bucks the "tropical" trend of the other Hawaiian Islands with African kiawe trees, Cook pines, and eucalyptus in place of palm trees, and deep blue sea where you might expect shallow turquoise bays. Abandoned pineapple fields are overgrown with drought-resistant grasses, Christmas berry, and lantana; native plants, *aalii* and *ilima*, are found in uncultivated areas. Axis deer from India dominate the ridges, and wild turkeys lumber around the resorts. Whales can be seen December through April, and a family of resident spinner dolphins rests and fishes regularly in Hulopoe Bay.

ON LANAI TODAY
Despite its fancy resorts, Lanai still has that languid-Hawaii feel. The island is 97% owned by billionaire Larry Ellison, who plans to revitalize the island. Old-time residents are a mix of just about everything—Hawaiian, Chinese, German, Portuguese, Filipino, Japanese, French, Puerto Rican, English, Norwegian—you name it. When Dole owned the island in the early 20th century and grew pineapples, the plantation was divided into ethnic camps, which helped retain cultural cuisines. Potluck dinners feature sashimi, Portuguese bean soup, *laulau* (morsels

of pork, chicken, butterfish, or other ingredients steamed in ti leaves), potato salad, teriyaki steak, chicken *hekka* (a gingery Japanese chicken stir-fry), and Jell-O. The local language is pidgin, a mix of words as complicated and rich as the food. Newly arrived residents have added to the cultural mix.

PLANNING

WHEN TO GO

Lanai has an ideal climate year-round, hot and sunny at the sea and a few delicious degrees cooler Upcountry. In Lanai City and Upcountry the nights and mornings can be almost chilly when a fog or harsh trade winds settle in. Winter months are known for *slightly* rougher weather—periodic rain showers, occasional storms, and higher surf.

As higher mountains on Maui capture the trade-wind clouds, Lanai receives little rainfall and has a near-desert ecology. Consider the wind direction when planning your day. If it's blowing a gale on the windward beaches, head for the beach at Hulopoe or check out Garden of the Gods. Overcast days, when the wind stops or comes lightly from the southwest, are common in whale season. At that time, try a whale-watching trip or the windward beaches.

Whales are seen off Lanai's shores from December through April. A Pineapple Festival on the July 4 Saturday in Dole Park features traditional entertainment, a pineapple-eating contest, and fireworks. Buddhists hold their annual outdoor Obon Festival, honoring departed ancestors with joyous dancing, local food, and drumming, in early July. During hunting-season weekends, from mid-February through mid-May, and mid-July through mid-October, watch out for hunters on dirt roads even though there are designated safety zones. Sunday is a day of rest in Lanai City, and shops and most restaurants are closed.

GETTING HERE AND AROUND

AIR TRAVEL

Island Air is the only commercial airline serving Lanai City. All flights to the island depart from Oahu's Honolulu International Airport.

If you're staying at the Hotel Lanai or either Four Seasons hotel, you'll be met at the airport or ferry dock by a bus that shuttles between the resorts and Lanai City. A different shuttle will pick you up if you're renting a Jeep or minivan from Lanai City Service.

If you're not taking a shuttle, bus drivers at the ferry docks will herd you onto the appropriate bus and take you into town for $10 per person. Advance reservations aren't necessary (or even possible), but be prepared for a little confusion at the dock.

Information Island Air ☎ *800/652–6541* ⊕ *www.islandair.com.*

CAR TRAVEL

Lanai has only 30 miles of paved roads. Keomuku Highway starts just past the Lodge at Koele and runs northeast to the dirt road that goes to Shipwreck Beach and Lopa Beach. Manele Road (Highway 440) runs south down to Manele Bay, the Four Seasons Resort Lanai at Manele Bay, and Hulopoe Beach. Kaumalapau Highway (also Highway 440) heads west to Kaumalapau Harbor. The rest of your driving takes place on bumpy, dusty roads that remain unpaved and unmarked. Driving in thick mud is not recommended, and the rental agency will charge a stiff cleaning fee. Watch out for blind curves on narrow roads.

Renting a four-wheel-drive vehicle is expensive but almost essential if you'd like to explore beyond the resorts and Lanai City. Make reservations far in advance of your trip, because Lanai's fleet of vehicles is limited. Lanai City Service, where you'll find a branch of Dollar Rent A Car, is open daily 7 to 7.

Bring along a good topographical map, and keep in mind your directions. Stop from time to time to find landmarks and gauge your progress. Never drive or walk to the edge of lava cliffs, as rock can give way under you. Directions on the island are often given as *mauka* (toward the mountains) and *makai* (toward the ocean).

Information Lanai City Service ✉ *1036 Lanai Ave., Lanai City* ☏ *808/565–7227, 800/533–7808.*

FERRY TRAVEL

Ferries operated by Expeditions cross the channel four times daily between Lahaina on Maui to Manele Bay Harbor on Lanai. The crossing takes 45 minutes and costs $30. Be warned: passage can be rough, especially in winter.

Contact Expeditions ☏ *808/661–3756, 800/695–2624* ⊕ *www.go-lanai.com.*

SHUTTLE TRAVEL

A shuttle transports hotel guests between the Hotel Lanai, the Four Seasons Resort Lodge at Koele, the Four Seasons Resort Lanai at Manele Bay, and the airport. A $47.50 fee added to the room rates covers all transportation during the length of your stay.

RESTAURANTS

Lanai has a wide range of choices for dining, from simple plate-lunch local eateries to fancy, upscale, gourmet resort restaurants.

HOTELS

The range of lodgings is limited on Lanai. Essentially there are only three options: the two Four Seasons Resorts Lanai (at Manele Bay and Upcountry at the Lodge at Koele) and the venerable Hotel Lanai. A good alternative is looking into house rentals, which give you a feel for everyday life on the island. Make sure to book far in advance. **Note:** Maui County has regulations concerning vacation rentals; to avoid disappointment, always contact the property manager or owner and ask if the accommodation has the proper permits and is in compliance with local laws.

Ocean views provide a backdrop to the eroded rocks at Garden of the Gods.

EXPLORING LANAI

You can easily explore Lanai City and the island's two resorts without a car; just hop on the hourly shuttle. A small fee applies. To access the rest of this untamed island, rent a four-wheel-drive vehicle. Take a map, be sure you have a full tank, and bring a snack and plenty of water. Ask the rental agency or your hotel's concierge about road conditions before you set out. Although roads may be dry on the coast they may be impassable upland. It's always good to carry a cell phone. The main road on Lanai, Highway 440, refers to both Kaumalapau Highway and Manele Road.

LANAI CITY, GARDEN OF THE GODS, AND MANELE BAY

Lanai City is 3 miles northeast of the airport; Manele Bay is 9 miles southeast of Lanai City; Garden of the Gods is 6 miles northwest of Lanai City.

Pineapples once blanketed the Palawai, the great basin south of Lanai City. Although it looks like a volcanic crater, it isn't. Some say that the name Palawai is descriptive of the mist that sometimes fills the basin at dawn and looks like a huge shining lake.

The area northwest of Lanai City is wild; the Garden of the Gods is one of its highlights.

GETTING HERE AND AROUND

Lanai City serves as the island's hub, with roads leading to Manele Bay, Kaumalapau Harbor, and windward Lanai. Garden of the Gods is usually possible to visit by car, but beyond that you will need four-wheel drive.

EXPLORING

TOP ATTRACTIONS

Fodor's Choice
★

Garden of the Gods. This preternatural plateau is scattered with boulders of different sizes, shapes, and colors, the products of a million years of wind erosion. Time your visit for sunset, when the rocks begin to glow—from rich red to purple—and the fiery globe sinks to the horizon. Magnificent views of the Pacific Ocean, Molokai, and, on clear days, Oahu, provide the perfect backdrop for photographs.

The ancient Hawaiians shunned Lanai for hundreds of years, believing the island was the inviolable home of spirits. Standing beside the oxide-red rock spires of this strange, raw landscape, you might be tempted to believe the same. This lunar savanna still has a decidedly eerie edge, but the shadows disappearing on the horizon are those of mouflon sheep and axis deer, not the fearsome spirits of lore. According to tradition, Kawelo, a Hawaiian priest, kept a perpetual fire burning on an altar at the Garden of the Gods, in sight of the island of Molokai. As long as the fire burned, prosperity was assured for the people of Lanai. Kawelo was killed by a rival priest on Molokai and the fire went out. The Hawaiian name for this area is Keahiakawelo, meaning the "fire of Kawelo."

Garden of the Gods is 6 miles north of Lanai City. From the Stables at Koele, follow a dirt road through a pasture, turn right at a crossroad marked by carved boulder, and head through abandoned fields and ironwood forests to an open red-dirt area marked by a carved boulder. ⊠ *Off Polihua Rd.*

Ka Lokahi o Ka Malamalama Church. Built in 1938, this picturesque painted wooden church provided services for Lanai's growing population. (For many people, the only other Hawaiian church, in coastal Keomuku, was too far away.) A classic structure of ranching days, the one-room church was moved from its original site when the Lodge at Koele was built. It's open all day and Sunday services are still held in Hawaiian and English; visitors are welcome but are requested to attend quietly. The church is north of the entrance to the Four Seasons Resort Lodge at Koele. ⊠ *1 Keomuku Hwy.*

Kanepuu Preserve. Hawaiian sandalwood, olive, and ebony trees characterize Hawaii's largest example of a rare native dryland forest. Thanks to the combined efforts of volunteers at the Nature Conservancy and Castle & Cooke Resorts, the 590-acre remnant forest is protected from the axis deer and mouflon sheep that graze on the land beyond its fence. More than 45 native plant species, including *nau,* the endangered Hawaiian gardenia, can be seen here. A short, self-guided loop trail, with eight signs illustrated by local artist Wendell Kahoohalahala, reveals this ecosystem's beauty and the challenges it faces. The reserve is adjacent to the sacred hill, Kane Puu, dedicated to

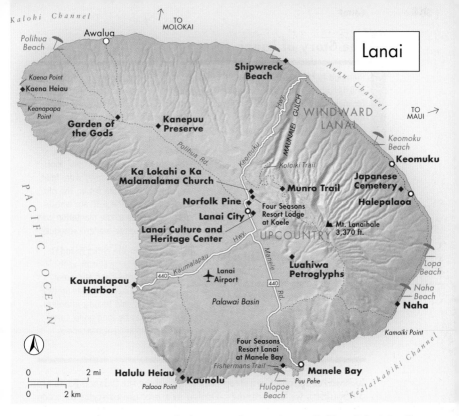

the Hawaiian god of water and vegetation. ⊠ *Polihua Rd., 4.8 miles north of Lanai City.*

Kaumalapau Harbor. Built in 1926 by the Hawaiian Pineapple Company, this is Lanai's principal commercial seaport. A native fishing village once thrived here. The cliffs that flank the western shore reach up to 1,000 feet. Water activities aren't allowed here, but it's a dramatic sunset spot and is perfect for stargazing. The area is closed to visitors on barge days: Tuesday, Wednesday, and Thursday. ⊠ *West end of Hwy. 440, 6 miles west of Lanai City.*

Fodor's Choice
★

Lanai City. A tidy plantation town, built in 1924 by Jim Dole to accomodate workers for his pineapple business, Lanai City is home to old-time residents, recently arrived resort workers, and second-home owners. A simple grid of roads is lined with stately Cook pines. Despite recent growth, the pace is still calm and the people are friendly. **Dole Park,** in the center of Lanai City, is surrounded by small shops and restaurants and is a favorite spot among locals for sitting, strolling, and talking story. Try a picnic lunch in the park and visit the **Lanai Culture and Heritage Center** in the old Dole administration building to glimpse this island's rich past, purchase historical publications and maps, and get directions to anywhere on the island.

The Story of Lanai

Rumored to be haunted by hungry ghosts, Lanai was sparsely inhabited for many centuries. Most of the earliest settlers lived along the shore and made their living from fishing the nearby waters. Others lived in the Uplands near seasonal water sources and traded their produce for seafood. The high chiefs sold off the land bit by bit to foreign settlers, and by 1910 the island was owned by the Gay family.

When the Hawaiian Pineapple Company purchased Lanai for $1.1 million in 1922, it built the town of Lanai City, opened the commercial harbor, and laid out the pineapple fields. Field workers came from overseas to toil in what quickly became the world's largest pineapple plantation. Exotic animals and birds were imported for hunting. Cook pines were planted to catch the rain, and eucalyptus windbreaks anchored the blowing soil.

Everything was stable for 70 years, until the plantation closed in 1992. When the resorts opened their doors, newcomers arrived, homes were built, and other ways of life set in. The old pace, marked by the 6:30 am whistle calling everyone to the plantation was replaced by a more modern schedule.

Because almost the entire island is now owned by Larry Ellison, vast areas remain untouched and great views abound. Deer and birds provide glimpses of its wild beauty. Although the ghosts may be long gone, Lanai still retains its ancient mysterious presence.

Luahiwa Petroglyphs. On a steep slope overlooking the Palawai Basin are 34 boulders with engravings. Drawn in a mixture of styles between the late 1700s and early 1800s, the simple stick figures depict animals, people, and mythical beings. A no longer visible *heiau*, or temple, was used to summon the rain and was dedicated to the god Kane. Do not draw on or deface the images, and do not add to the collection. From Lanai City, head south on Highway 440, turn left on the first dirt road, and follow it for 1.2 miles. Do not go left uphill, but continue straight. When you see boulders on a hillside, park and walk up to the petroglyphs. Watch your step, wear sturdy shoes, and carry water. ⊠ *Off Hwy. 440.*

Manele Bay. The site of a Hawaiian village dating from AD 900, Manele Bay is flanked by lava cliffs hundreds of feet high. Ferries from Maui dock four times a day, and visiting yachts pull in here, as it's the island's only small boat harbor. Public restrooms, grassy lawns, and picnic tables make it a busy pit stop—you can watch the boating activity as you rest.

Just offshore to the west is **Puu Pehe.** Often called Sweetheart Rock, the isolated 80-foot-high islet carries a romantic Hawaiian legend that is probably not true. The rock is said to be named after Pehe, a woman so beautiful that her husband kept her hidden in a sea cave. One day, the surf surged into the cave and she drowned. Her grief-stricken husband buried her on this rock and jumped to his death. A more likely story is that the enclosure on the summit is a shrine to

The calm crescent of Hulopoe Beach is perfect for swimming, snorkeling, or just relaxing.

birds, built by bird-catchers. Protected shearwaters nest in the nearby sea cliffs from July through November. ⊠ *Hwy. 440, 9 miles south of Lanai City, Manele.*

WORTH NOTING

Halulu Heiau. The well-preserved remains of an impressive *heiau* (temple) at Kaunolu village, which was actively used by Lanai's earliest residents, attest to this spot's sacred history. As late as 1810, this hilltop temple was considered a place of refuge, where those who had broken *kapu* (taboos) were forgiven and where women and children could find safety in times of war. If you explore the area, be respectful and leave nothing behind. Be sure to bring along water and wear sturdy shoes.

This place is hard to find, and hard to reach. The four-wheel-drive-only road is alternately rocky, sandy, and soft at the bottom. From Lanai City, follow Highway 440 west toward Kaumalapau Harbor. Past the airport, look for a carved boulder on the hill on your left. Turn left on the dirt road and follow it 3 miles to another carved boulder, where you'll turn right and head downhill. ⊠ *On a dirt road off Hwy. 440.*

Kaunolu. Close to the island's highest cliffs, Kaunolu was once a prosperous fishing village. This important archaeological site includes a major *heiau* (temple), stone floors, and house platforms. The impressive 90-foot drop to the ocean through a gap in the lava rock is called **Kahekili's Leap.** Warriors made the dangerous leap into the shallow water below to prove their courage. King Kamehameha came here for the superb fishing and to collect taxes. The road is rocky, then gets soft and sandy at the bottom. From Lanai City, follow Highway 440 west past the airport. At a carved boulder on your left, turn left onto an unmarked dirt road. Continue 3 miles until you reach the second carved boulder, then go downhill 3 miles to village. At the end of the road, walk across the streambed and up the hill. Take water, wear shoes. Hawaiians request that you do not move or stack rocks. ✉ *On a dirt road off Hwy. 440.*

Lanai Culture and Heritage Center. Small and carefully arranged, this historical museum features artifacts and photographs from Lanai's varied and rich history. Plantation-era clothing and tools, ranch memorabilia, old maps, precious feather lei, poi pounders, and family portraits combine to give you a good idea of the history of the island and its people. Postcards, maps, books, and pamphlets are for sale. The friendly staff can orient you to the island's historical sites and provide directions. This is the best place to start your explorations of the island. ✉ *730 Lanai Ave.* ☎ *808/565–7177* ⊕ *www.lanaihc.org* ✆ *Free* ☉ *Weekdays 8:30–3:30, Sat. 9–1.*

Norfolk Pine. Considered the "mother" of all the pines on the island, this 160-foot-tall tree was planted here, at the former site of the ranch manager's house, in 1875. Almost 30 years later, George Munro, the manager, observed how, in foggy weather, water collected on its foliage, dripping off rain. This led Munro to supervise the planting of Cook pines along the ridge of Lanaihale and throughout the town in order to add to the island's water supply. This majestic tree is just in front of the south wing of Four Seasons Resort Lodge at Koele. ✉ *Four Seasons Resort Lodge at Koele, 1 Keomuku Hwy.*

WINDWARD LANAI

9 miles northeast of Lodge at Koele to end of paved road.

The eastern shore of Lanai is mostly deserted. A few inaccessible *heiau*, or temples, rock walls and boulders marking old shrines, and a restored church at Keomuku reveal traces of human habitation. Four-wheel-drive vehicles are a must to explore this side of the isle. Be prepared for hot, rough conditions. Pack a picnic lunch, a hat and sunscreen, and plenty of drinking water. A cell phone is also a good idea.

GETTING HERE AND AROUND

Once you leave paved Keomuku Highway and turn left toward Shipwreck Beach or right to Naha, the roads are dirt and sand; conditions vary with the seasons. Mileage doesn't matter much here, but figure on 20 minutes from the end of the paved road to Shipwreck Beach, and about 45 minutes to Lopa Beach.

For information about Shipwreck Beach and Lopa Beach, see Beaches, below.

EXPLORING

TOP ATTRACTIONS

Munro Trail. This 12.8-mile four-wheel-drive trail along a fern- and pine-clad narrow ridge was named after George Munro, manager of the Lanai Ranch Company, who began a reforestation program in the 1950s to restore the island's much-needed watershed. The trail climbs

Lanaihale (House of Lanai), which, at 3,370 feet, is the island's highest point; on clear days you'll be treated to a panorama of canyons and almost all the Hawaiian Islands. ■ TIP→ The road gets very muddy, and trade winds can be strong. Watch for sheer drop-offs, and keep an eye out for hikers. You can also hike the Munro Trail, although it's steep, the ground is uneven, and there's no water. From the Four Seasons Resort Lodge at Koele, head north on Highway 440 for 1¼ miles, then turn right onto Cemetery Road. Keep going until you're headed downhill on the main dirt road. It's a one-way road, but you may meet Jeeps coming from the opposite direction. ⊠ *Cemetery Rd., Lanai City.*

WORTH NOTING

Halepalaoa. Named for the whales that once washed ashore here, Hale-palaoa, or the "House of Whale Ivory," was the site of the wharf used by the short-lived Maunalei Sugar Company in 1899. Some say the sugar company failed because the sacred stones of nearby **Kahea Heiau** were used for the construction of the cane railroad. The brackish well water turned too salty, forcing the sugar company to close in 1901, after just two years. The remains of the *heiau* (temple), once an important place of worship for the people of Lanai, are now difficult to find through the *kiawe* (mesquite) overgrowth. There's good public-beach access here and clear shallow water for swimming, but no other facilities. Take Highway 440 (Keomuku Highway) to its eastern terminus; then turn right on the dirt road and continue south for 5½ miles. ⊠ *On dirt road off Hwy. 440, Lanai City.*

Japanese Cemetery. In 1899 sugarcane came to this side of Lanai. The 2,400-acre plantation promised to be a profitable proposition, but that same year disease wiped out the labor force. This Buddhist shrine commemorates the Japanese workers who died, and the local congregation comes down to clean this sacred place each year. Take Highway 440 to its eastern terminus, then turn right on dirt road and continue south for 6½ miles. The shrine is uphill on your right. ⊠ *On dirt road off Hwy. 440.*

Keomuku. There's a peaceful beauty about the former fishing village of Keomuku. During the late 19th century this small Lanai community served as the headquarters of Maunalei Sugar Company. After the company failed, the land was abandoned. Although there are no other signs of previous inhabitation, its church, **Ka Lanakila O Ka Malamalama,** built in 1903, has been restored by volunteers. Visitors often leave some small token, a shell or lei, as an offering. Take Highway 440 to its eastern terminus, then turn right onto a dirt road and continue south for 5 miles. The church is on your right in the coconut trees. ⊠ *On dirt road off Hwy. 440.*

Naha. An ancient rock-walled fishpond—visible at low tide—lies where the sandy shore ends and the cliffs begin their rise along the island's shores. Accessible by four-wheel-drive vehicle, the beach is a frequent dive spot for local fishermen. ■ TIP→ Treacherous currents make this a dangerous place for swimming. Take Highway 440 to its eastern terminus, then turn right onto a sandy dirt road and continue south for 11 miles. The shoreline dirt road ends here. ⊠ *On dirt road off Hwy. 440, Lanai City.*

BEACHES

Lanai offers miles of secluded white-sand beaches on its windward side, plus the moderately developed Hulopoe Beach, which is adjacent to the Four Seasons Resort Lanai at Manele Bay. Hulopoe is accessible by car or hotel shuttle bus; to reach the windward beaches you need a four-wheel-drive vehicle. Reef, rocks, and coral make swimming on the windward side problematic, but it's fun to splash around in the shallow water. Expect debris on the windward beaches due to the Pacific convergence ocean currents. Driving on the beach itself is illegal and can be dangerous. *Beaches in this chapter are listed alphabetically.*

> **THE COASTAL ROAD**
>
> Road conditions can change overnight and become impassable due to rain in the Uplands. Car-rental agencies should be able to give you updates before you hit the road. Some of the spur roads leading to the windward beaches from the coastal dirt road cross private property and are closed off by chains. Look for open spur roads with recent tire marks (a fairly good sign that they are safe to drive on). It's best to park on firm ground and walk in to avoid getting your car mired in the sand.

Fodor's Choice ★ **Hulopoe Beach.** A short stroll down from the Four Seasons Resort Lanai at Manele Bay, Hulopoe is one of the best beaches in Hawaii. The sparkling crescent of this Marine Life Conservation District beckons with calm waters safe for swimming almost year-round, great snorkeling reefs, tide pools, and, sometimes, spinner dolphins. A shady, grassy beach park is perfect for picnics. If the shore break is pounding, or if you see surfers riding big waves, stay out of the water. In the afternoon, watch Lanai High School students heave outrigger canoes down the steep shore break and race one another just offshore. To get here, take Highway 440 south to the bottom of the hill and turn right. The road dead-ends at the beach's parking lot. **Amenities:** parking (no fee); showers; toilets. **Best for:** snorkeling; swimming; surfing. ⊠ *Off Hwy. 440, Lanai City.*

Lopa Beach. A difficult surfing spot that tests the mettle of experienced locals, Lopa is also an ancient fishpond. With majestic views of West Maui and Kahoolawe, this remote white-sand beach is a great place for a picnic. ⚠ **Don't let the sight of surfers fool you: the channel's currents are too strong for swimming.** Take Highway 440 to its eastern terminus, turn right onto a dirt road, and continue south for 7 miles. **Amenities:** none. **Best for:** solitude; sunrise; walking. ⊠ *On dirt road off Hwy. 440.*

Polihua Beach. This often-deserted beach gets a star for its long, wide stretches of white sand and unobstructed views of Molokai. The northern end of the beach ends at a rocky lava cliff with some interesting tide pools, and sea turtles that lay their eggs in the sand. (Do not drive on the beach and endanger their nests.) However, the dirt road leading here has deep, sandy places that are difficult in dry weather and impassable when it rains. In addition, strong currents and a sudden drop in the ocean floor make swimming dangerous, and strong trade winds can make walking uncomfortable. Thirsty wild bees sometimes gather around your car. To get rid of them, put out water some distance away

11

and wait. The beach is in windward Lanai, 11 miles north of Lanai City. To get here, turn right onto the marked dirt road past Garden of the Gods. **Amenities:** none. **Best for:** solitude; sunrise; walking. ⊠ *East end of Polihua Rd., Lanai City.*

Shipwreck Beach. The rusting World War II tanker abandoned off this 8-mile stretch of sand adds just the right touch to an already photogenic beach. Strong trade winds have propelled vessels onto the reef since at least 1824, when the first shipwreck was recorded. Beachcombers come to this fairly accessible beach for shells and washed-up treasures, and photographers take great shots of Molokai, just across the Kalohi Channel. A deserted plantation era fishing settlement adds to the charm. It's still possible to find glass-ball fishing floats as you wander along. Kaiolohia, its Hawaiian name, is a favorite local diving spot. ■TIP➔ An offshore reef and rocks in the water mean that it's not for swimmers, though you can play in the shallow water on the shoreline. To get here, take Highway 440 to its eastern terminus, then turn left onto a dirt road and continue to the end. **Amenities:** none. **Best for:** solitude; windsurfing; stargazing. ⊠ *Off Hwy. 440, Lanai City.*

WATER SPORTS AND TOURS

The easiest way to enjoy the water on Lanai is to wade in at Hulopoe Beach and swim or snorkel. If you prefer an organized excursion, a fishing trip is a good bet (you keep some of the fish). Snorkel trips are a great way to see the island, above and below the surface, and scuba divers can marvel at one of the top cave-dive spots in the Pacific.

DEEP-SEA FISHING

Some of the best fishing grounds in Maui County are off the southwest shoreline of Lanai, the traditional fishing grounds of Hawaiian royalty. Pry your eyes open and go deep-sea fishing in the early morning, with departures at 6 or 6:30 am from Manele Harbor. Console yourself with the knowledge that Maui anglers have to leave an hour earlier to get to the same prime locations. Peak seasons are spring and summer, although good catches have been landed year-round. Mahimahi, *ono* (a mackerel-like fish; the word means "delicious" in

Lanai has miles of good coasts for a variety of water sports.

Hawaiian), *ahi* (yellowfin tuna), and marlin are prized catches and preferred eating.

BOATS AND CHARTERS

Fish-N-Chips. This 36-foot Twin-Vee with a tuna tower will get you to the fishing grounds in comfort. Friendly Captain Jason will do everything except reel in the big one for you. Plan on trolling along the south coast for ono and around the point at Kaunolu for mahimahi or marlin. A trip to the offshore buoy often yields skipjack tuna or big ahi. Whales are often spotted during the season. Fishing gear, soft drinks, and water are included. A four-hour charter (six-passenger maximum) is $700; each additional hour costs $110. Guests can keep a third of all fish caught. Shared charters on Sunday are $150 per person. ☎ *808/565–7676* ⊕ *www.sportfishinglanai.com.*

SCUBA DIVING

When you have a dive site such as Cathedrals—with eerie pinnacle formations and luminous caverns—it's no wonder that scuba-diving buffs consider exploring the waters off Lanai akin to having a religious experience.

BEST SPOTS

Cathedrals. Just outside Hulopoe Bay, Cathedrals was named the best cavern dive site in the Pacific by *Skin Diver* magazine. Shimmering light makes the many openings resemble stained-glass windows. A current generally keeps the water crystal clear, even if it's turbid outside.

In these unearthly chambers, large *ulua* and small reef sharks add to the adventure. Tiger sharks may appear in certain seasons. ⊠ *Manele.*

Sergeant Major Reef. Off Kamaiki Point, Sergeant Major Reef is named for big schools of yellow- and black-striped *manini* (sergeant major fish) that turn the rocks silvery as they feed. There are three parallel lava ridges separated by rippled sand valleys, a cave, and an archway. Depths range 15 to 50 feet. Depending on conditions, the water may be clear or cloudy. ⊠ *Lanai City.*

EQUIPMENT, LESSONS, AND TOURS

Trilogy Oceansports Lanai. Serious certified divers should go for Trilogy's four-hour, two-tank dive. Locations depend on the weather. The $189 fee includes a light breakfast of cinnamon rolls and coffee, wet suits, and all the equipment you need. Noncertified beginners over age 11 can try a one-tank introductory dive lasting 20 to 30 minutes for $102. You can wade into Hulopoe Bay with an instructor at your side. Certified divers can choose a 35- to 40-minute wade-in dive at Hulopoe, also for $102. ⊠ *Manele Small Boat Harbor, Manele Rd., Manele* ☎ *888/628–4800* ⊕ *www.sailtrilogy.com.*

SNORKELING

Snorkeling is the easiest ocean sport available on the island, requiring nothing but a snorkel, mask, fins, and good sense. Borrow equipment from your hotel or purchase some in Lanai City if you didn't bring your own. Wait to enter the water until you are sure no big sets of waves are coming; and observe the activity of locals on the beach. If little kids are playing in the shore break, it's usually safe to enter. ■TIP→ **To get into the water safely, always swim in past the breakers, and in the comparative calm put on your fins, then mask and snorkel.**

BEST SPOTS

Hulopoe Beach. Hulopoe Beach is an outstanding snorkeling destination. The Four Seasons Manele Resort overlooks this beach and has guest amenities. The bay is a State of Hawaii Marine Conservation District, and no spearfishing or diving is allowed. Schools of *manini* (sergeant major fish) feeding on the coral coat the rocks with flashing silver, and you can view *kala* (unicorn fish), *uhu* (parrot fish), and *papio* (small trevally) in all their rainbow colors. As you wade in from the sandy beach, the best snorkeling is toward the left. Beware of rocks and surging waves. When the resident spinner dolphins are in the bay, watch them from the shore. If swimmers and snorkelers go out, the dolphins may leave and be deprived of their necessary resting place. ⊠ *Manele, Lanai City.*

Manele Small Boat Harbor. A wade-in snorkel spot is beyond the break wall at Manele Small Boat Harbor. Enter over the rocks, just past the boat ramp. ■TIP→ **It's dangerous to enter if waves are breaking.** ⊠ *Manele, Lanai City.*

EQUIPMENT, LESSONS, AND TOURS

Trilogy Oceansports Lanai. A 4½-hour snorkeling trip aboard a spacious catamaran explores Lanai's pristine coastline with this company's experienced captain and crew. The trip includes lessons, equipment, and lunch served on board. Tours are offered Monday, Wednesday, Friday, and Saturday for $181 per person. ✉ *Manele Small Boat Harbor, Manele Rd., Manele, Lanai City* ☎ *888/628–4800* ⊕ *www. sailtrilogy.com.*

SURFING

Surfing on Lanai can be truly enjoyable. Quality, not quantity, characterizes this isle's few breaks. Be considerate of the locals and they will be considerate of you—surfing takes the place of megaplex theaters and pool halls here, serving as one of the island's few recreational luxuries.

BEST SPOTS

Don't try to hang 10 at **Hulopoe Bay** without watching the conditions for a while. When it "goes off," it's a tricky left-handed shore break that requires some skill. Huge summer south swells are for experts only. The southeast-facing breaks at **Lopa Beach** on the east side are inviting for beginners, but hard to get to. Give them a try in summer, when the swells roll in nice and easy.

EQUIPMENT AND LESSONS

Lanai Surf School. Nick Palumbo offers the only surf instruction on the island. Sign up for his "4x4 Safari"—a four-hour adventure that includes hard- or soft-top boards, snacks, and transportation to windward "secret spots." Palumbo, who was born on Lanai, is a former Hawaii State Surfing Champion. Lessons are $200 (minimum of two people). Experienced riders can rent boards overnight for $58. Palumbo also has the only paddleboard permit for Hulopoe Bay, and gives lessons and rents equipment. He will pick you up at your hotel. ☎ *808/306–9837* ⊕ *www.lanaisurfsafari.com.*

GOLF, HIKING, AND OUTDOOR ACTIVITIES

The island's two world-class championship golf courses will certainly test your skill on the green. Experienced hikers can choose from miles of dirt roads and trails, but note that you're on your own—there's no water or support. Remember that Lanai is privately owned, and all land-based activities are at the owner's discretion.

BIKING

Many of the same red-dirt roads that invite hikers are excellent for biking, offering easy, flat terrain and long clear views. There's only one hitch: you may have to bring your own bike, as there are no rentals or tours available except at the resorts.

BEST SPOTS

A favorite biking route is along the fairly flat red-dirt road northward from Lanai City through the old pineapple fields to Garden of the Gods. Start your trip on Keomuku Highway in town. Take a left just before the Lodge at Koele's tennis courts, and then a right where the road ends at the fenced pasture, and continue on to the north end and the start of Polihua and Awalua dirt roads. If you're really hardy you could bike down to Polihua Beach and back, but it would be a serious all-day trip. In wet weather these roads turn to mud and are not advisable. Go in the early morning or late afternoon, because the sun gets hot in the middle of the day. Take plenty of water, spare parts, and snacks.

For the exceptionally fit, it's possible to bike from town down the Keomuku Highway to the windward beaches and back, or to bike the Munro Trail *(see Hiking)*. Experienced bikers also travel up and down the Manele Highway from Manele Bay to town.

GOLF

Lanai has two gorgeous resort courses that offer very different environments and challenges. They are so diverse that it's hard to believe they're on the same island, let alone just 20 minutes apart by resort shuttle.

The Challenge at Manele. Designed by Jack Nicklaus in 1993, this course sits right over the water of Hulopoe Bay. Built on lava outcroppings, it features three holes on cliffs that use the Pacific Ocean as a water hazard. The five-tee concept challenges the best golfers—tee shots over natural gorges and ravines must be precise. This unspoiled natural terrain is a stunning backdrop, and every hole offers ocean views. Early morning tee times are recommended to avoid the midday heat. ⊠ *Four Seasons Resort Lanai at Manele Bay, Challenge Dr., Manele, Lanai City* ☎ *808/565–2222* ⊕ *www.fourseasons.com/manelebay/golf* ⚡ *18 holes. 6310 yds. Par 72, slope 126. Greens fees: hotel guests $210, nonguests $225* ⚲ *Facilities: driving range, putting green, golf carts, rental clubs, pro shop, lessons, restaurant, bar.*

The Experience at Koele. Designed by Greg Norman in 1991, this challenging layout begins at an elevation of 2,000 feet. The front 9 move dramatically through ravines wooded with pine, koa, and eucalyptus trees; seven lakes and streams with cascading waterfalls dot the course. No other course in Hawaii offers a more incredible combination of highland terrain, inspired landscape architecture, and range of play challenges. Beware of the superfast greens and high winds on the back 9. ⊠ *Four Seasons Resort Lodge at Koele, 1 Keomuku Hwy., Lanai City* ☎ *808/565–4653* ⊕ *www.fourseasons.com/koele/golf* ⚡ *18 holes. 6310 yds. Par 72, slope 134. Greens fees: hotel guests $210, nonguests $225* ⊙ *Closed Mon. and Tues.* ⚲ *Facilities: driving range, putting green, golf carts, rental clubs, pro shop, lessons.*

Some holes at the Challenge at Manele use the Pacific Ocean as a water hazard.

HIKING

Only 30 miles of Lanai's roads are paved, but red-dirt roads and trails, ideal for hiking, will take you to sweeping overlooks, isolated beaches, and shady forests. Take a self-guided walk through Kane Puu, Hawaii's largest native dryland forest. You can also explore the Munro Trail over Lanaihale with views of plunging canyons, hike along an old coastal fisherman trail, or head out across Koloiki Ridge. Wear hiking shoes, a hat, and sunscreen, and carry a windbreaker, cell phone, and plenty of water.

BEST SPOTS

Koloiki Ridge. This marked trail starts behind the Lodge at Koele and takes you along the cool and shady Munro Trail to overlook the windward side, with impressive views of Maui, Molokai, Maunalei Valley, and Naio Gulch. The average time for the 5-mile round-trip is two hours. Bring snacks, water, and a windbreaker, wear good shoes, and take your time. A map is available from the concierge at the Four Seasons Resort Lodge at Koele, and notify them you are taking the hike. *Moderate.* ⊠ *Lanai City.*

Lanai Fisherman Trail. Local anglers still use this trail to get to their favorite fishing spots. The trail takes about 1½ hours and follows the rocky shoreline below the Four Seasons Resort at Lanai Manele Bay. The marked trail entrance begins at the west end of Hulopoe Beach. Keep your eyes open for spinner dolphins cavorting offshore and the silvery flash of fish feeding in the pools below you. The condition of the trail varies with weather and frequency of maintenance; it can be slippery and rocky. Take your time, wear a hat and enclosed shoes, and carry water. *Moderate.* ⊠ *Manele, Lanai City.*

Munro Trail. This is the real thing: a strenuous 12.8-mile trek that begins behind the Four Seasons Resort Lodge at Koele and follows the ridge of Lanaihale through the rain forest. The island's most demanding hike, it has an elevation gain of 1,400 feet and leads to a lookout at the island's highest point, Lanaihale. It's also a narrow dirt road; watch out for careening four-wheel-drive vehicles. The trail is named after George Munro, who supervised the planting of Cook pine trees and eucalyptus windbreaks. Mules used to wend their way up the mountain carrying the pine seedlings. Unless you arrange for someone to pick you up at the trail's end, you have a 3-mile hike back through the Palawai Basin to return to your starting point. The summit is often cloud-shrouded and can be windy and muddy, so check conditions before you start. *Difficult.* ⊠ *Four Seasons Resort Lodge at Koele, 1 Keomuku Hwy., Lanai City.*

Puu Pehe Trail. Beginning to the left of Hulopoe Beach, this trail travels a short distance around the coastline, and then climbs up a sharp, rocky rise. At the top, you're level with the offshore stack of Puu Pehe and can overlook miles of coastline in both directions. The trail is not difficult, but it's hot and steep. Be aware of nesting seabirds and don't approach their nests. ⚠ **Stay away from the edge, as the cliff can easily give way.** The hiking is best in the early morning or late afternoon, and it's a perfect place to look for whales in season (December–April). Wear a hat and shoes, and take water so you can spend some time at the top admiring the view. *Moderate.* ⊠ *Manele, Lanai City.*

HORSEBACK RIDING

A horseback ride can be a memorable experience on the island.

Stables at Koele. The subtle beauty of the high country slowly reveals itself to horseback riders. Two-hour adventures traverse leafy trails with scenic overlooks. Well-trained horses take riders (must be over 8 years old and under 225 pounds) of all skill levels. Prices range from $130 for a 90-minute group ride to $300 for a two-hour private ride. A four-person carriage ride is $150 an hour. Lessons are also available. Book rides at the Four Seasons Resort Lodge at Koele or with Lanai Grand Adventures. ⊠ *1 Keomuku Hwy., Lanai City* ☏ *808/563–9385* ⊕ *www.lanaigrandadventures.com.*

SPORTING CLAYS AND ARCHERY

For something different, you can try your hand at clay shooting or archery.

Lanai Pine Sporting Clays and Archery Range. Outstanding rustic terrain, challenging targets, and a well-stocked pro shop make this sporting-clays course top-flight in the expert's eyes. Sharpshooters can complete the meandering 14-station course in 1½ hours, with the help of a golf cart. There are group tournaments, and even kids can enjoy skilled instruction at the archery range and compressed-air rifle gallery. The $60 archery introduction includes an amusing "pineapple challenge"—contestants are given five arrows with which to hit a paper pineapple target. The winner takes home a crystal pineapple as a nostalgic souvenir of the old Dole Plantation days. Prices depend on amount of ammunition and activity. The range is on the Keomoku Road just past Cemetery Road on the windward side of island. ⊠ *1 Keomoku Hwy., Lanai City* ☎ *808/565–9385* ⊕ *www. lanaigrandadventures.com.*

SHOPPING

A cluster of Cook pines in the center of Lanai City surrounded by small shops and restaurants, Dole Park is the closest thing to a mall on Lanai. Except for the high-end resort boutiques and pro shops, it's the island's only shopping. A morning or afternoon stroll around the park offers an eclectic selection of gifts and clothing, plus a chance to chat with friendly shopkeepers. Well-stocked general stores are reminiscent of the 1920s, and galleries and a boutique have original art and fashions for everyone.

ARTS AND CRAFTS

Dis 'n Dat. This tiny, jungle-green shop packs in thousands of gift and jewelry items in a minuscule space enlivened by a glittering crystal ceiling. Fanciful garden ornaments and Asian antiques add to the inventory. ⊠ *418 8th St., Lanai City* ☎ *808/565–9170* ⊕ *www.disndatshop.com.*

CLOTHING

Cory Labang Studio. This tiny studio shop near Dole Park reflects its owner's life-long love of vintage clothing. Cory Labang's old piano and her Hawaiian family photos are a nice backdrop for handmade bags and clutches in antique fabrics. Crystal glassware, glittering costume jewelry, and one-of-a-kind accessories complete this unique collection. ⊠ *431A 7th St., Lanai City* ☎ *808/315–6715* ⊕ *www. corylabangstudio.com.*

Lanai Beach Walk. The shop may be small, but it's crammed with many styles and colors of the now indispensable "crocs," as well as colorful resort clothing, swimwear, and classy skirts and dresses. Tropical knickknacks and jewelry complete the whimsical inventory. Gail, the owner, is always up for a bit of local conversation and advice. ⊠ *850 Fraser Ave., Lanai City* ☎ *808/565–9249.*

The Local Gentry. Spacious and classy, this store has clothing for every need, from casual men's and women's beachwear to evening resort wear, shoes, jewelry, and hats. Fancy fashions for tots as well. A selection of original Lanai-themed clothing is also available, including the signature "What happens on Lanai everybody knows" T-shirts. Proprietor Jenna Gentry Majkus will mail your purchases. ⊠ *363 7th St., Lanai City* ☎ *808/565–9130.*

FOOD

Pine Isle Market. One of Lanai City's two all-purpose markets, Pine Isle stocks everything from beach toys and electronics to meats and vegetables. The staff is friendly, and it's the best place around to buy fresh fish. The market is closed Sunday. ⊠ *356 8th St., Lanai City* ☎ *808/565–6488.*

Richard's. Along with fresh meats, fine wines, and imported gourmet items, Richard's stocks everything from camping gear to household items. ⊠ *434 8th St., Lanai City* ☎ *808/565–3780.*

GALLERIES

Lanai Art Center. Local artists display their work at this dynamic center staffed by volunteers. Workshops in pottery, photography, woodworking, and painting welcome visitors. The gift shop sells Lanai handicrafts and special offerings like handmade Swarovski crystal bracelets, whose sale underwrites children's art classes. There are occasional concerts and special events. Closed Sundays. ⊠ *339 7th St., Lanai City* ☎ *808/565–7503* ⊕ *www.lanaiart.org.*

Mike Carroll Gallery. The dreamy, soft-focus oil paintings of award-winning painter Mike Carroll are inspired by island scenes. His work is showcased along with those of other local artists and visiting plein air painters. You can also find handcrafted jewelry and antiques. ⊠ *443 7th St., Lanai City* ☎ *808/565–7122* ⊕ *www.mikecarrollgallery.com.*

GENERAL STORES

International Food and Clothing Center. You may not find everything the name implies, but this old-fashioned emporium stocks everything from fishing and camping gear to fine wine to imported beer. It's a good place to pick up last-minute items when other stores are closed on Sunday. ⊠ *833 Ilima Ave., Lanai City* ☎ *808/565–6433.*

Lanai City Service. In addition to being Lanai's only gas station, auto-parts store, and car-rental operation, this outfit sells resort wear, *manapua* (steamed buns with pork filling), hot dogs, beer, soda, and bottled water. It's open 6:30 am to 8:30 pm daily. ⊠ *1036 Lanai Ave., Lanai City* ☎ *808/565–7227.*

SPAS

If you're looking for rejuvenation, the whole island could be considered a spa, though the only full spa is at the Manele Bay Four Seasons Resort.

The Spa at Manele. Granite floors, eucalyptus steam rooms, and private cabanas set the scene for indulgence. State-of-the-art pampering enlists a panoply of oils and lotions that would have pleased Cleopatra. The Tropical Bliss Ritual includes a full-body exfoliation, massage, and body wrap followed by a scalp massage. The banana-coconut scrub and pineapple-citrus polish treatments are delicious. You can then also relax in the sauna or steam room. Massages in private oceanfront *hale* (houses) are available for singles or couples. ⊠ *Four Seasons Resort Lanai at Manele Bay, 1 Manele Bay Rd., Manele, Lanai City* ☎ *808/565–2088* ⊕ *www.fourseasons.com/manelebay/spa* ⌇ *$165–$190 50-min massage; $325 per person Topical Bliss Ritual. Gym with: cardiovascular equipment, free weights. Services: aromatherapy, body wraps, facials, hair salon, hair care, reflexology, wax-*

ing. Classes and programs: aquaerobics, guided hikes, hula classes, personal training, tai chi, yoga.

NIGHTLIFE

When it comes to nightlife, Lanai is beginning to come alive. A handful of places now feature live music and stay open past 9 pm. At the resorts, pianists add to the romantic settings. An alternative is stargazing from the beaches or watching the full moon rise from secluded vantage points.

The Bar. This intimate lounge at the Four Seasons Resort Lodge at Koele has a lively atmosphere. It's open until 11 pm, so you can enjoy a late-night cocktail and plan your next day's activities. The resort also features quiet music every evening in its Great Hall, as well as performances by well-known Hawaiian entertainers and local hula dancers. ✉ *Four Seasons Resort Lodge at Koele, 1 Keomuku Hwy., Lanai City* ☎ *808/565–4000* ⊕ *www.fourseasons.com.*

Hotel Lanai. A visit to this small, lively bar lets you chat with locals and find out more about the island. Enjoy performances by local and visiting musicians in the big green tent on Friday nights. Get here early, as last call is at 9:30. ✉ *Hotel Lanai, 828 Lanai Ave., Lanai City* ☎ *808/565–7211* ⊕ *www.hotellanai.com.*

The Lounge. With commanding views of the ocean, The Lounge at Four Seasons Resort Lanai at Manele Bay offers sunset cocktails and after-dinner drinks along with a world-class selection of wines and sparkling wines by the glass. Local entertainers offer live music nightly to add to the festive air. ✉ *Four Seasons Resort Lanai at Manele Bay, 1 Manele Rd., Manele, Lanai City* ☎ *808/565–2000* ⊕ *www.fourseasons.com.*

Sports Bar. At the Four Seasons Resort Lanai at Manele Bay, the oceanfront Sports Bar is an open-air lounge serving such casual fare as chicken wings and burgers. Pool tables, shuffleboard courts, and two 90-inch TVs make for an amusing time out. An added bonus: dolphins playing in the bay below. ✉ *Four Seasons Resort Lanai at Manele Bay, 1 Manele Bay Rd., Manele, Lanai City* ☎ *808/565–2000* ⊕ *www.fourseasons.com.*

WHERE TO EAT

Lanai's own version of Hawaii Regional Cuisine draws on the fresh bounty provided by local farmers and fishermen, combined with the skills of well-regarded chefs. The upscale menus at the Four Seasons Resort Lodge at Koele and the Four Seasons Resort at Lanai Manele Bay encompass European-inspired cuisine as well as innovative preparations of international favorites and vegetarian delights. All Four Seasons Resort restaurants offer children's menus. Lanai City's eclectic ethnic fare runs from construction-worker-size local plate lunches to *poke* (raw fish), pizza, and pasta. ■TIP➔ Lanai "City" is really a small town; restaurants sometimes close their kitchen early, and only a few are open on Sunday.

Prices in the reviews are the average cost of a main course at dinner or, if dinner is not served, at lunch.

MANELE BAY

Dining at Manele Bay offers the range of options provided by Four Seasons Lanai resorts, from informal poolside meals to relaxed, eclectic dining.

$$
AMERICAN
⨯**The Challenge at Manele Clubhouse.** A stunning view of the legendary Puu Pehe island only enhances the imaginative fare of this open-air restaurant. Spot frolicking dolphins from the terrace. Tuck into a Hulopoe Bay prawn BLT, or the crispy battered fish-and-chips with Meyer lemon tartar sauce. The fish tacos are splendid, and specialty drinks add to the informal fun. ⑤ *Average main: $25* ⊠ *Four Seasons Resort Lanai at Manele Bay, 1 Manele Bay Rd.* ☎ *808/565–2230* ⊕ *www.fourseasons. com/manelebay* ⊗ *No dinner.*

$$$$
AMERICAN
⨯**One Forty.** Named after the island's 140 square miles, this ocean-view restaurant offers an extensive steak and seafood menu that emphasizes local ingredients. Prime cuts of beef and the freshest local fish are served in airy comfort on the hotel terrace, which overlooks the wide sweep of Hulopoe Bay. Retractable awnings provide shade on sunny days. Comfy rattan chairs, potted palms, and tropical decor create an inviting backdrop. At breakfast, fresh-baked pastries and made-to-order omelets ensure that your day starts well. ⑤ *Average main: $45* ⊠ *Four Seasons Resort Lanai at Manele Bay, 1 Manele Bay Rd.* ☎ *808/565–2290* ⊕ *www.fourseasons.com/manelebay* ⌕ *Reservations essential* ⊗ *No lunch.*

$$$$
ITALIAN
⨯**Kailani.** Poolside at the Four Seasons Resort Lanai at Manele Bay, Kailani offers contemporary Italian cuisine in a setting with a stunning view of Hulopoe Bay. The big umbrellas are cool and cheerful, and upholstered chairs deliciously comfortable. If you're a coffee drinker, a Kona cappuccino freeze by the pool is a must. For a satisfying lunch try the crunchy fish-and-chips or an old-fashioned burger. Spaghetti with manila clams and a creamy Prosecco sauce and lava-salt-crusted ahi are good choices for dinner. The service is the brand of cool aloha always offered by the Four Seasons. ⑤ *Average main: $35* ⊠ *Four Seasons Resort Lanai at Manele Bay, 1 Manele Bay Rd.* ☎ *808/565–2092* ⊕ *www.fourseasons.com/manelebay* ⌕ *Reservations essential.*

$$$
JAPANESE
Fodor's Choice
★
⨯**Nobu.** Chef Nobuyuki "Nobu" Matsuhisa offers his signature new-style Japanese cuisine in this open-air, relaxed luxury venue. This is fine dining without the stress, as black-clad waiters present dish after dish of beautifully seasoned, raw and lightly cooked seafood flown in directly from Alaska and Japan. Pale grey wicker couches on the veranda provide comfortable sink-in seating, while inside diners relax around natural wood tables. The lively and friendly waitstaff regale you with the life history of every fish on your ceramic black plates, and go into great detail about the elaborate aging processes of their sakes. This simple yet elegant place is definitely worth the indulgence, but brace yourself for a significant bill at meal's end. ⑤ *Average main: $30* ⊠ *1*

Manele Bay Rd. ☎ *808/565–2832* ⊕ *www.noburestaurants.com/lanai* ⌥ *Reservations essential* ⊘ *No lunch.*

LANAI CITY AND UPCOUNTRY

In Lanai City you can enjoy everything from local-style plate lunches to upscale gourmet meals. For a small area, there are a number of good places to eat and drink, but remember that Lanai City closes down on Sunday.

$ ✕ **Blue Ginger Café.** Owners Joe and Georgia Abilay made this cheery
HAWAIIAN place into a Lanai City institution with simply prepared, consistent, tasty food. Local paintings and photos line the walls inside, while townspeople parade by the outdoor tables. For breakfast, try the Portuguese sausage omelet with rice or fresh pastries. Lunch selections range from burgers to such local favorites as saimin noodles. For dinner you can sample generous portions of stir-fried shrimp or roasted pork. Phone ahead for takeout. ⑤ *Average main: $15* ⊠ *409 7th St.* ☎ *808/565–6363* ⊕ *www.bluegingercafelanai.com* ⌥ *Reservations not accepted* ▭ *No credit cards.*

$$$$ ✕ **The Dining Room.** Reflecting the resort's country-manor ambience, this
HAWAIIAN peaceful and romantic octagonal restaurant is fine dining at its infor-
Fodor's Choice mal best. Terra-cotta walls and soft peach lighting flatter everyone, and
★ intimate tables are spaced to allow for private conversations. Choose from a four-course tasting menu that might include such delicacies as goat-cheese ravioli, seafood stew, pan-seared fish, and pineapple crème brûlée, or go à la carte with rack of lamb or duck breast. Finish with a warm vanilla or chocolate soufflé (order in advance). A master sommelier provides perfect wine pairings, and the service is quietly attentive. ⑤ *Average main: $60* ⊠ *Four Seasons Resort Lodge at Koele, 1 Keomuku Hwy.* ☎ *808/565–4580* ⊕ *www.fourseasons.com/koele* ⌥ *Reservations essential* ⊘ *No lunch.*

$ ✕ **565 Café.** Named after the oldest telephone prefix on Lanai, 565 Café
HAWAIIAN is a convenient stop for plate lunches, sandwiches like Palawai chicken breast on freshly baked focaccia, or platters of chicken *katsu* (Japanese-style breaded and fried chicken) to take along for an impromptu picnic. Phone ahead to order pizza. Bring your own beer or wine for lunch or dinner. The patio and outdoor tables are kid-friendly, and an outdoor Saturday afternoon flea market adds to the quirkiness. ⑤ *Average main: $12* ⊠ *408 8th St.* ☎ *808/565–6622* ⌥ *Reservations not accepted* ⊘ *Closed Sun.*

$$$$ ✕ **Lanai City Grille.** Simple white walls hung with local art, lazily turning
AMERICAN ceiling fans, and unobtrusive service provide the backdrop for a menu designed and supervised by celebrity-chef Beverly Gannon. Oysters on the half shell, pulled-pork wontons, or steamed manila clams are a great way to start the evening. Baby field greens are a special treat. The entrées are on the meaty side for Hawaii, and should satisfy serious appetites. The dining room is a friendly and comfortable alternative to the Four Seasons, and a convenient, if sometimes noisy, gathering place for large parties. ⑤ *Average main: $36* ⊠ *Hotel Lanai, 828 Lanai*

Ave. ☎ *808/565–4700* ⊕ *www.hotellanai.com* ⌂ *Reservations essential* ⊘ *Closed Mon. and Tues. No lunch.*

$ ✗**Lanai Coffee.** A block from Dole Park, this Northern California–style
AMERICAN café offers an umbrella-covered deck where you can sip cappuccinos
and get in tune with the slow pace of life. Bagels with lox, deli sandwiches, and pastries add to the caloric content, while blended espresso
shakes and gourmet ice cream complete the coffeehouse vibe. $ *Average
main: $8* ⊠ *604 Ilima St.* ☎ *808/565–6962* ⌂ *Reservations not accepted*
⊘ *Closed Sun. No dinner.*

$ ✗**Lanai Ohana Poke Market.** This is the closest you can come to dining on
HAWAIIAN traditional cuisine on Lanai. Enjoy fresh food prepared by a Hawaiian
family and served in a cool, shady garden. The emphasis is on *poke*,
which is raw ahi tuna flavored with Hawaiian salt and seaweed. Hawaiian plate lunches, take-out kimchi shrimp, and ahi and aku tuna steaks
complete the menu. The place also caters picnics and parties. $ *Aver-
age main: $9* ⊠ *834A Gay St.* ☎ *808/559–6265* ⌂ *Reservations not
accepted* ⊟ *No credit cards* ⊘ *Closed Sun. No dinner.*

$ ✗**No Ka Oi Grindz Lanai.** A local favorite, this lunchroom-style café has
HAWAIIAN a shaded picnic table in the landscaped front yard and five more tables
FAMILY in the no-frills interior. The innovative menu, which changes frequently,
includes such delicacies as kimchi fried rice, pork fritter sandwiches,
and massive plate lunches. Sit outside and watch the town drive by.
$ *Average main: $10* ⊠ *335 9th St.* ☎ *808/565–9413* ⌂ *Reservations
not accepted* ⊟ *No credit cards* ⊘ *Closed Sun.*

$$ ✗**Pele's Other Garden.** Small and colorful, Pele's is a deli and bistro
ITALIAN all in one. For lunch, sandwiches or daily hot specials satisfy hearty
appetites. At night it's transformed into a busy bistro, complete with
tablecloths and soft jazz. Designer beers and fine wines enhance an
Italian-inspired menu. Start with bruschetta, then choose from a selec-
tion of pizzas or pasta dishes. An intimate back-room bar adds to the
liveliness, and entertainers often drop in for impromptu jam sessions.
$ *Average main: $22* ⊠ *811 Houston St., at 8th St.* ☎ *808/565–9628,
888/764–3354* ⊕ *www.pelesothergarden.com* ⌂ *Reservations essen-
tial* ⊘ *Closed Sun.*

$$$$ ✗**The Terrace.** Floor-to-ceiling glass doors at this spacious lounge open
AMERICAN onto formal gardens and lovely vistas of the mist-clad mountains. A
comfort-food menu features a hearty breakfast to start the day, and
Kauai shrimp ravioli to finish it. The Sunday brunch is a special treat. In
the evening the soothing sounds of Hawaiian music or the grand piano
in the Great Hall complete the ambience. $ *Average main: $38* ⊠ *Four
Seasons Resort Lodge at Koele, 1 Keomuku Hwy.* ☎ *808/565–4500*
⊕ *www.fourseasons.com/koele* ⌂ *Reservations essential.*

WHERE TO STAY

For expanded hotel reviews, visit Fodors.com.

Though Lanai has few properties, it does have a range of price options.
Four Seasons manages both the Lodge at Koele and Four Seasons Resort
Lanai at Manele Bay. Although the room rates are different, guests can
partake of all the resort amenities at both properties. If you're on a

Four Seasons Lanai at Manele Bay

Four Seasons Lanai at Koele

budget, consider the Hotel Lanai. Note that room rates do not include 13.42% sales tax.

Prices in the reviews are the lowest cost of a standard double room in high season.

$

B&B/INN

Dreams Come True. Antiques gleaned from many trips through South Asia add to the atmosphere at Michael and Susan Hunter's four-bedroom, four-bathroom plantation home on the main street of Lanai City. **Pros:** convenient location; outdoor barbecue; nice garden. **Cons:** two-night minimum stay on weekends; on a busy street. $ *Rooms from: $129* ⊠ *1168 Lanai Ave., Lanai City* ☎ *808/565–6961, 800/566–6961* ⊕ *www.dreamscometruelanai.com* ⇌ *4 rooms* ⦿ *Breakfast.*

$$$$

RESORT

FAMILY

Fodor's Choice

★

Four Seasons Resort Lanai at Manele Bay. Overlooking Hulopoe Bay, this newly renovated retreat offers beachside urban chic with stunning views of the deep blue sea and astonishing rocky coastline. **Pros:** fitness center with ocean views; nearby beach; friendly pool bar. **Cons:** 20 minutes from town; need a car to explore the area; caged parrots strike a sour note. $ *Rooms from: $459* ⊠ *1 Manele Rd.* ☎ *808/565–2000, 800/321–4666* ⊕ *www.fourseasons.com/manelebay* ⇌ *215 rooms, 21 suites.*

$$$$

RESORT

Fodor's Choice

★

Four Seasons Resort Lodge at Koele. In the highlands above Lanai City, this grand country estate exudes luxury and romance with paths meandering through formal gardens, a huge reflecting pond, and an orchid greenhouse. **Pros:** beautiful surroundings; impeccable service; walking distance to Lanai City. **Cons:** doesn't seem much like Hawaii; can get chilly, especially in winter; not much to do in rainy weather. $ *Rooms from: $429* ⊠ *1 Keomoku Rd., Lanai City* ☎ *808/565–4000, 800/321–4666* ⊕ *www.fourseasons.com/koele* ⇌ *94 rooms, 8 suites* ⦿ *No meals.*

$

HOTEL

Hotel Lanai. Built in 1923 to house visiting pineapple executives, this historic inn has South Pacific–style rooms with country quilts, ceiling fans, and bamboo shades. **Pros:** historic atmosphere; walking distance to town. **Cons:** rooms are a bit plain; noisy at dinnertimes; no room phones. $ *Rooms from: $149* ⊠ *828 Lanai Ave., Lanai City* ☎ *808/565–7211, 800/795–7211* ⊕ *www.hotellanai.com* ⇌ *10 rooms, 1 cottage* ⦿ *Breakfast.*

HAWAIIAN VOCABULARY

Although an understanding of Hawaiian is by no means required on a trip to the Aloha State, a *malihini*, or newcomer, will find plenty of opportunities to pick up a few of the local words and phrases. Traditional names and expressions are widely used in the Islands. You're likely to read or hear at least a few words each day of your stay.

With a basic understanding and some uninhibited practice, anyone can have enough command of the local tongue to ask for directions and to order from a restaurant menu. One visitor announced she would not leave until she could pronounce the name of the state fish, the *humuhumunukunukuāpua'a*.

Simplifying the learning process is the fact that the Hawaiian language contains only eight consonants—H, K, L, M, N, P, W, and the silent *'okina*, or glottal stop, written '—plus one or more of the five vowels. All syllables, and therefore all words, end in a vowel. Each vowel, with the exception of a few diphthongized double vowels such as *au* (pronounced "ow") or *ai* (pronounced "eye"), is pronounced separately. Thus *'Iolani* is four syllables (ee-oh-la-nee), not three (yo-la-nee). Although some Hawaiian words have only vowels, most also contain some consonants, but consonants are never doubled.

Pronunciation is simple. Pronounce *A* "ah" as in *father*; *E* "ay" as in *weigh*; *I* "ee" as in *marine*; *O* "oh" as in *no*; *U* "oo" as in *true*.

Consonants mirror their English equivalents, with the exception of *W*. When the letter begins any syllable other than the first one in a word, it is usually pronounced as a *V*. *'Awa*, the Polynesian drink, is pronounced "ava," *'ewa* is pronounced "eva."

Almost all long Hawaiian words are combinations of shorter words; they are not difficult to pronounce if you segment them. *Kalaniana'ole*, the highway running east from Honolulu, is easily understood as *Kalani ana 'ole*. Apply the standard pronunciation rules—the stress falls on the next-to-last syllable of most two- or three-syllable Hawaiian words—and Kalaniana'ole Highway is as easy to say as Main Street.

Now about that fish. Try *humu-humu nuku-nuku āpu a'a*.

The other unusual element in Hawaiian language is the *kahakō*, or macron, written as a short line (ˉ) placed over a vowel. Like the accent (´) in Spanish, the kahakō puts emphasis on a syllable that would normally not be stressed. The most familiar example is probably *Waikīkī*. With no macrons, the stress would fall on the middle syllable; with only one macron, on the last syllable, the stress would fall on the first and last syllables. Some words become plural with the addition of a macron, often on a syllable that would have been stressed anyway. No Hawaiian word becomes plural with the addition of an *S*, since that letter does not exist in the language.

The Hawaiian diacritical marks are not printed in this guide.

'a'ā: rough, crumbling lava, contrasting with *pāhoehoe,* which is smooth.

'ae: yes.

aikane: friend.

āina: land.

akamai: smart, clever, possessing savoir faire.

akua: god.

ala: a road, path, or trail.

ali'i: a Hawaiian chief, a member of the chiefly class.

aloha: love, affection, kindness; also a salutation meaning both greetings and farewell.

'ānuenue: rainbow.

'a'ole: no.

'apōpō: tomorrow.

'auwai: a ditch.

auwē: alas, woe is me!

'ehu: a red-haired Hawaiian.

'ewa: in the direction of 'Ewa plantation, west of Honolulu.

hala: the pandanus tree, whose leaves (*lau hala*) are used to make baskets and plaited mats.

hālau: school.

hale: a house.

hale pule: church, house of worship.

ha mea iki or **ha mea 'ole:** you're welcome.

hana: to work.

haole: ghost. Since the first foreigners were Caucasian, *haole* now means a Caucasian person.

hapa: a part, sometimes a half; often used as a short form of *hapa haole,* to mean a person who is part-Caucasian.

hau'oli: to rejoice. *Hau'oli Makahiki Hou* means Happy New Year. *Hau'oli lā hānau* means Happy Birthday.

heiau: an outdoor stone platform; an ancient Hawaiian place of worship.

holo: to run.

holoholo: to go for a walk, ride, or sail.

holokū: a long Hawaiian dress, somewhat fitted, with a yoke and a train. Influenced by European fashion, it was worn at court, and at least one local translates the word as "expensive mu'umu'u."

holomū: a post–World War II cross between a *holokū* and a mu'umu'u, less fitted than the former but less voluminous than the latter, and having no train.

honi: to kiss; a kiss. A phrase that some tourists may find useful, quoted from a popular hula, is *Honi Ka'ua Wikiwiki:* Kiss me quick!

honu: turtle.

ho'omalimali: flattery, a deceptive "line," bunk, baloney, hooey.

huhū: angry.

hui: a group, club, or assembly. A church may refer to its congregation as a *hui* and a social club may be called a *hui.*

hukilau: a seine; a communal fishing party in which everyone helps to drive the fish into a huge net, pull it in, and divide the catch.

hula: the dance of Hawai'i.

iki: little.

ipo: sweetheart.

ka: the. This is the definite article for most singular words; for plural nouns, the definite article is usually *nā.* Since there is no S in Hawaiian, the article may be your only clue that a noun is plural.

kahuna: a priest, doctor, or other trained person of old Hawai'i, endowed with special professional skills that often included prophecy or other supernatural powers; the plural form is kāhuna.

kai: the sea, saltwater.

kalo: the taro plant from whose root *poi* (paste) is made.

kamā'aina: literally, a child of the soil; it refers to people who were born in the Islands or have lived there for a long time.

kanaka: originally a man or humanity, it is now used to denote a male Hawaiian or part-Hawaiian, but is occasionally taken as a slur when used by non-Hawaiians. *Kanaka maoli,* originally a full-blooded Hawaiian person, is used by some native Hawaiian rights activists to embrace part-Hawaiians as well.

kāne: a man, a husband. If you see this word on a door, it's the men's room. If you see *kane* on a door, it's probably a misspelling; that is the Hawaiian name for the skin fungus tinea.

kapa: also called by its Tahitian name, *tapa,* a cloth made of beaten bark and usually dyed and stamped with a repeat design.

kapakahi: crooked, cockeyed, uneven. You've got your hat on *kapakahi.*

kapu: keep out, prohibited. This is the Hawaiian version of the more widely known Tongan word *tabu* (taboo).

kapuna: grandparent; elder.

kēia lā: today.

keiki: a child; *keikikāne* is a boy, *keikiwahine* a girl.

kona: the leeward side of the Islands, the direction (south) from which the *kona* wind and *kona* rain come.

kula: upland.

kuleana: a homestead or small plot of ground on which a family has been installed for some generations without necessarily owning it. By extension, *kuleana* is used to denote any area or department in which one has a special interest or prerogative. You'll hear it used this way: If you want to hire a surfboard, see Moki; that's his *kuleana.*

lā: sun.

lamalama: to fish with a torch.

lānai: a porch, a balcony, an outdoor living room. Almost every house in Hawaii has one. Don't confuse this two-syllable word with the three-syllable name of the island, Lāna'i.

lani: heaven, the sky.

lau hala: the leaf of the *hala,* or pandanus tree, widely used in handicrafts.

lei: a garland of flowers.

limu: sun.

lolo: stupid.

luna: a plantation overseer or foreman.

mahalo: thank you.

makai: toward the ocean.

malihini: a newcomer to the Islands.

mana: the spiritual power that the Hawaiian believed inhabited all things and creatures.

manō: shark.

manuwahi: free, gratis.

mauka: toward the mountains.

mauna: mountain.

mele: a Hawaiian song or chant, often of epic proportions.

Mele Kalikimaka: Merry Christmas (a transliteration from the English phrase).

Menehune: a Hawaiian pixie. The *Menehune* were a legendary race of little people who accomplished prodigious work, such as building fishponds and temples in the course of a single night.

moana: the ocean.

mu'umu'u: the voluminous dress in which the missionaries enveloped Hawaiian women. Now made in bright printed cottons and silks, it is an indispensable garment. Culturally sensitive locals have embraced the Hawaiian spelling but often shorten the spoken word to "mu'u." Most English dictionaries include the spelling "muumuu."

nani: beautiful.

nui: big.

ohana: family.

'ono: delicious.

pāhoehoe: smooth, unbroken, satiny lava.

Pākē: Chinese. This *Pākē* carver makes beautiful things.

palapala: document, printed matter.

pali: a cliff, precipice.

pānini: prickly pear cactus.

paniolo: a Hawaiian cowboy, a rough transliteration of *español,* the language of the Islands' earliest cowboys.

pau: finished, done.

pilikia: trouble. The Hawaiian word is much more widely used here than its English equivalent.

puka: a hole.

pupule: crazy, like the celebrated Princess Pupule. This word has replaced its English equivalent in local usage.

pu'u: volcanic cinder cone.

waha: mouth.

wahine: a female, a woman, a wife, and a sign on the ladies' room door; the plural form is *wāhine.*

wai: freshwater, as opposed to saltwater, which is *kai.*

wailele: waterfall.

wikiwiki: to hurry, hurry up (since this is a reduplication of *wiki,* quick, neither W is pronounced as a V).

Note: Pidgin is the unofficial language of Hawaii. It is a Creole language, with its own grammar, evolved from the mixture of English, Hawaiian, Japanese, Portuguese, and other languages spoken in 19th-century Hawaii, and it is heard everywhere.

TRAVEL SMART MAUI

GETTING HERE AND AROUND

▮ AIR TRAVEL

Flying time to Hawaii is about 10 hours from New York, 8 hours from Chicago, and 5 hours from Los Angeles.

Hawaii is a major destination link for flights traveling between the U.S. mainland, Asia, Australia, New Zealand, and the South Pacific. Island hopping is easy, with several daily interisland flights connecting all the major islands. International travelers also have options: Oahu and the Big Island are gateways to the United States.

Although Maui's airports are smaller and more casual than Oahu's Honolulu International, during peak times they can also be quite busy. Allow extra travel time to either airport during morning and afternoon rush-hour traffic periods, and allow time if you are returning a rental car. Plan to arrive at the airport at least two hours before departure for interisland flights.

Plants and plant products are subject to regulation by the Department of Agriculture, both when entering and leaving Hawaii. Upon leaving the Islands, you're required to have your bags X-rayed and tagged at one of the airport's agricultural-inspection stations before you proceed to check-in. Pineapples and coconuts with the packer's agricultural-inspection stamp pass freely; papayas must be treated, inspected, and stamped. All other fruits are banned for export to the U.S. mainland. Flowers pass except for gardenia, jade vine, and mauna loa. Also banned are insects, snails, soil, cotton, cacti, sugarcane, and all berry plants.

You'll have to leave dogs and other pets at home. A quarantine of up to 120 days is imposed to keep out rabies, which is nonexistent in Hawaii. If specific pre- and postarrival requirements are met, animals may qualify for 30-day or 5-day-or-less quarantine.

The Transportation Security Administration has answers for almost every question that might come up.

Airline-Security Issues Transportation Security Administration ⊕ www.tsa.gov.

Air-Travel Resources in Maui State of Hawaii Airports Division Offices ☎ 808/836–6413 ⊕ www.hawaii.gov/dot/airports.

AIRPORTS

All of Hawaii's major islands have their own airports, but Oahu's Honolulu International is the main stopover for most U.S. mainland and international flights. From Honolulu, daily flights to Maui leave almost every hour from early morning until evening. To travel interisland from Honolulu, you can depart from either the interisland terminal or the commuter-airline terminal, in two separate structures adjacent to the main overseas terminal building. A free bus service, the Wiki Wiki Shuttle, operates between terminals. In addition, several carriers offer nonstop service directly from the U.S. mainland to Maui. Flights from Honolulu into Lanai and Molokai are offered several times a day.

Maui has two major airports. Kahului Airport handles major airlines and interisland flights; it's the only airport on Maui that has direct service from the mainland. Kapalua–West Maui Airport is served by Hawaiian Airlines and Island Air. If you're staying in West Maui and you're flying in from another island, you can avoid the hour drive from the Kahului Airport by flying into Kapalua–West Maui Airport. Hana Airport in East Maui is small.

Molokai's Hoolehua Airport is small and centrally located, as is Lanai Airport. Both rural airports handle a limited number of flights per day. There's a small airfield at Kalaupapa on Molokai (you prebook your ground tour with Damien Tours). Visitors coming from the U.S. mainland to these islands must first stop in Oahu or Maui and change to an interisland flight. Lanai Airport has a federal agricultural inspection station, so guests departing to the mainland can check luggage directly.

Airport Information Hana Airport (HNM)
☎ 808/248-4861. **Honolulu International Airport (HNL)** ☎ 808/836-6411 ⊕ www. hawaii.gov/dot/airports. **Hooleehua Airport (MKK)** ☎ 808/567-9660. **Kahului Airport (OGG)** ☎ 808/872-3830. **Kalaupapa Airfield** ☎ 808/838-8701. **Kapalua-West Maui Airport (JHM)** ☎ 808/665-6108. **Lanai Airport (LNY)** ☎ 808/565-7942.

GROUND TRANSPORTATION

If you're not renting a car, you'll need to take a taxi. Maui Airport Taxi serves the Kahului Airport and charges $3.50, plus $3 for every mile. Cab fares to locations around the island are estimated as follows: Kaanapali $87, Kahului town $13, Kapalua $105, Kihei town $33 to $55, Lahaina $78, Makena $65, Wailea $57, and Wailuku $20.

SpeediShuttle offers transportation between the Kahului Airport and hotels, resorts, and condominium complexes throughout Maui. There is an online reservation and fare-quote system for information and bookings. You can expect to pay around $62 per couple to Kaanapali, and $43 to Wailea.

Information Maui Airport Taxi ☎ 808/281-9533 ⊕ www.nokaoitaxi.com. **Speedi-Shuttle Hawaii** ☎ 877/242-5777 ⊕ www. speedishuttle.com.

FLIGHTS

Service to Maui changes regularly, so it's best to check when you are ready to book. American has daily nonstop flights into Maui from Los Angeles and Dallas-Fort Worth. Alaska, Delta, United, and US Airways also have daily nonstops into Maui from Los Angeles. United has one nonstop flight from Newark Liberty near New York to Honolulu. Alaska Airlines flies a daily nonstop to Maui from Anchorage, Portland, Seattle, San Diego, and San Jose. Allegiant Air flies nonstop

to Maui from Bellingham twice a week. Delta serves Maui from Atlanta, Los Angeles, Minneapolis/St. Paul, Portland, Salt Lake City, San Francisco, and Seattle. Hawaiian Airlines serves Maui from Las Vegas, Los Angeles, New York (the only nonstop flight from JFK to Honolulu), Oakland, Phoenix, Portland, Sacramento, San Diego, San Francisco, San Jose, and Seattle. In addition to offering competitive rates and online specials, all have frequent-flyer programs that will entitle you to rewards and upgrades the more you fly.

Airline Contacts Alaska Airlines
☎ 800/252-7522 ⊕ www.alaskaairlines.com. **American Airlines** ☎ 800/433-7300 ⊕ www. aa.com. **Delta Airlines** ☎ 800/221-1212 for U.S. reservations, 800/241-4141 for international reservations ⊕ www.delta.com. **Hawaiian Airlines** ☎ 800/367-5320 ⊕ www. hawaiianair.com. **United Airlines** ☎ 800/864-8331 for U.S. reservations, 800/538-2929 for international reservations ⊕ www.united.com. **US Airways** ☎ 800/428-4322 for U.S. reservations, 800/622-1015 for international reservations ⊕ www.usairways.com.

INTERISLAND FLIGHTS

Hawaiian Airlines offers regular interisland service to Maui's Kahului and Kapalua airports. Island Air, go! Airlines, and Mokulele Airlines provide interisland service between Maui (Kahului), Lanai, Molokai (Hooleehua), Oahu, Kauai, and the Big Island. Island Air also services Maui's Kapalua airport and the Lanai City airport, and Mokulele Airlines services Hana airport twice daily from Kahului. Pacific Wings serves Maui's Kahului and Hana airports, Molokai's Hooleehua and Kalaupapa airports, and flies into Oahu and the Big Island.

Be sure to compare prices offered by all the interisland carriers. Plan ahead and be flexible with your dates and times if you're looking for an affordable round-trip.

Airline Contacts go! Airlines ☎ 888/435-9462 ⊕ www.iflygo.com. **Hawaiian Airlines** ☎ 800/367-5320 ⊕ www.hawaiianair.com. **Island Air** ☎ 800/652-6541 ⊕ www.islandair.

com. **Mokulele Airlines** ☎ 808/426–7070, 866/260–7070 ⊕ www.mokuleleairlines.com. **Pacific Wings** ☎ 888/575–4546 ⊕ www. pacificwings.com.

CHARTER FLIGHTS

In addition to its regular service between Honolulu, Maui, Molokai, and the Big Island, Pacific Wings offers charter options including premier (same-day departures on short notice), premium (24-hour notice), priority (48-hour notice), group, and cargo/courier. Should you want to explore Maui, Oahu, and the Big Island from the air and ground, you can book tours through Discover Hawaii Tours.

Charter Companies Discover Hawaii Tours ☎ 808/690–9050 ⊕ www.discoverhawaiitours. com. **Pacific Wings** ☎ 888/575–4546 ⊕ www. pacificwings.com.

▌BOAT TRAVEL

There is daily ferry service between Lahaina, Maui, and Manele Bay, Lanai, with Expeditions Lanai Ferry. The 9-mile crossing costs $60 round-trip and takes about 45 minutes or so, depending on ocean conditions (which can make this trip a rough one).

Molokai Ferry offers twice-daily ferry service between Lahaina, Maui, and Kaunakakai, Molokai. Travel time is about 90 minutes each way, and the one-way fare is $67.60. Reservations are recommended.

Ferry Contacts Expeditions Lanai Ferry ☎ 800/695–2624 ⊕ www.go-lanai.com. **Molokai Ferry** ☎ 866/307–6524 ⊕ www. molokaiferry.com.

CRUISES

For information about cruises, see Chapter 1, Experience Maui.

▌BUS TRAVEL

Maui Bus, operated by the tour company Roberts Hawaii, offers 12 routes in and between various Central, South, and West Maui communities. You can travel in and around Wailuku, Kahului, Lahaina, Kaanapali, Kapalua, Kihei, Wailea, Maalaea, the North Shore (Paia), and Upcountry (including Pukalani, Makawao, Haliimaile, and Haiku). The Upcountry and Haiku Islander routes include a stop at Kahului Airport. All routes cost $2.

Bus Contact Maui Bus ☎ 808/871–4838 ⊕ www.mauicounty.gov.

▌CAR TRAVEL

Should you plan to do any sightseeing on Maui, it's best to rent a car. Even if all you want to do is relax at your resort, you may want to hop in the car to check out one of the island's popular restaurants.

Many of Maui's roads are two lanes, so allow plenty of time to return your vehicle to the airport. Traffic can be bad during morning and afternoon rush hour, especially between Kahului and Paia, Kihei, and Lahaina. Give yourself about 3½ hours before departure time to return your vehicle.

On Molokai and Lanai four-wheel-drive vehicles are recommended for exploring off the beaten path. Many of the roads are poorly paved or unpaved.

Make sure you've got a GPS or a good map. Free visitor publications containing quality road maps can be found at airports, hotels, and shops.

Asking for directions will almost always produce a helpful explanation from the locals, but you should be prepared for an island term or two. Hawaii residents refer to places as being either *mauka* (toward the mountains) or *makai* (toward the ocean).

Hawaii has a strict seat-belt law. Those riding in the front seat must wear a seat belt, and children under the age of 18 in the backseat must be belted. The fine for not wearing a seat belt is $92. Jaywalking is also common, so pay careful attention to pedestrians. Turning right on a red light is legal in the state, except where noted.

Car Rental Resources

Local Agencies

AA Aloha Cars-R-Us	800/655–7989	www.hawaiicarrental.com
Adventure Lanai Eco-Centre (Lanai)	808/565–7373	www.adventurelanai.com
Aloha Campers (Maui)	808/281–8020	www.alohacampers.com
Aloha Toy Store	808/831–2660	www.alohatoystore.com
Bio-Beetle Eco Rental Cars	877/873–6121	www.bio-beetle.com
Discount Hawaii	888/292–1930	www.discounthawaiicarrental.com
Hawaiian Discount Car Rentals	888/292–1930	www.hawaiidrive-o.com
Island Rental Cars	800/440–7029	www.hawaiianriders.com
Maui Harley-Davidson	855/614–6171	www.hawaiiharleyrental.com

Your unexpired mainland driver's license is valid for rental cars for up to 90 days.

GASOLINE

Gas costs more on Maui than on the U.S. mainland. At this writing, the average price of a gallon of gas is about $4.29. Expect to pay more (sometimes significantly more) on Lanai and Molokai. The only gas station on Lanai is in Lanai City, at Lanai City Service.

PARKING

With a population of more than 155,000 and nearly 30,000 visitors on any given day, Maui has parking challenges. Lots sprinkled throughout West Maui charge by the hour. There are about 700 parking spaces in the Lahaina Center; shoppers can get validated parking here, as well as at Whalers Village. Parking along many streets is curtailed during rush hours, and towing is widely practiced. Read curbside parking signs before leaving your vehicle.

RENTALS

While on Maui you can rent anything from a subcompact to a Ferrari. Rates are usually better if you reserve though a rental agency's website. All the big national rental-car agencies have locations on Maui, but Dollar (⊕ www.dollar.com) is the only major company on Lanai and Alamo (⊕ www.alamo.com) is the only one on Molokai. There also are local rental-car companies, so be sure to compare prices before you book. It's wise to make reservations far in advance, especially if you're visiting during peak seasons or for major conventions or sporting events. *For more specifics about renting on Molokai and Lanai, see the planning sections of Chapters 10 and 11.*

Rates begin at about $27 to $31 a day for an economy car with air-conditioning, automatic transmission, and unlimited mileage, depending on your pickup location. This does not include the airport concession fee, general excise tax, rental-vehicle surcharge, or vehicle license fee. When you reserve a car, ask about cancellation penalties and drop-off charges should you plan to pick up the car in one location and return it to another. Many rental companies offer money-saving coupons for local attractions.

In Hawaii you must be 21 to rent a car, and you must have a valid driver's license and a major credit card. You can use a debit card at most rental agencies, but they will put a $500 hold on your account for the duration of the rental. Those under 25 will pay a daily surcharge of $10 to $25. Request car seats and extras such as a GPS when you make your reservation. Hawaii's Child Restraint Law requires that all children under age four be in an approved child-safety seat in the backseat of a vehicle. Children ages four to seven, and those who are less than 4 feet, 9 inches tall and weigh less than 80 pounds, must be seated in a rear booster seat or child restraint such as a lap and shoulder belt. Car seats and boosters range from $7 to $12 per day; some companies have a maximum charge per rental period.

Maui has some unusual rental options. Aloha Campers rents older VW Westfalia Campers for $115 per day, with a three-day minimum. And if exploring the island on two wheels is more your speed, Maui Harley-Davidson and Aloha Toy Store rent motorcycles. Aloha Toy Store also rents exotic cars, as do Hawaiian Discount Car Rentals and Island Rental Cars. Prefer an earth-friendly automobile that gets 35 to 50 miles to the gallon? Bio-Beetle Eco Rental Cars run on clean-burning diesel fuel that comes from renewable sources like recycled vegetable oil.

ROAD CONDITIONS

Getting around Maui is relatively easy, as only a few major roads hit the must-see sights. Honoapiilani Highway will get you from the central Maui towns of Wailuku and Kahului to the leeward coast and the towns of Lahaina, Kaanapali, Kahana, and Kapalua. Depending on traffic, it should take about 30 to 45 minutes to travel this route. Those gorgeous mountains that hug Honoapiilani Highway are the West Maui Mountains.

North and South Kihei Road will take you to the town of Kihei and the resort area of Wailea on the South Shore. The drive from the airport in Kahului to Wailea should take about 30 minutes, and the drive from Kaanapali in West Maui to Wailea on the South Shore will take about 45 to 60 minutes.

Your vacation to Maui must include a visit to Haleakala National Park, and you should plan on 2 to 2½ hours' driving time from Kaanapali or Wailea. The drive from Kaanapali or Wailea to the charming towns of Makawao and Kula will take about 45 to 60 minutes. And you must not miss the Road to Hana, a 55-mile stretch with one-lane bridges, hairpin turns, and breathtaking views. The Hawaii Visitors and Convention Bureau's red-caped King Kamehameha signs mark major attractions and scenic spots.

All major roads on Maui are passable with two-wheel-drive vehicles. You should exercise caution on Kahekili Highway between Waihee Point and Keawalua, which is somewhat treacherous due to sheer drop-offs, and the southern stretch of Piilani Highway between Ulupalakua and Kipahulu, which has sections of extremely rough and unpaved roadway. Both roads are remote, have no gas stations, and provide little or no cell-phone service, so plan accordingly.

In rural areas it's not unusual for gas stations to close early. Use caution during heavy downpours, especially if you see signs warning of falling rocks. If you're enjoying the views or need to study a map, pull over to the side. Remember the aloha spirit: allow other cars to merge, don't honk (it's considered rude), and use your headlights and turn signals.

Emergency Services AAA Help ☎ *800/222-4357* ⊕ *www.aaa.com.*

ESSENTIALS

▌ COMMUNICATIONS

INTERNET

If you've brought your laptop with you to Maui, you should have no problem checking email or connecting to the Internet. Most major hotels and resorts offer high-speed access in rooms or public areas. If you're staying at a small inn or bed-and-breakfast without Internet access, ask the proprietor for the nearest café or coffee shop with wireless access.

Contacts Cybercafés. Cybercafés lists more than 4,000 Internet cafés worldwide. ⊕ *www. cybercafes.com.* **JiWire.** This company has a free smartphone app for locating Wi-Fi hot-spots around the world. ⊕ *www.jiwire.com.*

▌ HEALTH

Hawaii is known as the Health State. The life expectancy here is 81.3 years, one of the longest in the nation. Balmy weather makes it easy to remain active year-round, and the low-stress aloha attitude certainly contributes to the general well-being. When visiting the Islands, however, there are a few health issues to keep in mind.

The Hawaii State Department of Health recommends that you drink 16 ounces of water per hour to avoid dehydration when hiking or spending time in the sun. Use sunblock, wear UV-reflective sunglasses, and protect your head with a visor or hat. If you're not used to warm, humid weather, allow plenty of time for rest stops and refreshments.

When visiting freshwater streams, be aware of the tropical disease leptospirosis, which is spread by animal urine. Symptoms include fever, headache, nausea, and red eyes. If left untreated it can cause liver and kidney damage, respiratory failure, internal bleeding, and even death. To avoid this, don't swim or wade in freshwater streams or ponds if you

have open sores, and don't drink from any freshwater streams or ponds.

On the Islands, fog is a rare occurrence, but there can often be "vog," an airborne haze of gases released from volcanic vents on the Big Island. During certain weather conditions such as "Kona Winds," the vog can settle over the Islands and wreak havoc with respiratory conditions, especially asthma or emphysema. If susceptible, stay indoors and get emergency assistance if needed.

The Islands have their share of insects. Most are harmless but annoying. When planning to spend time outdoors in hiking areas, wear long-sleeve clothing and pants and use mosquito repellent containing DEET. In damp places you may encounter the dreaded local centipedes, which are brown and blue and measure up to eight inches long. Their painful sting is similar to those of bees and wasps. When camping, shake out your sleeping bag and check your shoes, as the centipedes like cozy places. When hiking in remote areas, always carry a first-aid kit.

▌ HOURS OF OPERATION

Even people in paradise have to work. Generally, local business hours are weekdays 8 to 5. Banks are usually open Monday through Thursday 8:30 to 4 and until 6 on Friday. Some banks have Saturday-morning hours.

Many self-serve gas stations stay open around the clock, with full-service stations usually open from around 7 am until 9 pm; stations in rural spots may close earlier. U.S. post offices generally open between 8:30 and 9:30 am on weekdays, and close between 3:30 and 4:30 pm. Saturday hours are generally short, and vary from office to office.

Most museums generally open their doors between 9 am and 10 am and stay open until 4 or 4:30 pm. Many museums close on Sunday and Monday. Visitor-attraction hours vary throughout the state, but most sights are open daily with the exception of major holidays.

Stores in resort areas sometimes open as early as 8, with shopping-center opening hours varying from 9:30 to 10 on weekdays and Saturday, a bit later on Sunday. Bigger malls stay open until 9 weekdays and Saturday and close at 5 on Sunday. Boutiques in resort areas may stay open as late as 11.

▌ MONEY

Prices in listings are given for adults. Substantially reduced fees are almost always available for children, students, and senior citizens.

CREDIT CARDS

It's a good idea to inform your credit-card company before you travel, especially if you're going abroad and don't travel internationally very often. Otherwise, the credit-card company might put a hold on your card owing to unusual activity—not a good thing halfway through your trip. Record all your credit-card numbers—as well as the phone numbers to call if your cards are lost or stolen—in a safe place, so you're prepared should something go wrong. Both MasterCard and Visa have general numbers you can call (collect if you're abroad) if your card is lost, but you're better off calling the number of your issuing bank, since MasterCard and Visa usually just transfer you to your bank; your bank's number is usually printed on your card.

Reporting Lost Cards American Express ☎ 800/528–4800 ⊕ www.americanexpress. com. **Diners Club** ☎ 800/234–6377 ⊕ www. dinersclub.com. **Discover** ☎ 800/347– 2683 ⊕ www.discover.com. **MasterCard** ☎ 800/627–8372 ⊕ www.mastercard.com. **Visa** ☎ 800/847–2911 ⊕ www.visa.com.

▌ PACKING

Probably the most important thing to tuck into your suitcase is sunscreen. There are many tanning oils on the market in Hawaii, including coconut and *kukui* (the nut from a local tree) oils, but they can cause severe burns. Hats and sunglasses offer important sun protection, too.

Hawaii is casual: sandals, bathing suits, and comfortable, informal cotton clothing are the norm. In summer, synthetic slacks and shirts, although easy to care for, can be uncomfortably warm. The aloha shirt is accepted dress in Hawaii for business and most social occasions.

Shorts are acceptable daytime attire, along with a T-shirt or polo shirt. There's no need to buy expensive sandals on the mainland—here you can get flip-flops for a couple of bucks and off-brand sandals for $20 or less. Many golf courses have dress codes requiring a collared shirt. If you're visiting in winter or planning to visit a high-altitude area, bring a sweater, a light- to medium-weight jacket, or a fleece pullover.

If your vacation plans include an exploration of Maui's northeastern coast, including Hana and Upcountry Maui, pack a light rain jacket. And if you'll be exploring Haleakala National Park, make sure you pack appropriately, as weather at the summit can be very cold and windy. Bring good boots for hiking.

Transportation Security Administration (TSA) ⊕ www.tsa.gov.

▌ SAFETY

Hawaii is generally a safe tourist destination, but it's still wise to follow common-sense safety precautions. Rental cars are magnets for break-ins, so don't leave any valuables inside, not even in a locked trunk. Avoid poorly lighted areas, beach parks, and isolated areas after dark. When hiking, stay on marked trails, no matter how alluring the temptation might be to stray. Weather conditions can cause

LOCAL DO'S AND TABOOS

Hawaii was admitted to the Union in 1959, so residents can be sensitive when visitors refer to their own hometowns as "back in the States." Remember, when in Hawaii, refer to the contiguous 48 states as "the mainland" and not as the United States. When you do, you won't appear to be such a *malihini* (newcomer).

GREETINGS

Hawaii is a friendly place, and this is reflected in the day-to-day encounters with friends, family, and even business associates. Women will often hug and kiss one another on the cheek, and men will shake hands and sometimes combine that with a friendly hug. When a man and woman are greeting each other and are good friends, it is not unusual for them to hug and kiss on the cheek. Children are taught to call any elders "auntie" or "uncle," even if they aren't related. It's a way to show respect.

When you walk off a long flight, nothing quite compares with a Hawaiian lei greeting. The casual ceremony ranks as one of the fastest ways to make the transition from the worries of home to the joys of your vacation. Though the tradition has created an expectation that everyone receives this floral garland when they step off the plane, the state of Hawaii cannot greet each of its more than 7 million annual visitors.

If you've booked a vacation with a wholesaler or tour company, a lei greeting might be included in your package. If not, it's easy to arrange a lei greeting before you arrive at Kahului Airport with Kamaaina Leis, Flowers & Greeters. A dendrobium orchid lei is considered standard and costs about $24 per person.

Information Kamaaina Leis, Flowers & Greeters ☎ *808/836–3246, 800/367–5183* ⊕ *www.alohaleigreetings.com.*

LANGUAGE

English is the primary language on the Islands. Making the effort to learn some Hawaiian words can be rewarding, however. Hawaiian words you are most likely to encounter during your visit to the Islands are *aloha* (hello), *mahalo* (thank you), *keiki* (child), *haole* (Caucasian or foreigner), *mauka* (toward the mountains), *makai* (toward the ocean), and *pau* (finished, all done). If you'd like to learn more Hawaiian words, check out ⊕ *www.wehewehe.org.*

Hawaiian history includes waves of immigrants, each bringing their own language. To communicate with each other, they developed a language known as pidgin. If you listen closely, you will know what is being said by the inflections and by the body language. For an informative and sometimes hilarious view of things Hawaiian, check out Jerry Hopkins' books titled *Pidgin to the Max* and *Fax to the Max*, available at most local bookstores in the Hawaiiana sections.

VISITING AND ALOHA

If you've been invited to the home of friends living in Hawaii (an ultimate compliment), bring a small gift and don't forget to take off your shoes when you enter their house. Try to take part in a cultural festival during your stay in the Islands; there is no better way to get a glimpse of Hawaii's ethnic mosaic.

And finally, remember that *aloha* is not only the word for hello, good-bye, and love, but it also stands for the spirit that is all around the Islands. Take your time (after all, you're on "Hawaiian time"). Respect the *aina* (land): that is not only a precious commodity here but also stands at the core of the Polynesian belief system. "Living aloha" will transform your vacation, fill you with the warmth that is unique to Hawaii, and have you planning your return.

landscapes to become muddy, slippery, and tenuous, so staying on marked trails will lessen the possibility of a fall or getting lost.

Women traveling alone are generally safe on the Islands, but always follow the safety precautions you would use in any major destination. When booking hotels, request rooms closest to the elevator and always keep your hotel-room door and balcony doors locked. Stay away from isolated areas after dark; camping and hiking solo are not advised. If you stay out late visiting nightclubs and bars, use caution when returning to your lodging.

▮ TAXES

There's a 4.17% state sales tax on all purchases, including food. A hotel room tax of 9.25%, combined with the sales tax of 4.17%, equals a 13.42% rate added onto your hotel bill. A $7.50-per-day road tax is also assessed on each rental vehicle.

▮ TIME

Hawaii is on Hawaiian standard time, 5 hours behind New York, 2 hours behind Los Angeles, and 10 hours behind London.

When the U.S. mainland is on daylight saving time, Hawaii is not, so add an extra hour of time difference between the Islands and U.S. mainland destinations. You may find that things generally move more slowly here. That has nothing to do with your watch—it's just the laid-back way called Hawaiian time.

▮ TIPPING

As this is a major vacation destination and many of the people who work at the hotels and resorts rely on tips to supplement their wages, tipping is not only common but expected.

TIPPING GUIDELINES FOR MAUI	
Bartender	$1 to $5 per round of drinks, depending on the number of drinks
Bellhop	$1 to $5 per bag, depending on the level of the hotel and whether you have bulky items like golf clubs, surfboards, etc.
Hotel Concierge	$5 or more, depending on the service
Hotel Doorman	$1 to $5 if he helps you get a cab or helps with bags, golf clubs, etc.
Hotel Maid	$1 to $3 a day (either daily or at the end of your stay, in cash)
Hotel Room-Service Waiter	$1 to $2 per delivery, even if a service charge has been added
Porter at Airport	$1 per bag
Skycap at Airport	$1 to $3 per bag checked
Spa Personnel	15% to 20% of the cost of your service
Taxi Driver	15% to 20%, but round up the fare to the next dollar amount
Tour Guide	10% of the cost of the tour
Valet-Parking Attendant	$2 to $5, each time your car is brought to you
Waiter	15% to 20%, with 20% being the norm at high-end restaurants; nothing additional if a service charge is added to the bill

▮ TOURS

Guided tours are a good option when you don't want to do it all yourself. You travel along with a group (sometimes large, sometimes small), stay in prebooked hotels, eat with your fellow travelers (the cost of meals is sometimes included in the price of your tour, sometimes not), and follow a schedule.

Tours can be just the thing for first-time travelers to Maui or those who enjoy the group-traveling experience. None of the companies offering general-interest tours in Hawaii include Molokai or Lanai. When you book a guided tour, find out what's included and what isn't. A "land-only" tour includes all your ground transportation, but not necessarily your flights. Most prices in tour brochures don't include fees, taxes, and tips.

GENERAL-INTEREST TOURS

Globus has 10 Hawaii itineraries that include Maui. Tauck Travel and Trafalgar offer several land-based Hawaii itineraries that include two or three nights on Maui. Both companies offer similar itineraries with plenty of free time to explore the island. Tauck offers an 11-night multi-island tour called "The Best of Hawaii." Trafalgar has 7-, 9-, 10-, and 12-night multi-island tours. EscortedHawaiiTours.com, owned and operated by Atlas Cruises & Tours, sells several Hawaii trips ranging from 6 to 11 nights. These are operated by various tour companies, including Globus, Tauck, and Trafalgar.

Tour Contacts Atlas Cruises & Tours
☎ 800/942–3301 ⊕ www.atlastravelweb. com. **Globus** ☎ 866/755–8581 ⊕ www. globusjourneys.com. **Tauck Travel** ☎ 800/788–7885 ⊕ www.tauck.com. **Trafalgar** ☎ 866/544–4434 ⊕ www.trafalgar.com.

▌ VISITOR INFORMATION

Before you travel, contact the Hawaii Visitors & Convention Bureau for general information on Maui, Lanai, or Molokai, and to request a free official vacation planner. The Hawaii Tourism Authority's Travel Smart Hawaii site offers tips on everything from packing to flying. Also visit the Hawaii State Vacation Planner for personalized Hawaii vacation-planning help and to sign up for a free Best Places Hawaii Discount Card, which provides discounts on accommodations, activities, and wedding services on Maui, Oahu, Kauai, and the Big Island.

There are also special monthly deals and discounts offered by various hotels, condominiums, and vacation management companies.

Contacts Hawaii State Vacation Planner ⊕ www.bestplaceshawaii.com. **Hawaii Tourism Authority** ⊕ www.travelsmarthawaii. com. **Hawaii Visitors & Convention Bureau** ✉ 2270 Kalakaua Ave., Suite 801, Honolulu ☎ 808/923–1811, 800/464–2924 ⊕ www. gohawaii.com.

ALL ABOUT MAUI

Hawaii Beach Safety has the latest updates on Maui's beaches, including surf forecasts and safety tips. The Hawaii Department of Land and Natural Resources has information on hiking, fishing, and camping permits, online brochures on hiking safety and mountain and ocean preservation, and details on volunteer programs. Na Ala Hele, the state's trail and access program, has online maps and directions for hikes on Maui, Molokai, and Lanai.

The Maui Visitors Bureau, Lanai Visitors Bureau, and Molokai Visitors Association websites include information on accommodations, sights, events, and suggested itineraries for some of the most popular destinations and activities.

Contacts Hawaii Beach Safety ⊕ oceansafety.ancl.hawaii.edu. **Hawaii Department of Land and Natural Resources** ⊕ www.hawaii.gov/dlnr. **Lanai Visitors Bureau** ⊕ www.gohawaii.com/lanai. **Maui Visitors Bureau** ⊕ www.gohawaii.com/ maui. **Molokai Visitors Association** ⊕ www. gohawaii.com/molokai. **Na Ala Hele** ⊕ hawaiitrails.ehawaii.gov.

INDEX

PHOTO CREDITS

ABOUT OUR WRITERS

Eliza Escaño-Vasquez was raised in Manila, Philippines, and lived in California before falling deeply in aloha with Maui in 2005. She is a contributing writer for *Modern Luxury Hawaii*. For this edition, she updated the Water Sports and Tours, Shops and Spas, and Entertainment and Nightlife chapters. An ocean ninja in training, Eliza currently resides in Maui with her family, who makes living in paradise even more blissful than it sounds.

Bonnie Friedman, a native New Yorker, has made her home on Maui for more than 30 years. A well-published freelance writer, she also owns and operates Grapevine Productions, a public relations company. She traveled around Maui to get the latest news for the Experience Maui, Exploring Maui, and Where to Eat and Where to Stay chapters, adding some of her favorite places.

Heidi Pool is a freelance writer and personal fitness trainer who moved to Maui in 2003 after having been a frequent visitor for the previous two decades. An avid outdoor enthusiast, Heidi enjoys playing tour guide when friends or family members come to visit. She updated Beaches; Golf, Hiking, and Outdoor Activities; Molokai; and Travel Smart Maui.

Joana Varawa has lived on Lanai for more than 35 years and publishes a personal blog, joanaslanai.com, a collection of her prose, poetry, and painting. She has authored three books and many magazine and newspaper stories, and continues to explore her island with her beloved dog, Honey Girl. For this edition, Joana updated—no surprise—Lanai.